○○○

◀ ▶   ⊞ ▤ ▥ ▦   ⊙ ⚙▾   🔍 Magical Girl Site

▼ Summary   Display Images

Anazawa quit her idol job to pursue the Magical Girl who killed her friend and transferred to Aya's school. But why did she make contact with Shizukume...?! When Aya went to Yatsumura's house to check on her, she found Yatsumura unconscious on the floor and a man bound up in the house. Distressed by the scene in front of her, Aya is soon confronted by Shizukume, who attacks Aya with her yo-yo shaped wand.

Aya overcame the guilt she felt from having killed people and used her wand in Yatsumura's defense, after Anazawa called Shizukume to inform her that a magical barrier was put up in Shioi's hospital room. Once Shizukume learned that the barrier is Yatsumura's doing, she flew into an uncontrollable rage and sliced up Yatsumura's apartment with her yo-yo wand. The attack caused the building to crumble, and just as she was going to be crushed by falling rubble, she found herself back at the school. It was then she realized that Aya saved her life.

Meanwhile, Anazawa finally comes to the realization that it was Aya and Yatsumura who erected the barrier around Shioi. Upon arriving at Aya's house to confront the pair, Anazawa met Kaname and fell in love with him at first sight.

Back at the scene of the fallen building, Shizukume collected Aya and Yatsumura's wands and met with Site Manager Nana. When she asked the manager about a contradiction in the site's explanation of the Tempest, Nana shot Shizukume at point blank range. Meanwhile, Shioi finally awoke in her hospital room, healed by Amagai Kosame, a Magical Girl from another site?!

SEVEN SEAS ENTERTAINMENT PRESENTS

MAGICAL GIRL SITE

story and art by **KENTARO SATO**

VOLUME 4

TRANSLATION
Wesley Bridges

ADAPTATION
Janet Houck

LETTERING AND LAYOUT
Meaghan Tucker

COVER DESIGN
Nicky Lim

PROOFREADER
Brett Hallahan

ASSISTANT EDITOR
Jenn Grunigen

PRODUCTION ASSISTANT
CK Russell

PRODUCTION MANAGER
Lissa Pattillo

EDITOR-IN-CHIEF
Adam Arnold

PUBLISHER
Jason DeAngelis

MAHO SYOJYO SITE Volume 4

Originally published in Japan in 2015 by Akita Publishing Co., Ltd..
English translation rights arranged with Akita Publishing Co., Ltd. through TOHAN CORPORATION, Tokyo.

ISBN: 978-1-626925-80-9

Printed in Canada

First Printing: December 2017

10 9 8 7 6 5 4 3 2 1

FOLLOW US ONLINE: ***www.gomanga.com***

READING DIRECTIONS

This book reads from ***right to left***, Japanese style. If this is your first time reading manga, you start reading from the top right panel on each page and take it from there. If you get lost, just follow the numbered diagram here. It may seem backwards at first, but you'll get the hang of it! Have fun!!

1
2
3
4
5
6
7
8
9

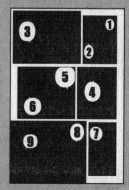

ENTER.20 FAKE

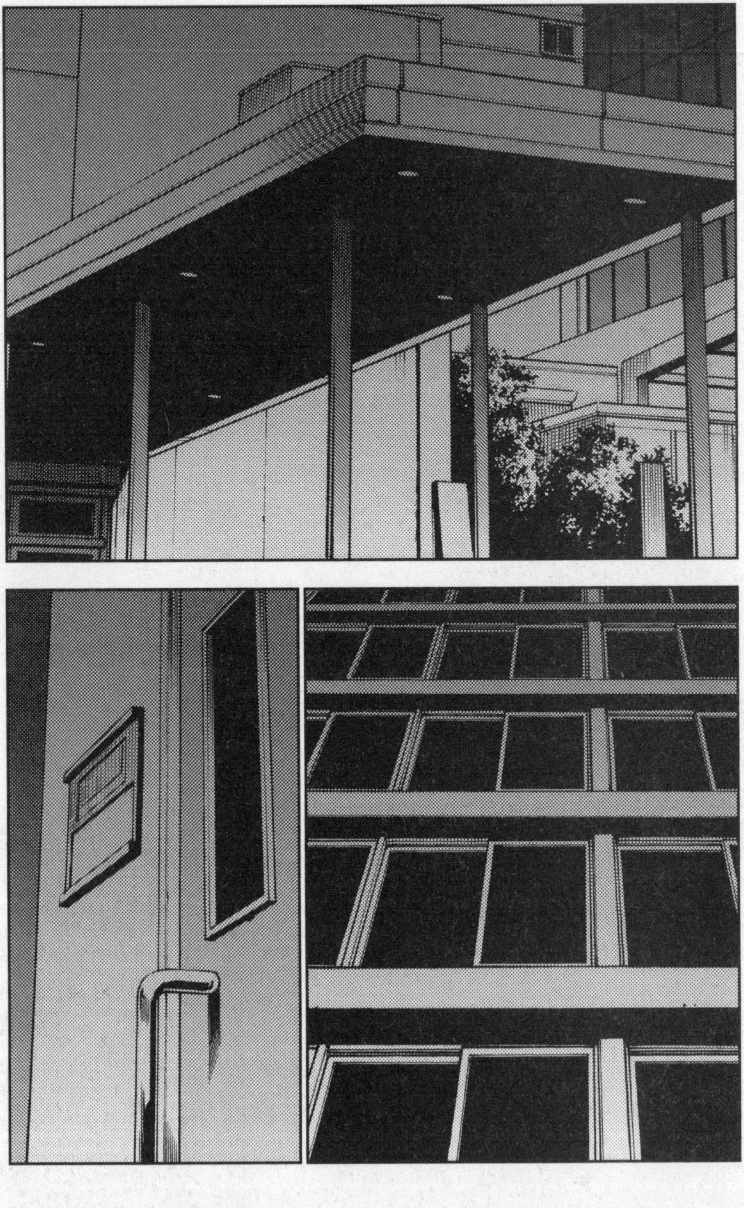

PLIP...
HUH ...?
WHERE ...?

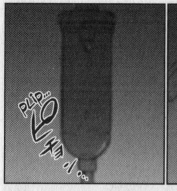

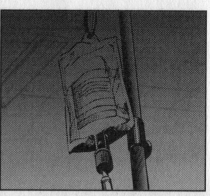

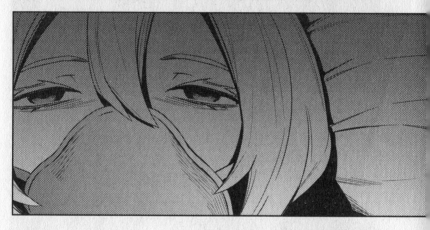

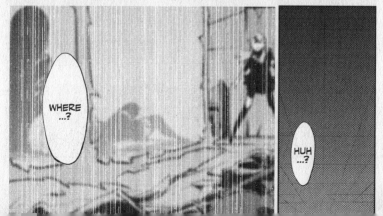

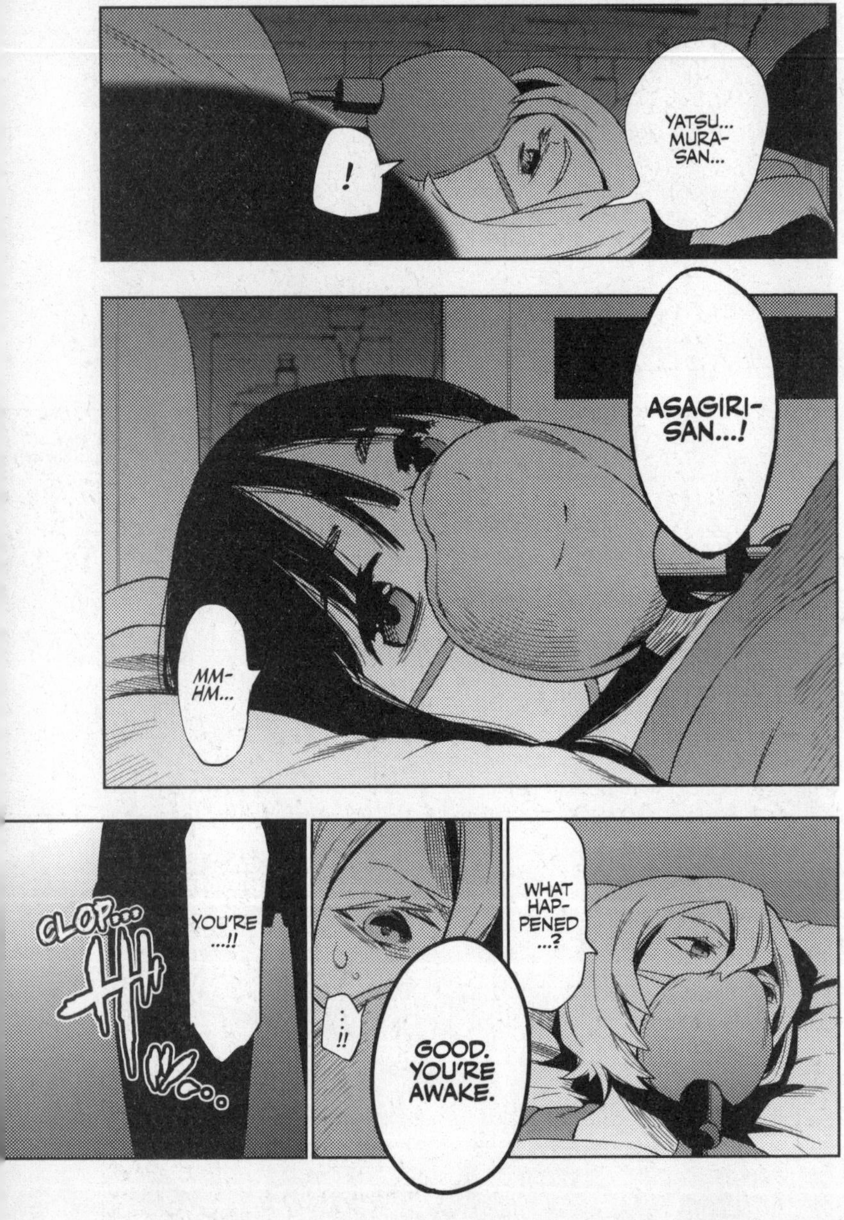
YATSU... MURA-SAN...
!
ASAGIRI-SAN...!
MM-HM...
WHAT HAP-PENED ...?
GOOD. YOU'RE AWAKE.
...!!
YOU'RE ...!!
CLOP...

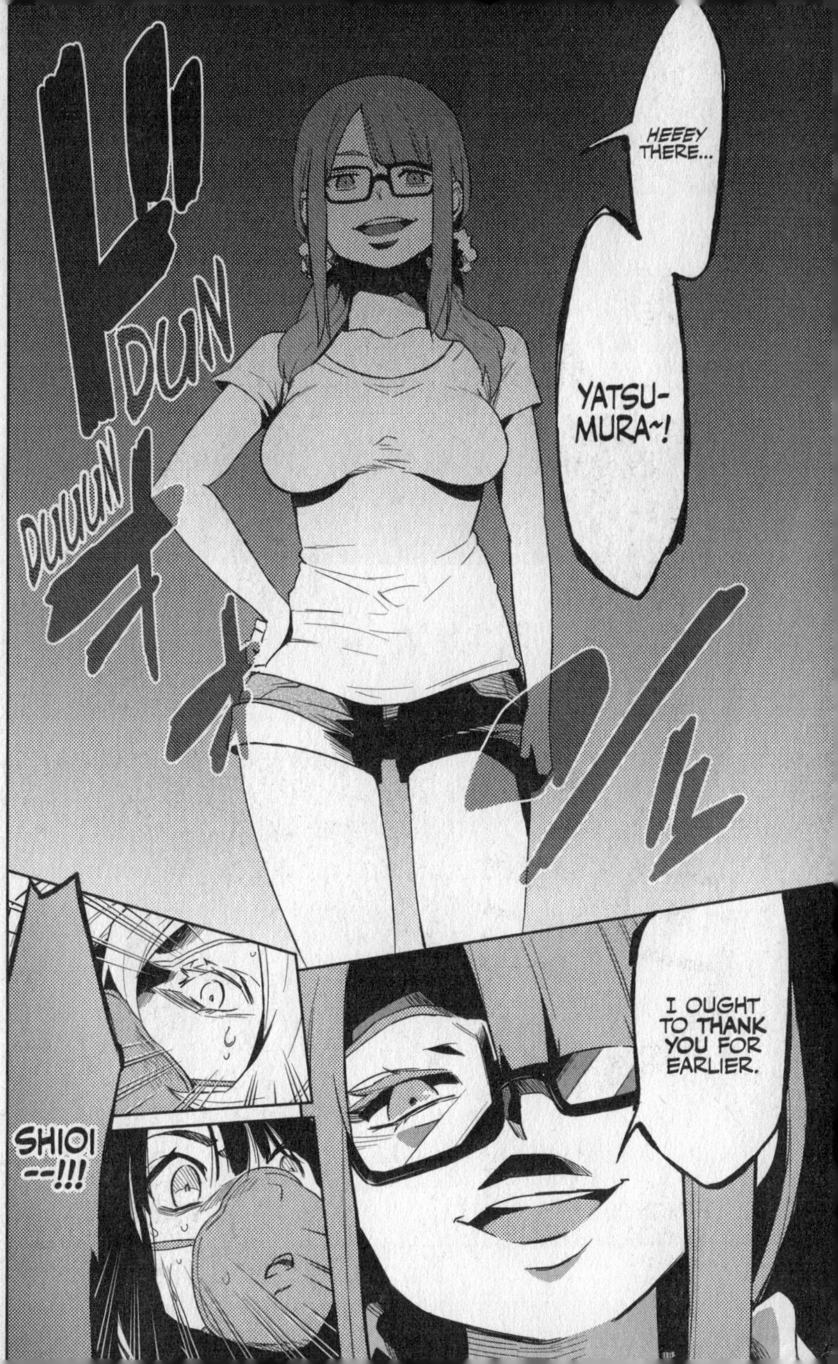
HEEEY THERE...
YATSU-MURA~!
DUN
DUUUN
I OUGHT TO THANK YOU FOR EARLIER.
SHIOI --!!!

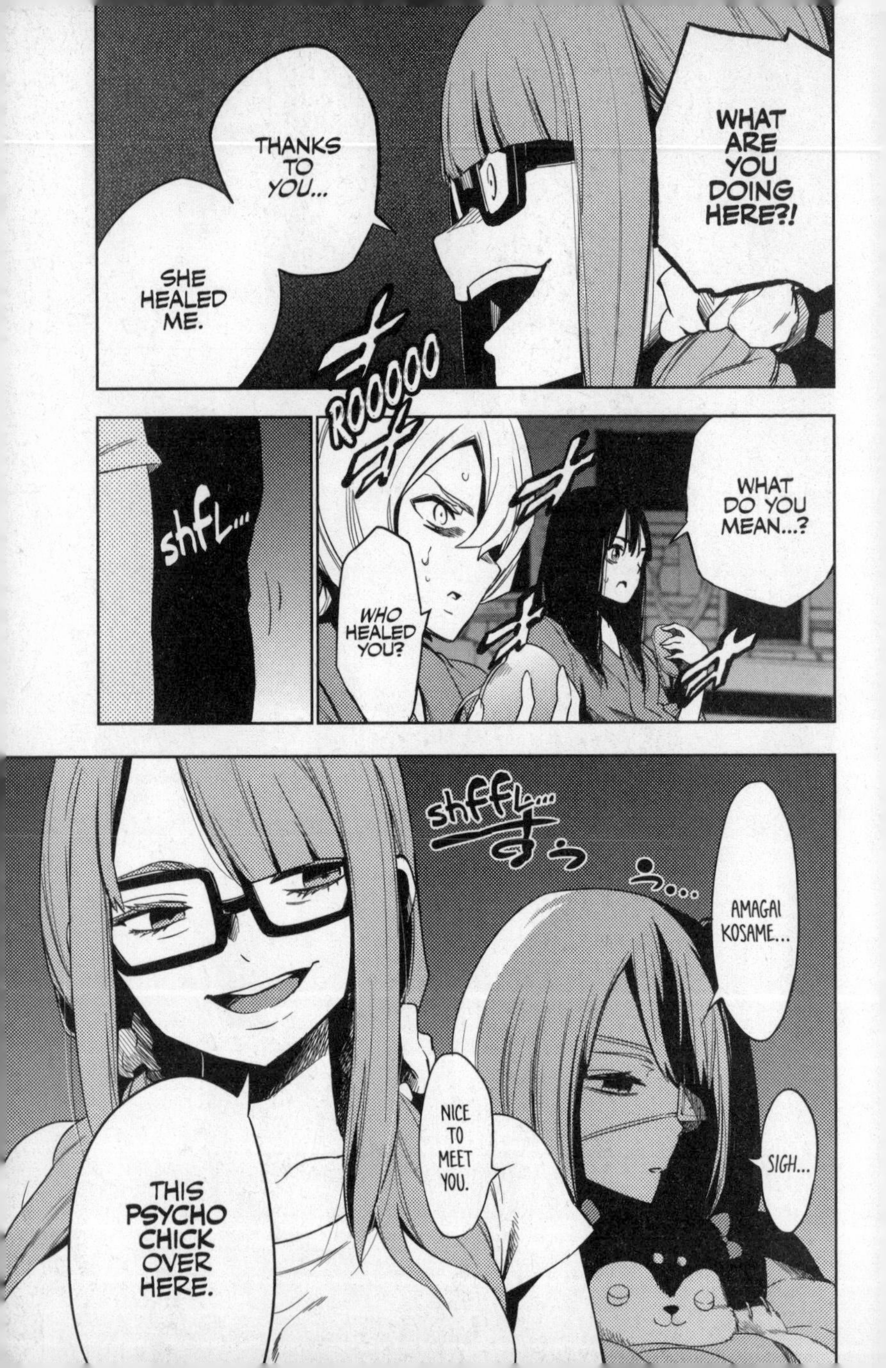
WHAT ARE YOU DOING HERE?!
THANKS TO YOU...
SHE HEALED ME.
ROOOOO
WHAT DO YOU MEAN...?
WHO HEALED YOU?
shfl...
shffl...
AMAGAI KOSAME...?
SIGH...
NICE TO MEET YOU.
THIS PSYCHO CHICK OVER HERE.

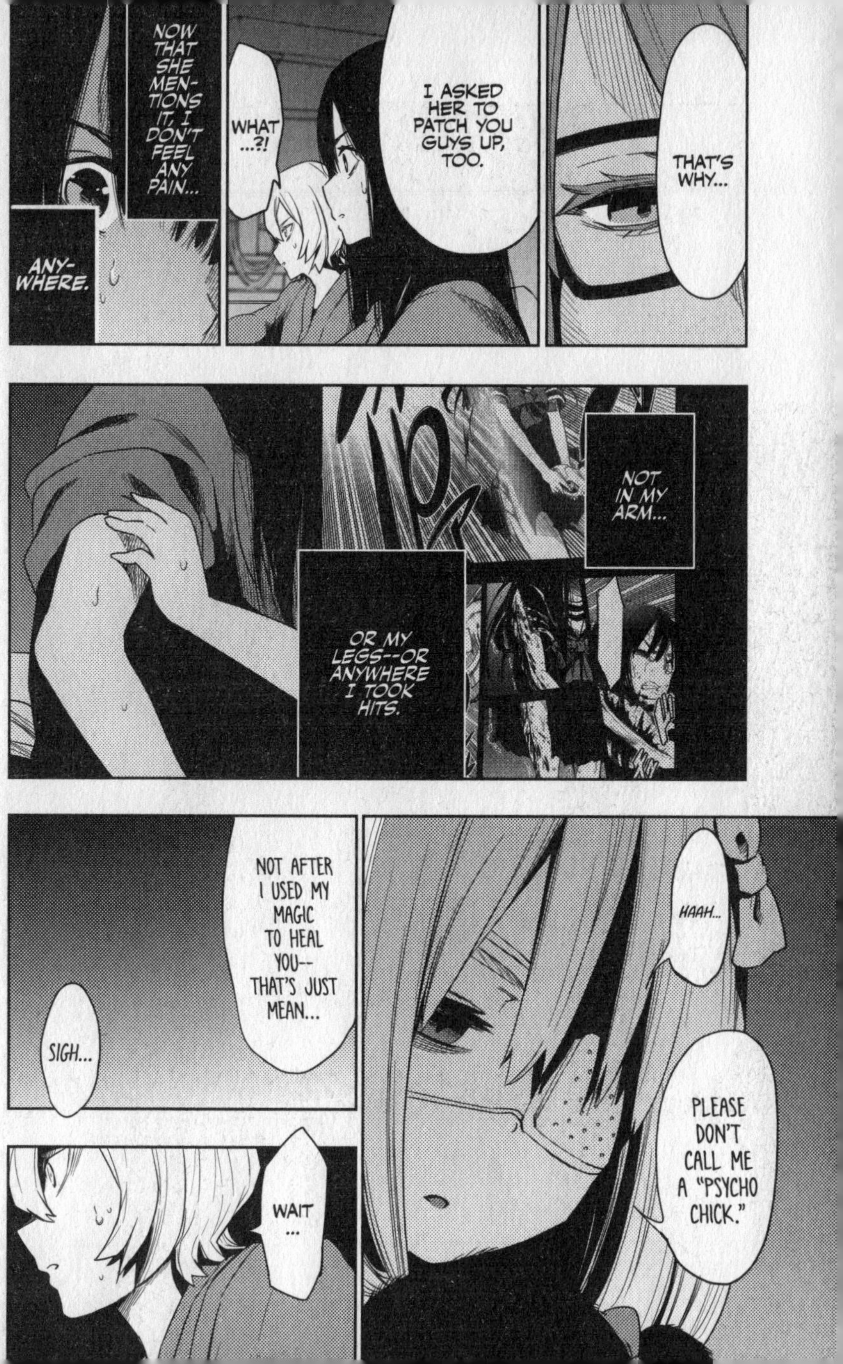
THAT'S WHY...
I ASKED HER TO PATCH YOU GUYS UP, TOO.
WHAT ...?!
NOW THAT SHE MEN-TIONS IT, I DON'T FEEL ANY PAIN...
ANY-WHERE.
NOT IN MY ARM...
OR MY LEGS--OR ANYWHERE I TOOK HITS.
HAAH...
PLEASE DON'T CALL ME A "PSYCHO CHICK."
NOT AFTER I USED MY MAGIC TO HEAL YOU--THAT'S JUST MEAN...
SIGH...
WAIT ...

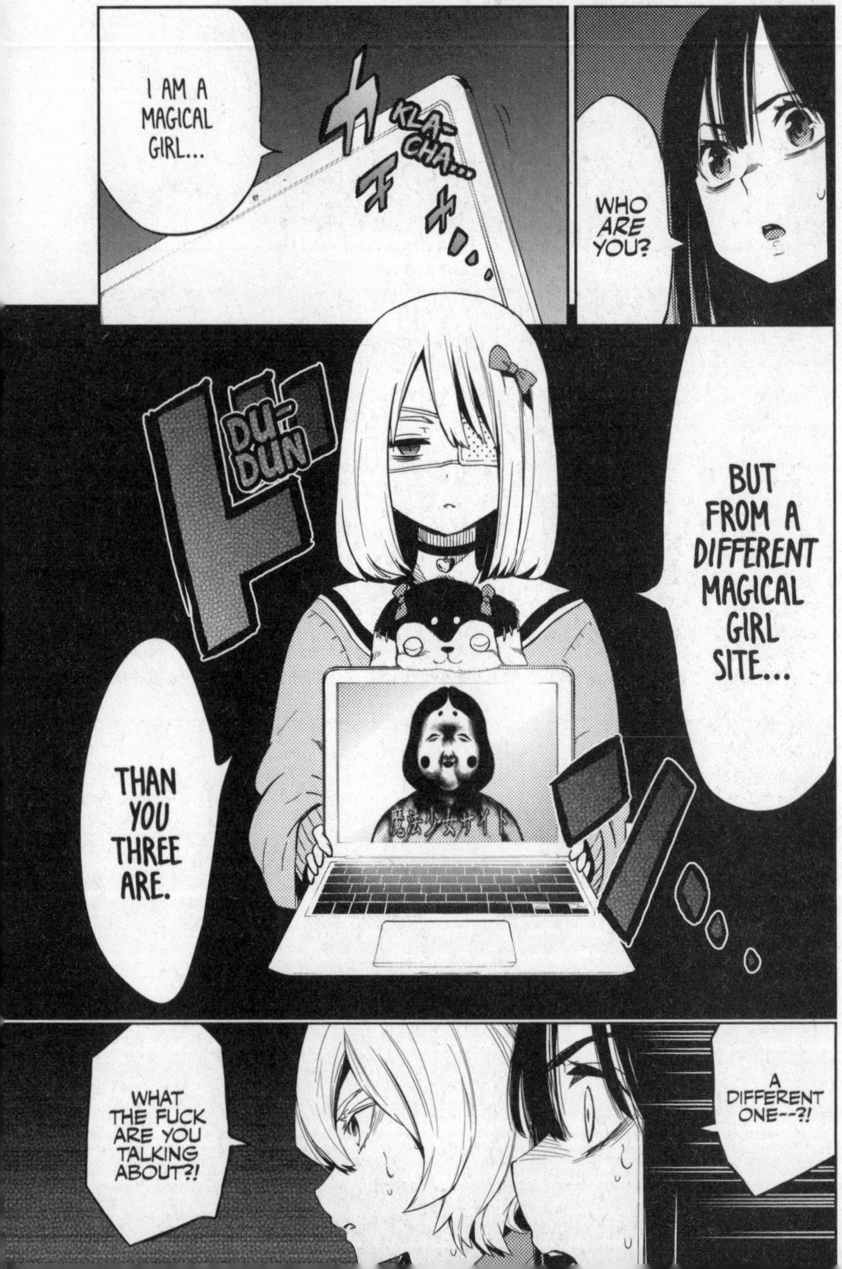
WHO ARE YOU?
I AM A MAGICAL GIRL...
KLA-CHA...
BUT FROM A DIFFERENT MAGICAL GIRL SITE...
DU-DUN
魔法少女サイト
THAN YOU THREE ARE.
A DIFFERENT ONE--?!
WHAT THE FUCK ARE YOU TALKING ABOUT?!

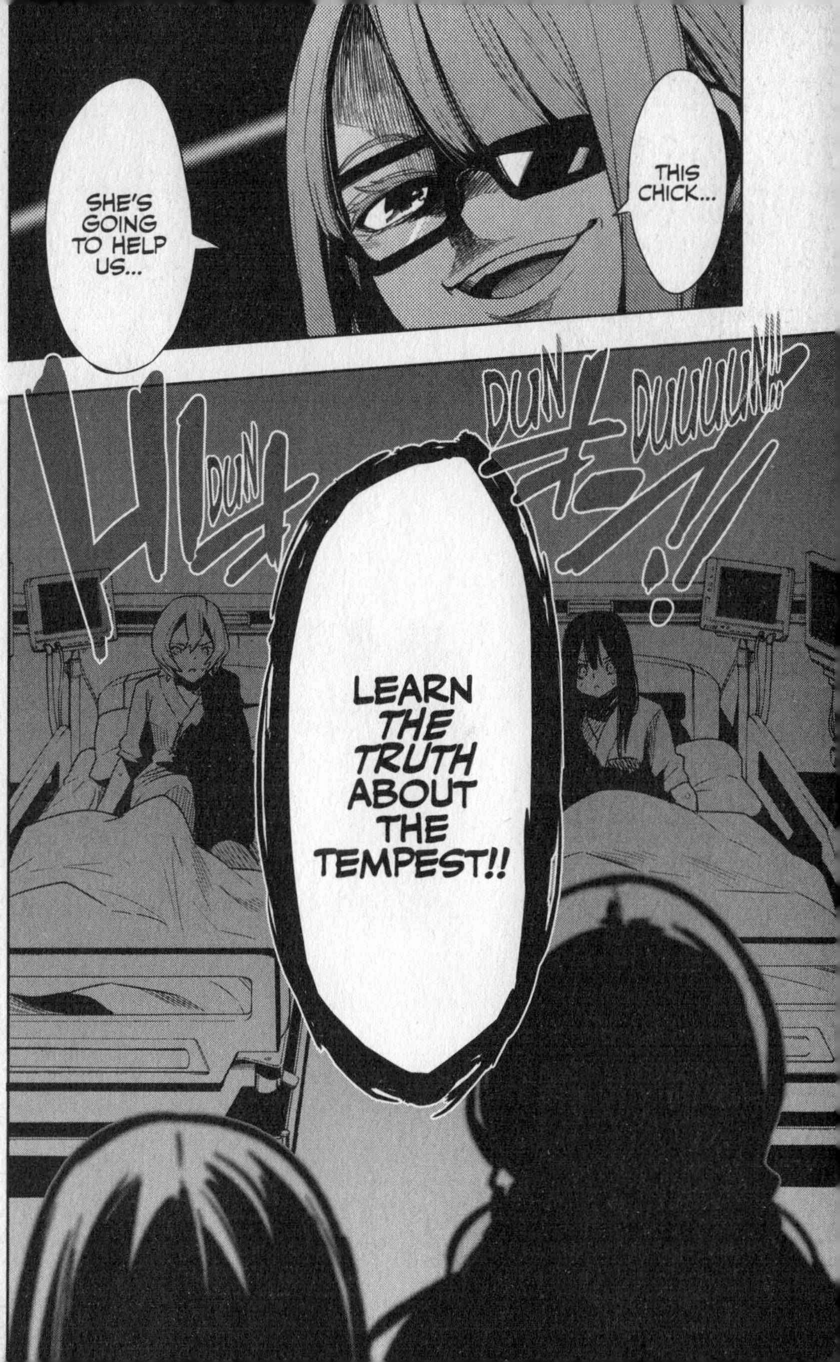
THIS CHICK...
SHE'S GOING TO HELP US...
DUN DUN DUN DUUUUN!!!
LEARN THE TRUTH ABOUT THE TEMPEST!!

ENTER.20 FAKE

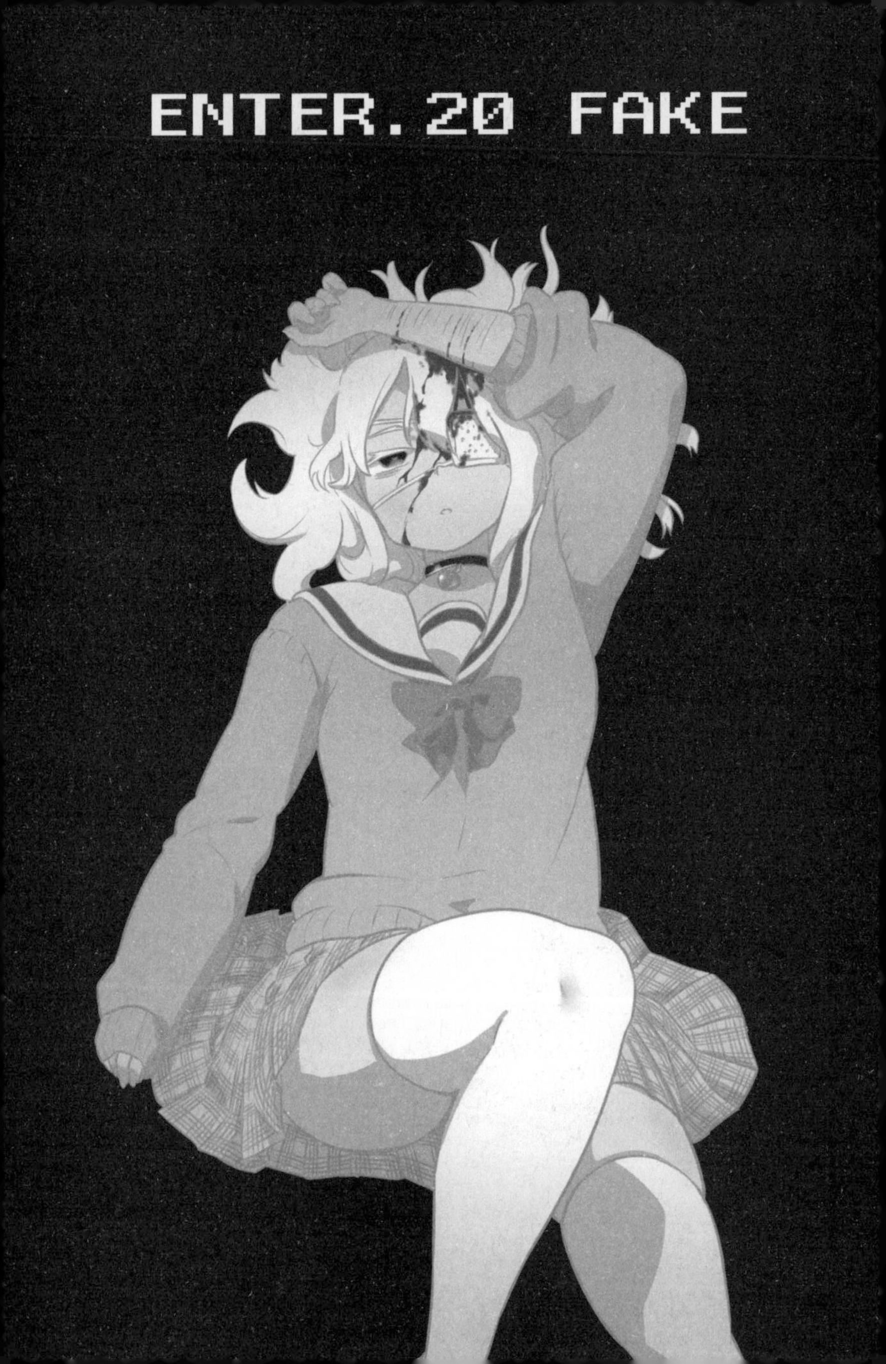

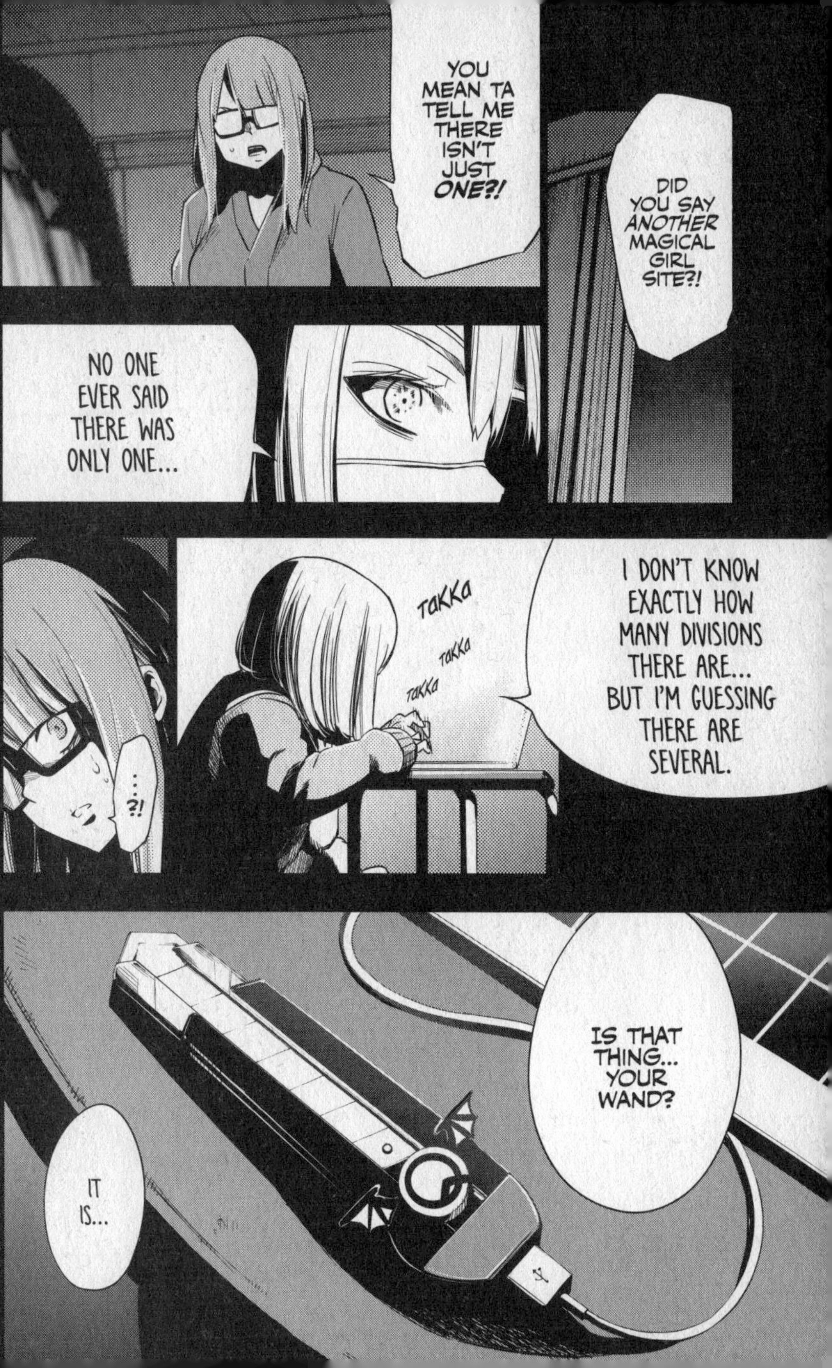
DID YOU SAY *ANOTHER* MAGICAL GIRL SITE?!
YOU MEAN TA TELL ME THERE ISN'T JUST *ONE?!*
NO ONE EVER SAID THERE WAS ONLY ONE...
I DON'T KNOW EXACTLY HOW MANY DIVISIONS THERE ARE... BUT I'M GUESSING THERE ARE SEVERAL.
TAKKA
TAKKA
TAKKA
...?!
IS THAT THING... YOUR WAND?
IT IS...

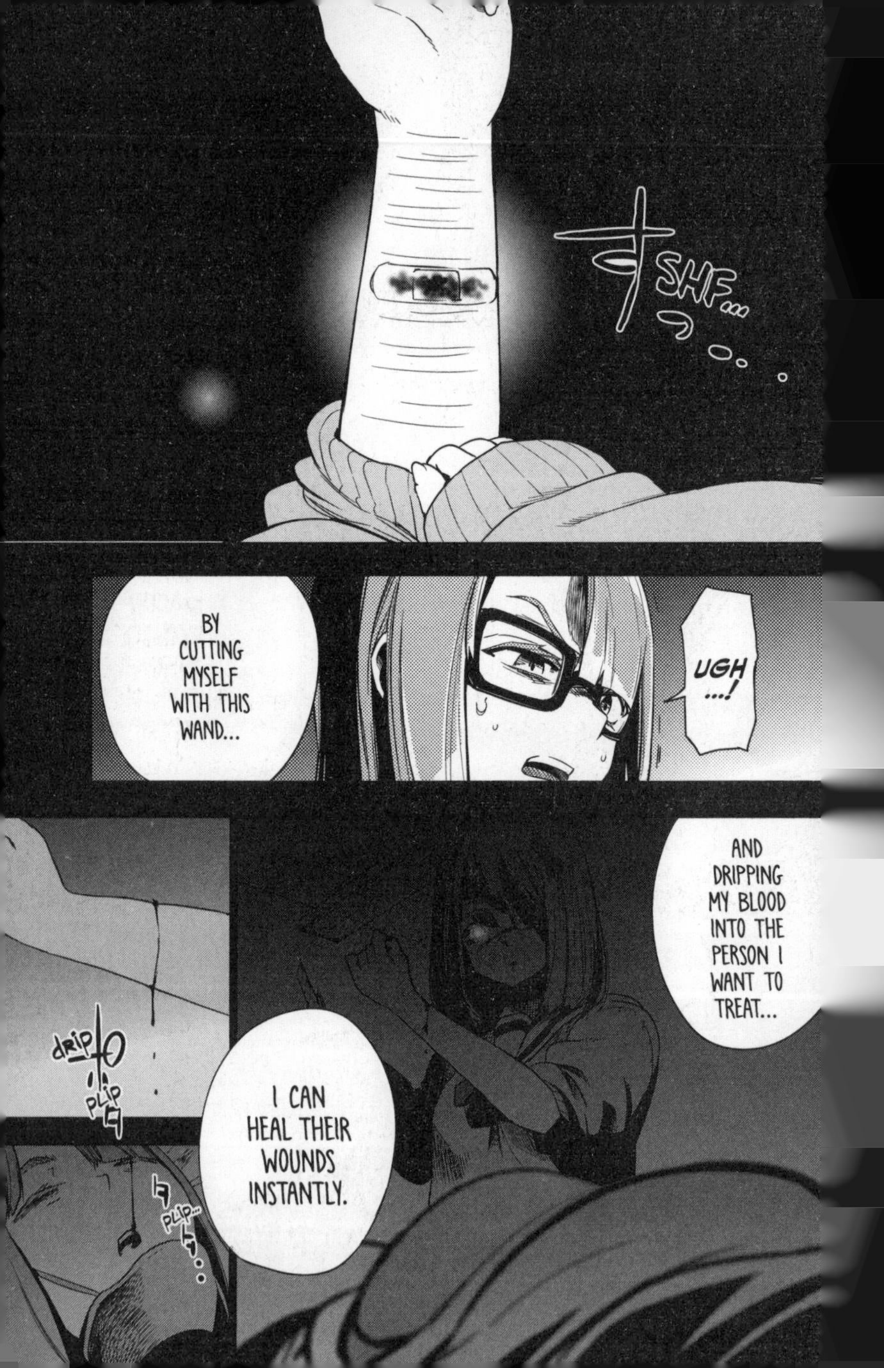
SHF...
UGH ...!
BY CUTTING MYSELF WITH THIS WAND...
AND DRIPPING MY BLOOD INTO THE PERSON I WANT TO TREAT...
I CAN HEAL THEIR WOUNDS INSTANTLY.
drip
plip
plip...

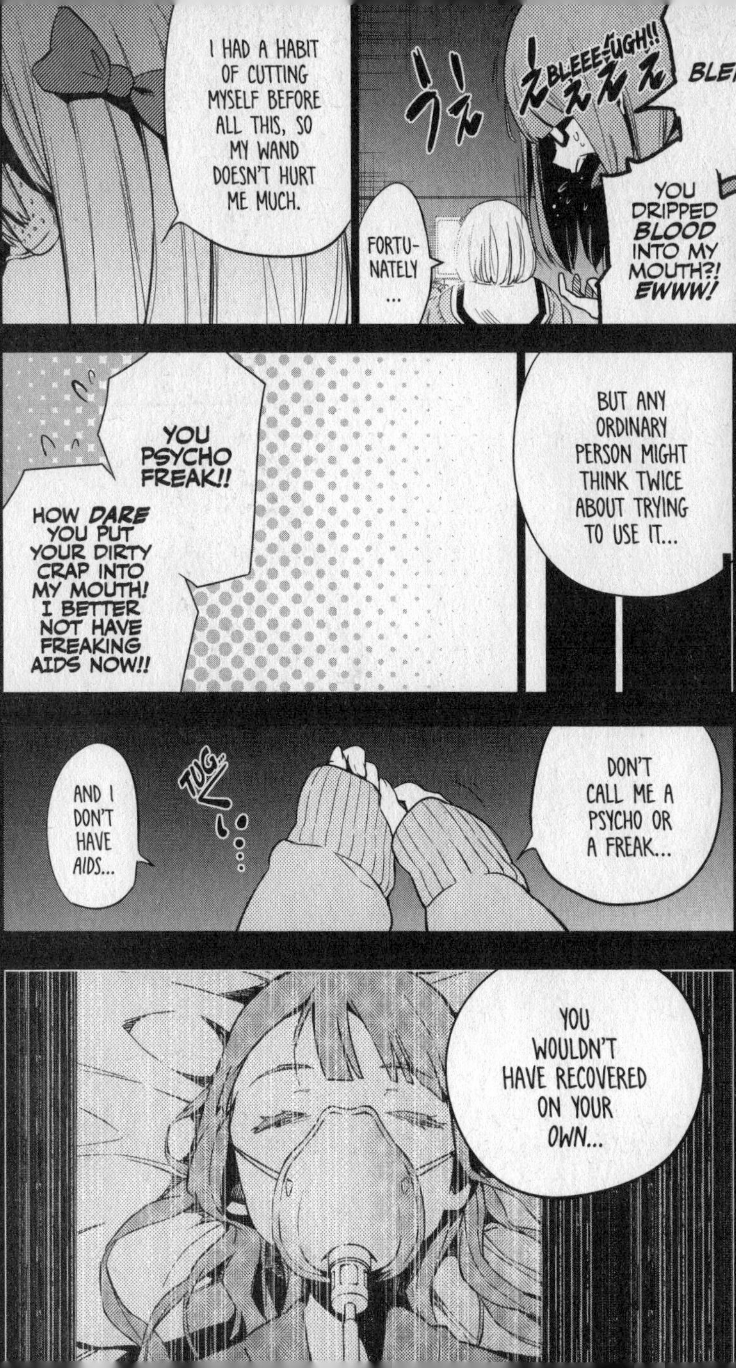
BLEH!!
BLEEEE-UGH!!
YOU DRIPPED BLOOD INTO MY MOUTH?! EWWW!
FORTUNATELY...
I HAD A HABIT OF CUTTING MYSELF BEFORE ALL THIS, SO MY WAND DOESN'T HURT ME MUCH.
BUT ANY ORDINARY PERSON MIGHT THINK TWICE ABOUT TRYING TO USE IT...
YOU PSYCHO FREAK!!
HOW DARE YOU PUT YOUR DIRTY CRAP INTO MY MOUTH! I BETTER NOT HAVE FREAKING AIDS NOW!!
DON'T CALL ME A PSYCHO OR A FREAK...
TUG...
AND I DON'T HAVE AIDS...
YOU WOULDN'T HAVE RECOVERED ON YOUR OWN...

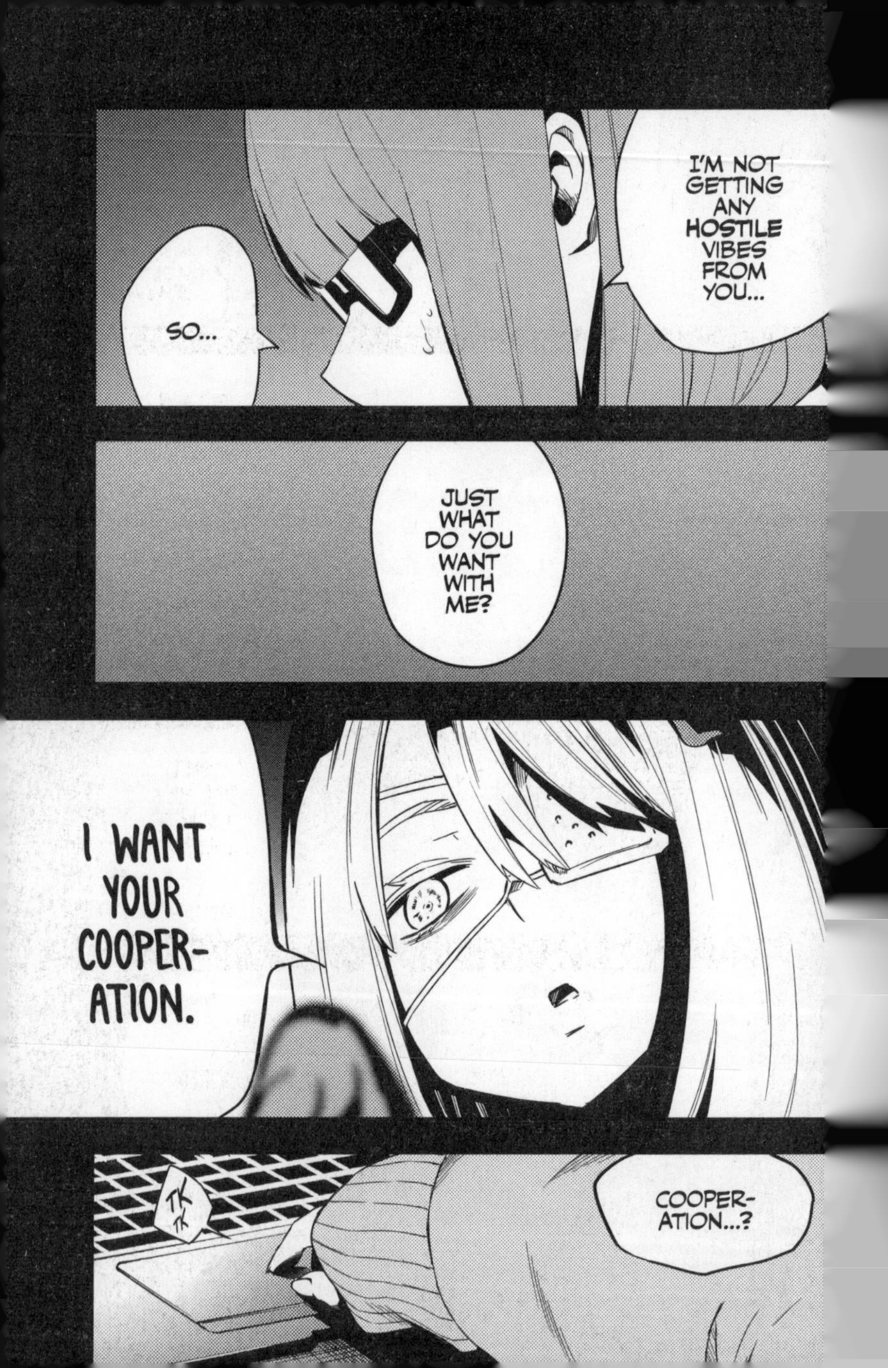
I'M NOT GETTING ANY HOSTILE VIBES FROM YOU...
SO...
JUST WHAT DO YOU WANT WITH ME?
I WANT YOUR COOPER-ATION.
COOPER-ATION...?
TK TK

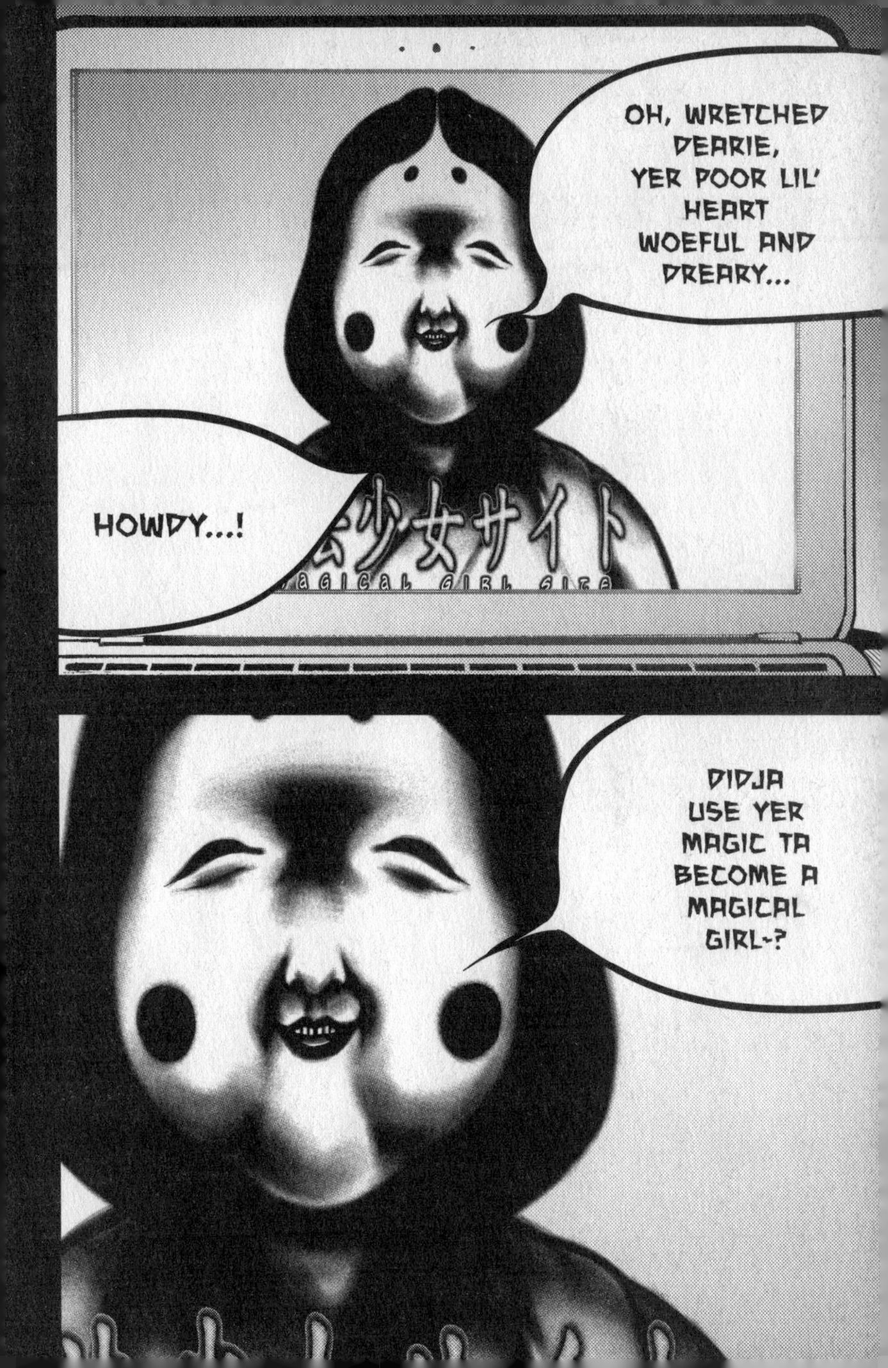
OH, WRETCHED DEARIE, YER POOR LIL' HEART WOEFUL AND DREARY...
HOWDY...!
DIDJA USE YER MAGIC TA BECOME A MAGICAL GIRL~?

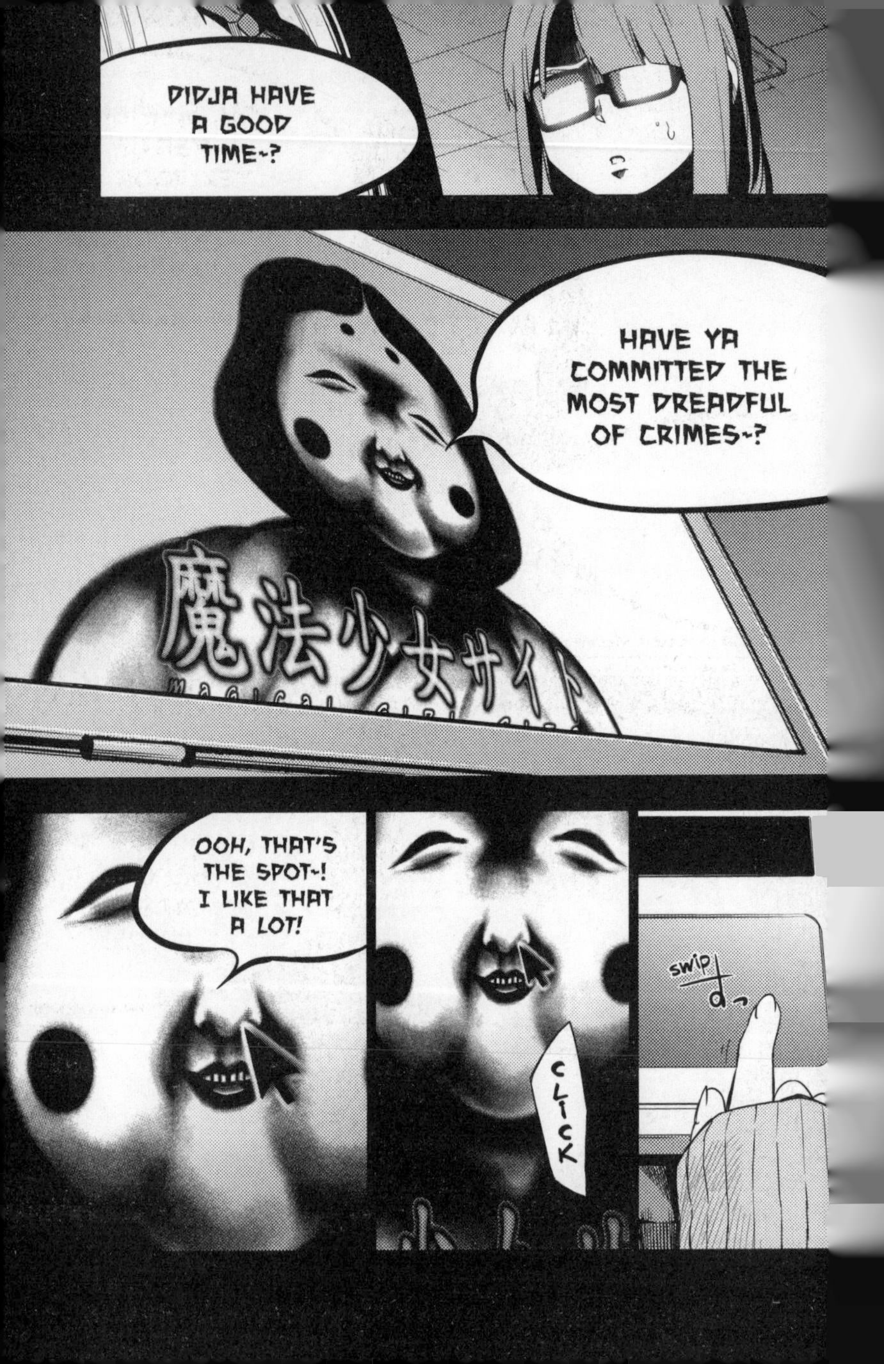
DIDJA HAVE A GOOD TIME~?
HAVE YA COMMITTED THE MOST DREADFUL OF CRIMES~?
魔法少女サイト
swip
CLICK
OOH, THAT'S THE SPOT~! I LIKE THAT A LOT!

BWAAAN

THE TEMPEST...

DA-DUUUN

YES...

Until the Tempest Begins

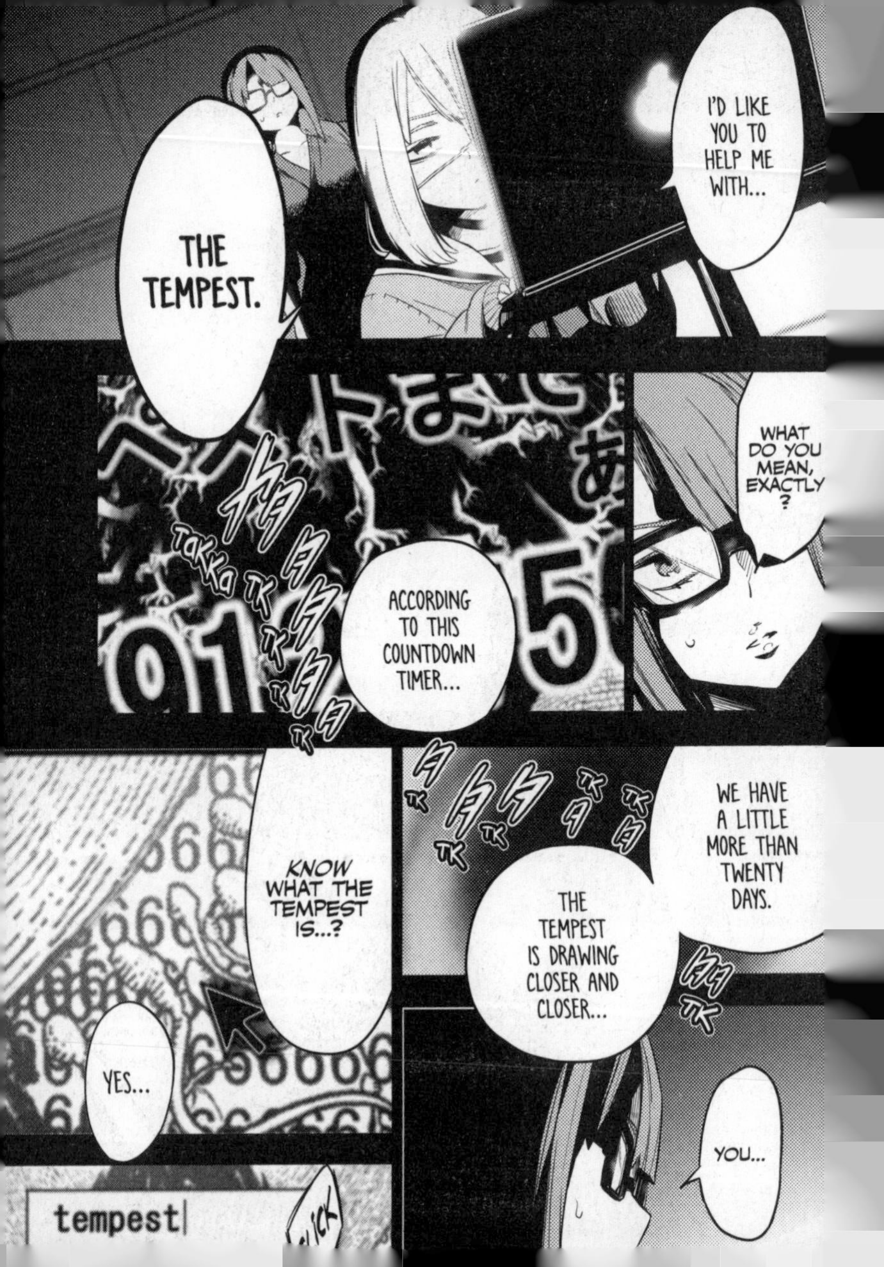
I'D LIKE YOU TO HELP ME WITH...
THE TEMPEST.
WHAT DO YOU MEAN, EXACTLY?
TAKKA TK TK TK TK
ACCORDING TO THIS COUNTDOWN TIMER...
TK TK TK TK TK TK
WE HAVE A LITTLE MORE THAN TWENTY DAYS.
THE TEMPEST IS DRAWING CLOSER AND CLOSER...
YOU...
KNOW WHAT THE TEMPEST IS...?
YES...
tempest|
CLICK

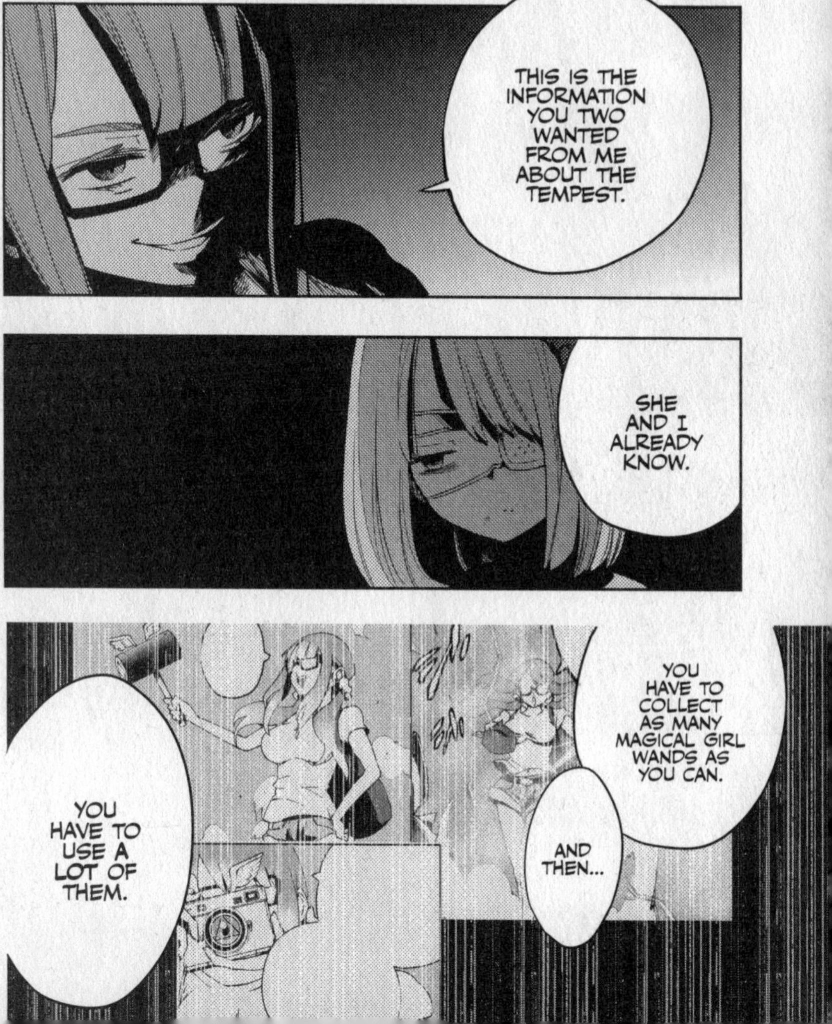
THIS IS THE INFORMATION YOU TWO WANTED FROM ME ABOUT THE TEMPEST.
SHE AND I ALREADY KNOW.
YOU HAVE TO COLLECT AS MANY MAGICAL GIRL WANDS AS YOU CAN.
AND THEN...
YOU HAVE TO USE A LOT OF THEM.

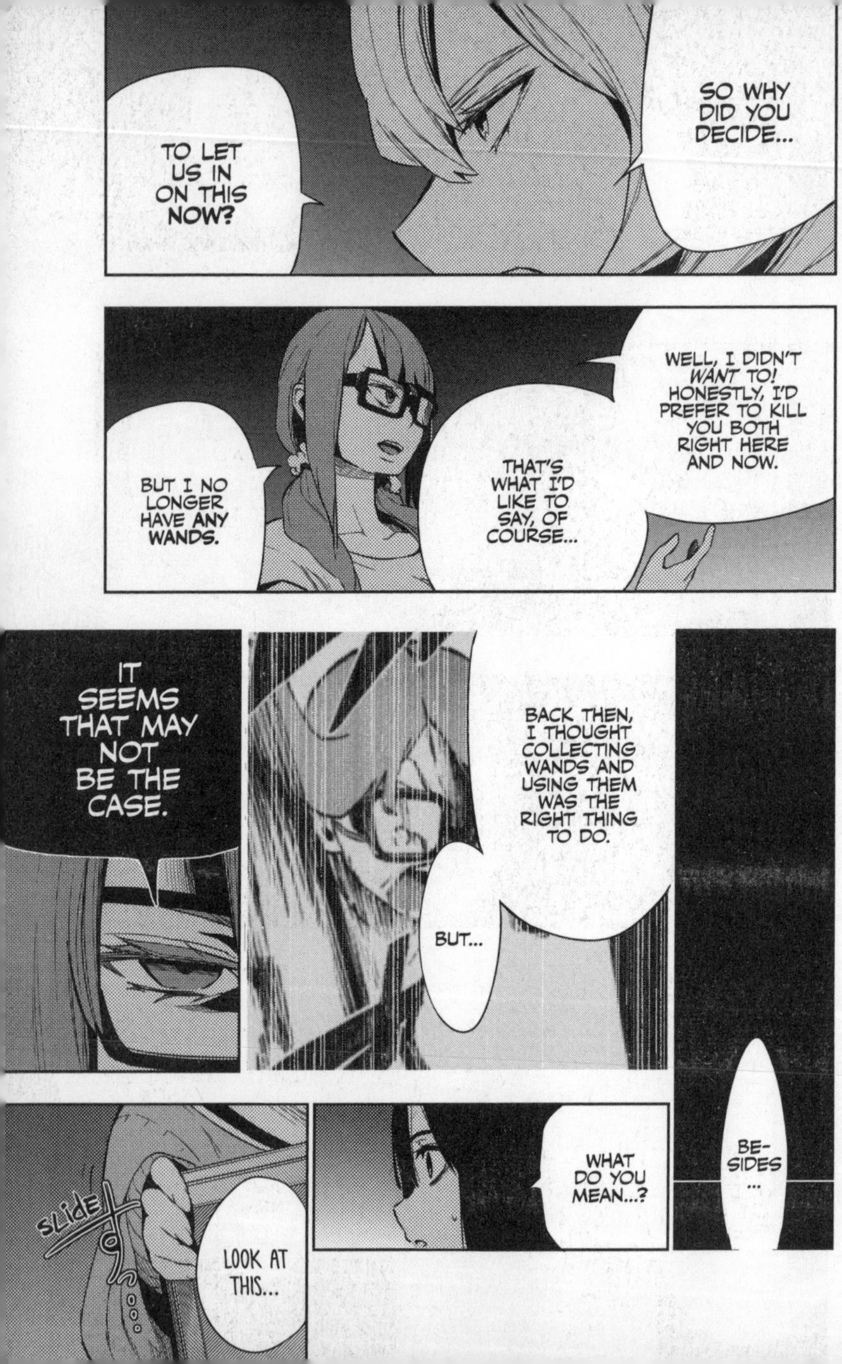
SO WHY DID YOU DECIDE...
TO LET US IN ON THIS NOW?
WELL, I DIDN'T *WANT* TO! HONESTLY, I'D PREFER TO KILL YOU BOTH RIGHT HERE AND NOW.
THAT'S WHAT I'D LIKE TO SAY, OF COURSE...
BUT I NO LONGER HAVE ANY WANDS.
BACK THEN, I THOUGHT COLLECTING WANDS AND USING THEM WAS THE RIGHT THING TO DO.
BUT...
IT SEEMS THAT MAY NOT BE THE CASE.
BE-SIDES ...
WHAT DO YOU MEAN...?
SLIDE
LOOK AT THIS...

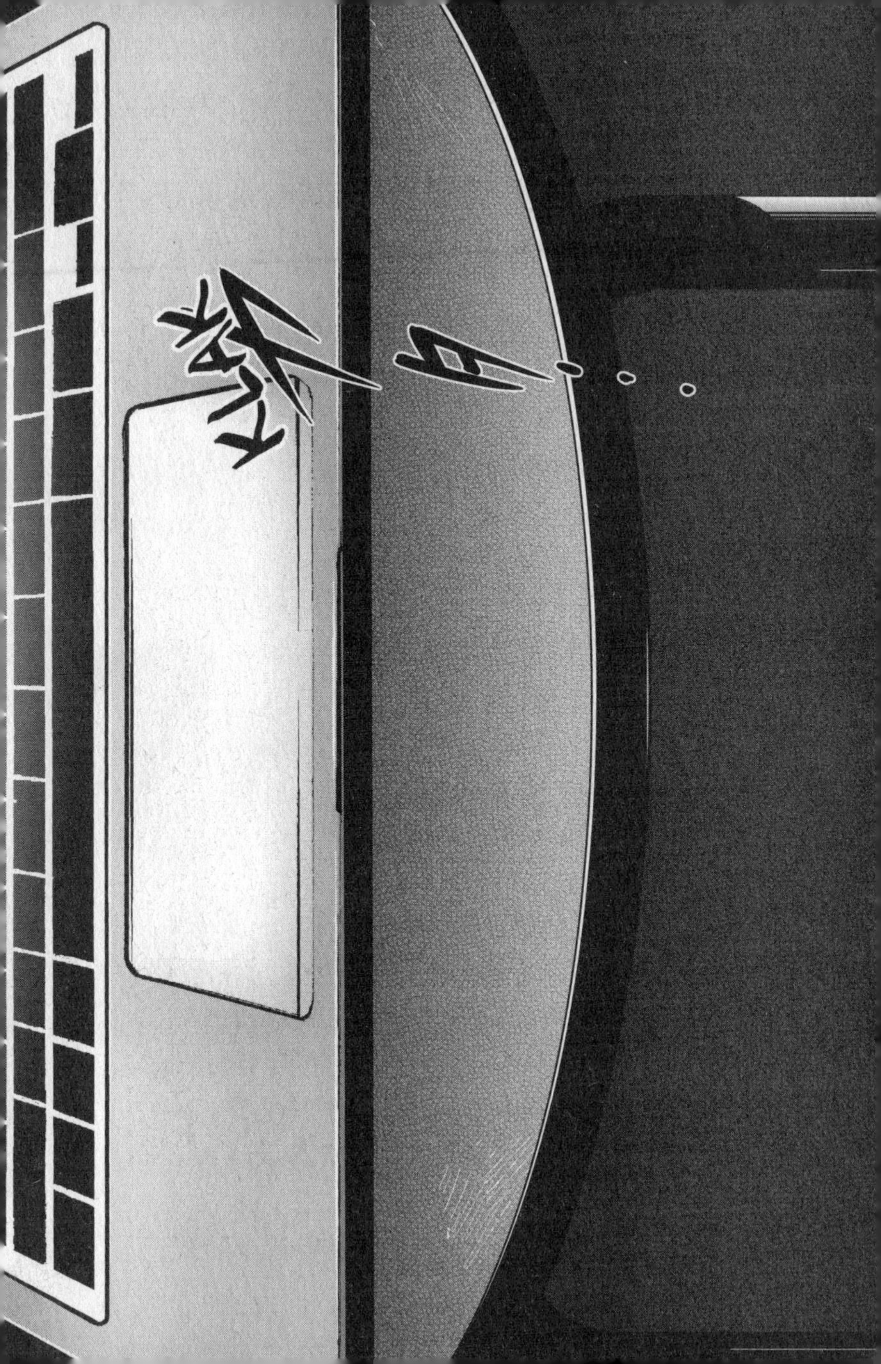
KLAK

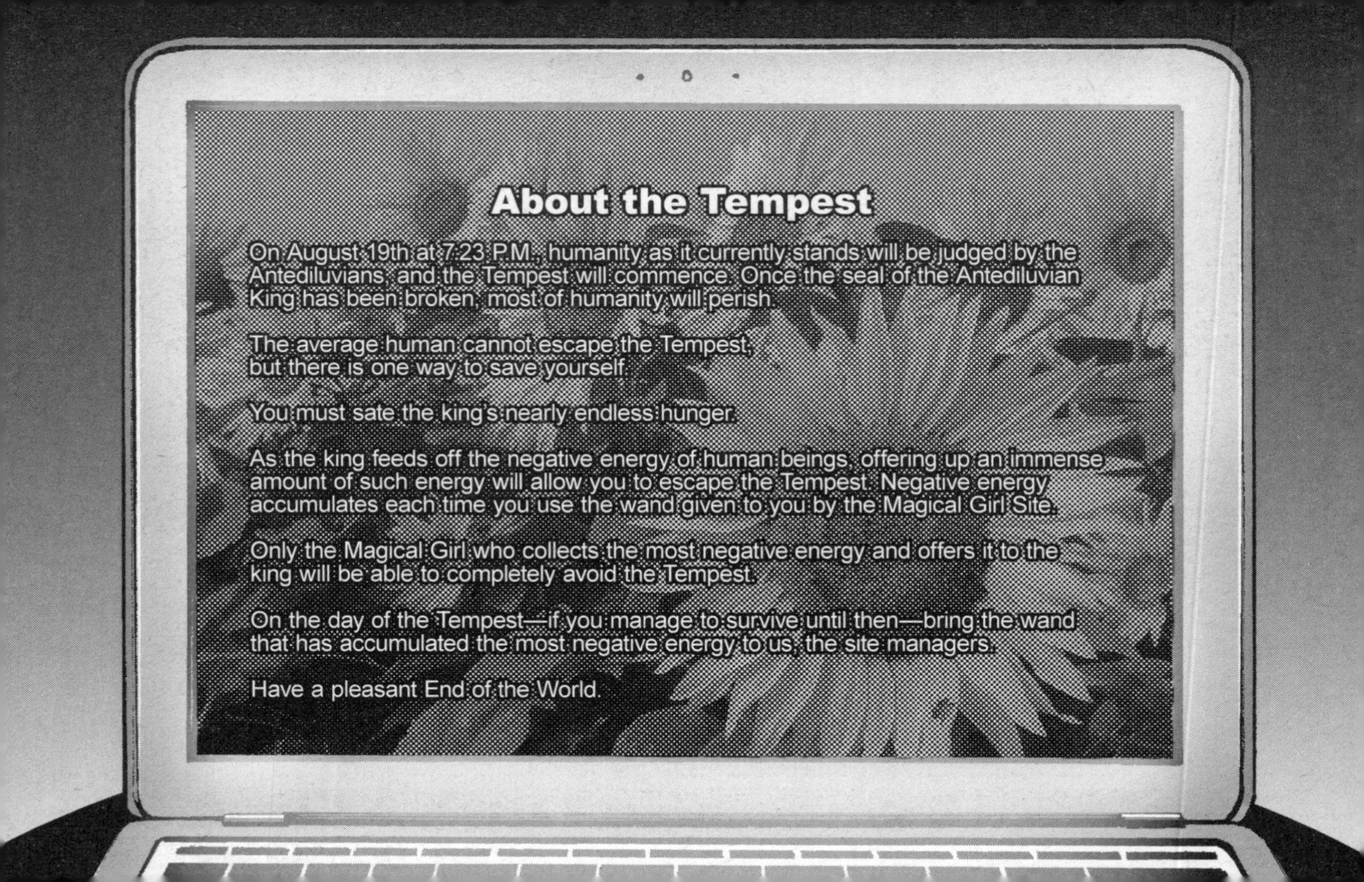
About the Tempest
On August 19th at 7:23 P.M., humanity as it currently stands will be judged by the Antediluvians, and the Tempest will commence. Once the seal of the Antediluvian King has been broken, most of humanity will perish.
The average human cannot escape the Tempest, but there is one way to save yourself.
You must sate the king's nearly endless hunger.
As the king feeds off the negative energy of human beings, offering up an immense amount of such energy will allow you to escape the Tempest. Negative energy accumulates each time you use the wand given to you by the Magical Girl Site.
Only the Magical Girl who collects the most negative energy and offers it to the king will be able to completely avoid the Tempest.
On the day of the Tempest—if you manage to survive until then—bring the wand that has accumulated the most negative energy to us, the site managers.
Have a pleasant End of the World.

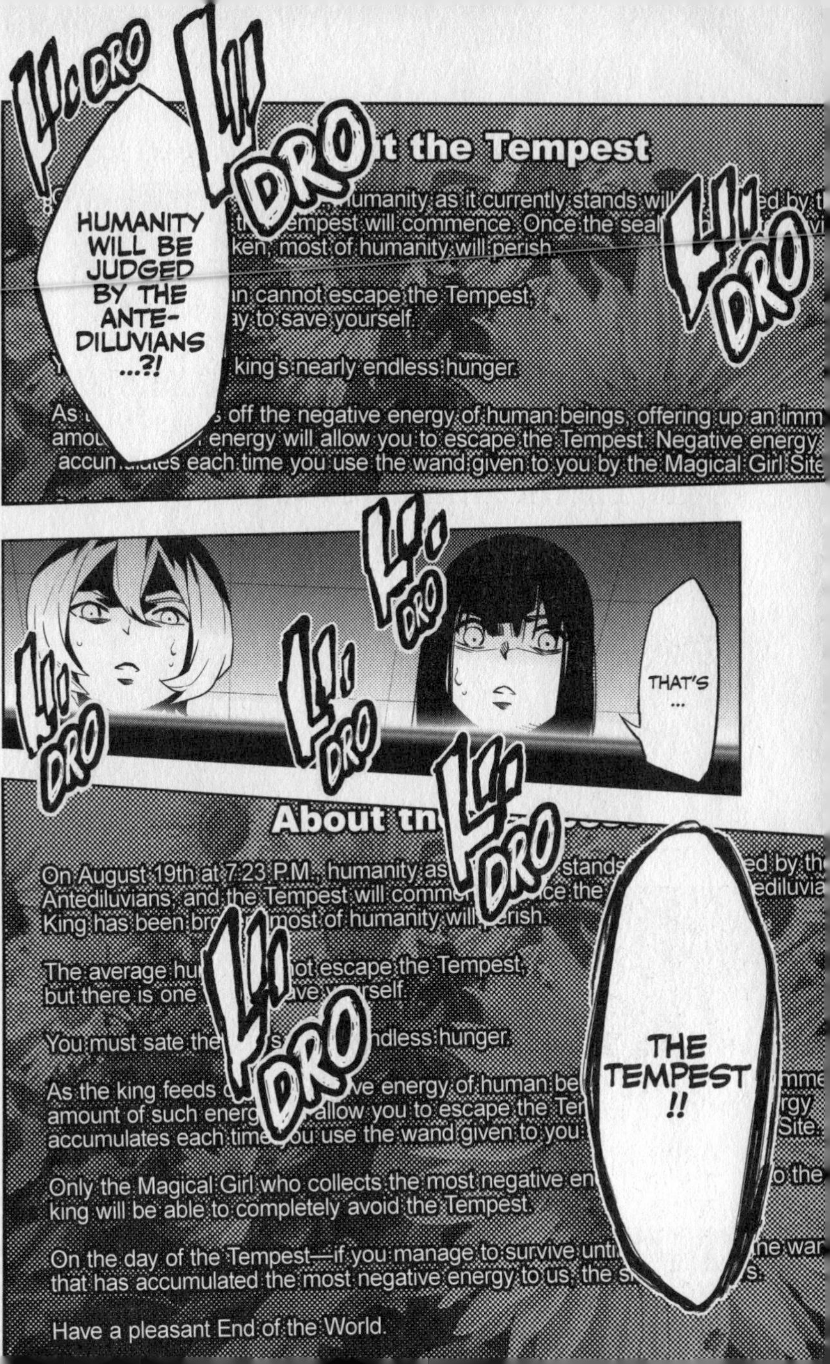
t the Tempest
humanity as it currently stands will
empest will commence. Once the seal
ken, most of humanity will perish.
n cannot escape the Tempest,
y to save yourself.
king's nearly endless hunger.
s off the negative energy of human beings, offering up an imm
energy will allow you to escape the Tempest. Negative energy
each time you use the wand given to you by the Magical Girl Site
HUMANITY WILL BE JUDGED BY THE ANTE-DILUVIANS ...?!
DRO
DRO
DRO
THAT'S ...
DRO
DRO
DRO
About th
On August 19th at 7:23 P.M., humanity as
Antediluvians, and the Tempest will comm
King has been bro most of humanity will perish.
The average hu not escape the Tempest,
but there is one ave yourself.
You must sate the ndless hunger.
As the king feeds ve energy of human be
amount of such energ allow you to escape the Te
accumulates each time you use the wand given to you
Only the Magical Girl who collects the most negative en
king will be able to completely avoid the Tempest.
On the day of the Tempest—if you manage to survive unti
that has accumulated the most negative energy to us, the s
Have a pleasant End of the World.
DRO
DRO
THE TEMPEST !!

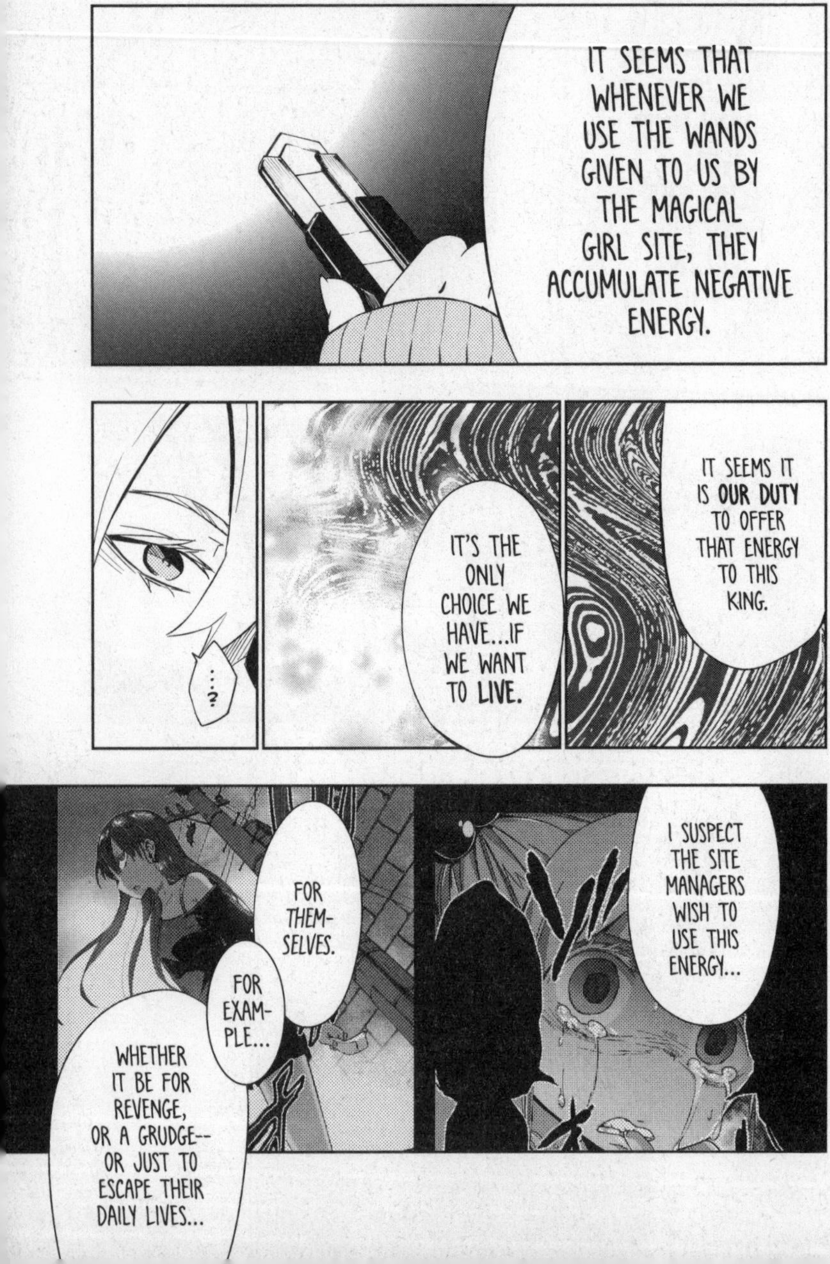
IT SEEMS THAT WHENEVER WE USE THE WANDS GIVEN TO US BY THE MAGICAL GIRL SITE, THEY ACCUMULATE NEGATIVE ENERGY.
IT SEEMS IT IS **OUR DUTY** TO OFFER THAT ENERGY TO THIS KING.
IT'S THE ONLY CHOICE WE HAVE...IF WE WANT TO **LIVE.**
...?
I SUSPECT THE SITE MANAGERS WISH TO USE THIS ENERGY...
FOR THEM-SELVES.
FOR EXAM-PLE...
WHETHER IT BE FOR REVENGE, OR A GRUDGE-- OR JUST TO ESCAPE THEIR DAILY LIVES...

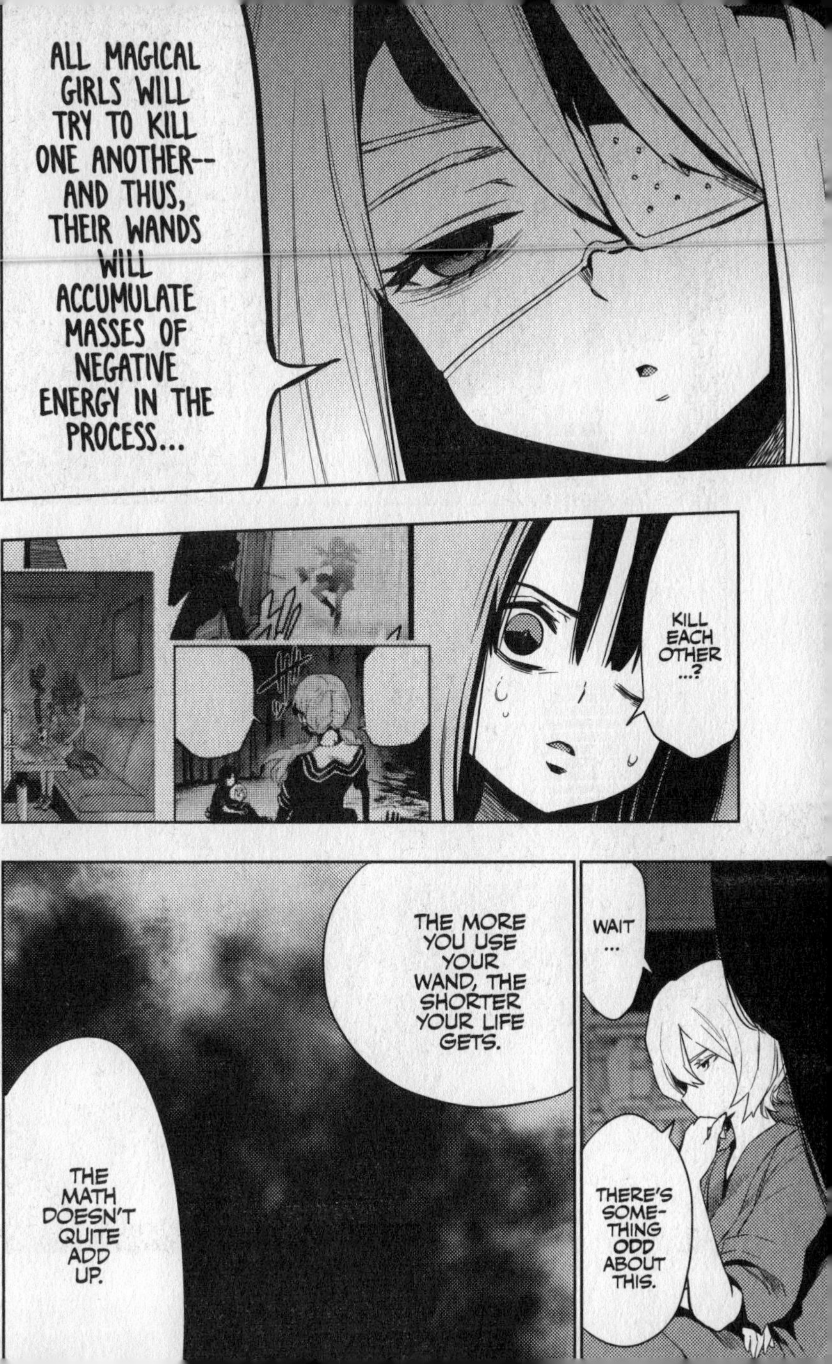
ALL MAGICAL GIRLS WILL TRY TO KILL ONE ANOTHER-- AND THUS, THEIR WANDS WILL ACCUMULATE MASSES OF NEGATIVE ENERGY IN THE PROCESS...
KILL EACH OTHER ...?
WAIT ...
THERE'S SOME-THING ODD ABOUT THIS.
THE MORE YOU USE YOUR WAND, THE SHORTER YOUR LIFE GETS.
THE MATH DOESN'T QUITE ADD UP.

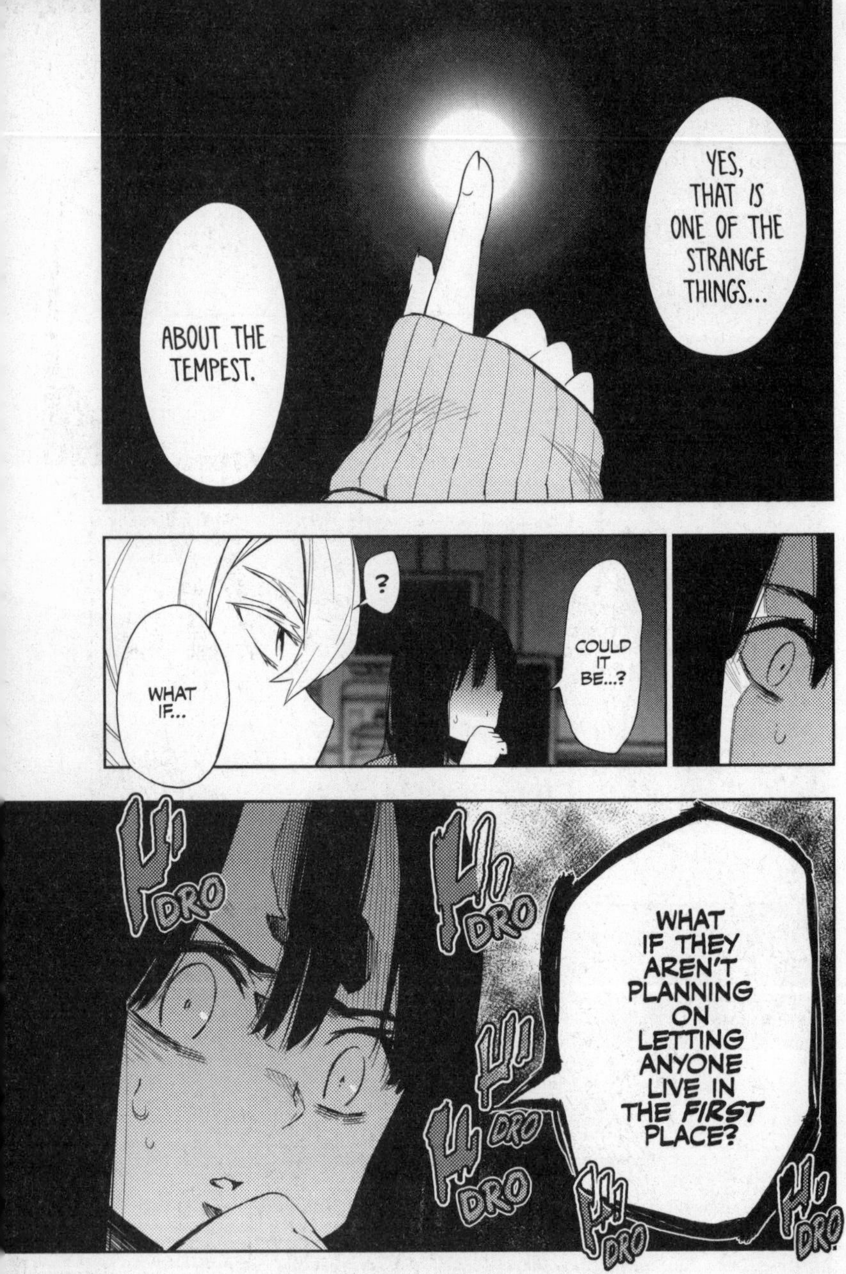
YES, THAT IS ONE OF THE STRANGE THINGS...
ABOUT THE TEMPEST.
COULD IT BE...?
?
WHAT IF...
DRO
WHAT IF THEY AREN'T PLANNING ON LETTING ANYONE LIVE IN THE *FIRST* PLACE?
DRO
DRO
DRO
DRO
DRO
DRO

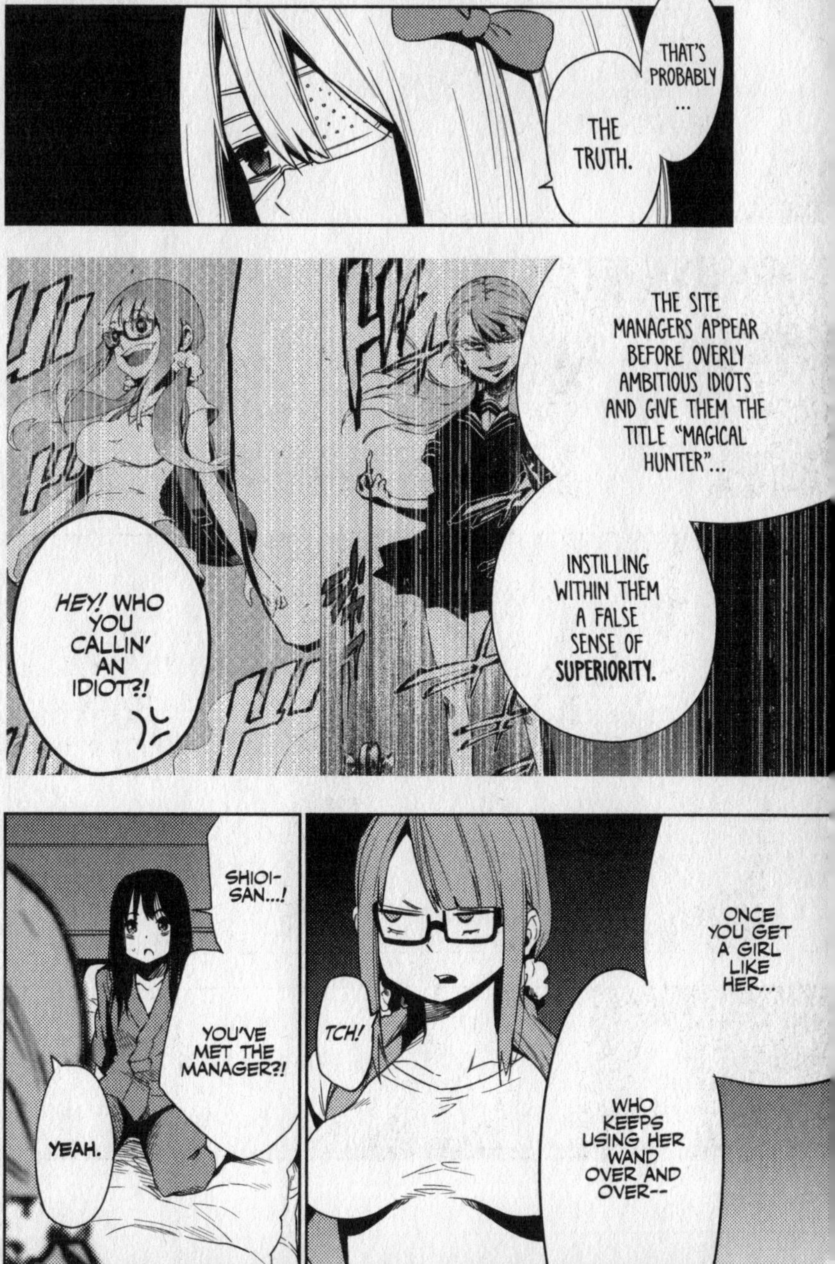
THAT'S PROBABLY...
THE TRUTH.
THE SITE MANAGERS APPEAR BEFORE OVERLY AMBITIOUS IDIOTS AND GIVE THEM THE TITLE "MAGICAL HUNTER"...
INSTILLING WITHIN THEM A FALSE SENSE OF SUPERIORITY.
HEY! WHO YOU CALLIN' AN IDIOT?!
ONCE YOU GET A GIRL LIKE HER...
WHO KEEPS USING HER WAND OVER AND OVER--
TCH!
SHIOI-SAN...!
YOU'VE MET THE MANAGER?!
YEAH.

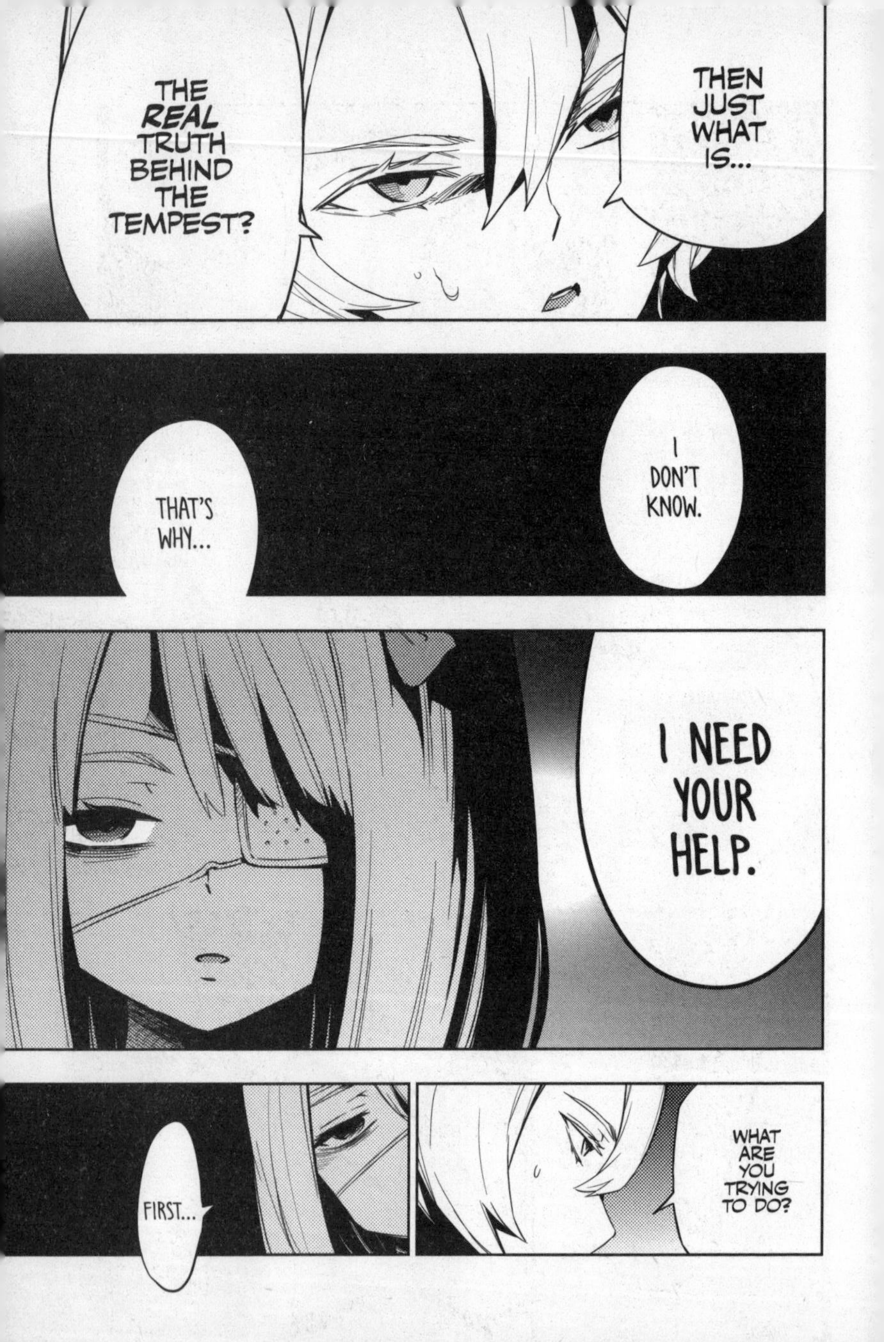
THEN JUST WHAT IS...
THE REAL TRUTH BEHIND THE TEMPEST?
I DON'T KNOW.
THAT'S WHY...
I NEED YOUR HELP.
WHAT ARE YOU TRYING TO DO?
FIRST...

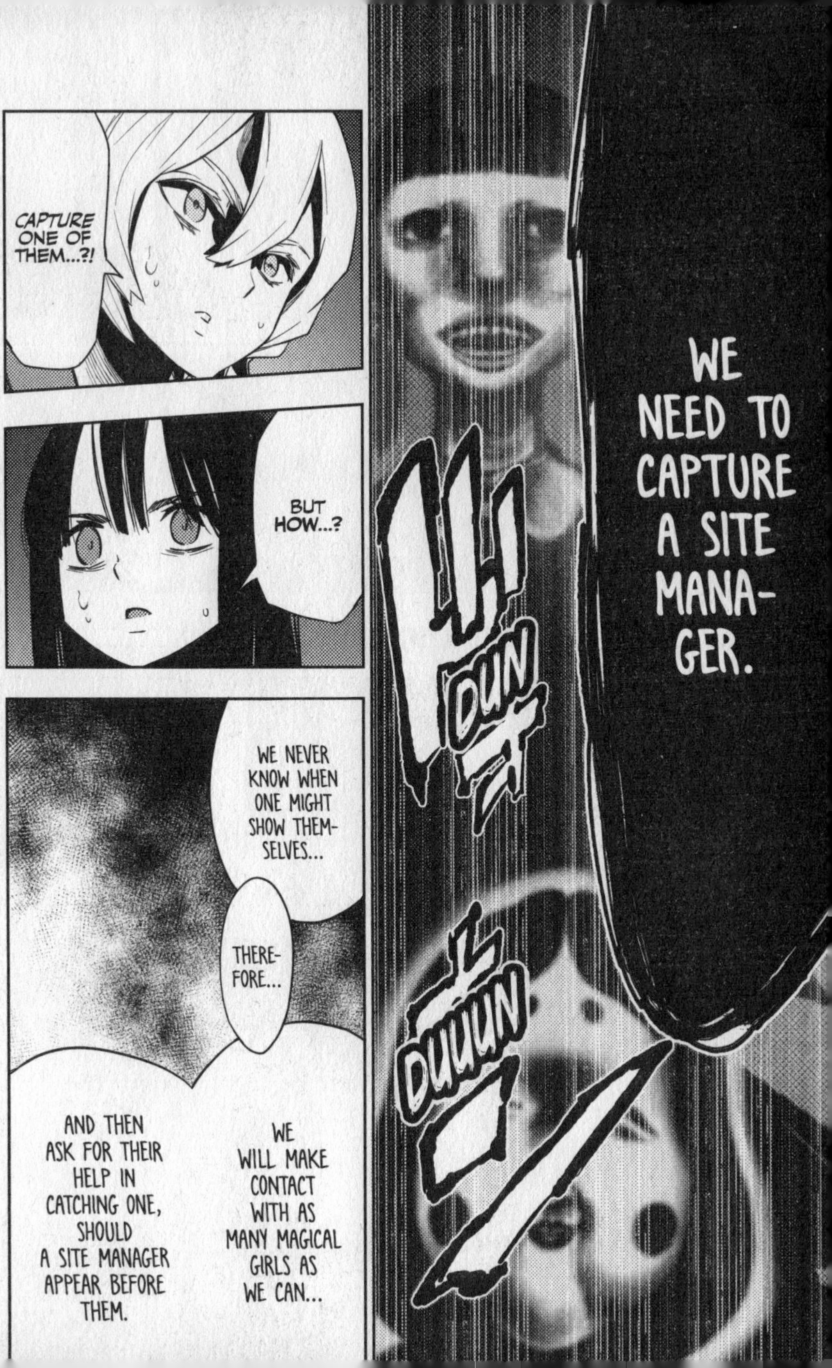
WE NEED TO CAPTURE A SITE MANA- GER.
DUN
DUUUN
CAPTURE ONE OF THEM...?!
BUT HOW...?
WE NEVER KNOW WHEN ONE MIGHT SHOW THEM- SELVES...
THERE- FORE...
WE WILL MAKE CONTACT WITH AS MANY MAGICAL GIRLS AS WE CAN...
AND THEN ASK FOR THEIR HELP IN CATCHING ONE, SHOULD A SITE MANAGER APPEAR BEFORE THEM.

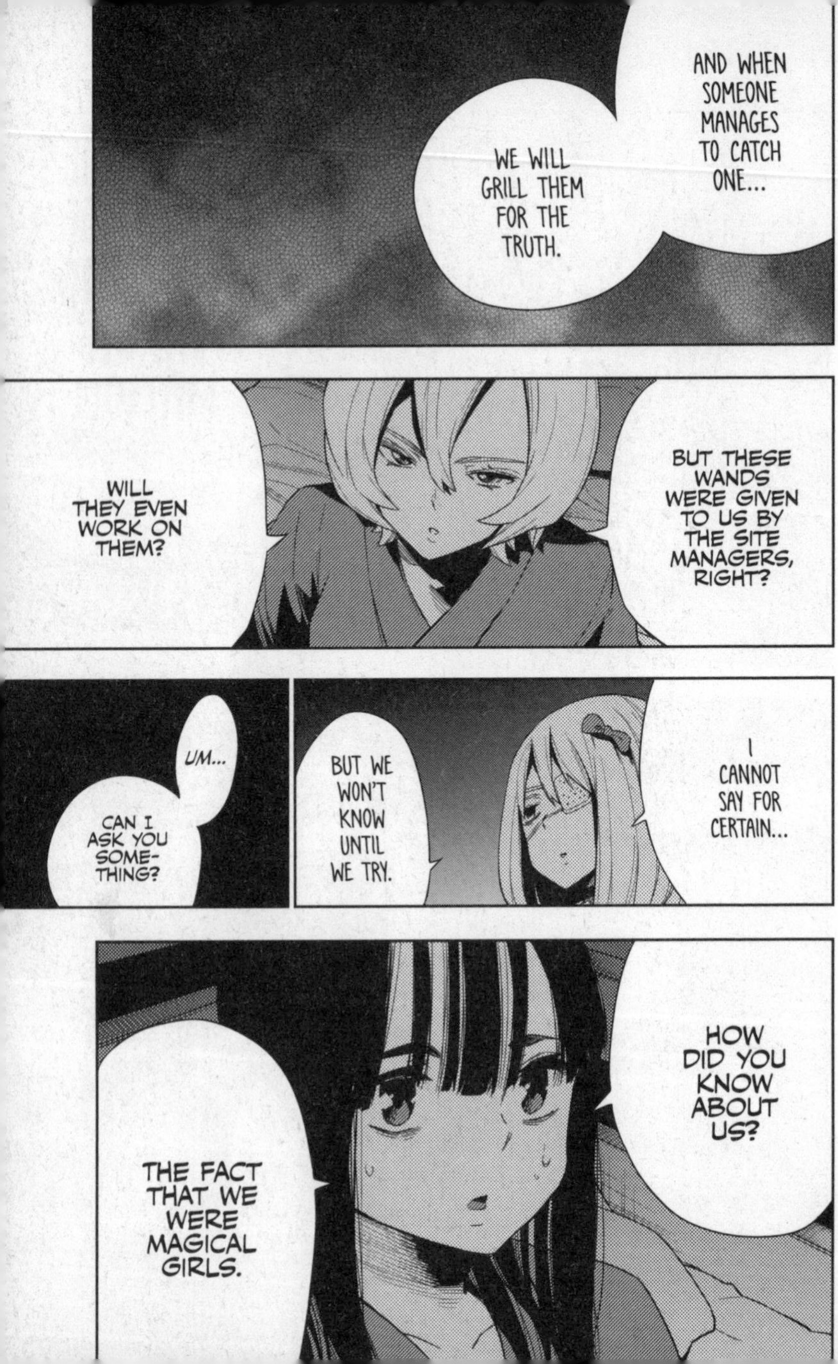
AND WHEN SOMEONE MANAGES TO CATCH ONE...
WE WILL GRILL THEM FOR THE TRUTH.
BUT THESE WANDS WERE GIVEN TO US BY THE SITE MANAGERS, RIGHT?
WILL THEY EVEN WORK ON THEM?
I CANNOT SAY FOR CERTAIN...
BUT WE WON'T KNOW UNTIL WE TRY.
UM...
CAN I ASK YOU SOME-THING?
HOW DID YOU KNOW ABOUT US?
THE FACT THAT WE WERE MAGICAL GIRLS.

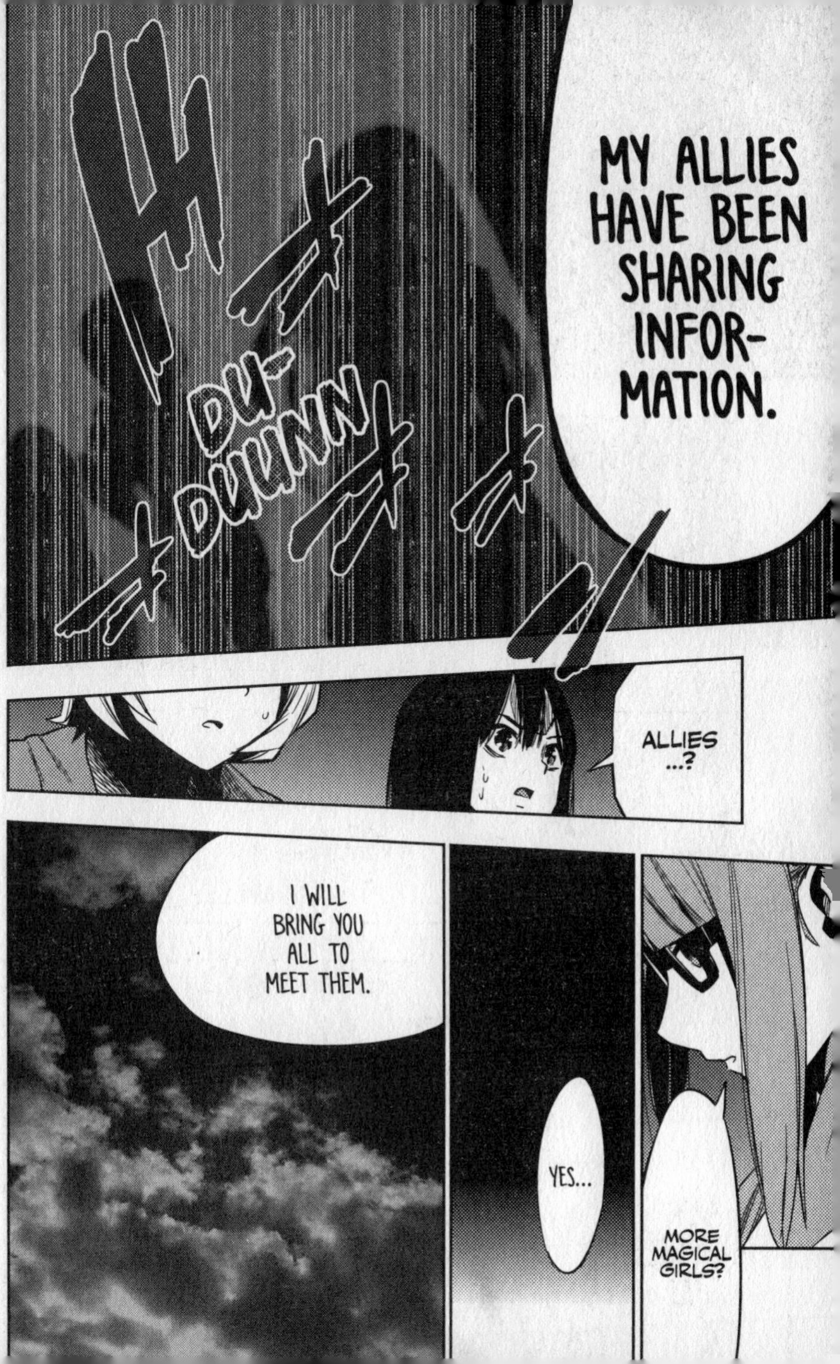
MY ALLIES HAVE BEEN SHARING INFOR-MATION.
DU-DUUNN
ALLIES ...?
MORE MAGICAL GIRLS?
YES...
I WILL BRING YOU ALL TO MEET THEM.

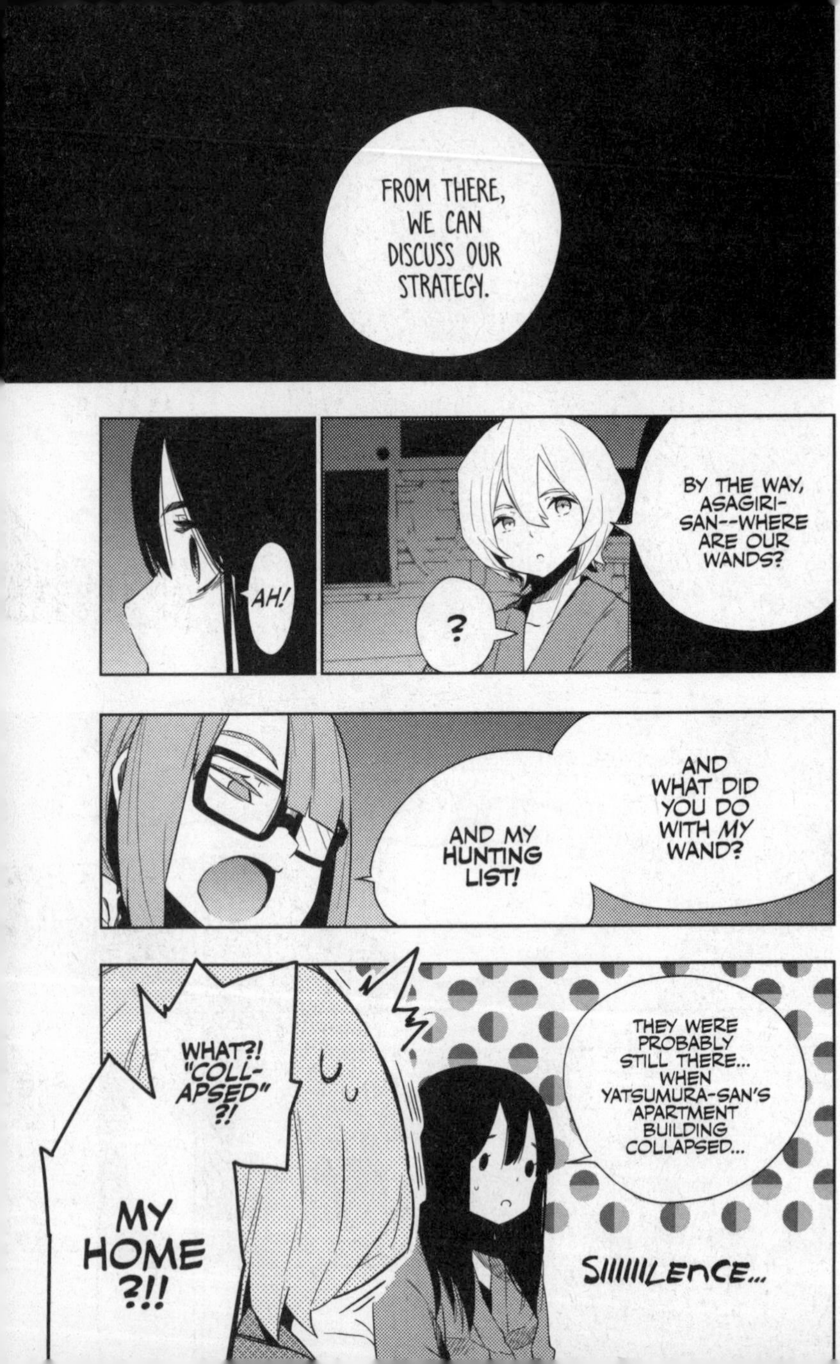
FROM THERE, WE CAN DISCUSS OUR STRATEGY.
BY THE WAY, ASAGIRI-SAN--WHERE ARE OUR WANDS?
?
AH!
AND WHAT DID YOU DO WITH *MY* WAND?
AND MY HUNTING LIST!
THEY WERE PROBABLY STILL THERE... WHEN YATSUMURA-SAN'S APARTMENT BUILDING COLLAPSED...
SIIIIIILENCE...
WHAT?! "COLL-APSED" ?!
MY HOME ?!!

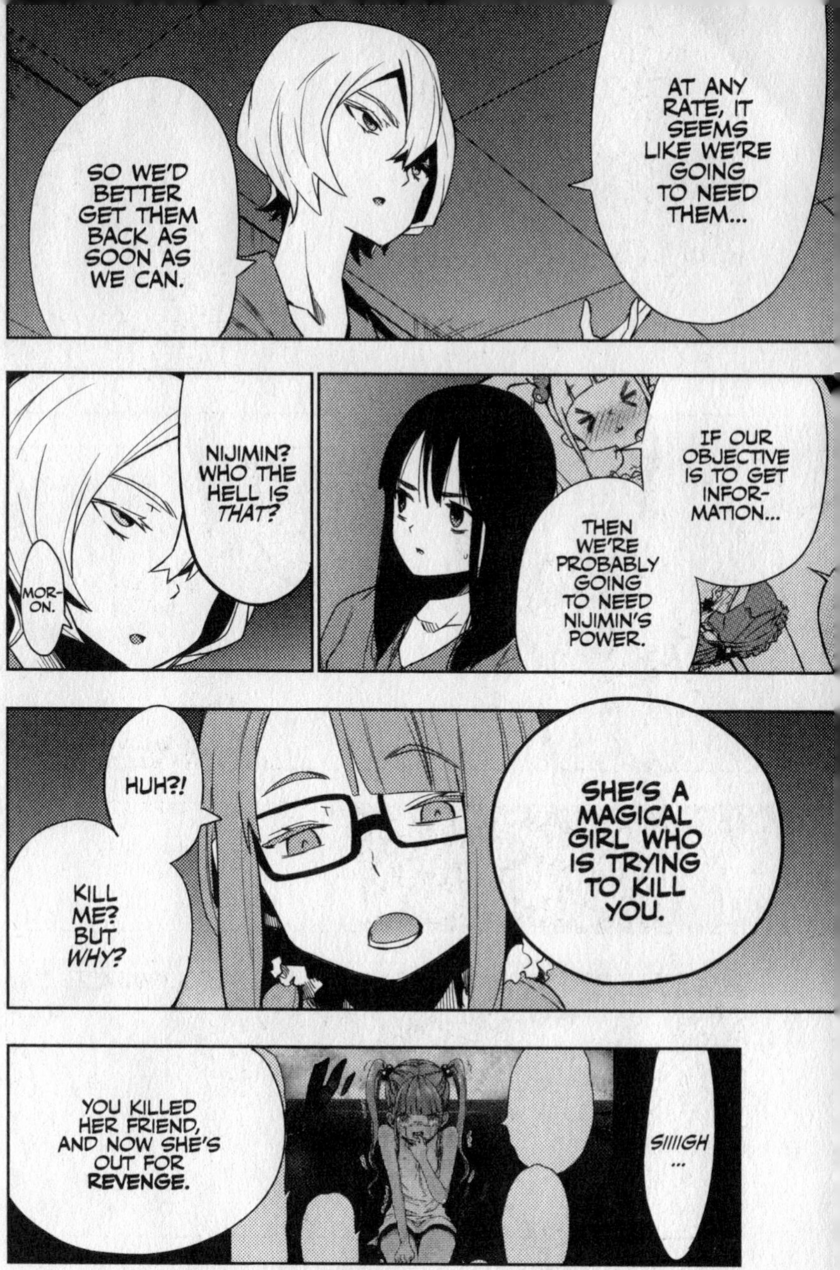
AT ANY RATE, IT SEEMS LIKE WE'RE GOING TO NEED THEM...
SO WE'D BETTER GET THEM BACK AS SOON AS WE CAN.
IF OUR OBJECTIVE IS TO GET INFOR-MATION...
THEN WE'RE PROBABLY GOING TO NEED NIJIMIN'S POWER.
NIJIMIN? WHO THE HELL IS *THAT?*
MOR-ON.
SHE'S A MAGICAL GIRL WHO IS TRYING TO KILL YOU.
HUH?!
KILL ME? BUT *WHY?*
SIIIGH ...
YOU KILLED HER FRIEND, AND NOW SHE'S OUT FOR REVENGE.

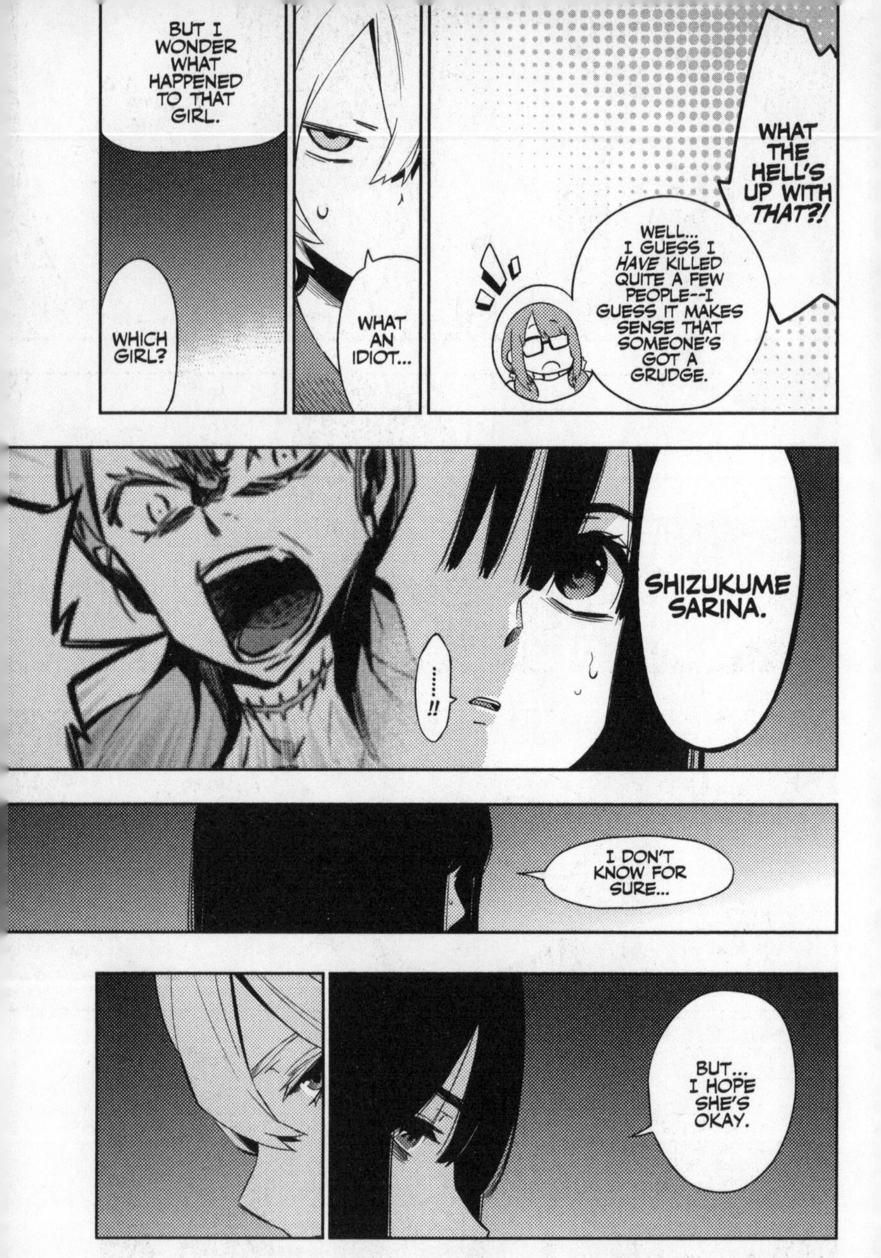
WHAT THE HELL'S UP WITH *THAT?!*
WELL... I GUESS I *HAVE* KILLED QUITE A FEW PEOPLE--I GUESS IT MAKES SENSE THAT SOMEONE'S GOT A GRUDGE.
WHAT AN IDIOT...
BUT I WONDER WHAT HAPPENED TO THAT GIRL.
WHICH GIRL?
SHIZUKUME SARINA.
......!!
I DON'T KNOW FOR SURE...
BUT... I HOPE SHE'S OKAY.

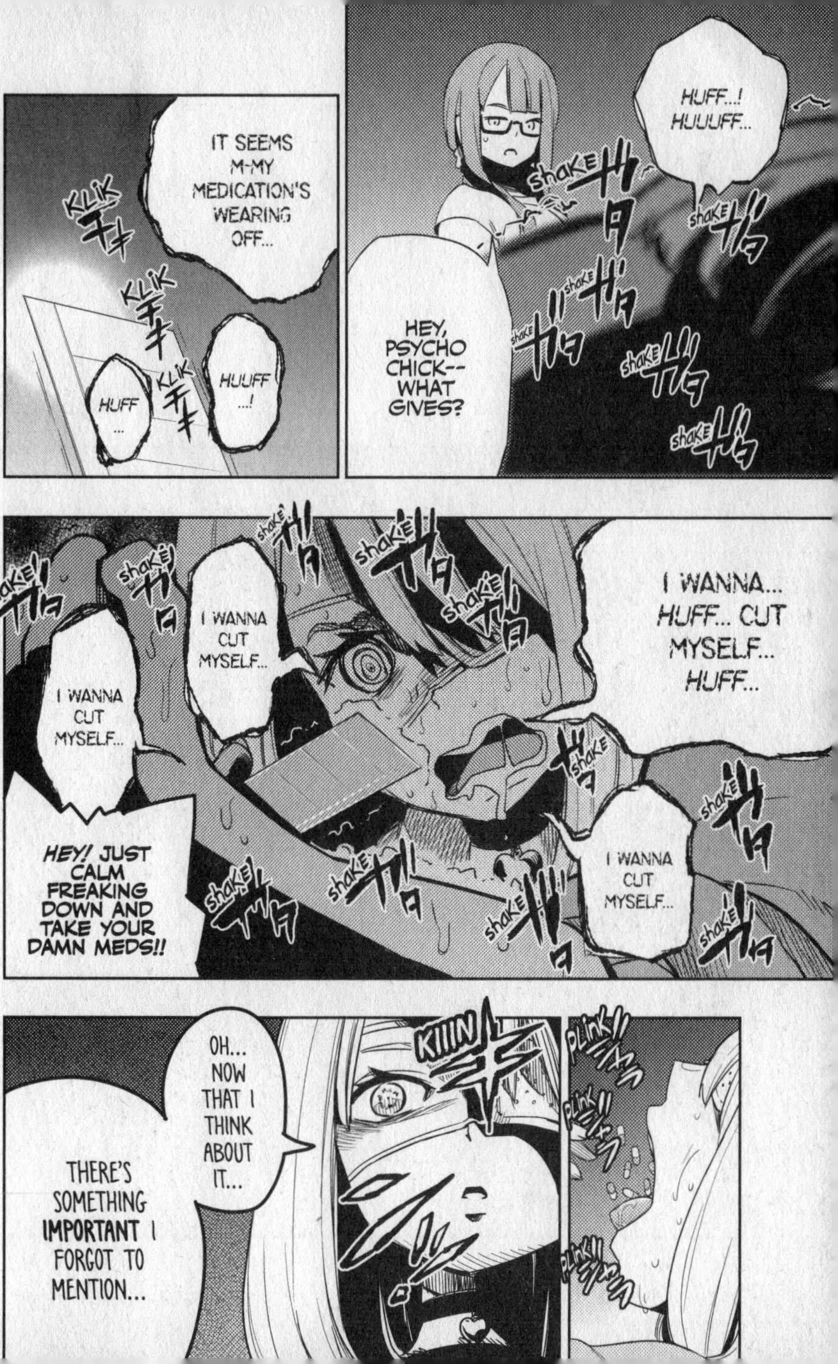
HUFF...! HUUUFF...
shake
shake
shake
shake
shake
shake
HEY, PSYCHO CHICK-- WHAT GIVES?
IT SEEMS M-MY MEDICATION'S WEARING OFF...
KLIK
KLIK
KLIK
HUUFF ...!
HUFF ...
I WANNA... HUFF... CUT MYSELF... HUFF...
shake
shake
shake
shake
I WANNA CUT MYSELF...
shake
shake
I WANNA CUT MYSELF...
shake
shake
I WANNA CUT MYSELF...
shake
shake
HEY! JUST CALM FREAKING DOWN AND TAKE YOUR DAMN MEDS!!
plink!!
plink!!
plink!!
KIIIN
OH... NOW THAT I THINK ABOUT IT...
THERE'S SOMETHING IMPORTANT I FORGOT TO MENTION...

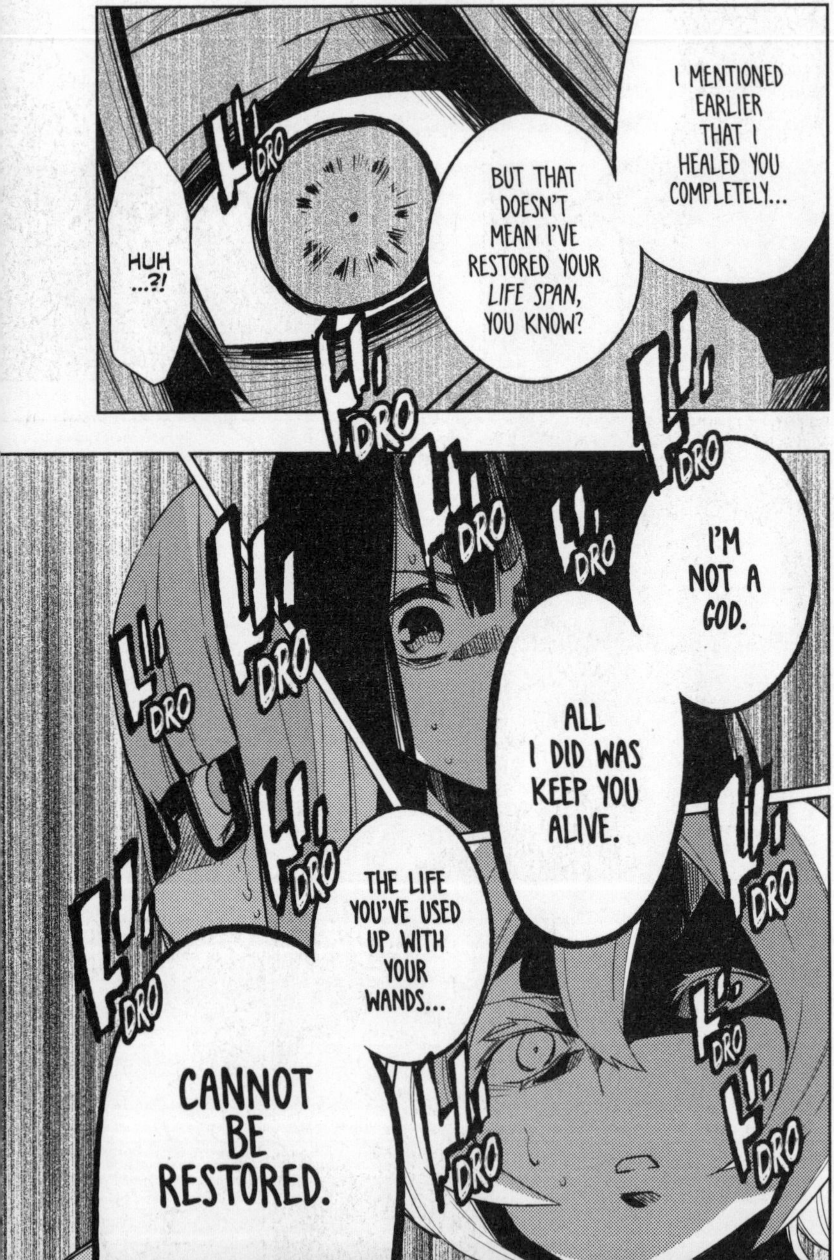
I MENTIONED EARLIER THAT I HEALED YOU COMPLETELY...
BUT THAT DOESN'T MEAN I'VE RESTORED YOUR *LIFE SPAN*, YOU KNOW?
DRO
HUH ...?!
DRO
DRO
I'M NOT A GOD.
DRO
DRO
DRO
DRO
ALL I DID WAS KEEP YOU ALIVE.
DRO
DRO
DRO
THE LIFE YOU'VE USED UP WITH YOUR WANDS...
DRO
DRO
CANNOT BE RESTORED.

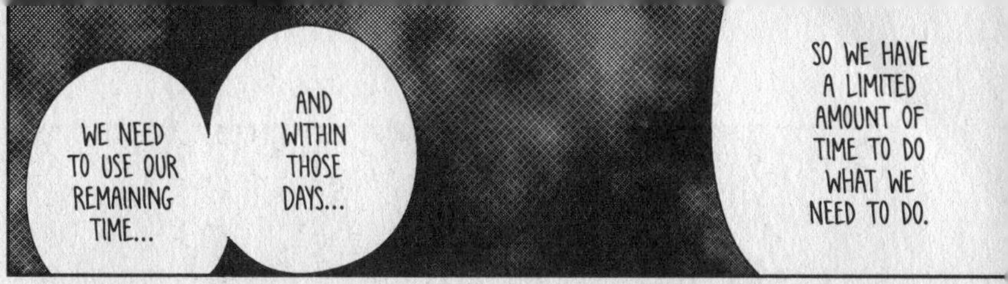
SO WE HAVE A LIMITED AMOUNT OF TIME TO DO WHAT WE NEED TO DO.
AND WITHIN THOSE DAYS...
WE NEED TO USE OUR REMAINING TIME...
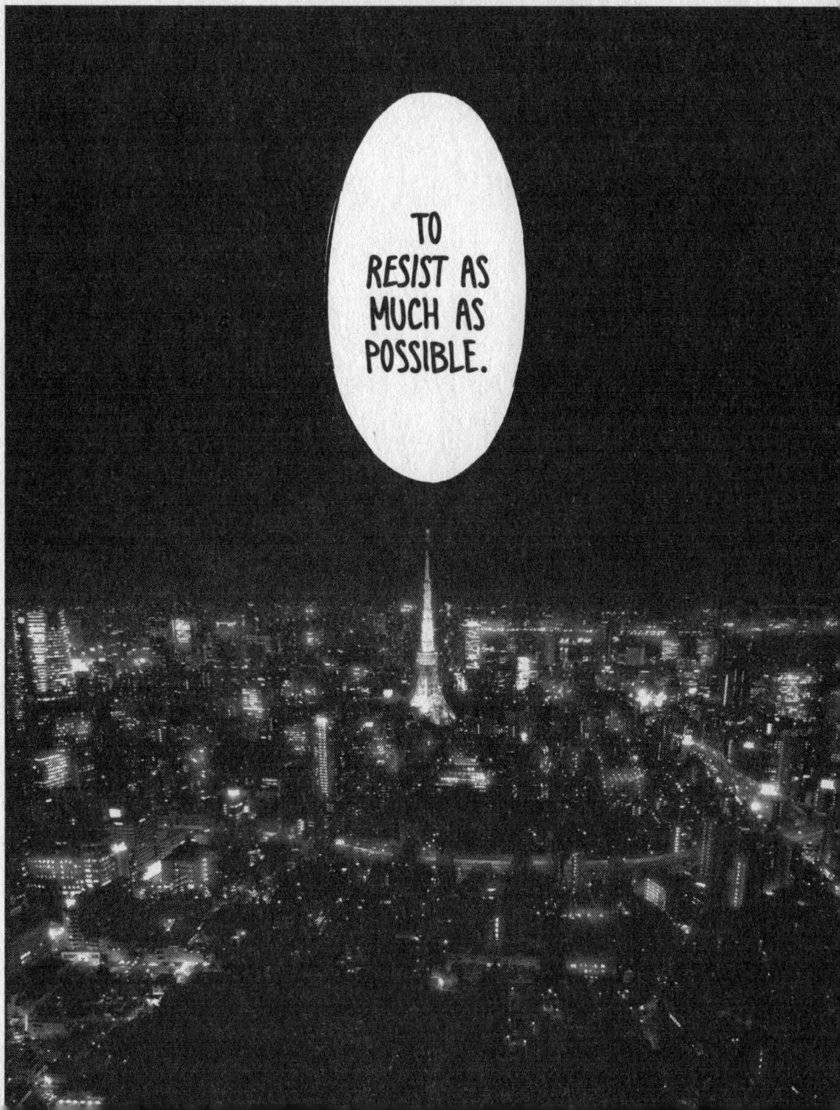
TO RESIST AS MUCH AS POSSIBLE.

ENTER. 21 THE TIME REMAINING

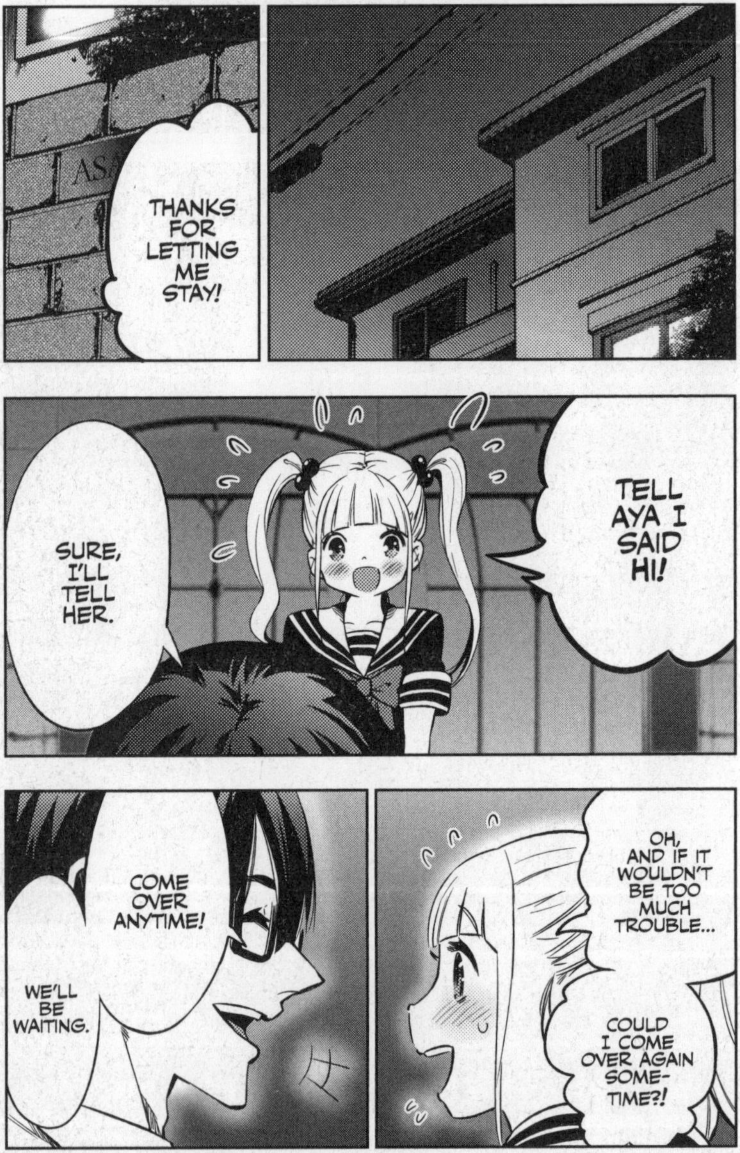
THANKS FOR LETTING ME STAY!
TELL AYA I SAID HI!
SURE, I'LL TELL HER.
OH, AND IF IT WOULDN'T BE TOO MUCH TROUBLE...
COULD I COME OVER AGAIN SOME-TIME?!
COME OVER ANYTIME!
WE'LL BE WAITING.

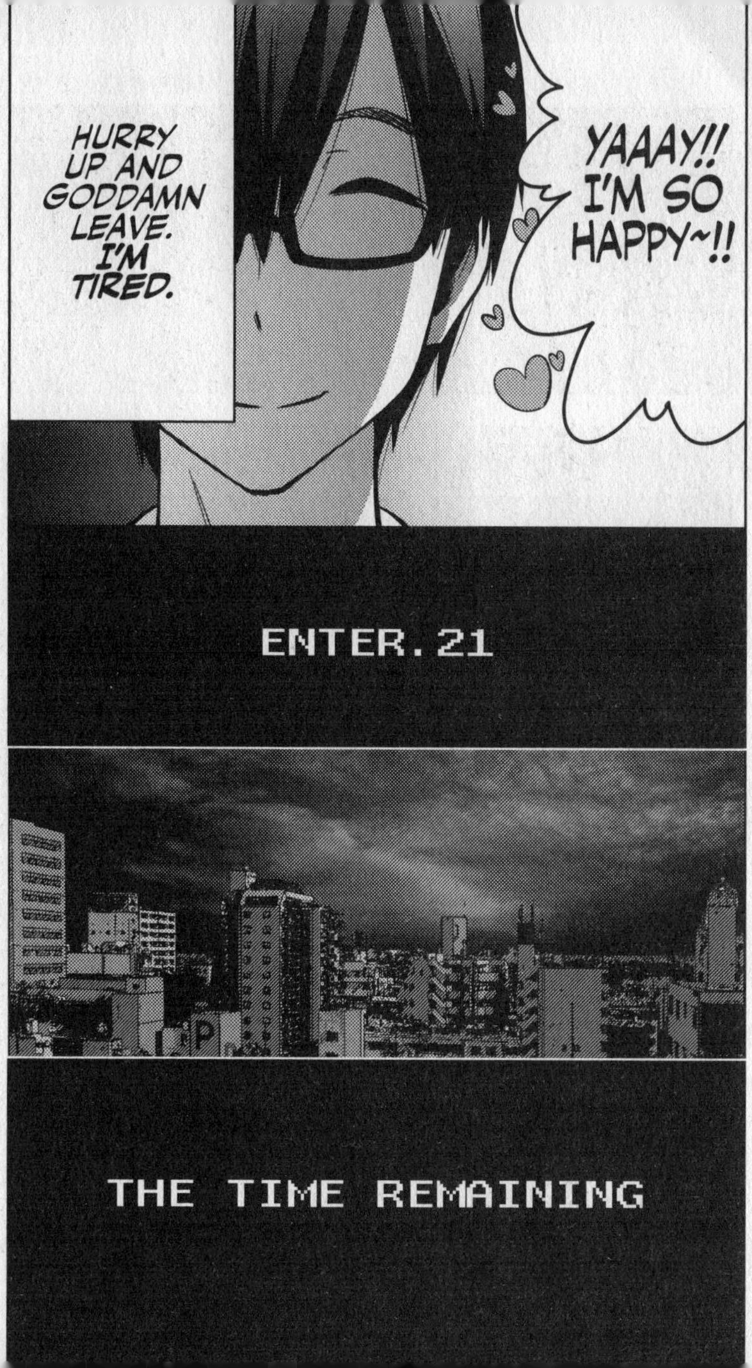
YAAAY!! I'M SO HAPPY~!!
HURRY UP AND GODDAMN LEAVE. I'M TIRED.
ENTER. 21
THE TIME REMAINING

Sign: Misashino General

......

?!

Ka-chak

OH, I MUST HAVE DRIFTED OFF...

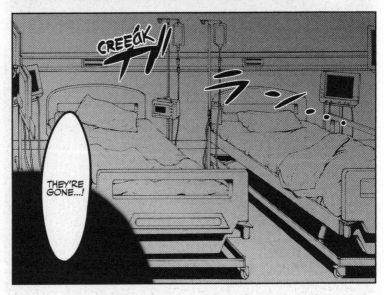

CREEAK

THEY'RE GONE...!

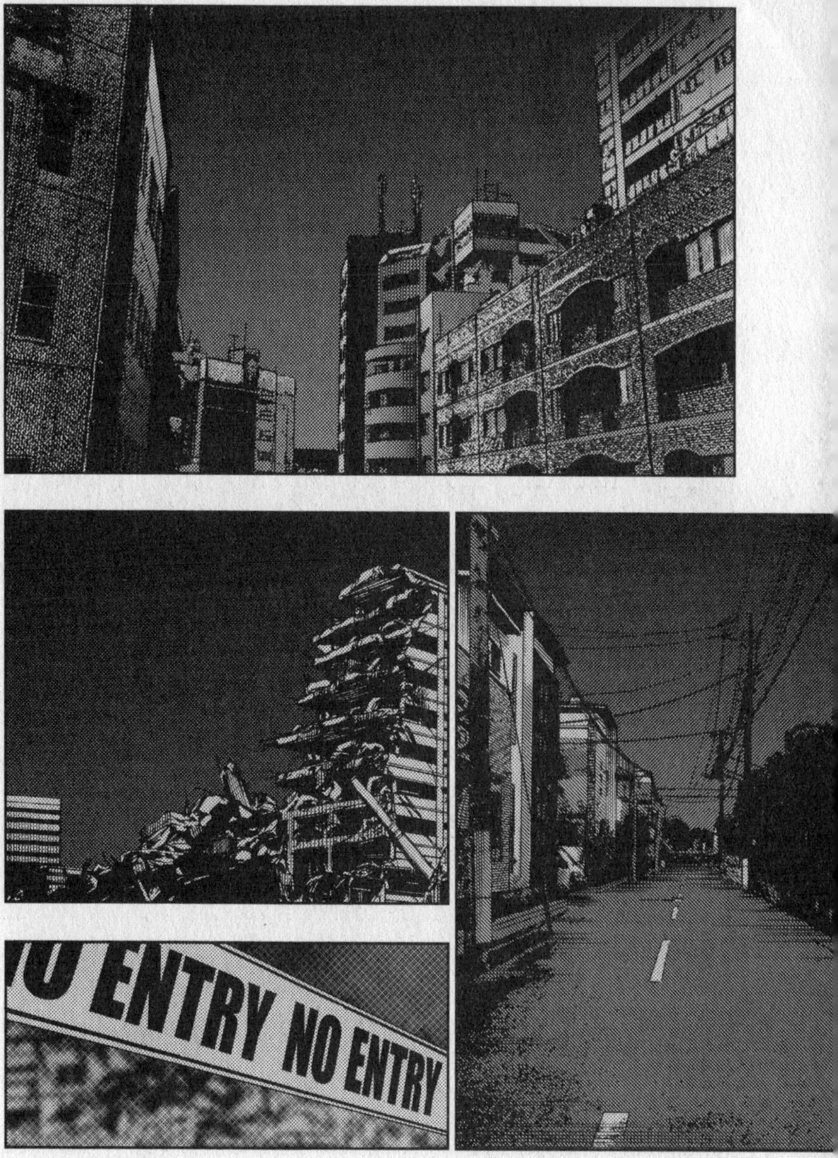
ENTRY NO ENTRY

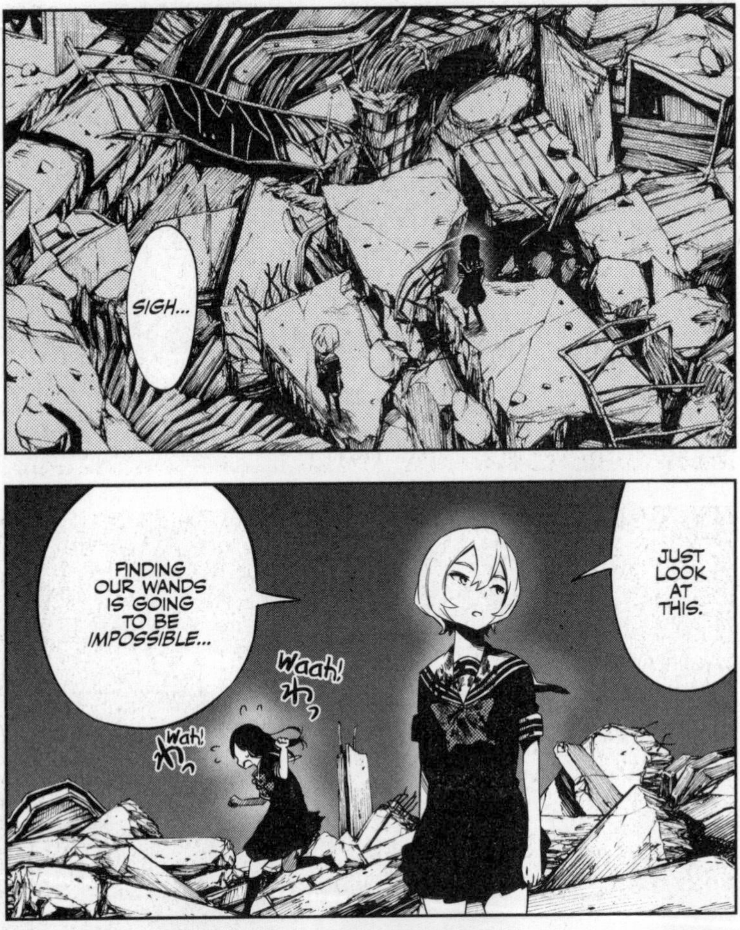
SIGH...
JUST LOOK AT THIS.
FINDING OUR WANDS IS GOING TO BE IMPOSSIBLE...
Waah!
わっ
Wah!
わっ
HEY, YATSUMURA-SAN...
CLOP

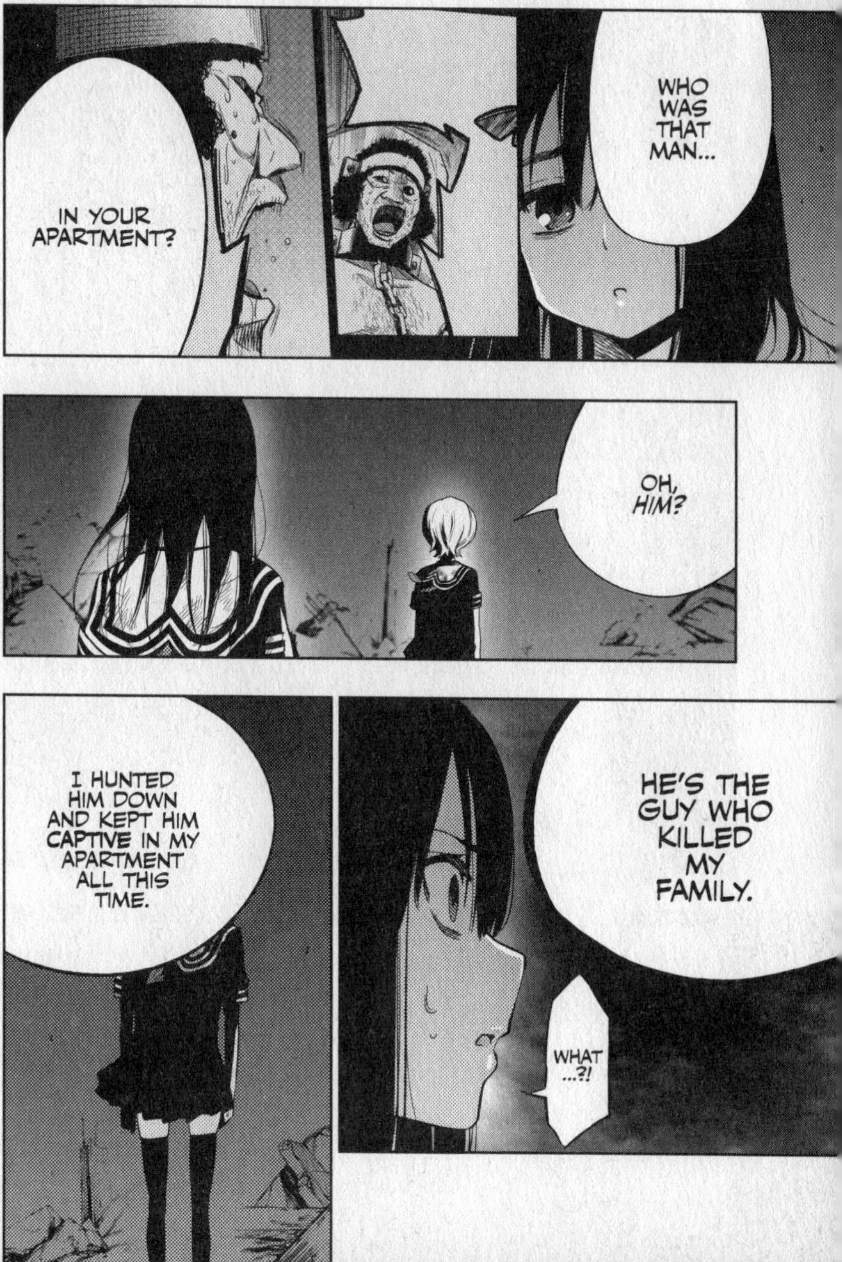
WHO WAS THAT MAN...
IN YOUR APARTMENT?
OH, *HIM?*
HE'S THE GUY WHO KILLED MY FAMILY.
WHAT ...?!
I HUNTED HIM DOWN AND KEPT HIM CAPTIVE IN MY APARTMENT ALL THIS TIME.

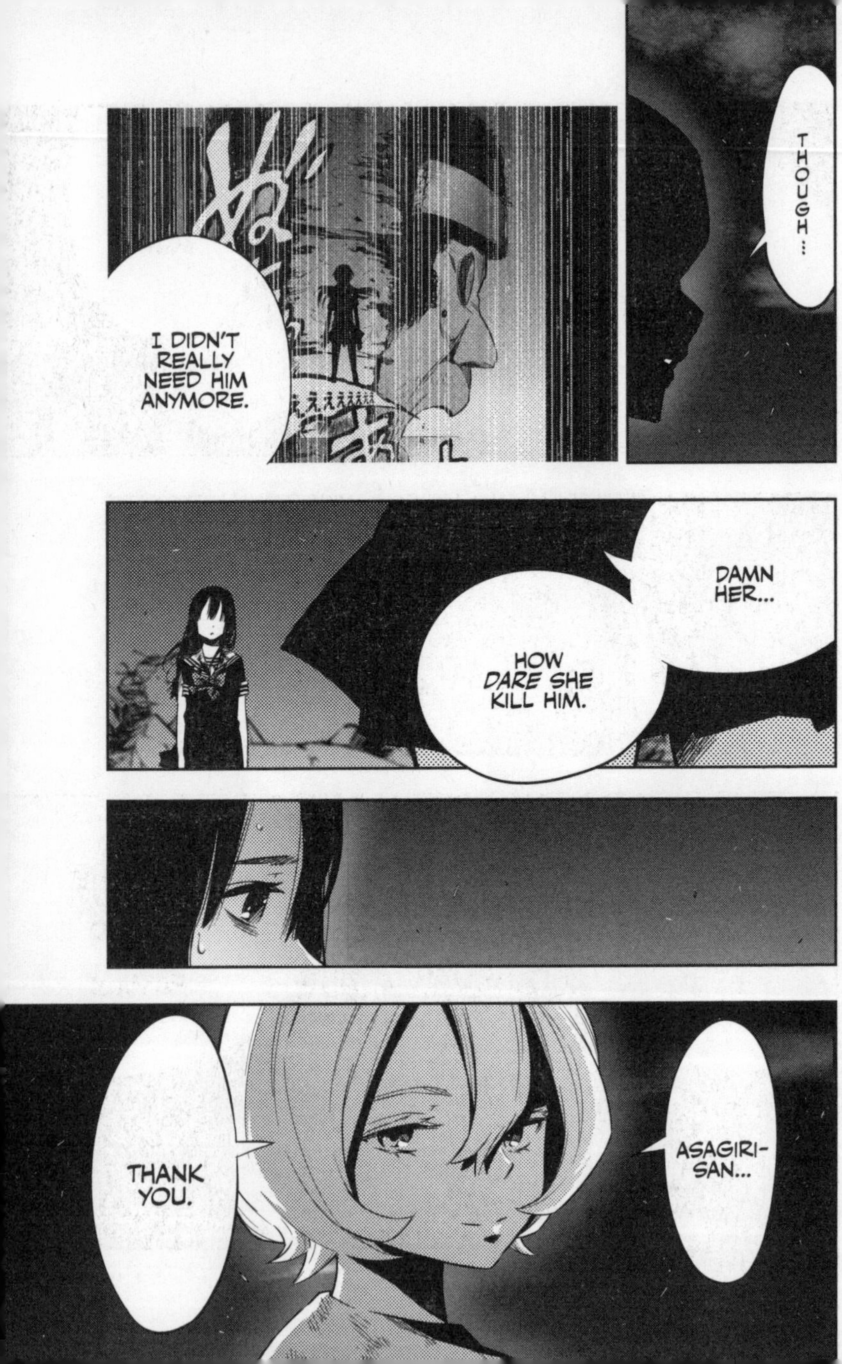
THOUGH...
I DIDN'T REALLY NEED HIM ANYMORE.
DAMN HER...
HOW *DARE* SHE KILL HIM.
ASAGIRI-SAN...
THANK YOU.

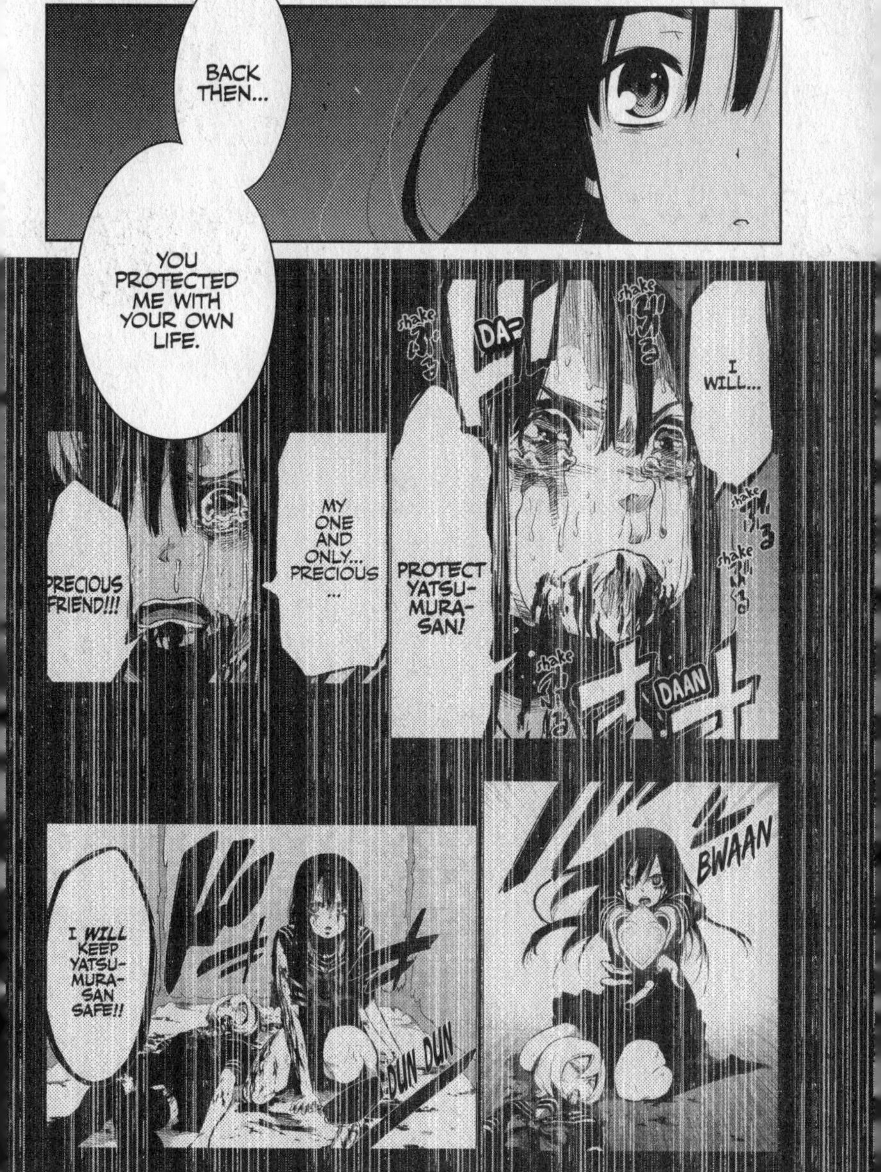

BACK THEN...
YOU PROTECTED ME WITH YOUR OWN LIFE.
I WILL...
shake
shake
DA-
shake
shake
PROTECT YATSUMURA-SAN!
shake
DAAN
MY ONE AND ONLY... PRECIOUS ...
PRECIOUS FRIEND!!!
BWAAN
I WILL KEEP YATSUMURA-SAN SAFE!!
DUN DUN

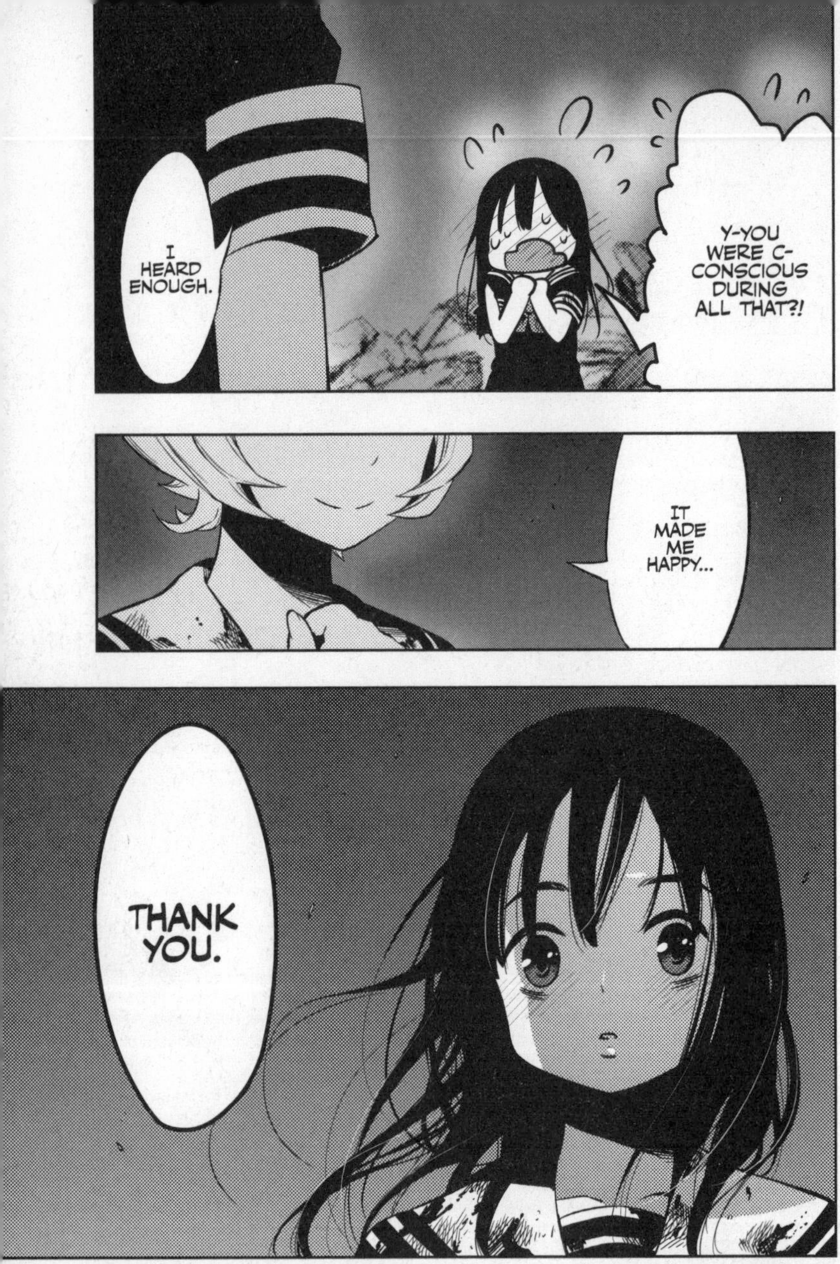
Y-YOU WERE C-CONSCIOUS DURING ALL THAT?!
I HEARD ENOUGH.
IT MADE ME HAPPY...
THANK YOU.

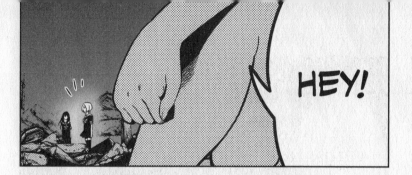

HEY!

THERE'S NO WAY WE'RE GOING TO FIND *ANYTHING* IN THIS JUNKPILE!

LET'S GO!

UH, YOU'RE RIGHT.

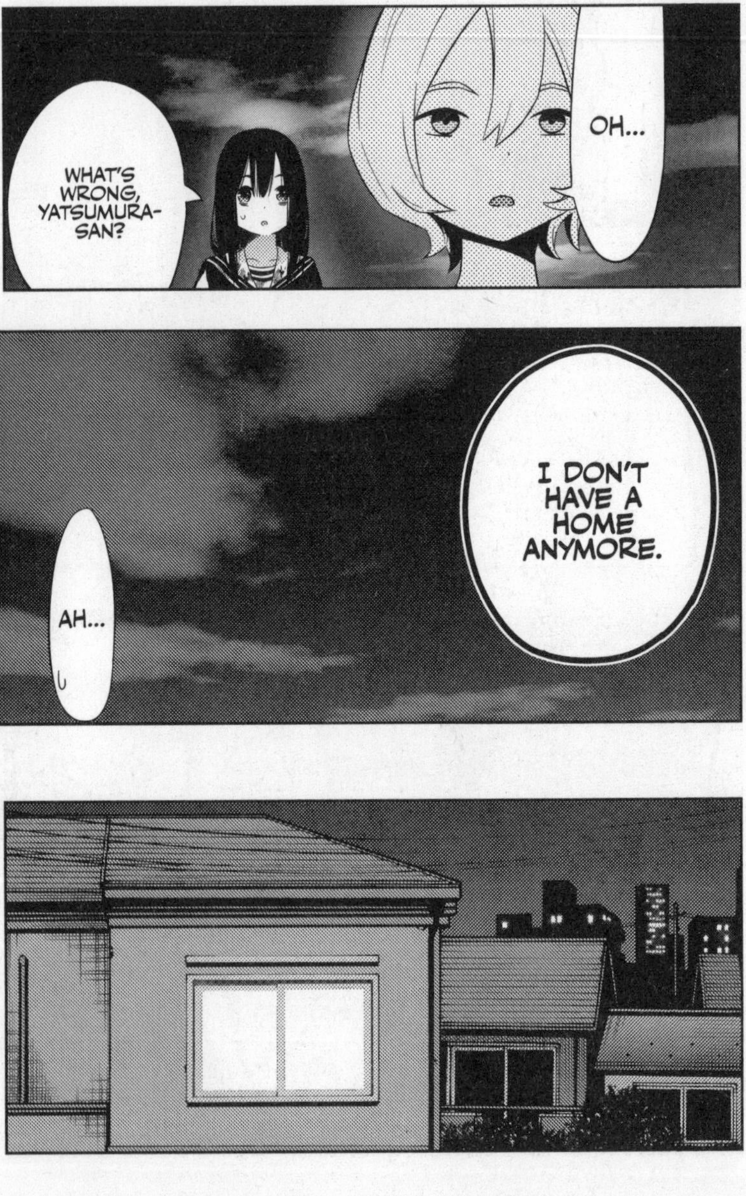
OH...
WHAT'S WRONG, YATSUMURA-SAN?
I DON'T HAVE A HOME ANYMORE.
AH...

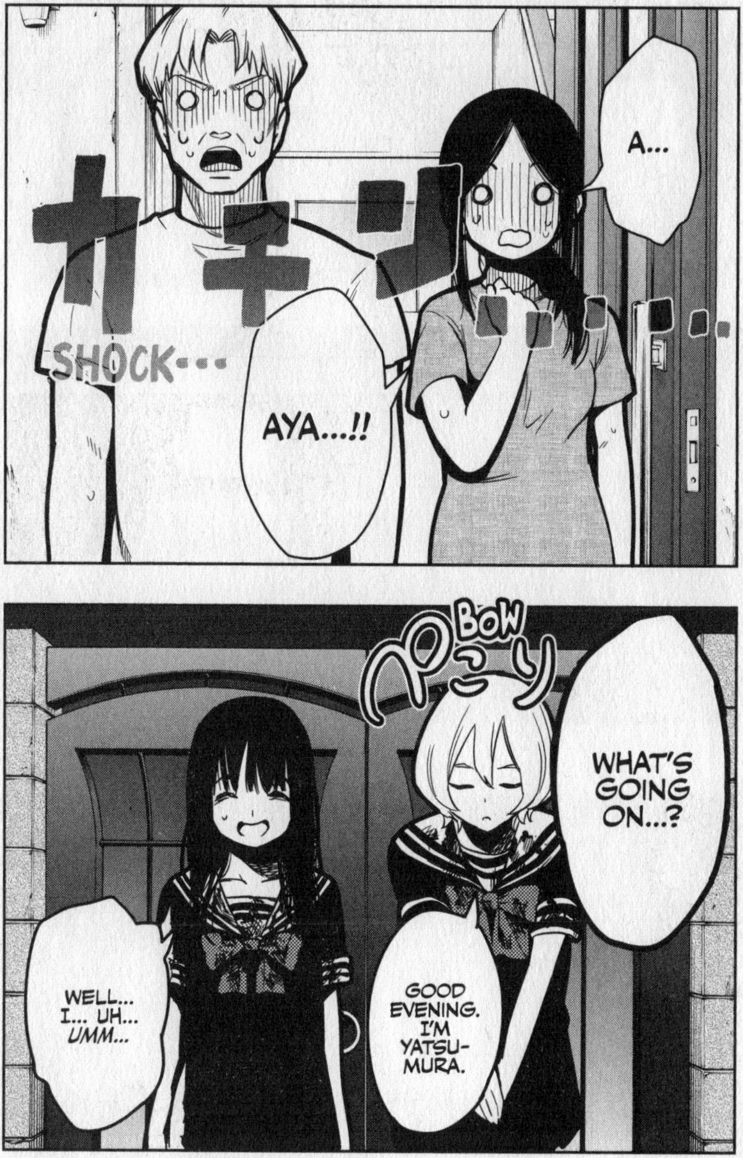
A...
AYA...!!
SHOCK...
BOW
WHAT'S GOING ON...?
GOOD EVENING. I'M YATSU-MURA.
WELL... I... UH... UMM...

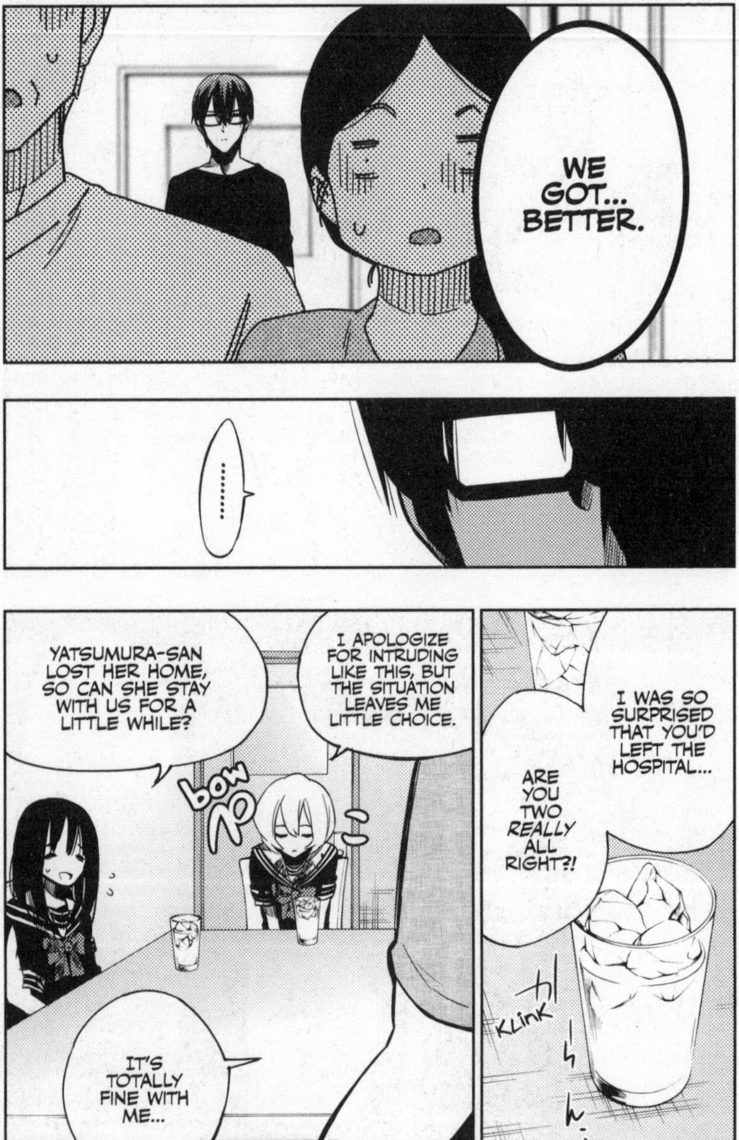
WE GOT... BETTER.
......
I WAS SO SURPRISED THAT YOU'D LEFT THE HOSPITAL...
ARE YOU TWO REALLY ALL RIGHT?!
KLink
I APOLOGIZE FOR INTRUDING LIKE THIS, BUT THE SITUATION LEAVES ME LITTLE CHOICE.
YATSUMURA-SAN LOST HER HOME, SO CAN SHE STAY WITH US FOR A LITTLE WHILE?
bow
IT'S TOTALLY FINE WITH ME...

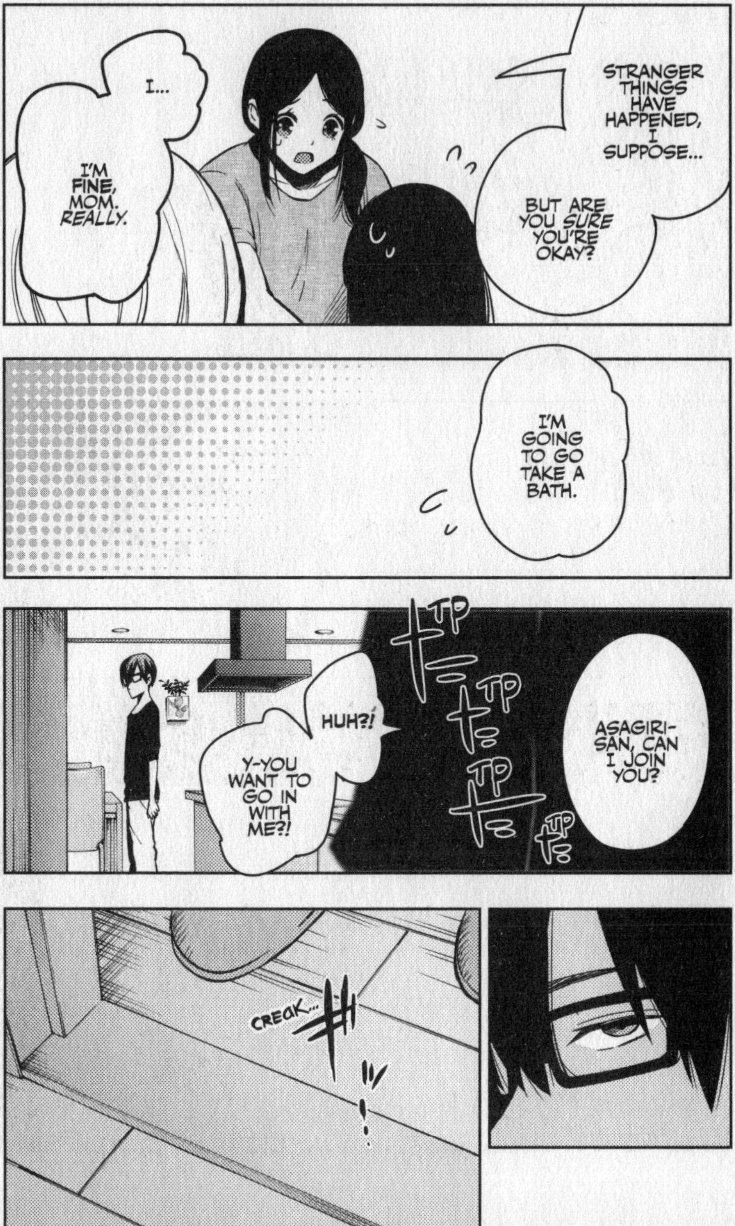
STRANGER THINGS HAVE HAPPENED, I SUPPOSE...
BUT ARE YOU SURE YOU'RE OKAY?
I...
I'M FINE, MOM. REALLY.
I'M GOING TO GO TAKE A BATH.
ASAGIRI-SAN, CAN I JOIN YOU?
TP
TP
TP
TP
HUH?!
Y-YOU WANT TO GO IN WITH ME?!
CREAK...

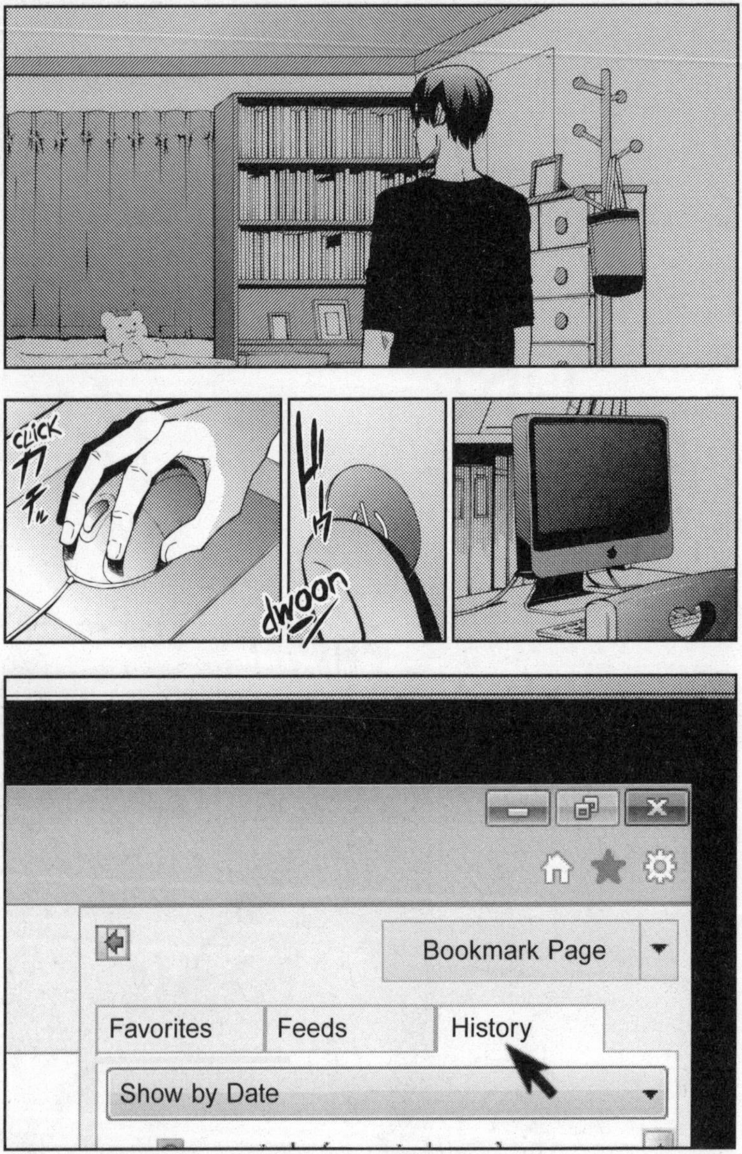
dwoon
CLICK
Bookmark Page
Favorites
Feeds
History
Show by Date

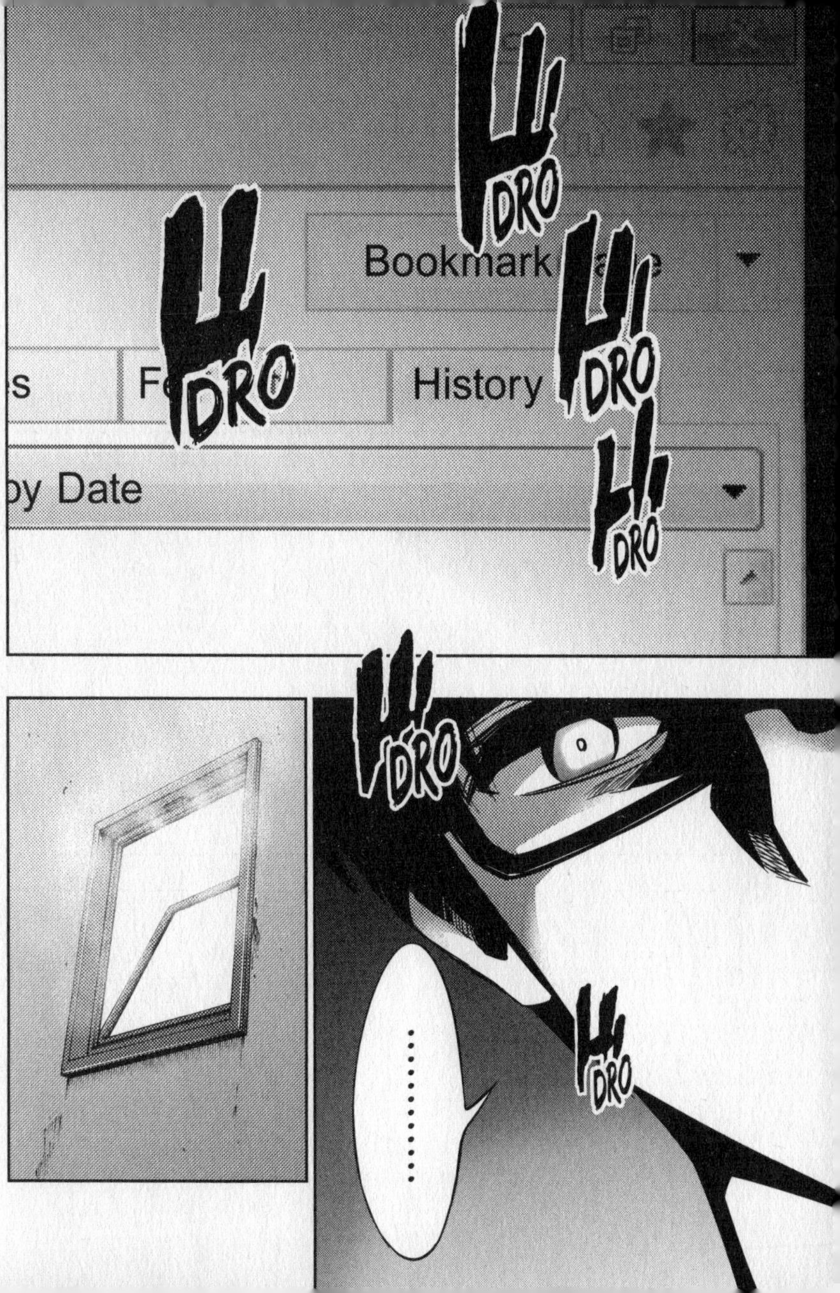
DRO
Bookmark
DRO
History
DRO
DRO
DRO
DRO
DRO
......

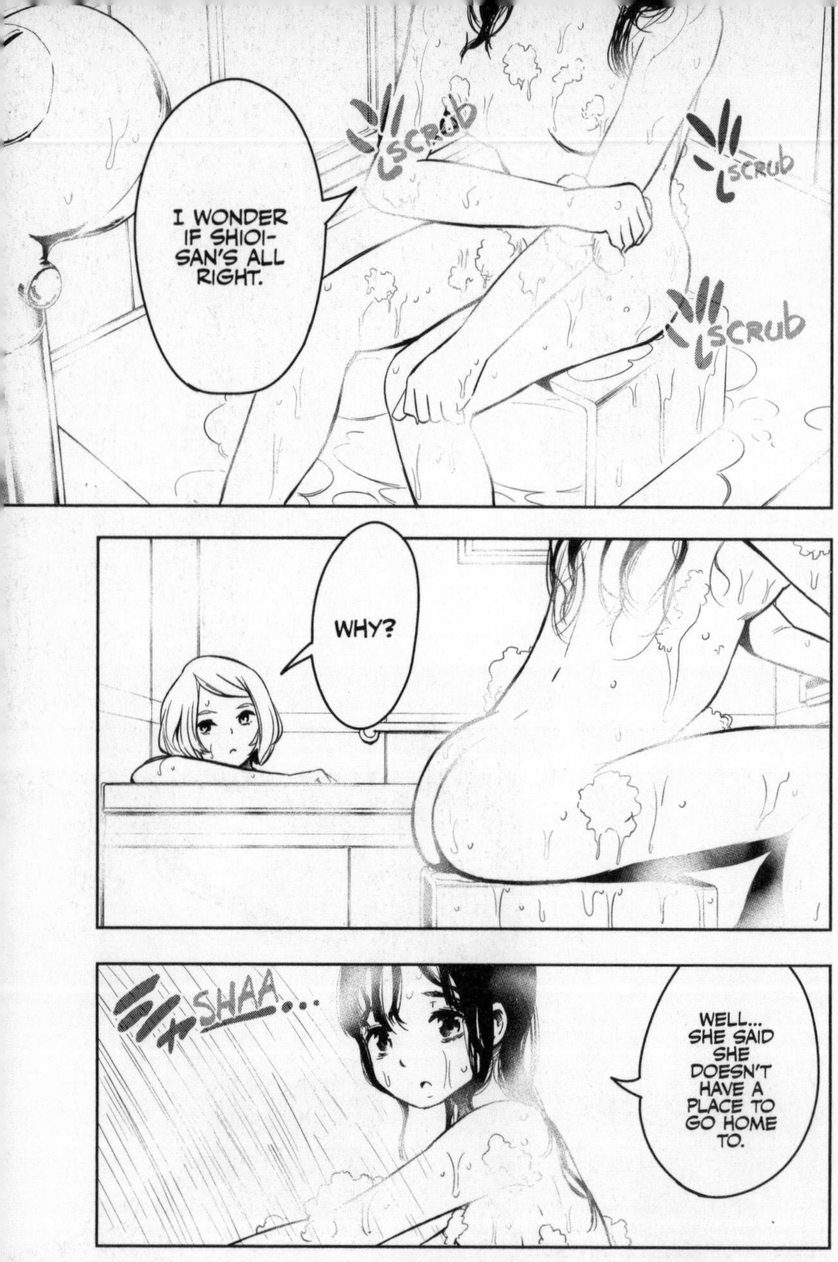
SCRUB
SCRUB
SCRUB
I WONDER IF SHIOI-SAN'S ALL RIGHT.
WHY?
WELL... SHE SAID SHE DOESN'T HAVE A PLACE TO GO HOME TO.
SHAA...

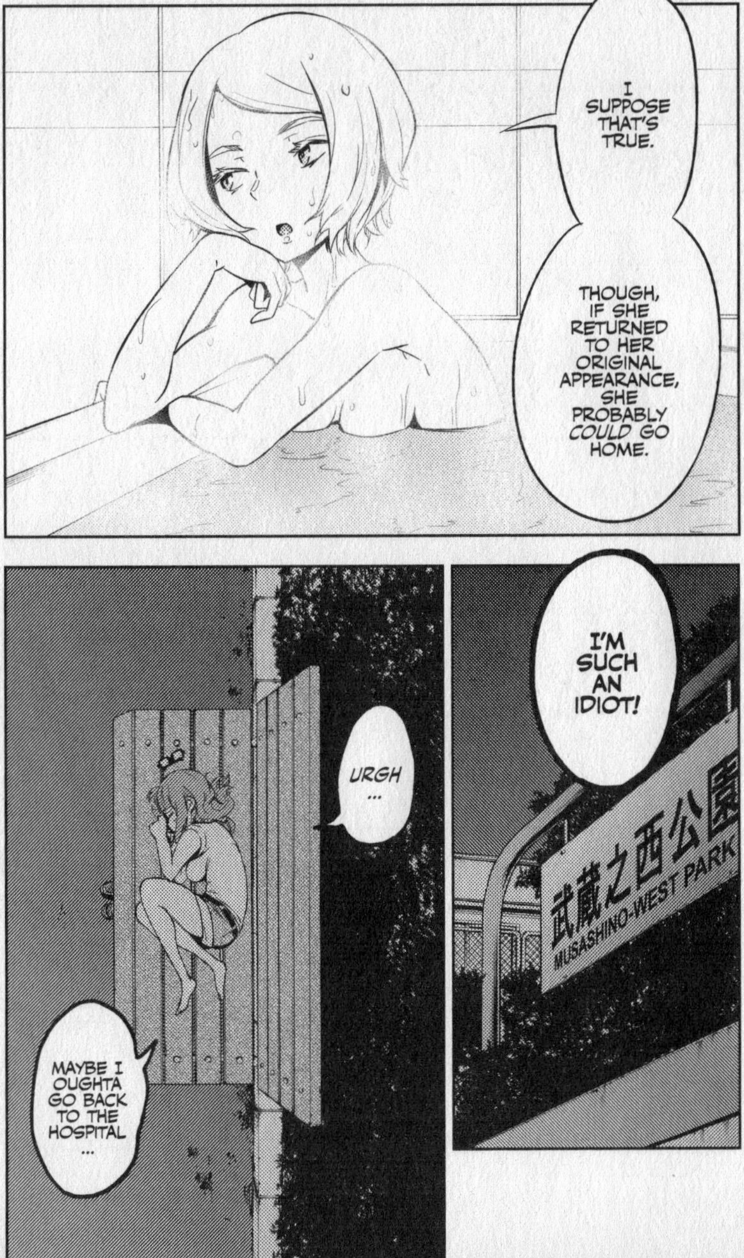
I SUPPOSE THAT'S TRUE.
THOUGH, IF SHE RETURNED TO HER ORIGINAL APPEARANCE, SHE PROBABLY *COULD* GO HOME.
I'M SUCH AN IDIOT!
武蔵之西公園
MUSASHINO-WEST PARK
URGH ...
MAYBE I OUGHTA GO BACK TO THE HOSPITAL ...

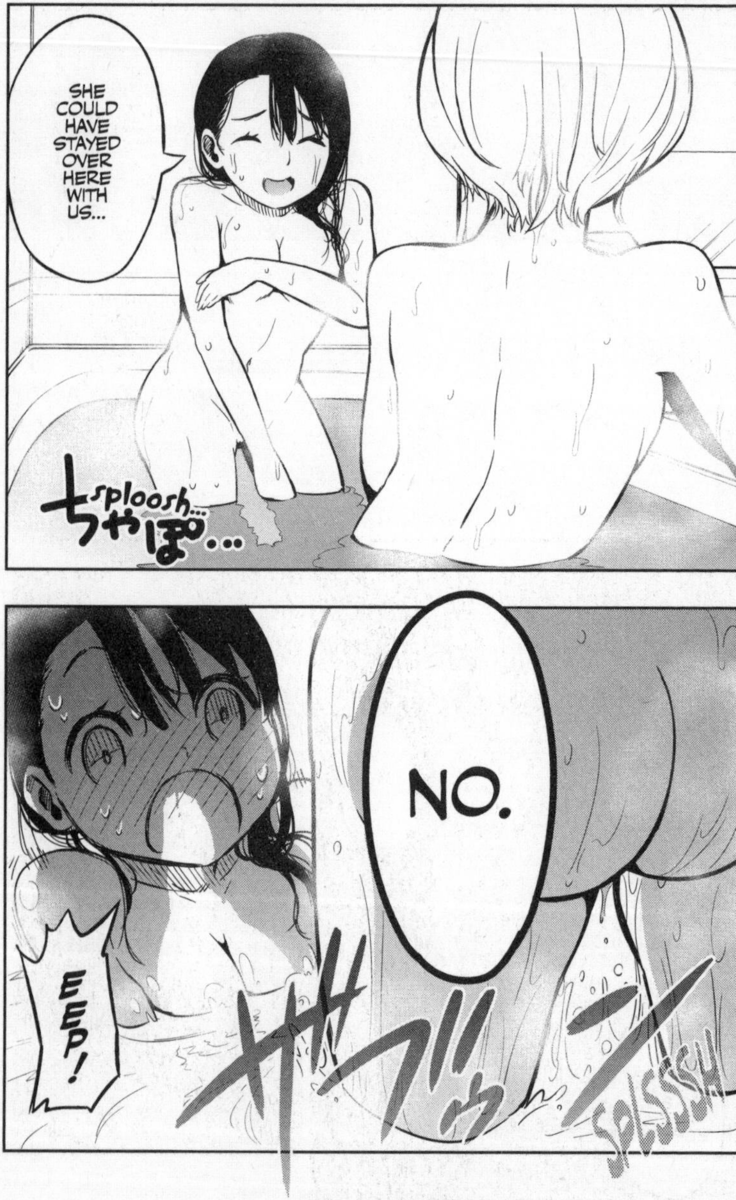
SHE COULD HAVE STAYED OVER HERE WITH US...
ちゃぽ...
sploosh...
NO.
SPLSSSH
EEP!

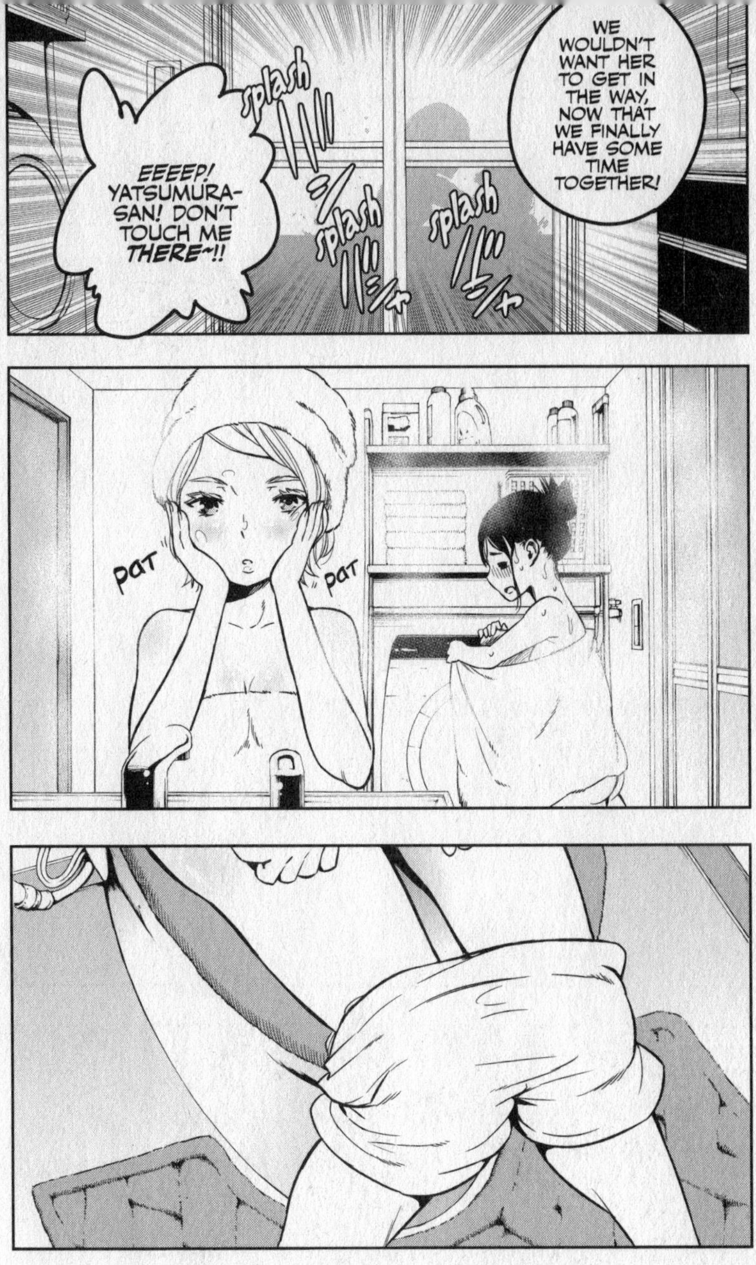
WE WOULDN'T WANT HER TO GET IN THE WAY, NOW THAT WE FINALLY HAVE SOME TIME TOGETHER!
splash
splash
splash
EEEEP! YATSUMURA-SAN! DON'T TOUCH ME THERE~!!
pat
pat

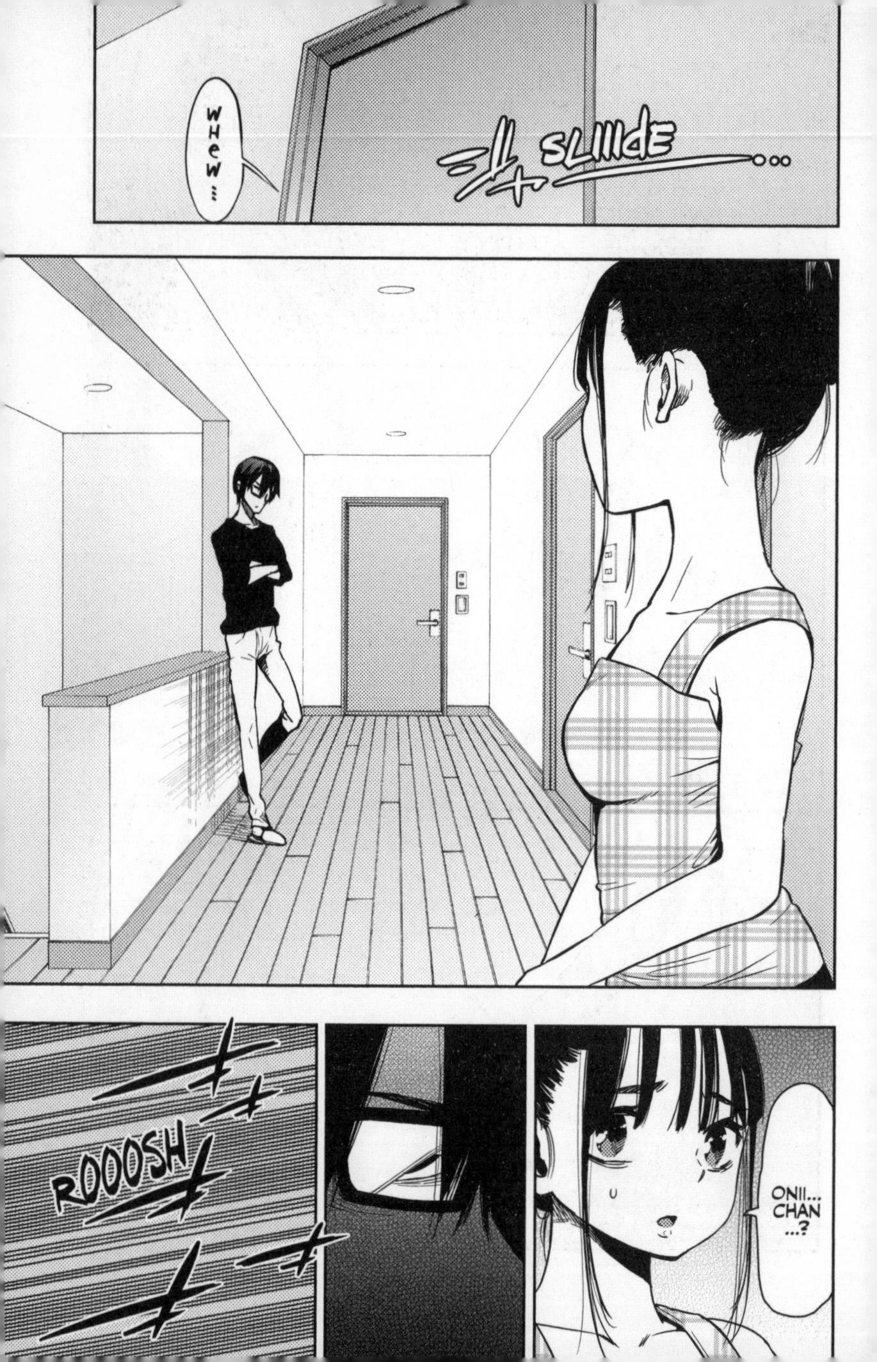
SLIIIDE
whew...
ONII... CHAN ...?
ROOOSH

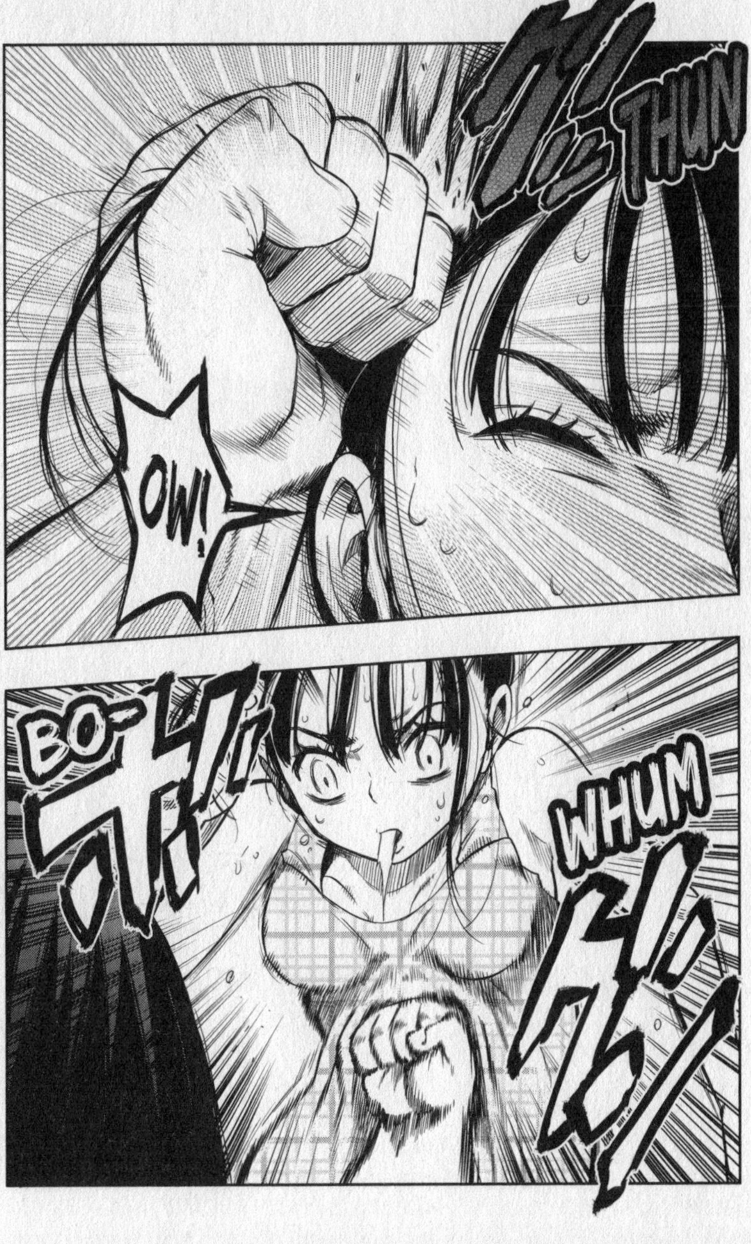
THUN
OW!
WHUM
BO-

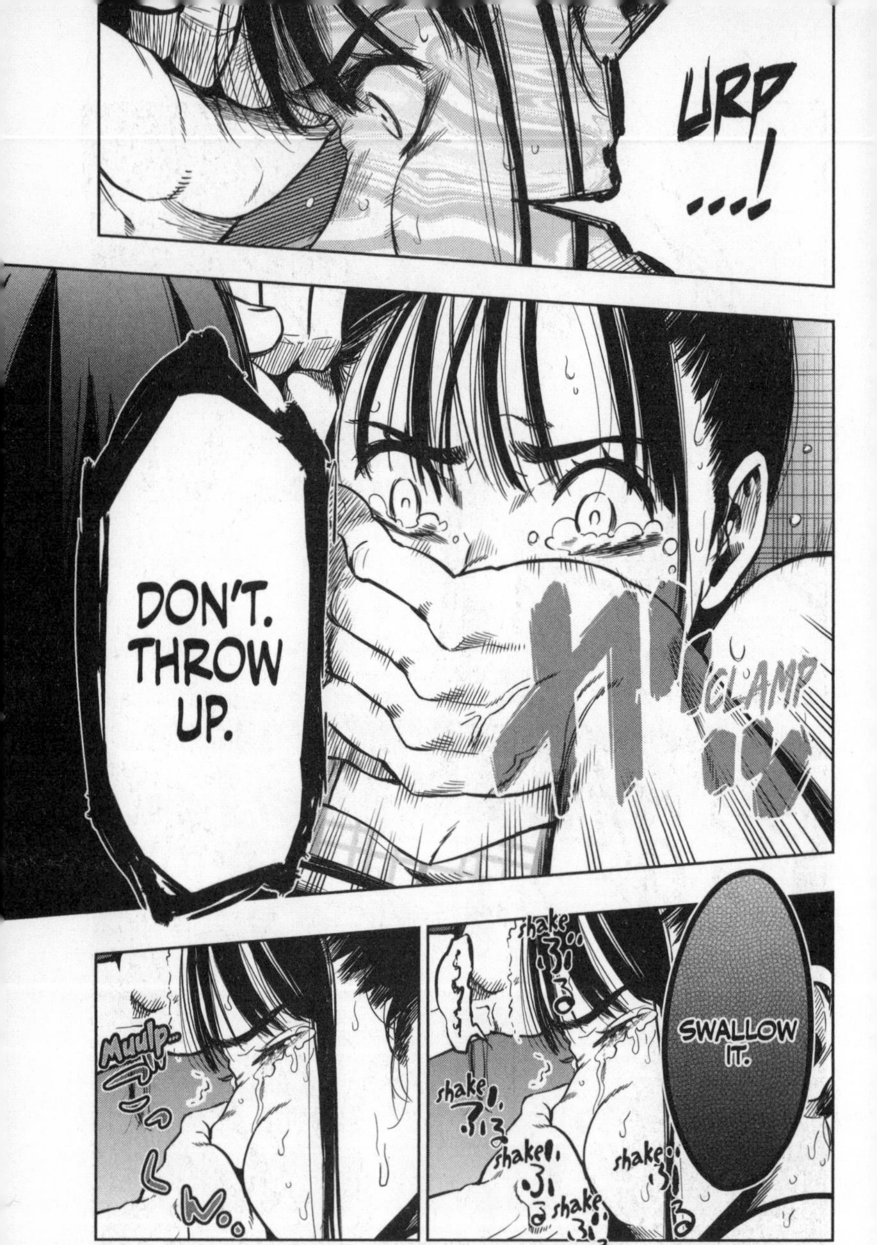
URP ...!
DON'T. THROW UP.
CLAMP
SWALLOW IT.
shake
shake
shake
shake
shake
Muulp...

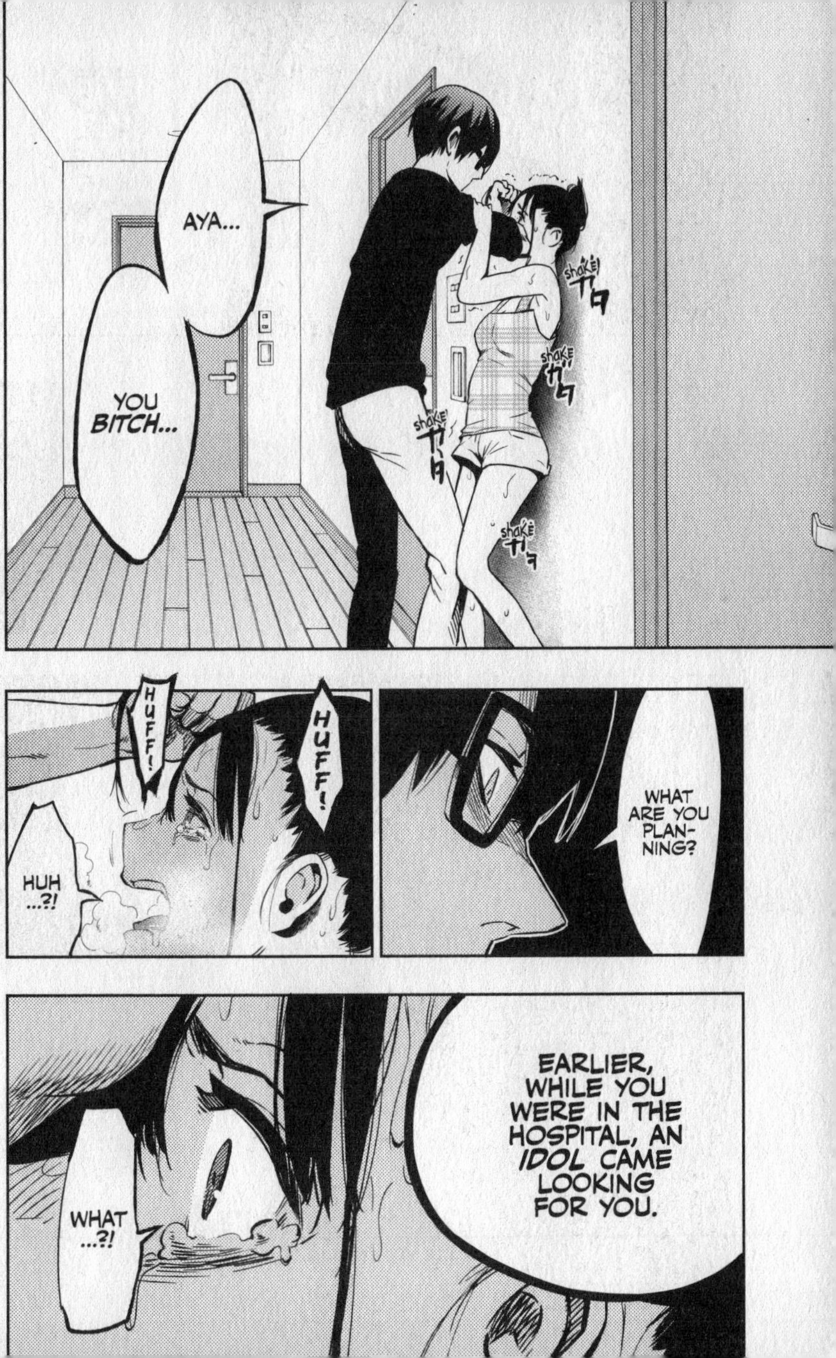
AYA...
YOU BITCH...
shake!
shake
shake!
shake
WHAT ARE YOU PLAN-NING?
HUFF!
HUFF!
HUH ...?!
EARLIER, WHILE YOU WERE IN THE HOSPITAL, AN *IDOL* CAME LOOKING FOR YOU.
WHAT ...?!

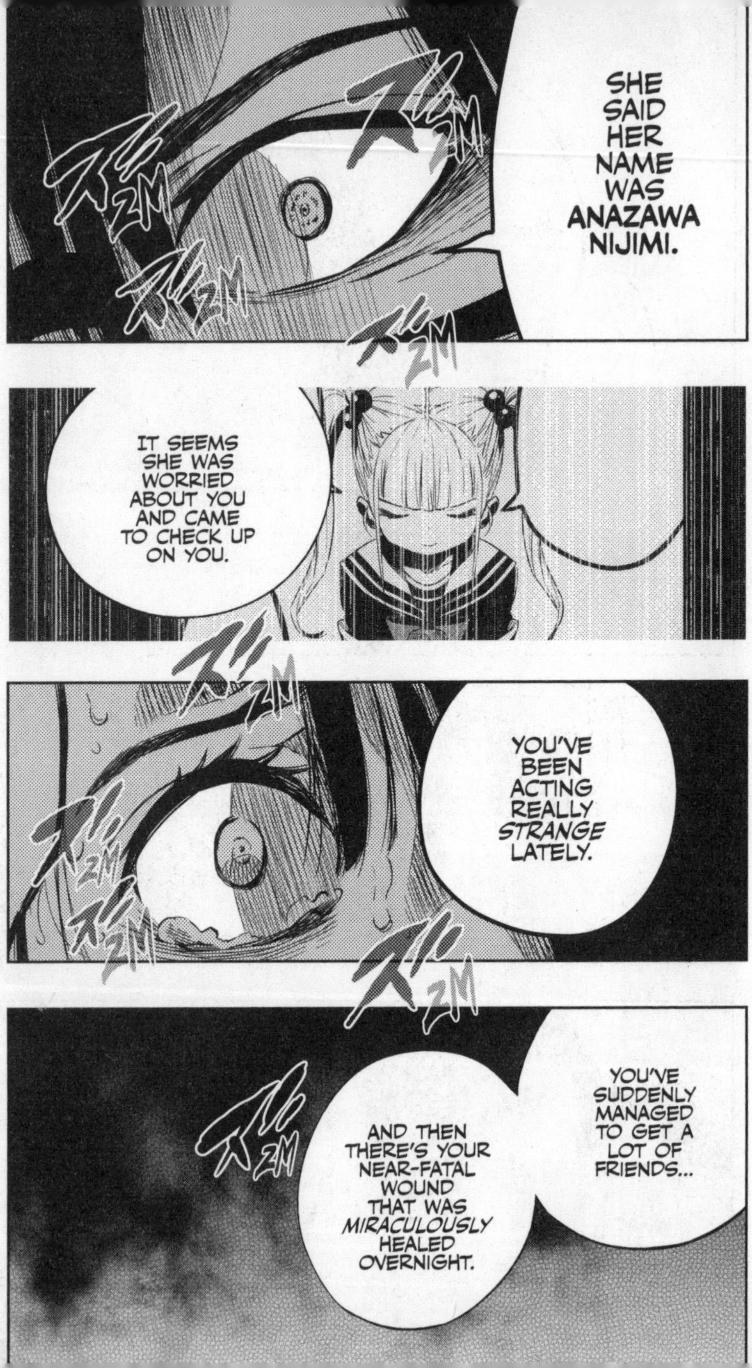
SHE SAID HER NAME WAS ANAZAWA NIJIMI.
IT SEEMS SHE WAS WORRIED ABOUT YOU AND CAME TO CHECK UP ON YOU.
YOU'VE BEEN ACTING REALLY *STRANGE* LATELY.
YOU'VE SUDDENLY MANAGED TO GET A LOT OF FRIENDS...
AND THEN THERE'S YOUR NEAR-FATAL WOUND THAT WAS *MIRACULOUSLY* HEALED OVERNIGHT.

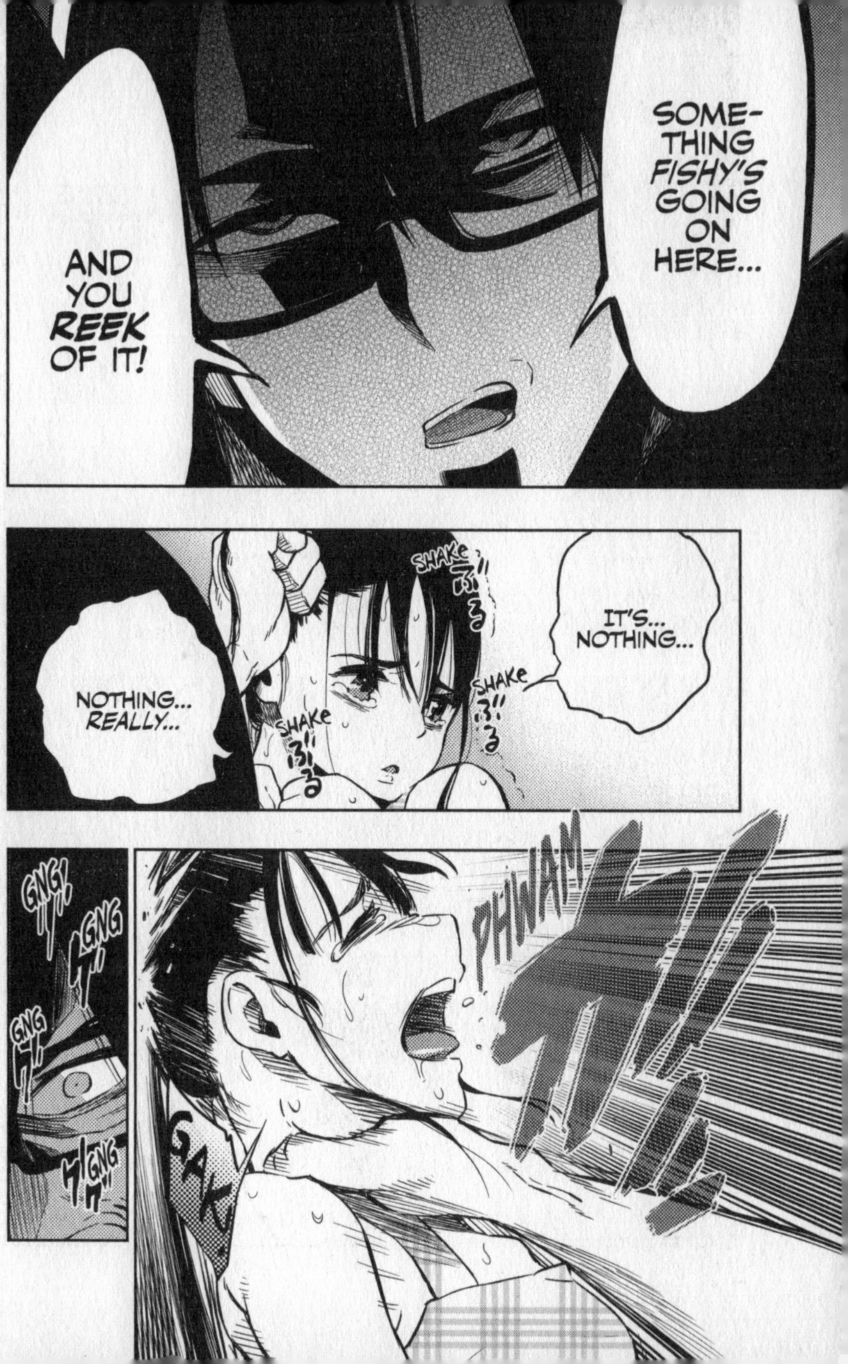
SOME-THING FISHY'S GOING ON HERE...
AND YOU REEK OF IT!
SHAKE
IT'S... NOTHING...
SHAKE
SHAKE
NOTHING... REALLY...
PHWAM
GAK
GNG
GNG
GNG
GNG

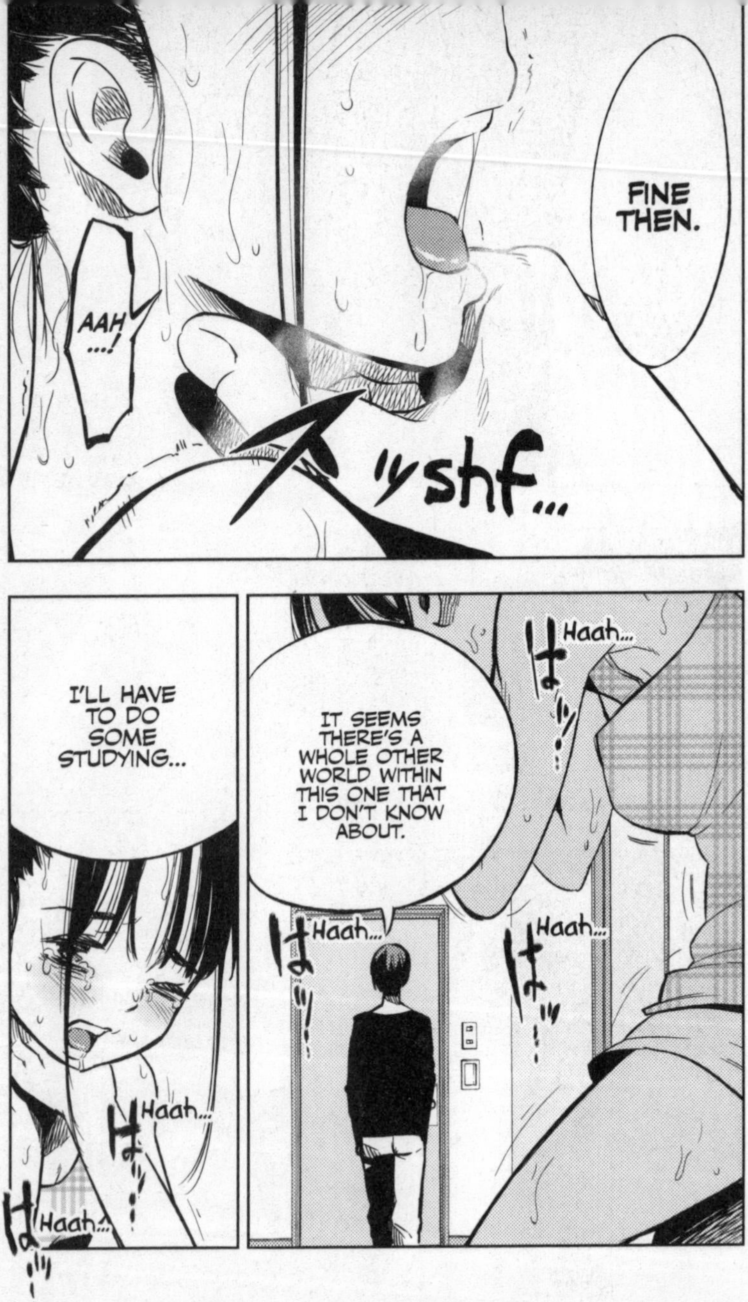
FINE THEN.
AAH ...!
shf...
Haah...
IT SEEMS THERE'S A WHOLE OTHER WORLD WITHIN THIS ONE THAT I DON'T KNOW ABOUT.
Haah...
Haah...
I'LL HAVE TO DO SOME STUDYING...
Haah...
Haah...

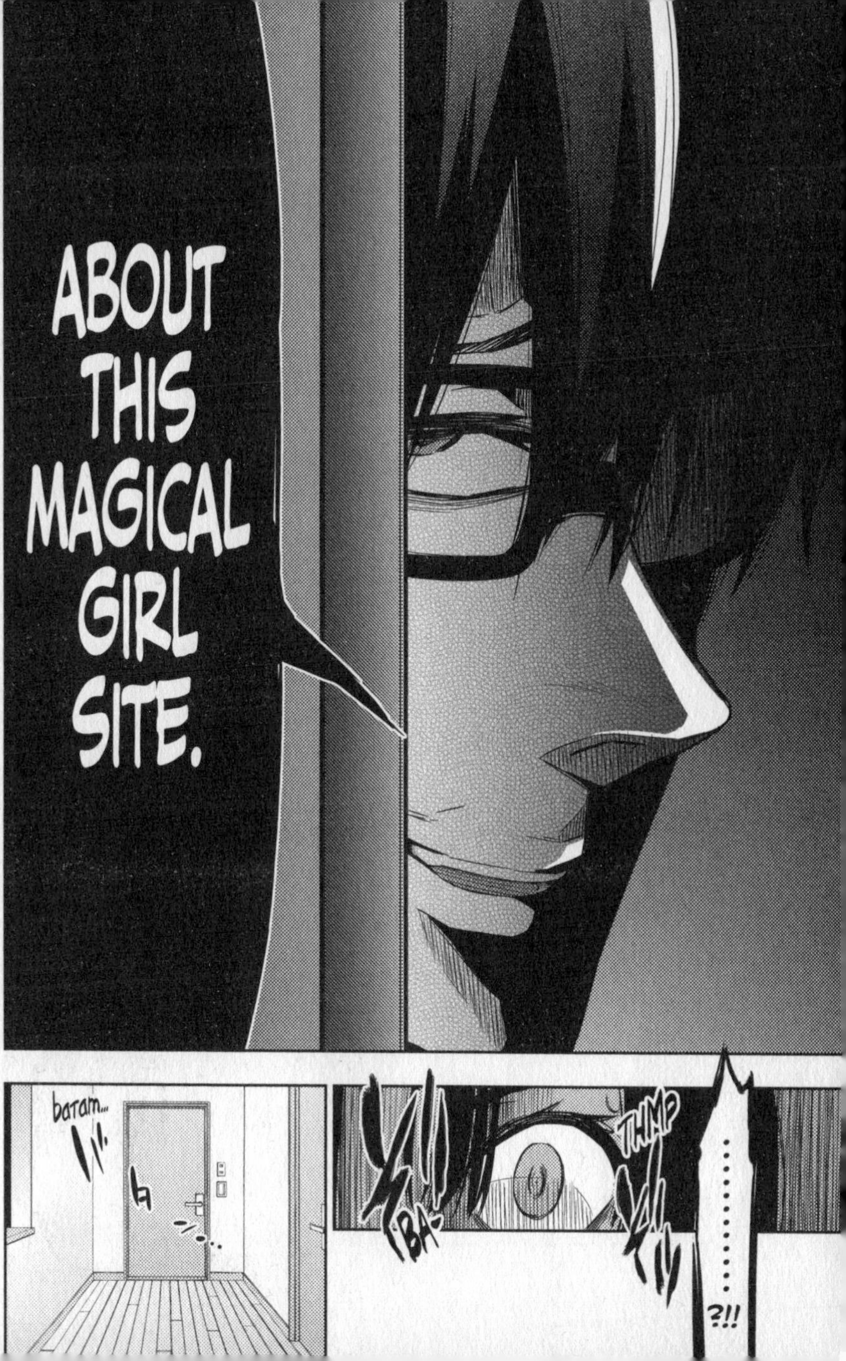
ABOUT THIS MAGICAL GIRL SITE.
......?!!
THMP
BA-
batam...

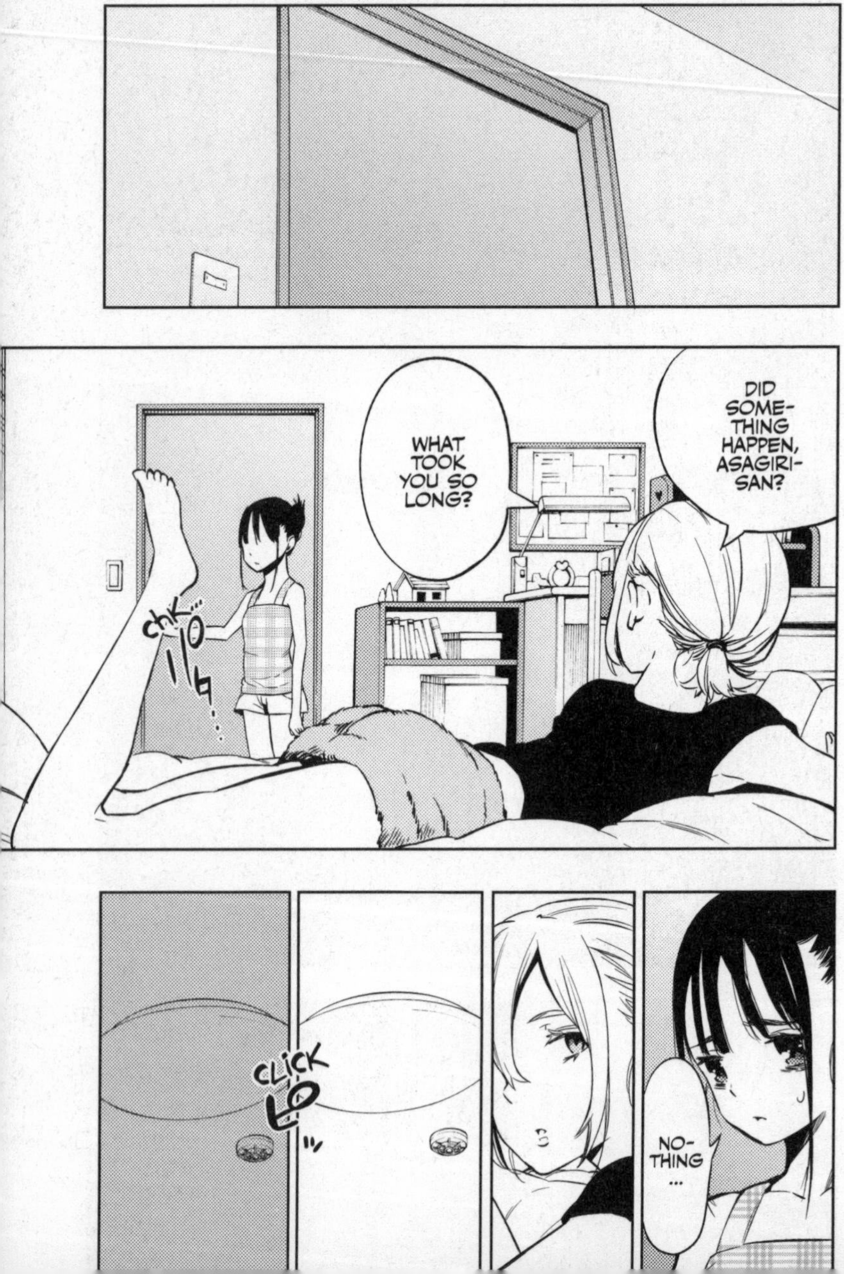
DID SOME-THING HAPPEN, ASAGIRI-SAN?
WHAT TOOK YOU SO LONG?
chk...
NO-THING ...
CLICK

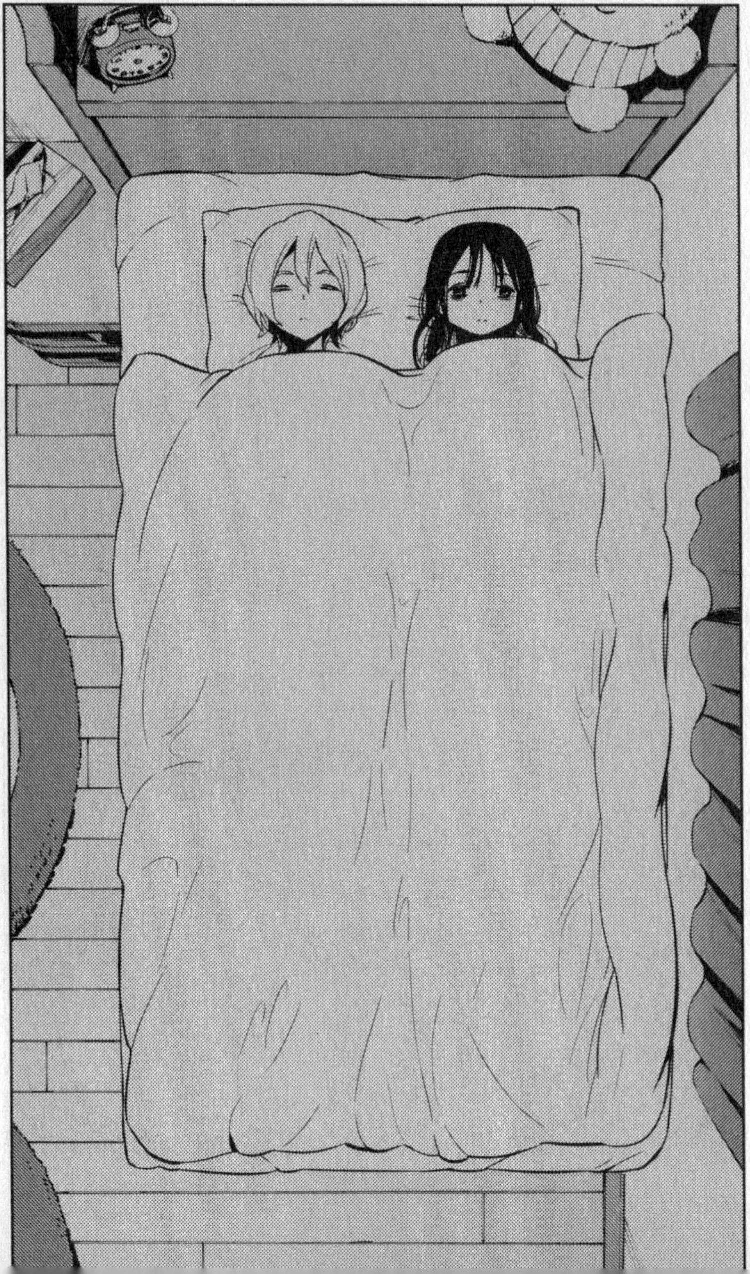

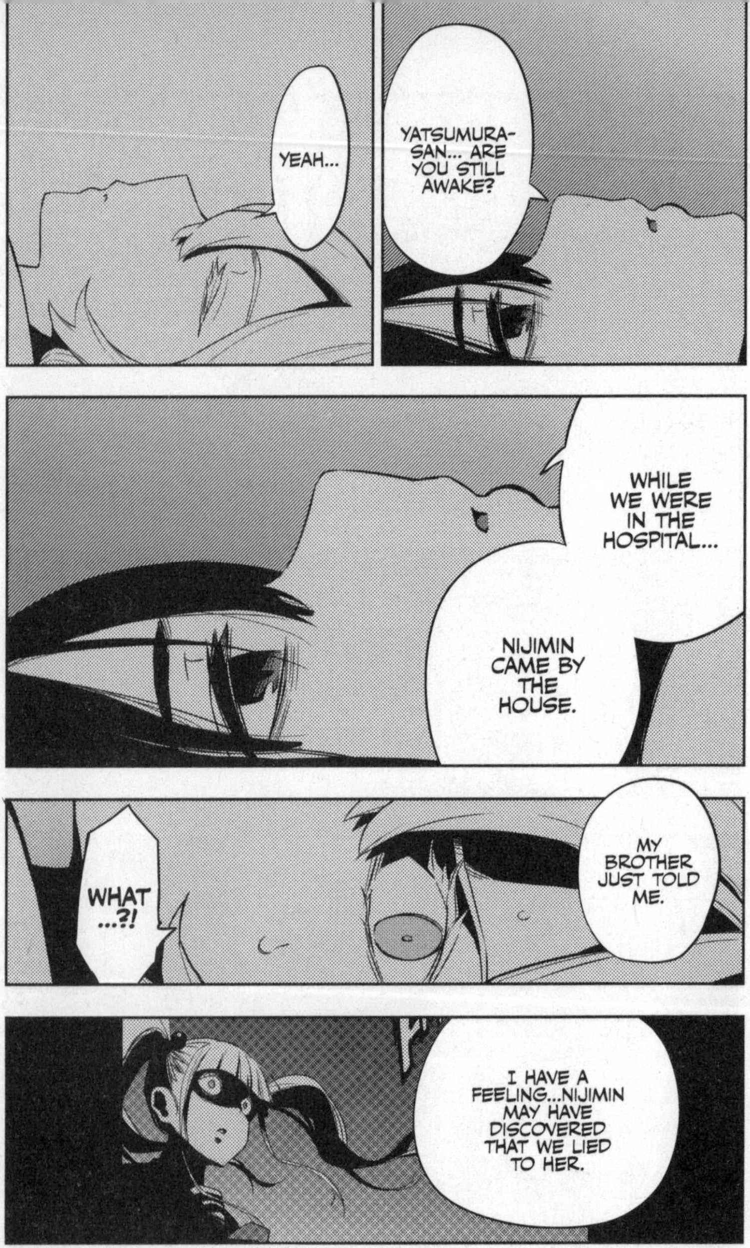
YATSUMURA-SAN... ARE YOU STILL AWAKE?
YEAH...
WHILE WE WERE IN THE HOSPITAL...
NIJIMIN CAME BY THE HOUSE.
MY BROTHER JUST TOLD ME.
WHAT ...?!
I HAVE A FEELING...NIJIMIN MAY HAVE DISCOVERED THAT WE LIED TO HER.

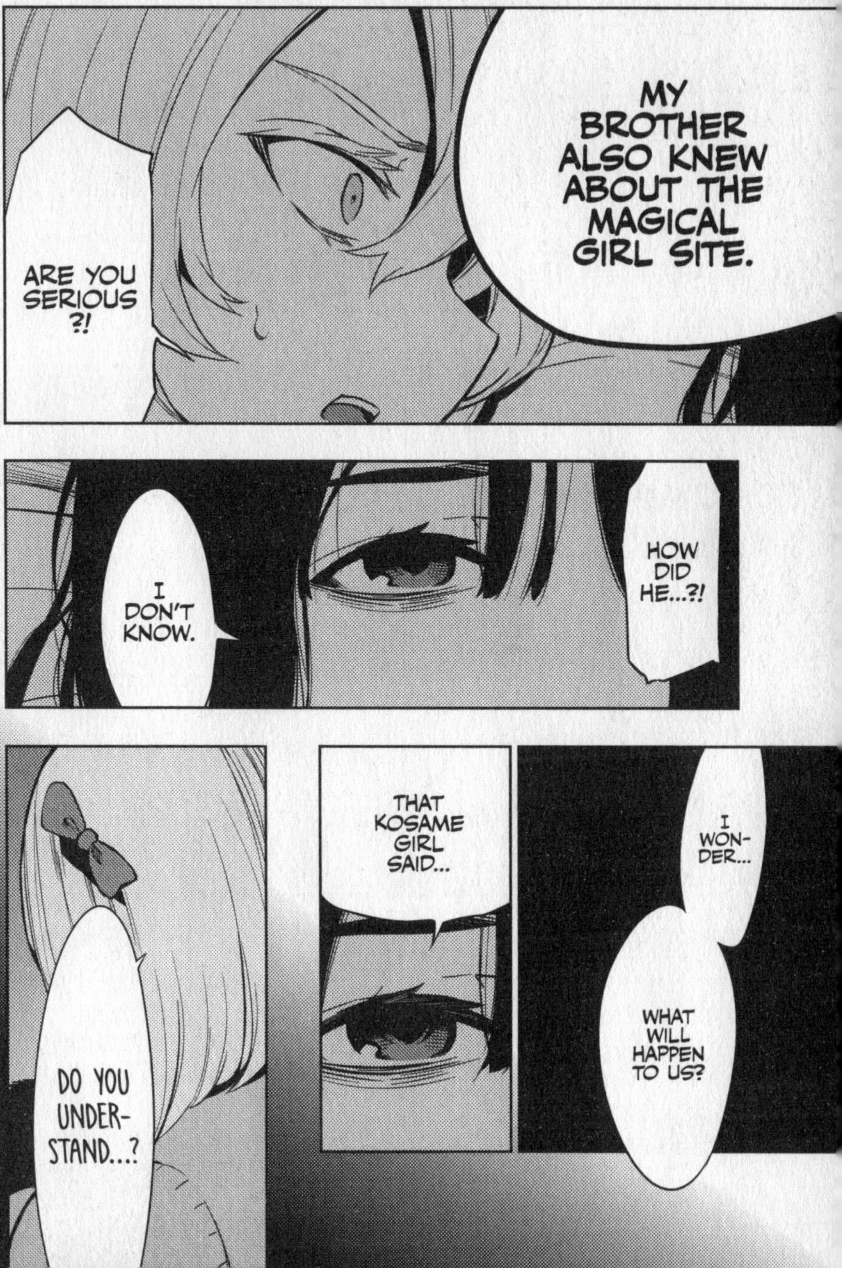
MY BROTHER ALSO KNEW ABOUT THE MAGICAL GIRL SITE.
ARE YOU SERIOUS?!
HOW DID HE...?!
I DON'T KNOW.
I WON-DER...
WHAT WILL HAPPEN TO US?
THAT KOSAME GIRL SAID...
DO YOU UNDER-STAND...?

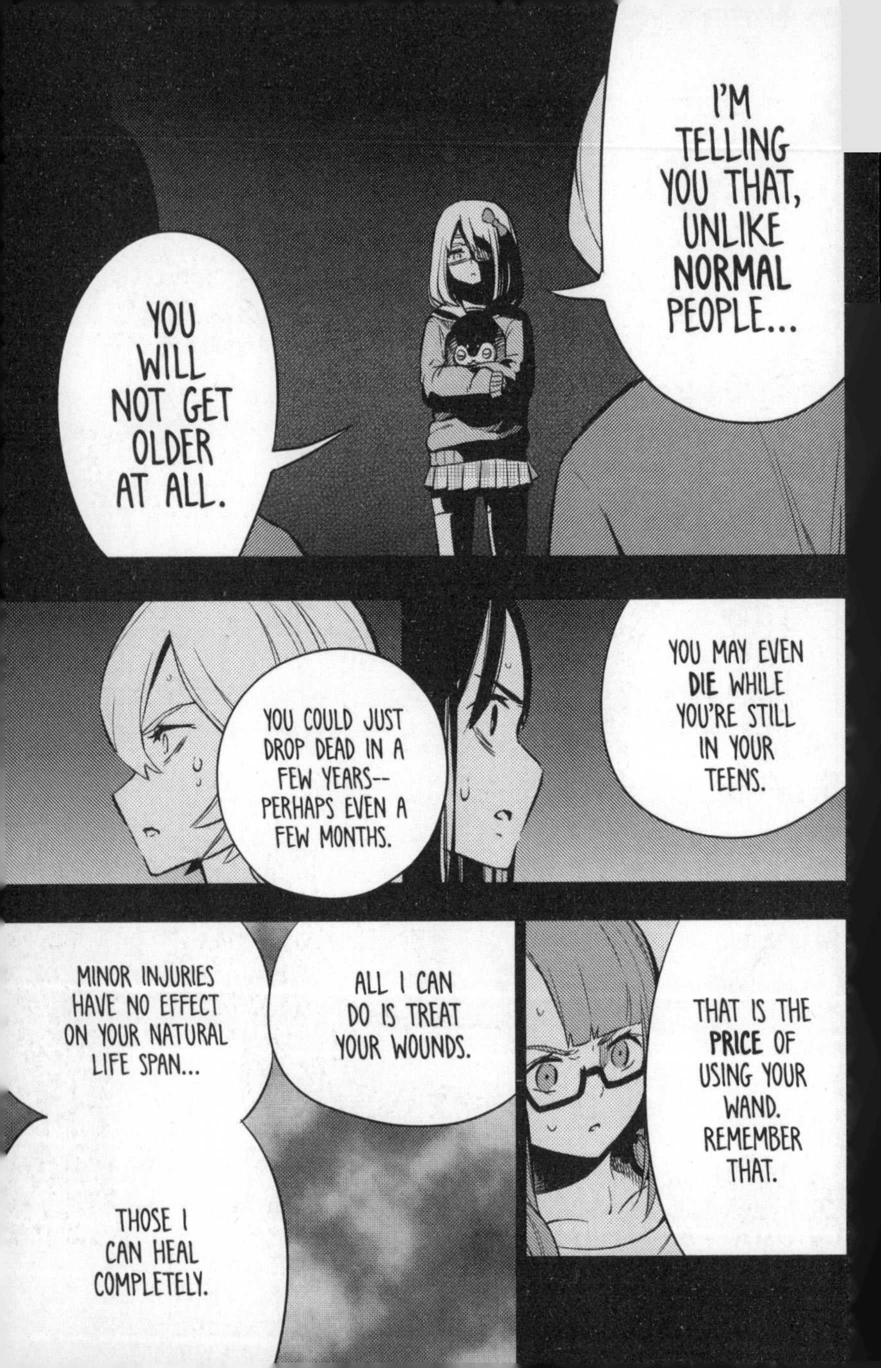
I'M TELLING YOU THAT, UNLIKE NORMAL PEOPLE...
YOU WILL NOT GET OLDER AT ALL.
YOU MAY EVEN **DIE** WHILE YOU'RE STILL IN YOUR TEENS.
YOU COULD JUST DROP DEAD IN A FEW YEARS-- PERHAPS EVEN A FEW MONTHS.
THAT IS THE **PRICE** OF USING YOUR WAND. REMEMBER THAT.
ALL I CAN DO IS TREAT YOUR WOUNDS.
MINOR INJURIES HAVE NO EFFECT ON YOUR NATURAL LIFE SPAN...
THOSE I CAN HEAL COMPLETELY.

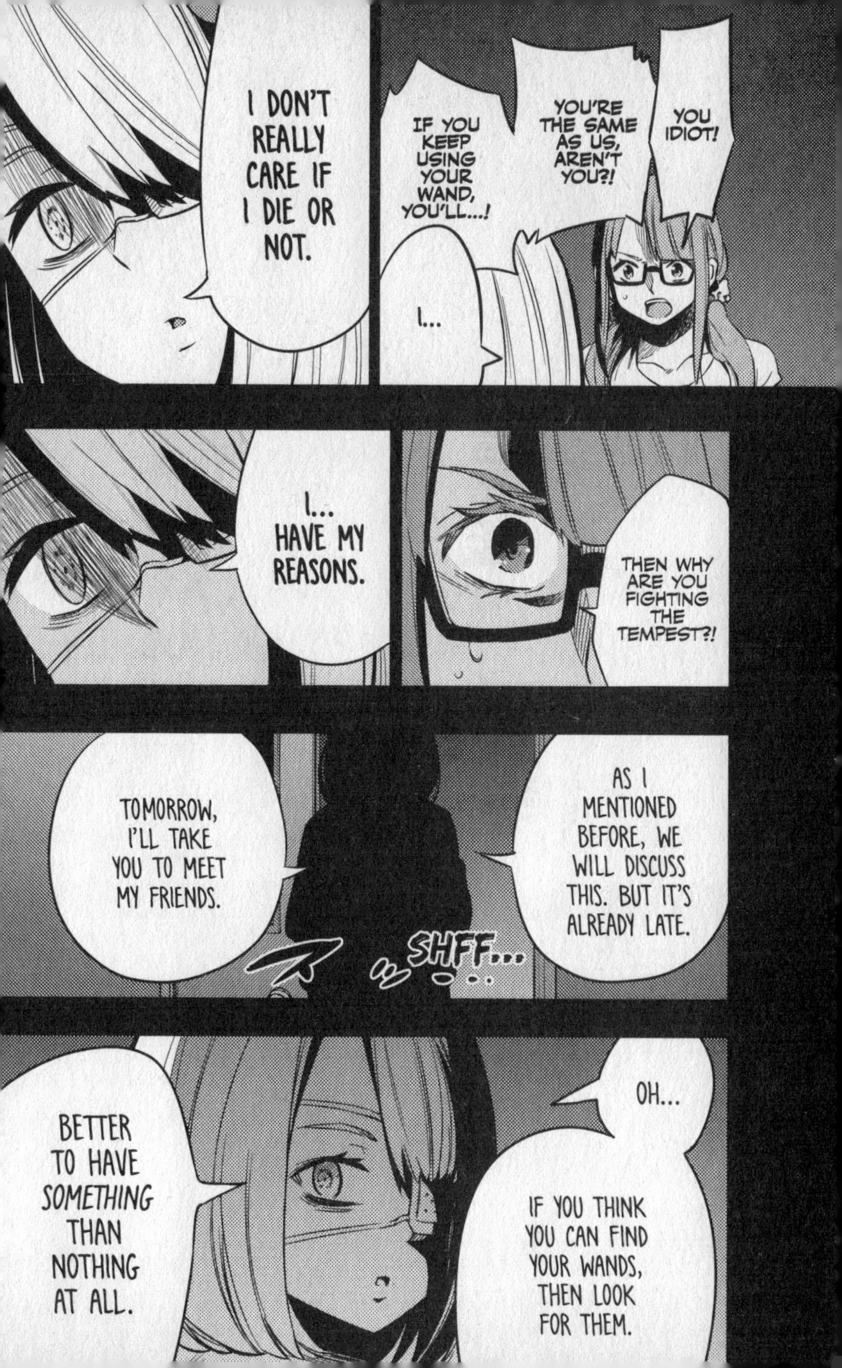
YOU IDIOT!
YOU'RE THE SAME AS US, AREN'T YOU?!
IF YOU KEEP USING YOUR WAND, YOU'LL...!
I...
I DON'T REALLY CARE IF I DIE OR NOT.
THEN WHY ARE YOU FIGHTING THE TEMPEST?!
I... HAVE MY REASONS.
AS I MENTIONED BEFORE, WE WILL DISCUSS THIS. BUT IT'S ALREADY LATE.
SHFF...
TOMORROW, I'LL TAKE YOU TO MEET MY FRIENDS.
OH...
IF YOU THINK YOU CAN FIND YOUR WANDS, THEN LOOK FOR THEM.
BETTER TO HAVE SOMETHING THAN NOTHING AT ALL.

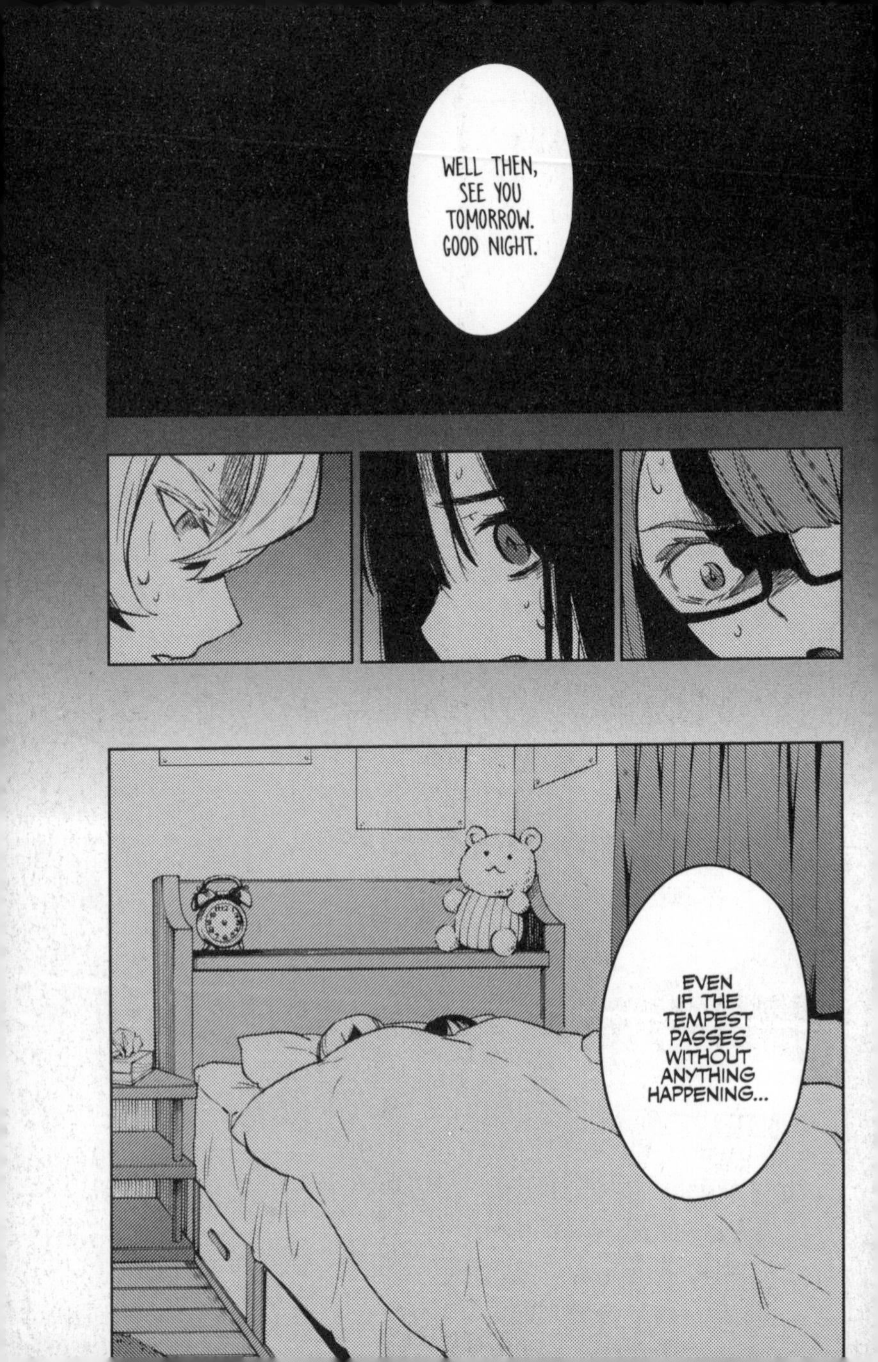
WELL THEN, SEE YOU TOMORROW. GOOD NIGHT.
EVEN IF THE TEMPEST PASSES WITHOUT ANYTHING HAPPENING...

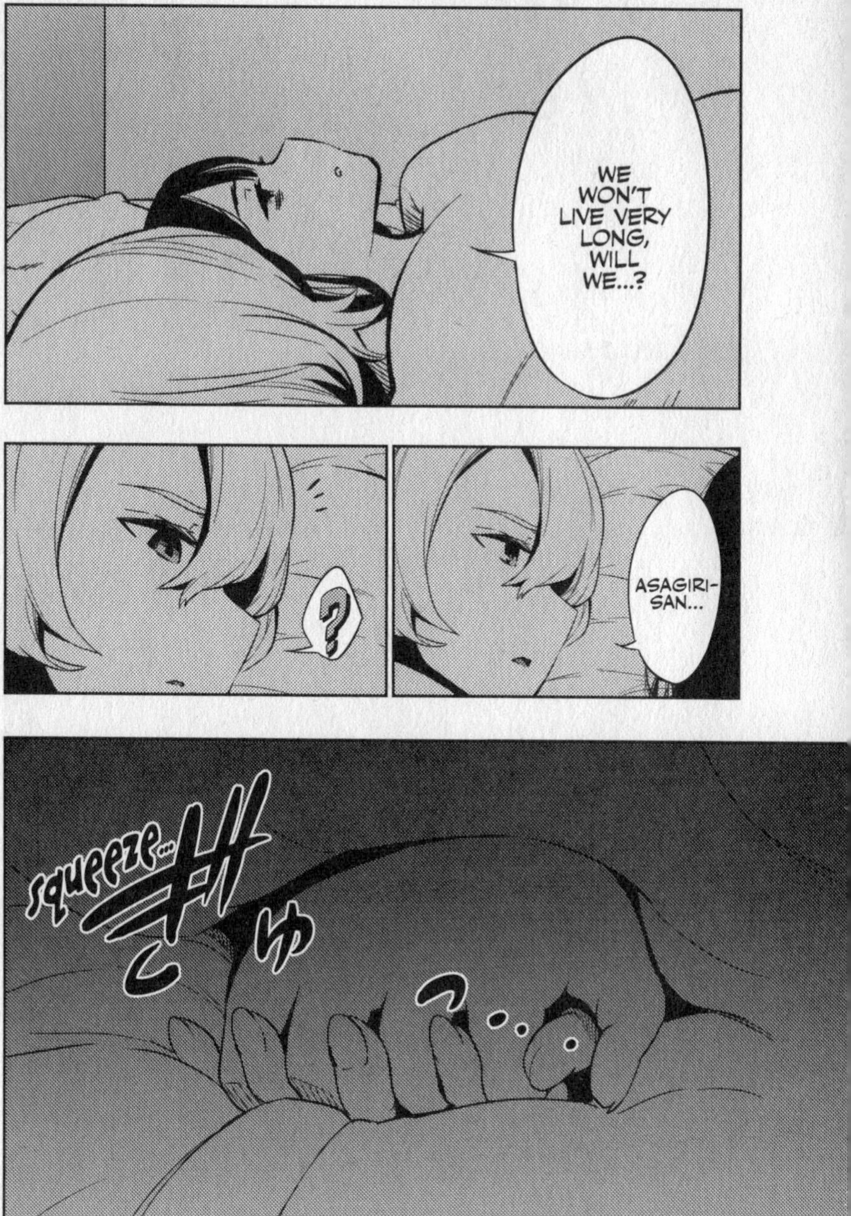
WE WON'T LIVE VERY LONG, WILL WE...?
ASAGIRI-SAN...
?
squeeze...

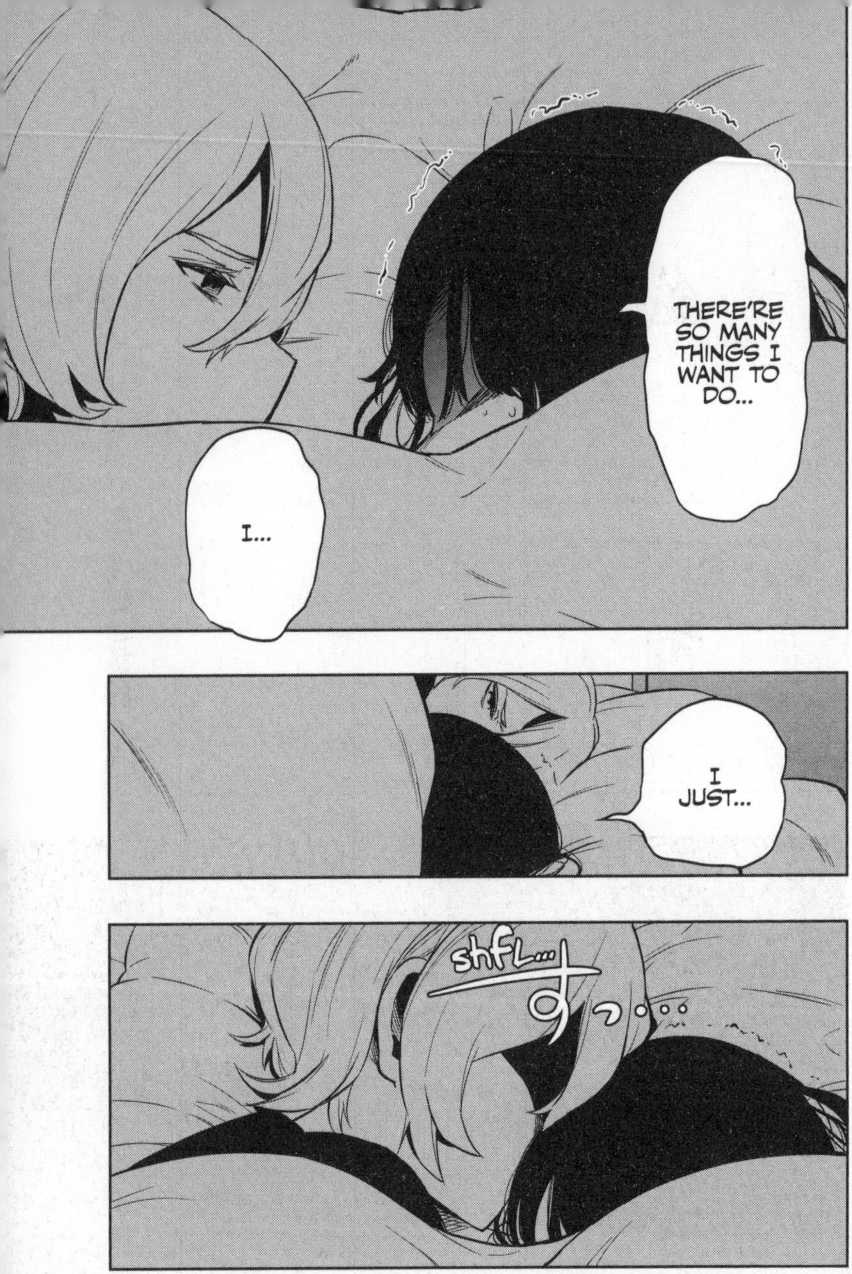
THERE'RE SO MANY THINGS I WANT TO DO...
I...
I JUST...
shfl...
すっ・・・

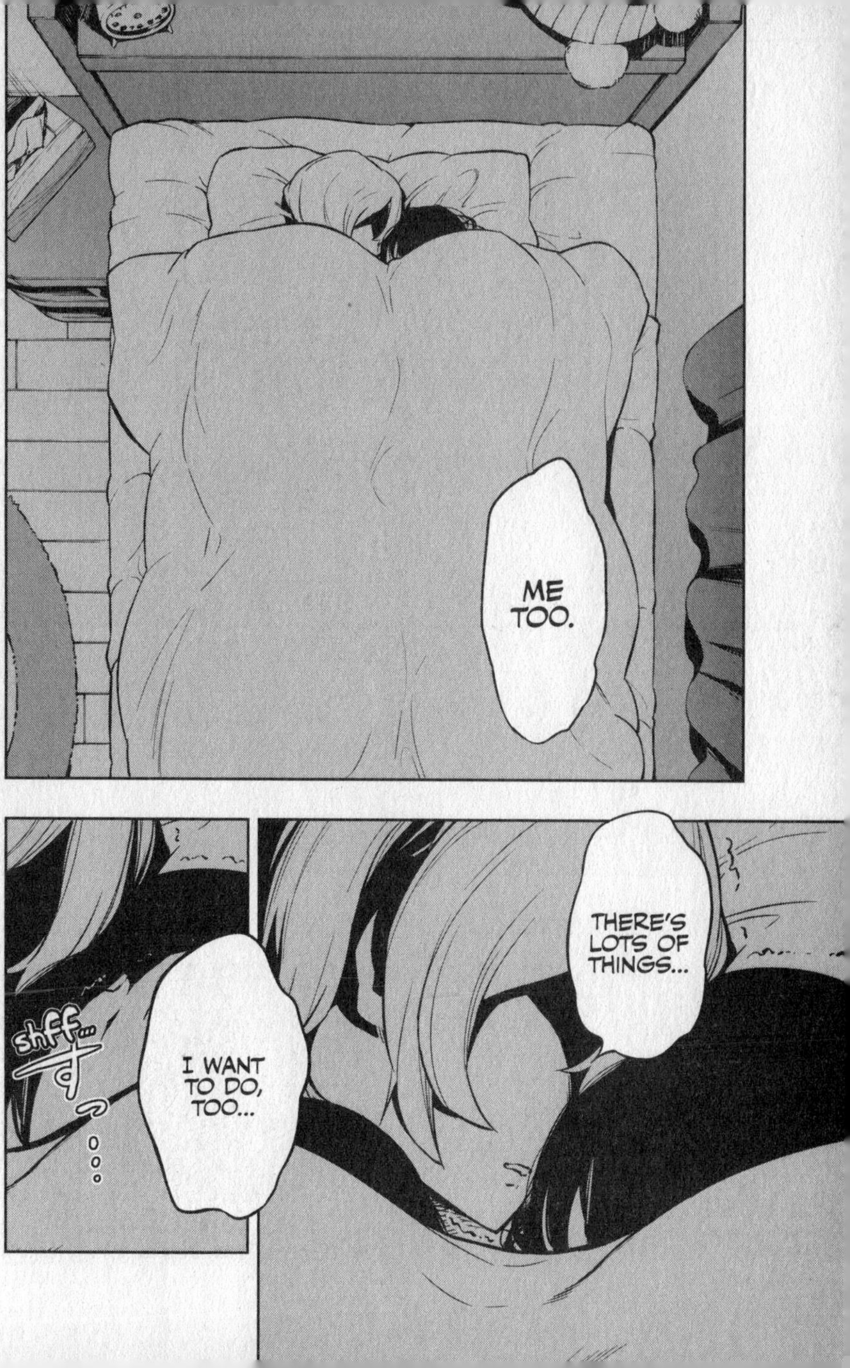
ME TOO.
THERE'S LOTS OF THINGS...
I WANT TO DO, TOO...
shff...

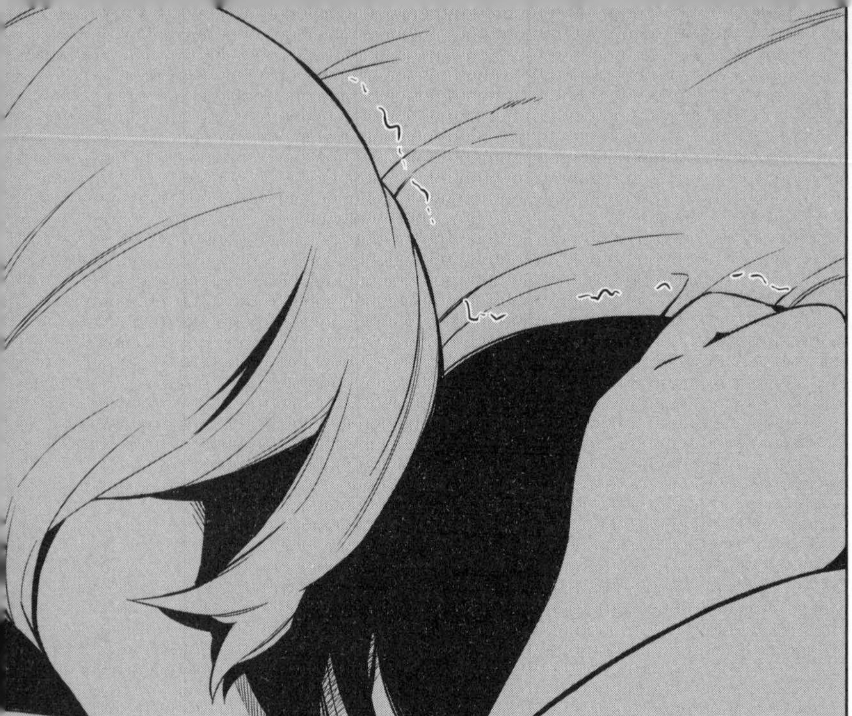
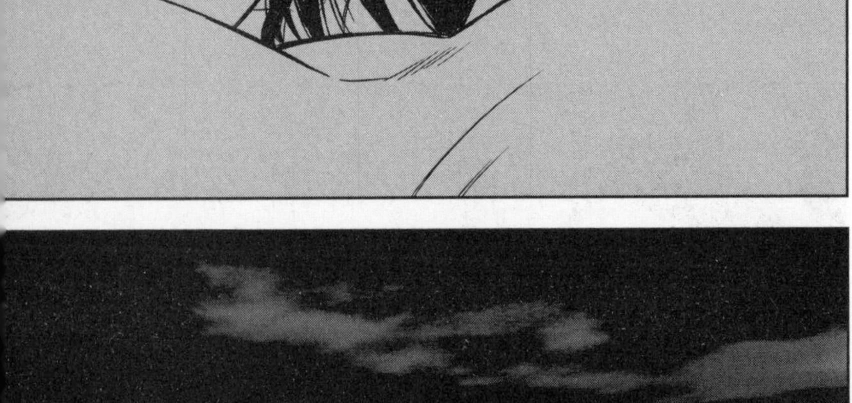

AMAGAI KOSAME

Sex: Female
Age: 13
Date of Birth: November 6 (Scorpio)
Height: 144cm
Weight: 42kg
Blood Type: AB
Birthplace: Kanagawa Prefecture

Hobbies/Interests: Online Games, Sleeping, SNS, Collecting Stuffed Animals, Anime, Online Shopping, Cutting Her Wrist

Strong Points: Being Quiet, Sewing

Weak Points: Crowds, Waking Up Early, Kids

Favorite Things: Sweets, The Occult

· Because she hurts herself, she has numerous cuts and scars on her body.

· People around her often say she has terrible fashion sense, which depresses her.

· Her past and the origin of her cutting habit are private at this time.

· She is a bit of a drama queen.

· Her skin is very white; you can see her blood vessels faintly underneath.

· Her favorite celebrity is NON STYLE's Yusuke Inoue.

ENTER.22 TWO MAGICAL GIRLS

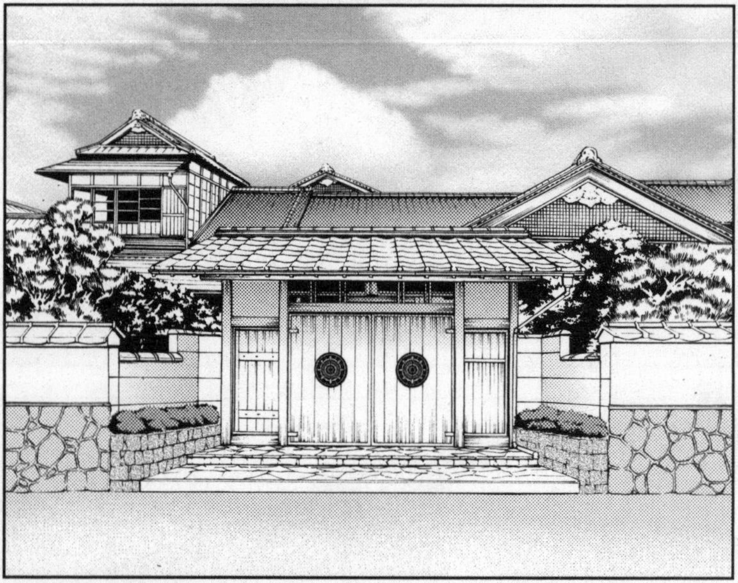

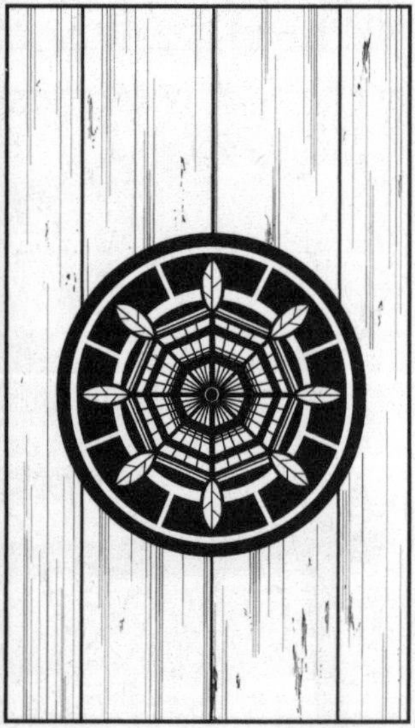

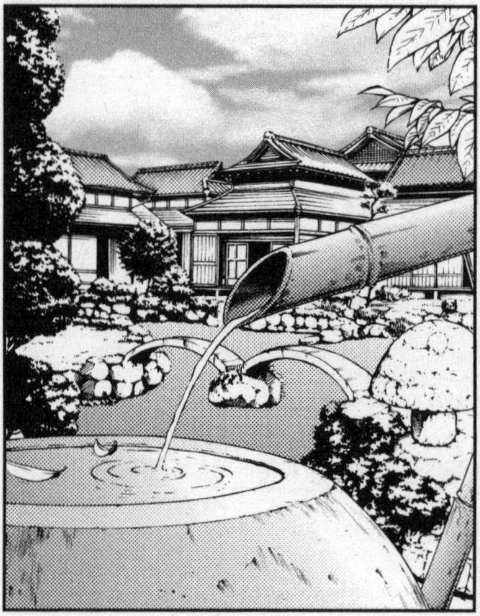

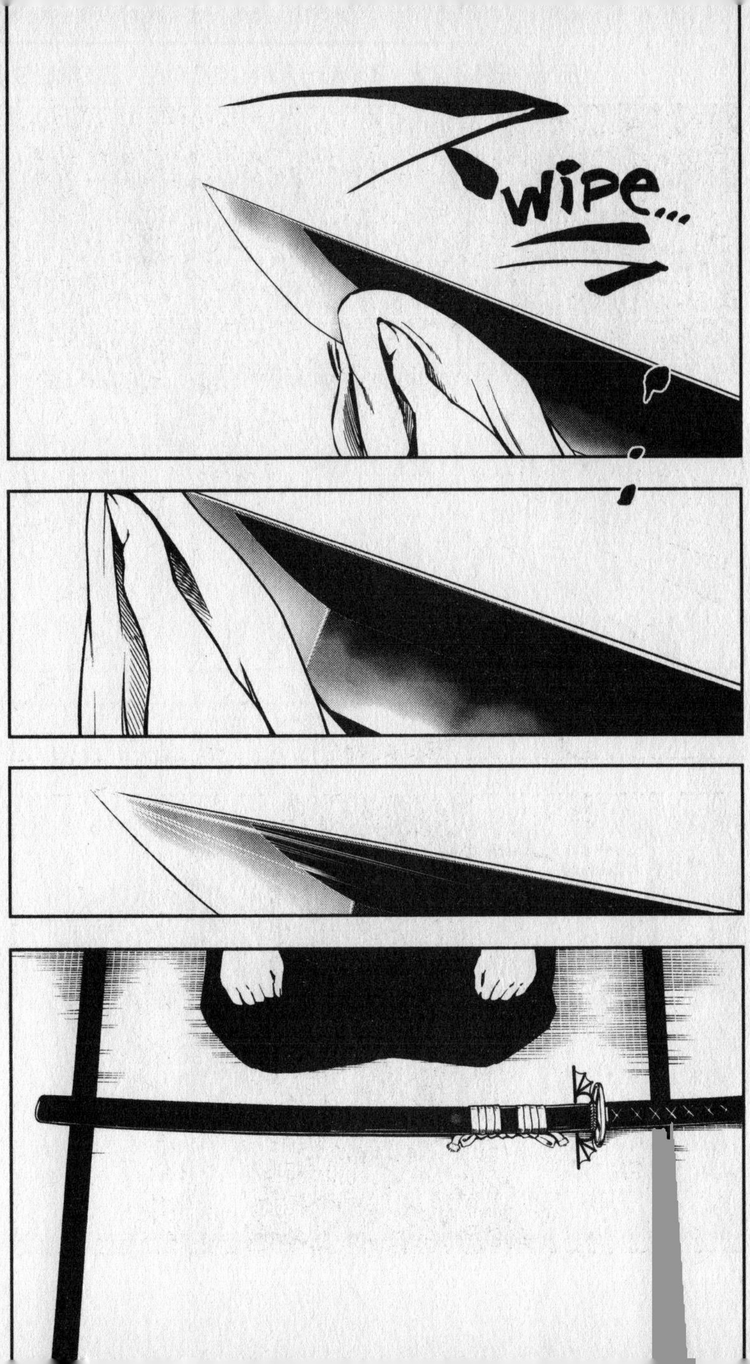
wipe...

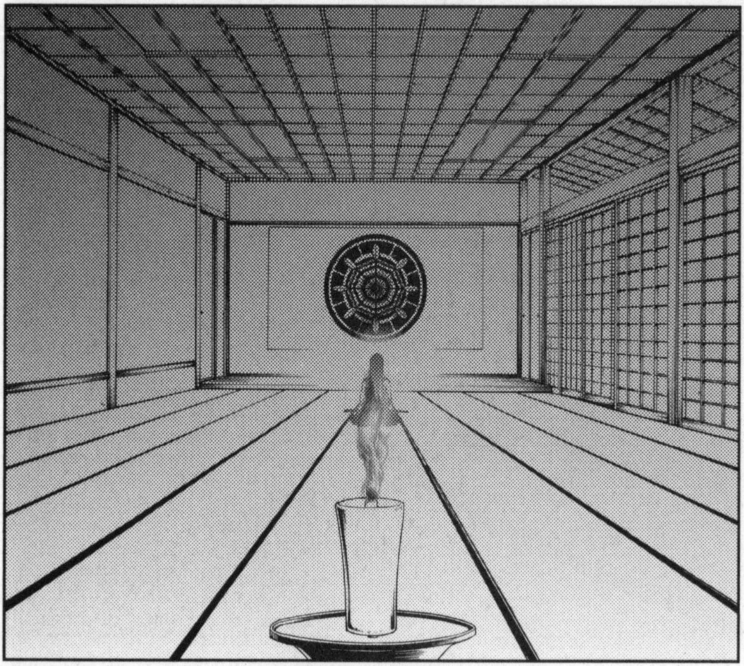
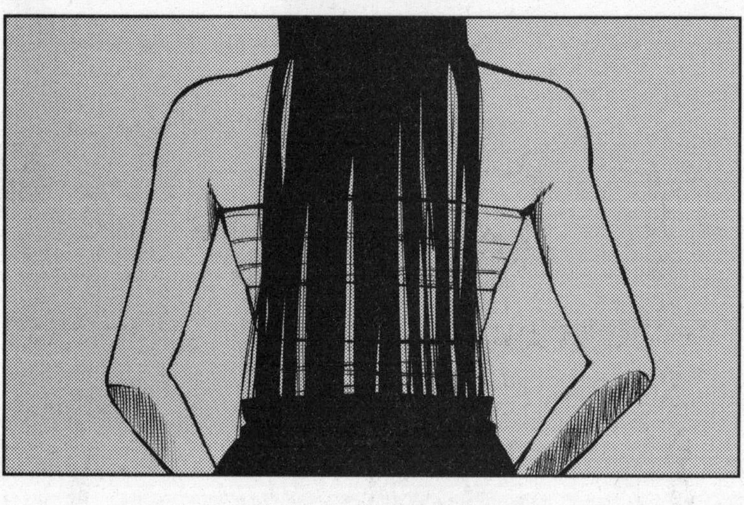

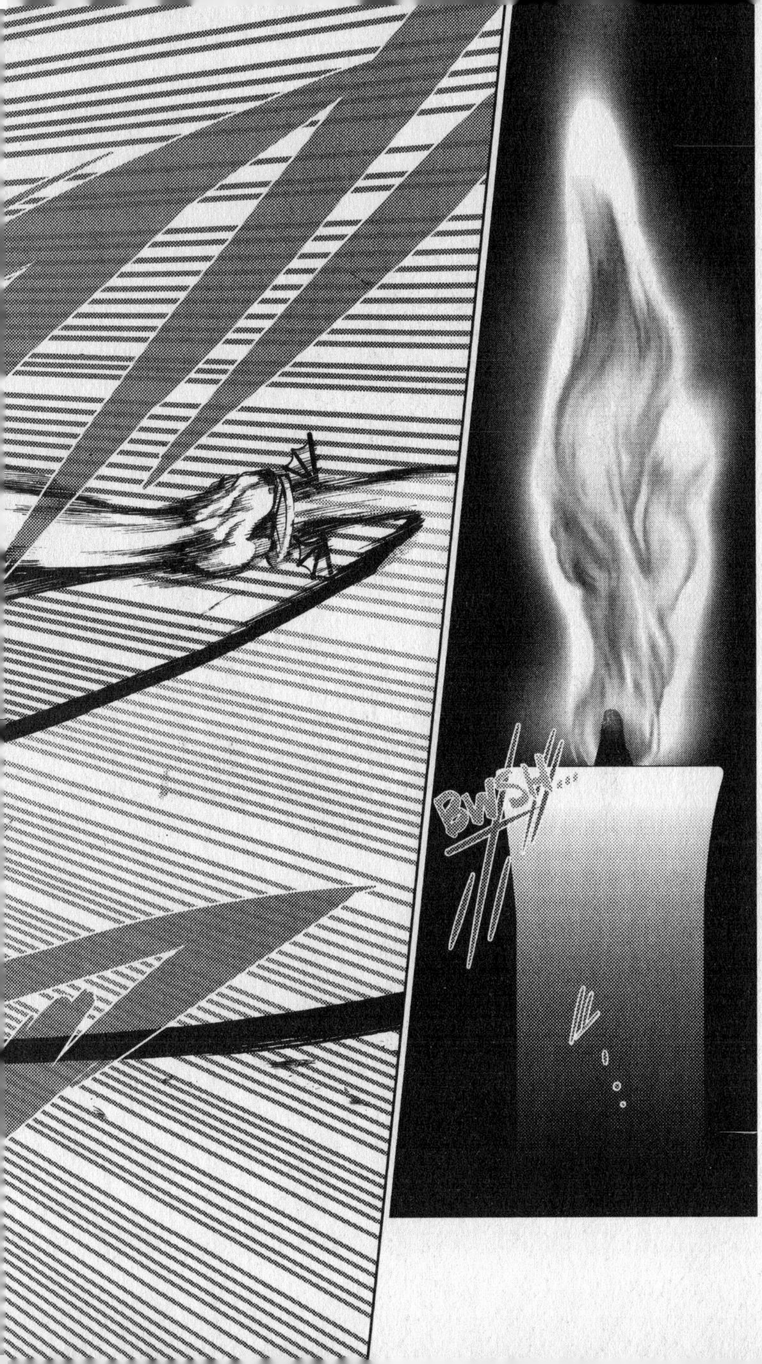
BWSH...

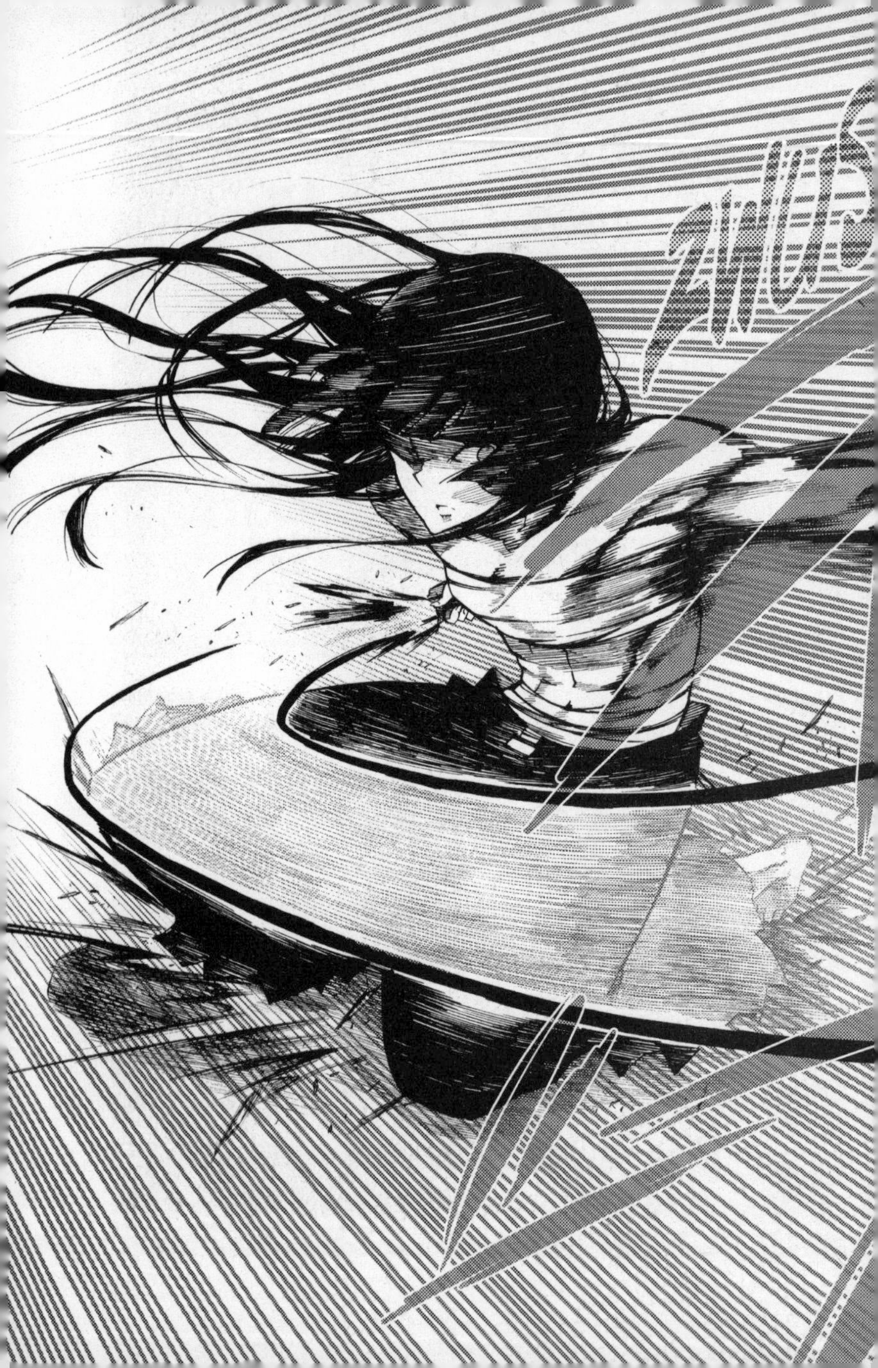

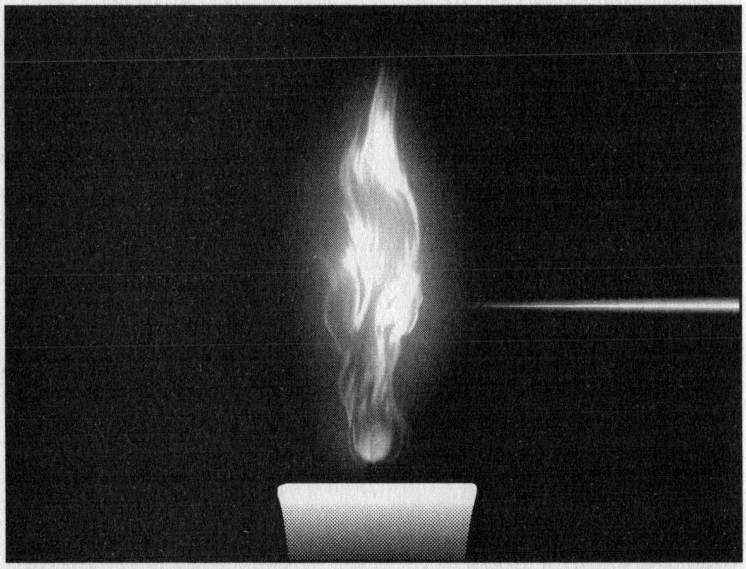

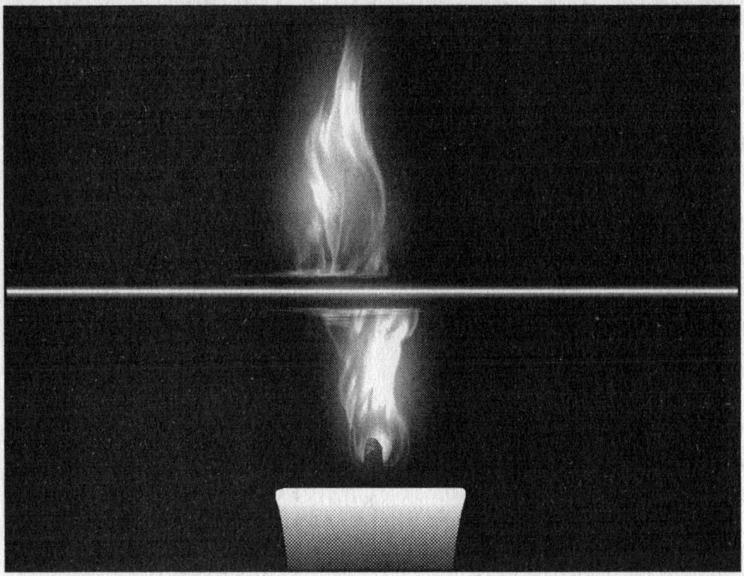

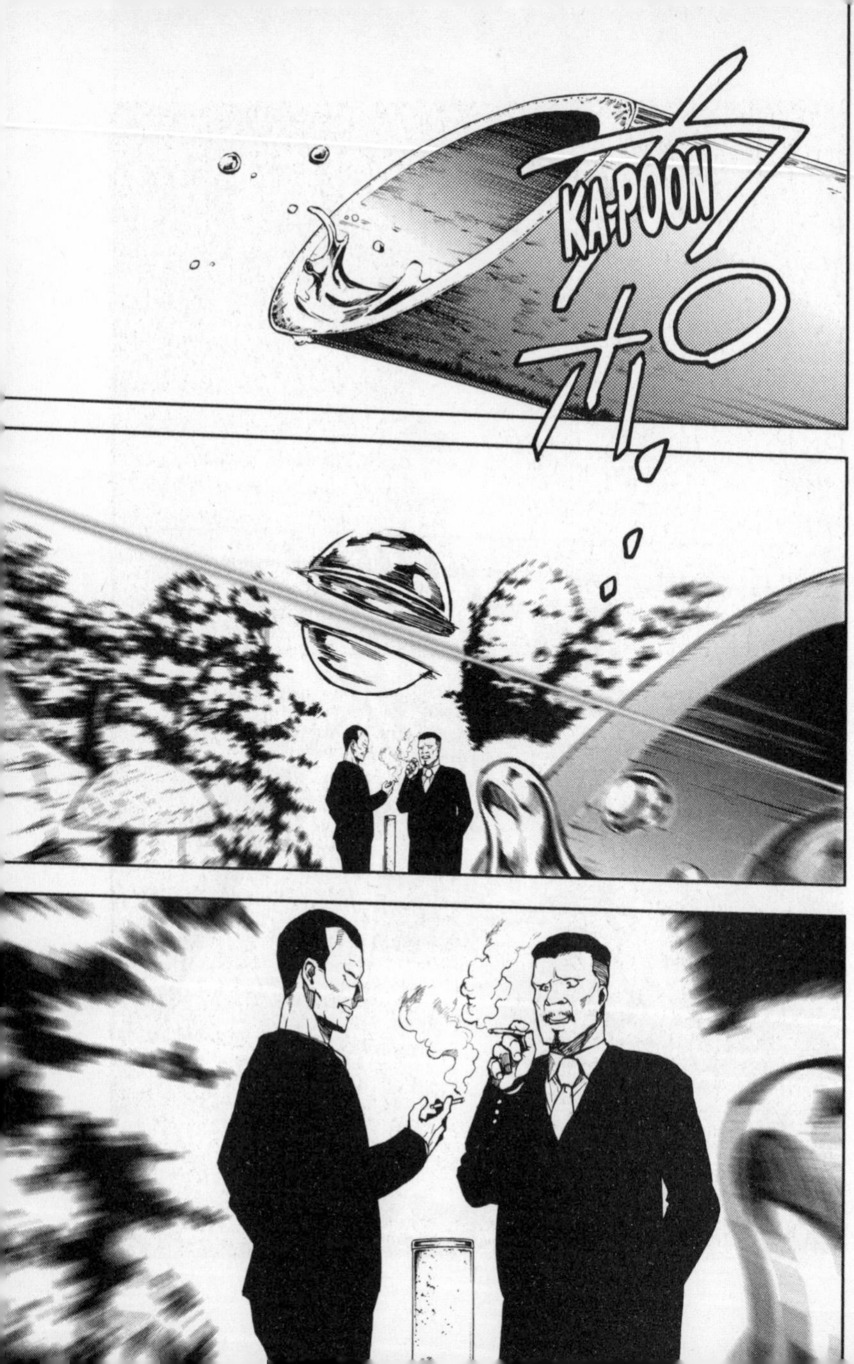
KA-POON

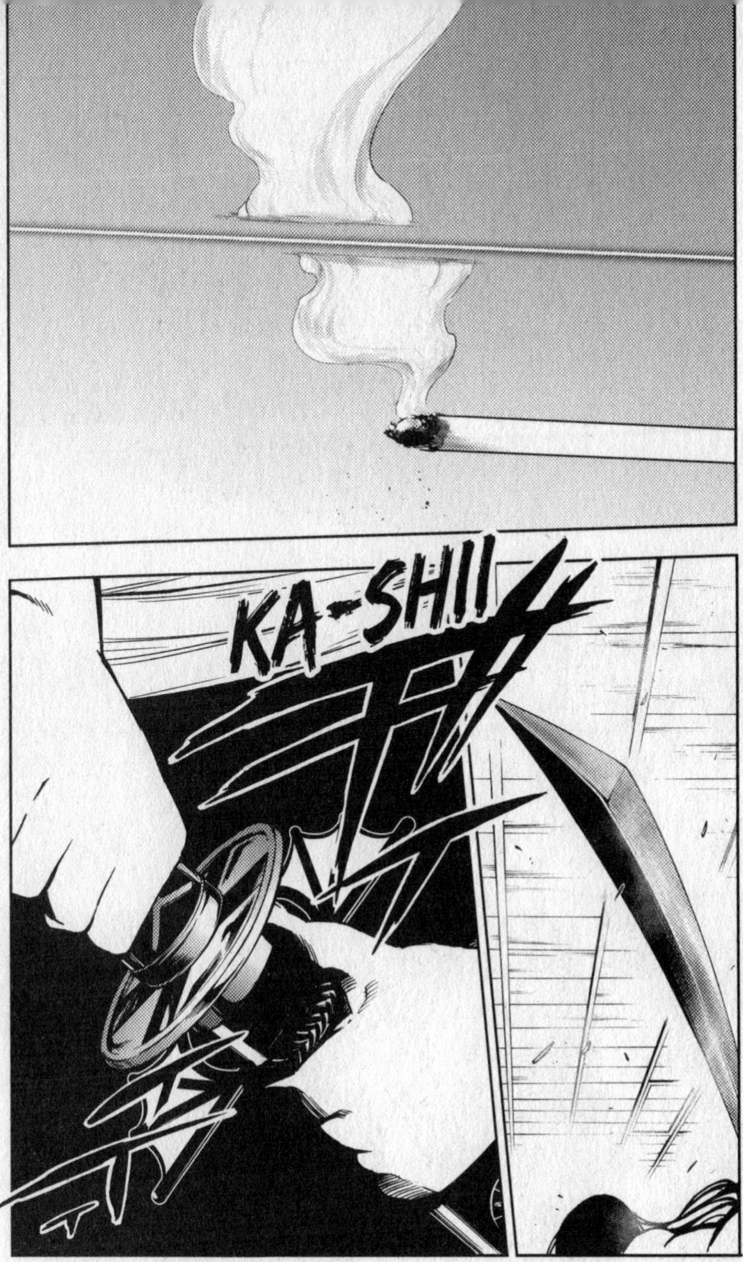
KA-SHII

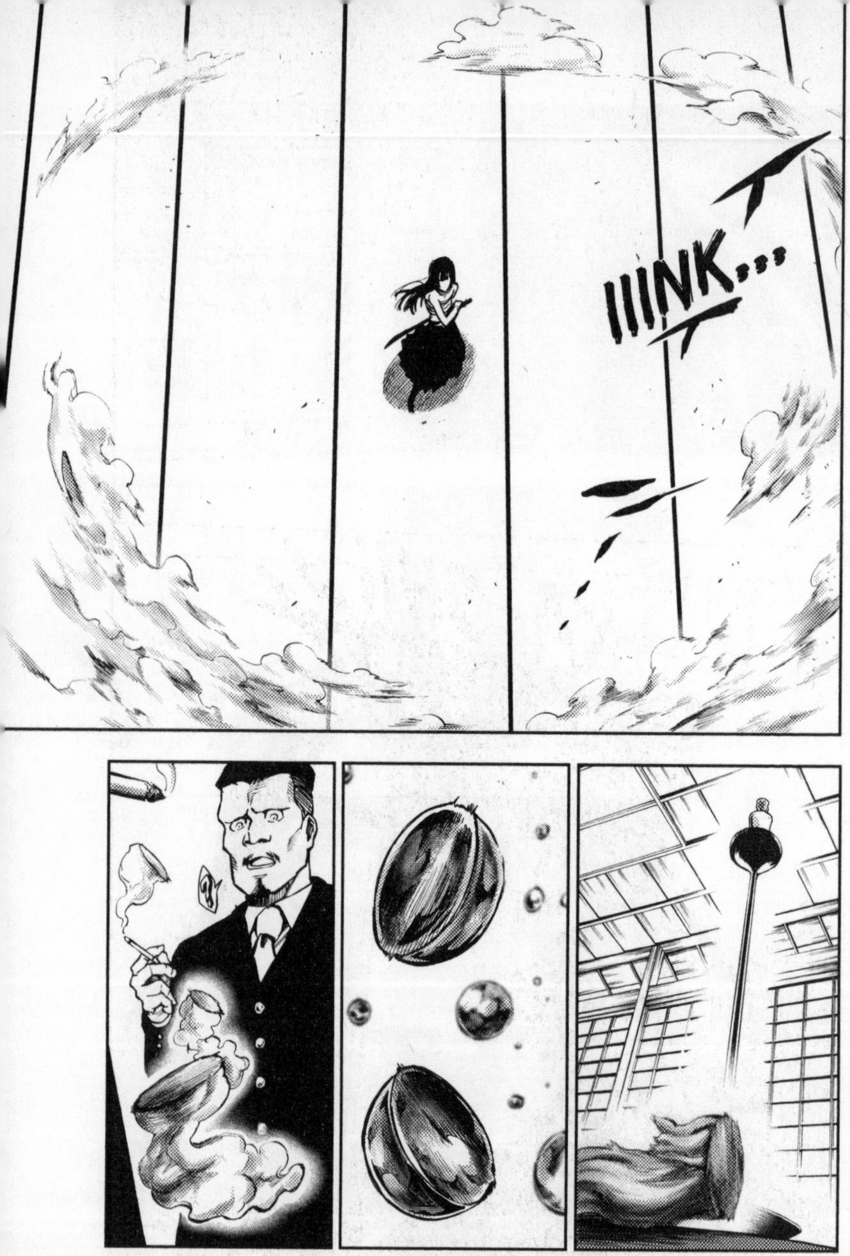
IIINK...

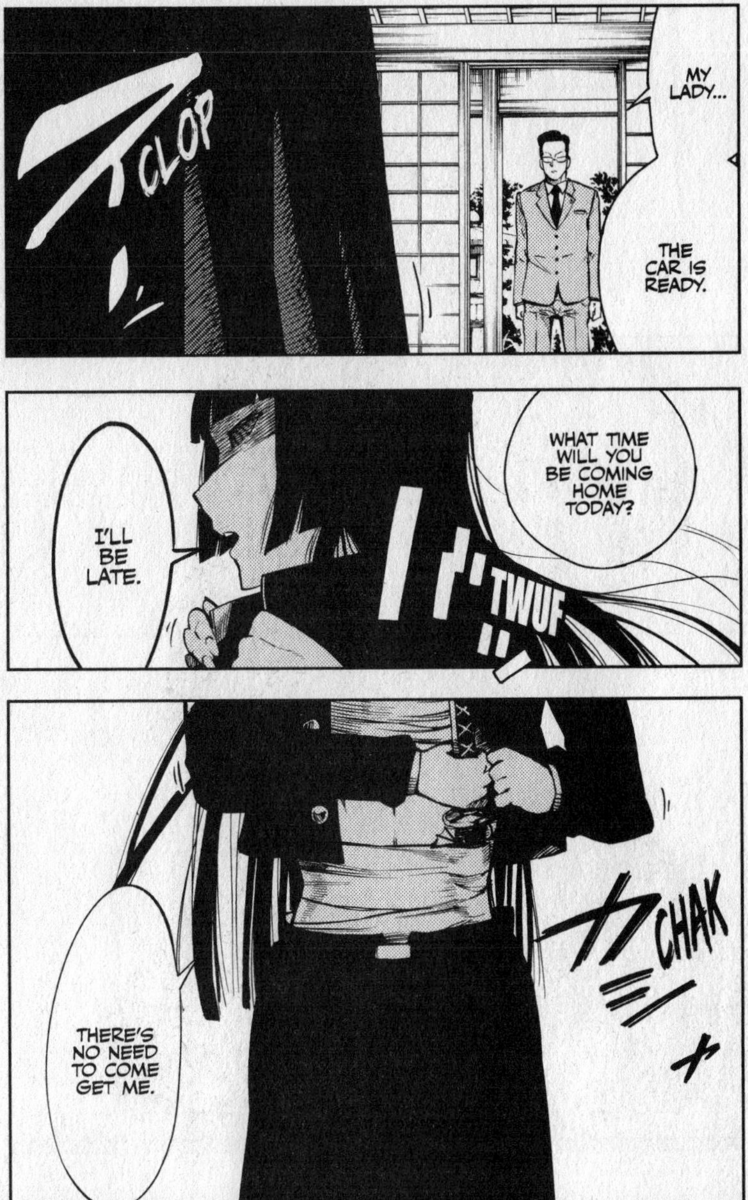
MY LADY...
THE CAR IS READY.
CLOP
WHAT TIME WILL YOU BE COMING HOME TODAY?
TWUF
I'LL BE LATE.
CHAK
THERE'S NO NEED TO COME GET ME.

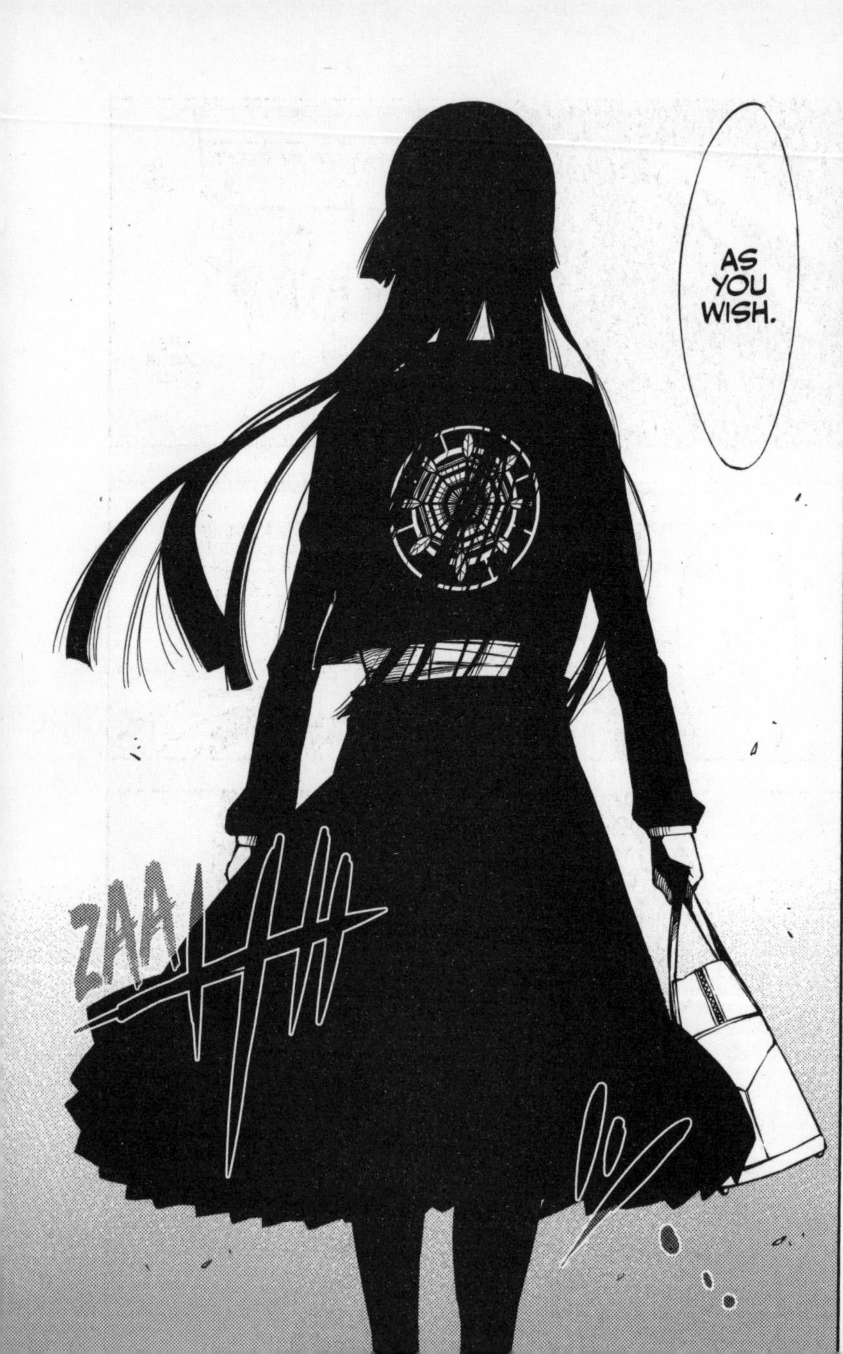
AS YOU WISH.
ZAAH

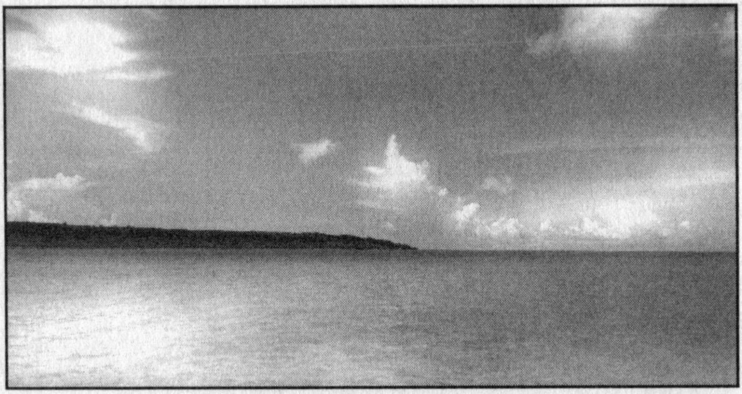
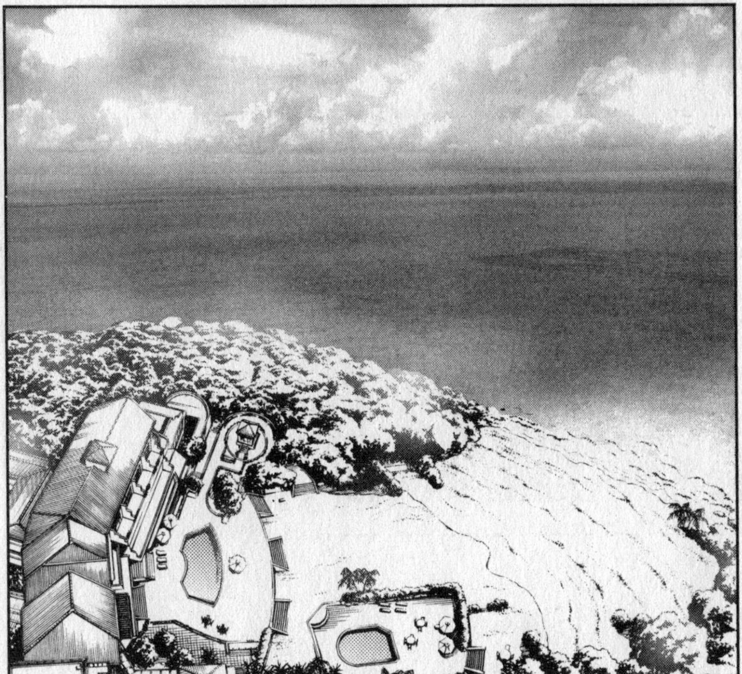

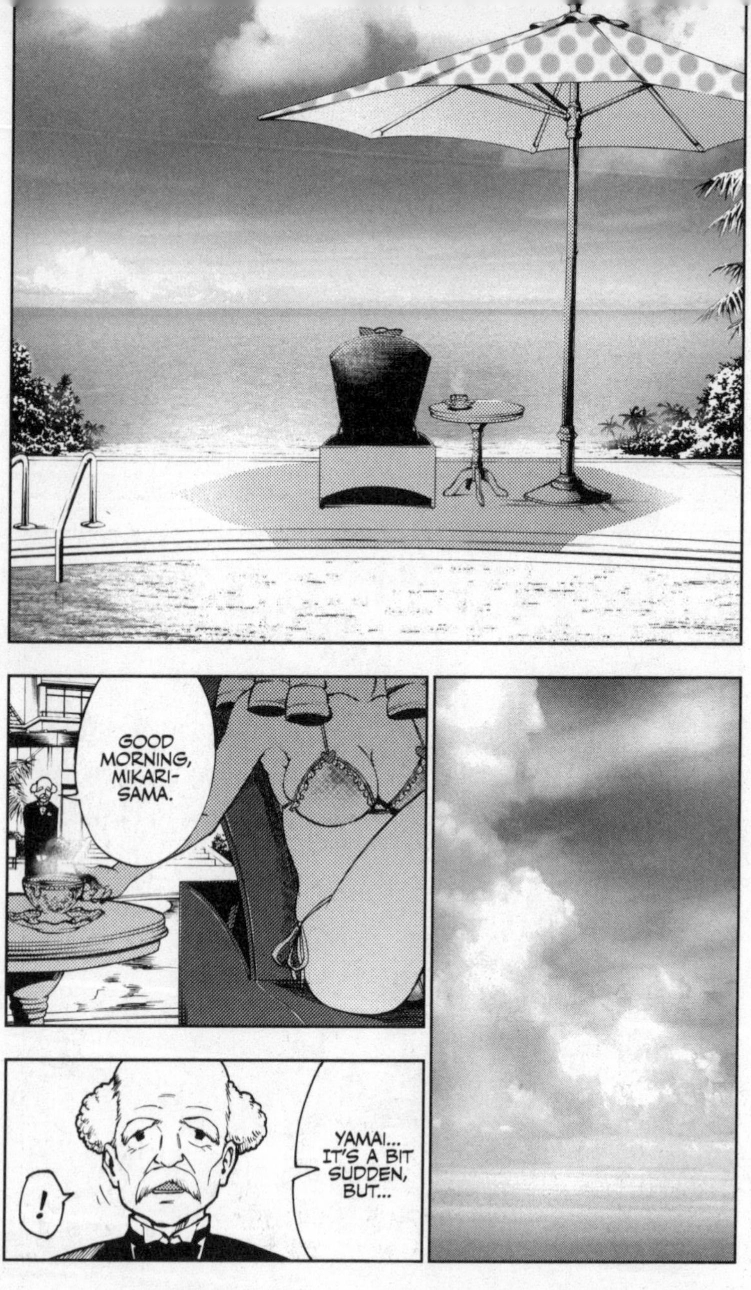
GOOD MORNING, MIKARI-SAMA.
YAMAI... IT'S A BIT SUDDEN, BUT...
!

STRIP.

NEXT...

GET DOWN ON ALL FOURS.

MI... MIKARI-SAMA...

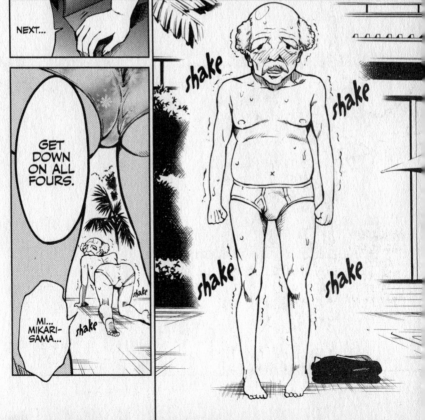

shake

shake

shake

shake

shake

shake

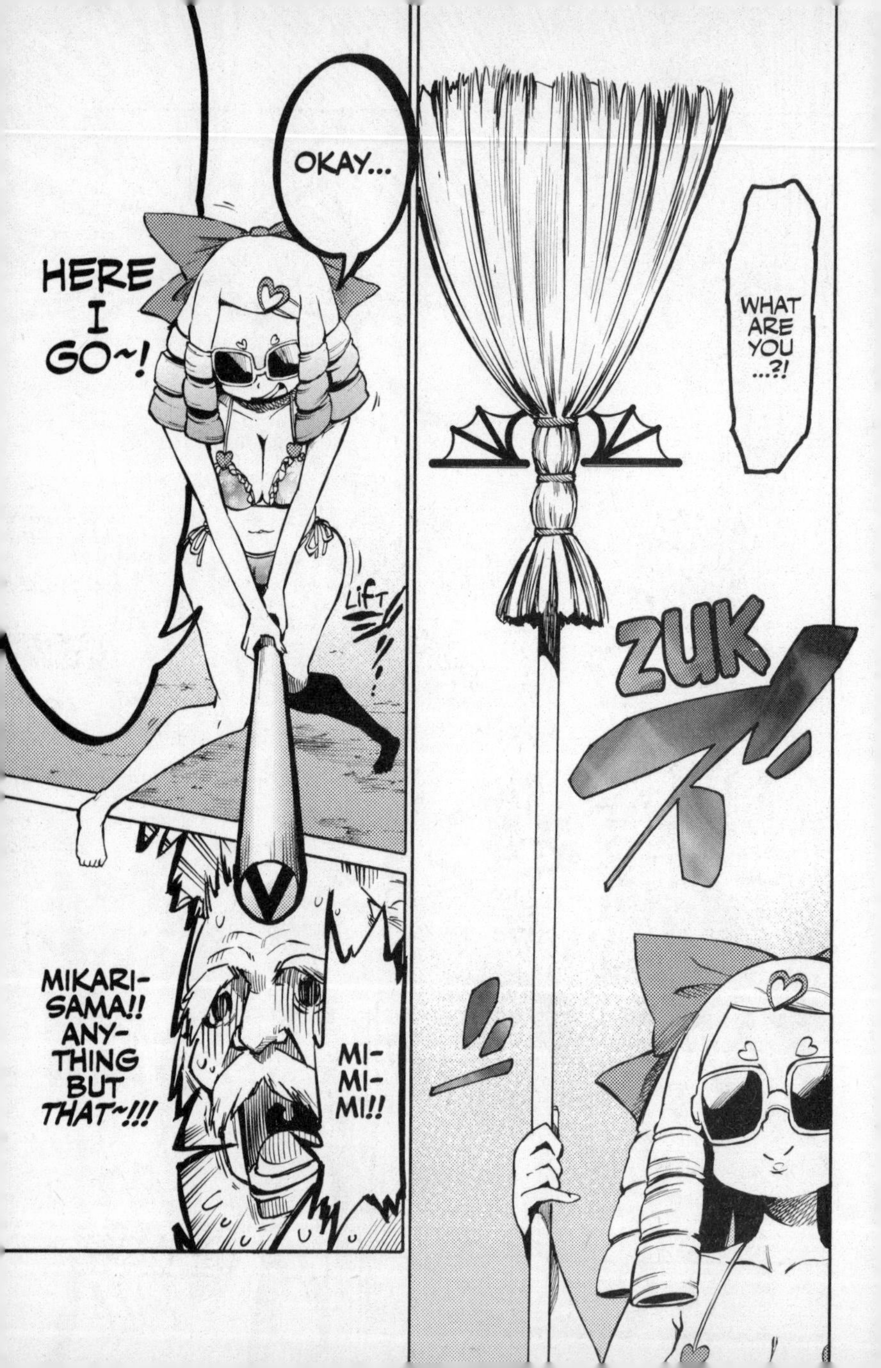
WHAT ARE YOU ...?!
ZUK
OKAY...
HERE I GO~!
LIFT
MI-MI-MI!!
MIKARI-SAMA!! ANYTHING BUT THAT~!!!

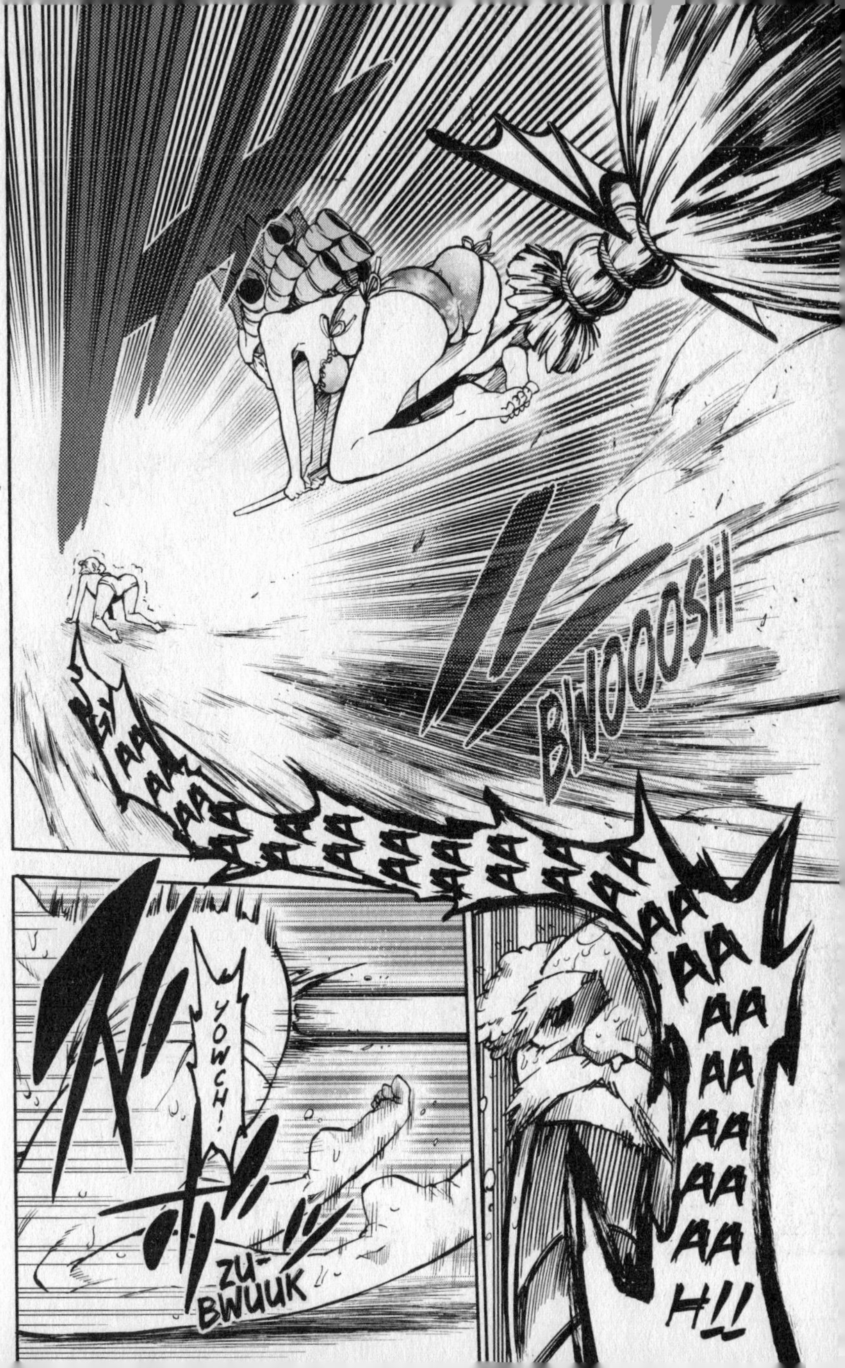
BWOOOSH
GYAAAAAAAAAAAAAAAAAAAAAAAAAAAAAAAAAAAAAAAAAAAH!!
YOWCH!
ZU-BWUUK

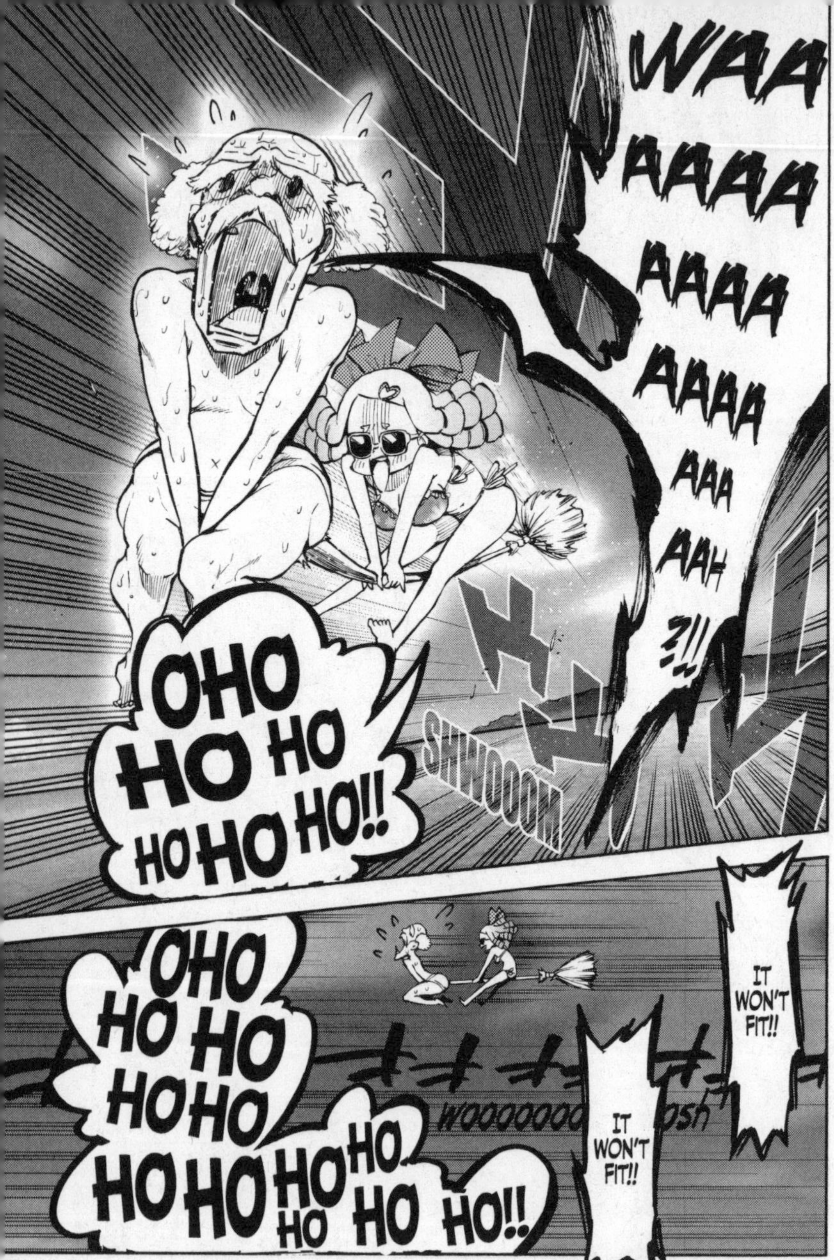
WAAAAAAAAAAAAAAAAAAAAAH?!!
OHO HO HO HO HO HO!!
SHWOOOM
IT WON'T FIT!!
IT WON'T FIT!!
WOOOOOOO OSH
OHO HO HO HO HO HO HO HO HO HO HO HO HO!!

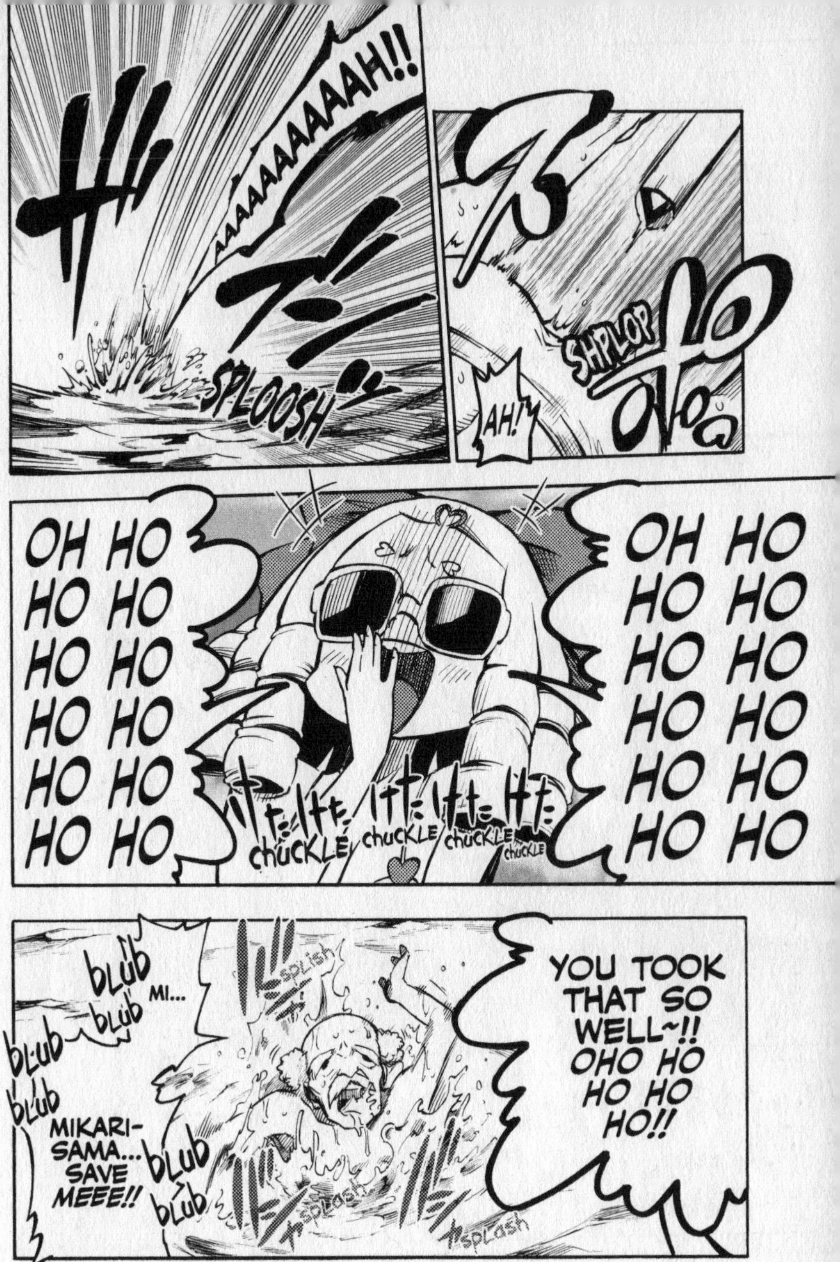
AH!
SHPLOP
AAAAAAAAAAAH!!
SPLOOSH
OH HO HO HO HO HO HO HO HO HO HO HO
chuckle chuckle chuckle chuckle
OH HO HO HO HO HO HO HO HO HO HO HO
YOU TOOK THAT SO WELL~!! OHO HO HO HO HO!!
splish
splash
splash
blub blub
MI...
blub blub
MIKARI-SAMA... SAVE MEEE!!
blub blub

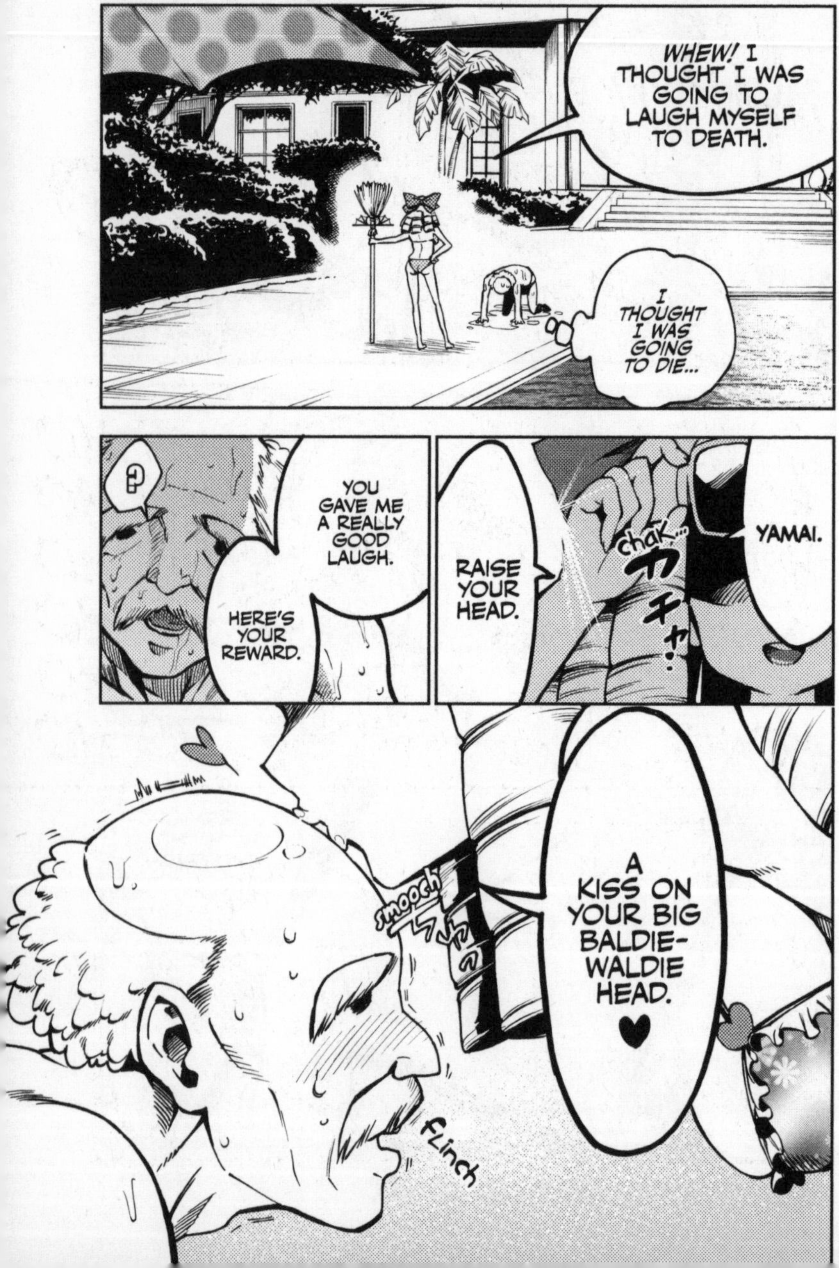
WHEW! I THOUGHT I WAS GOING TO LAUGH MYSELF TO DEATH.
I THOUGHT I WAS GOING TO DIE...
YAMAI.
chak...
RAISE YOUR HEAD.
?
YOU GAVE ME A REALLY GOOD LAUGH.
HERE'S YOUR REWARD.
A KISS ON YOUR BIG BALDIE-WALDIE HEAD. ♥
smooch
flinch

BALDIE!!!

DON'T YOU "SIGH" LIKE THAT AT ME...

THR-WHACK

D'OFF!

SIGH...

MUCH BETTER.

THANK YOU FOR KISSING MY BALDIE!!

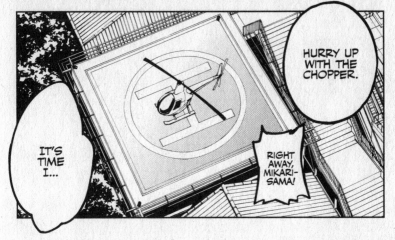

HURRY UP WITH THE CHOPPER.

IT'S TIME I...

RIGHT AWAY, MIKARI-SAMA!

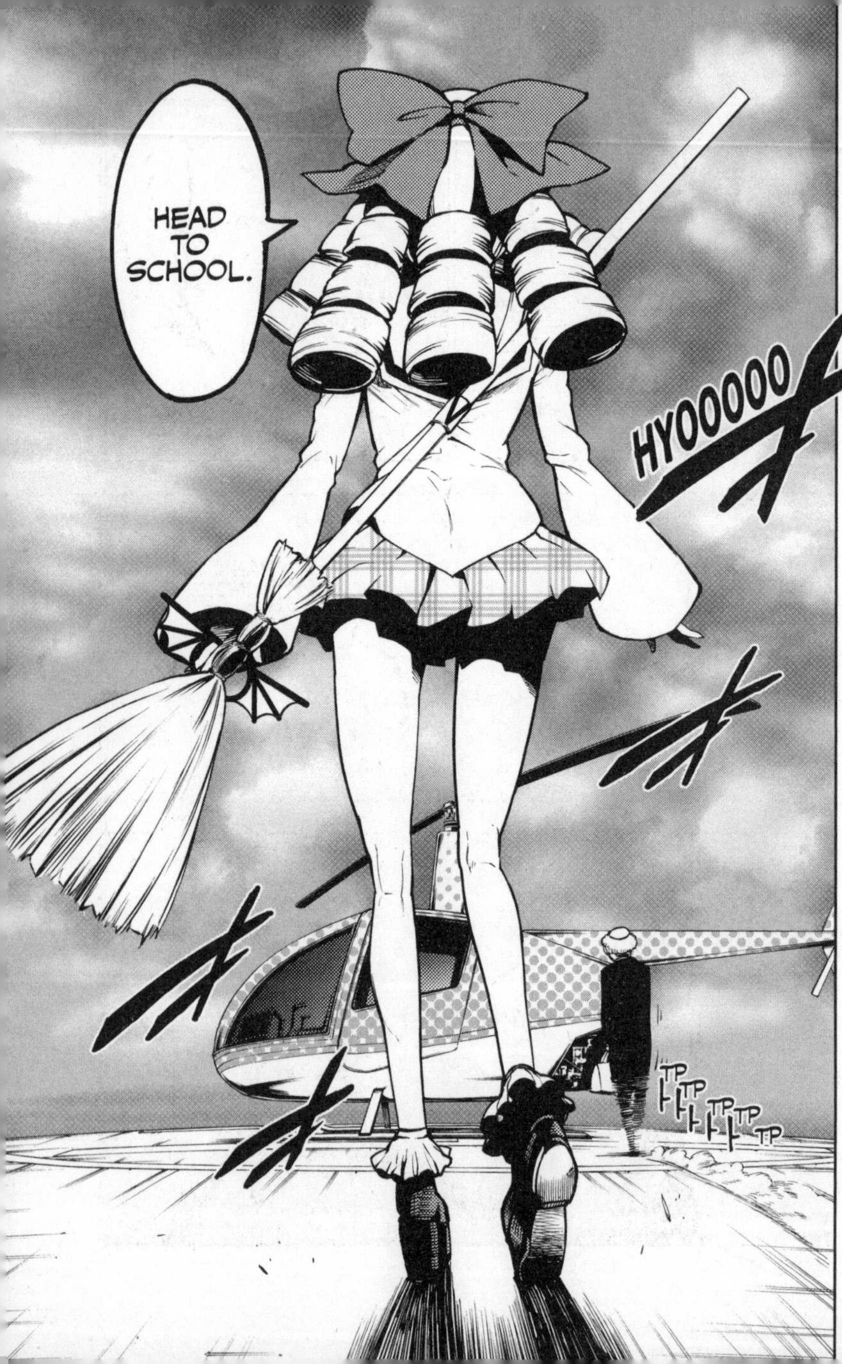
HYOOOOO
HEAD TO SCHOOL.
TP TP TP TP TP

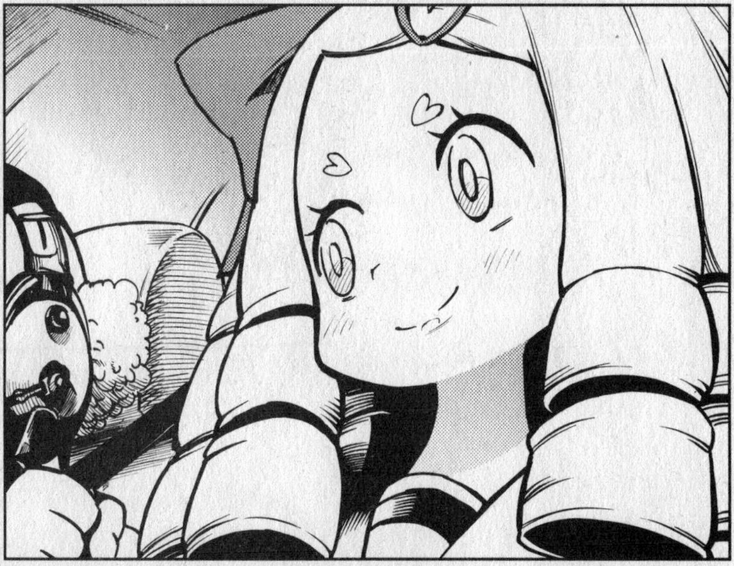
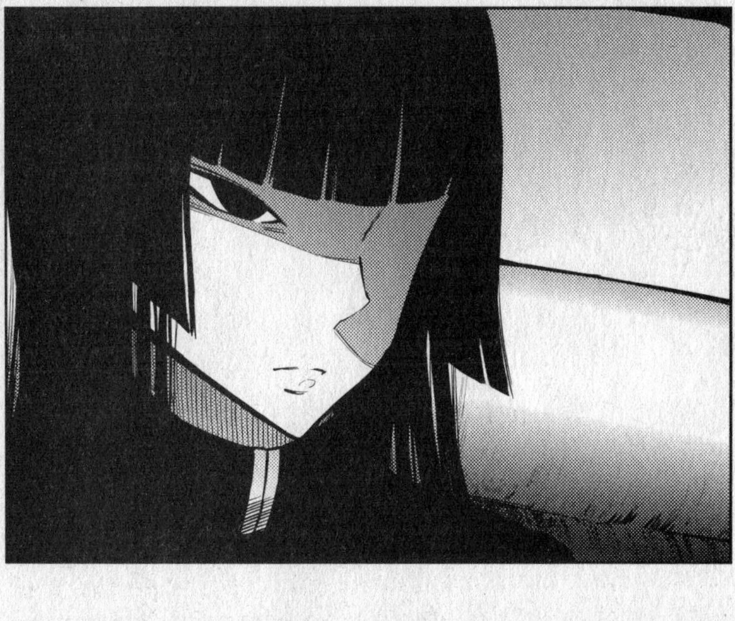

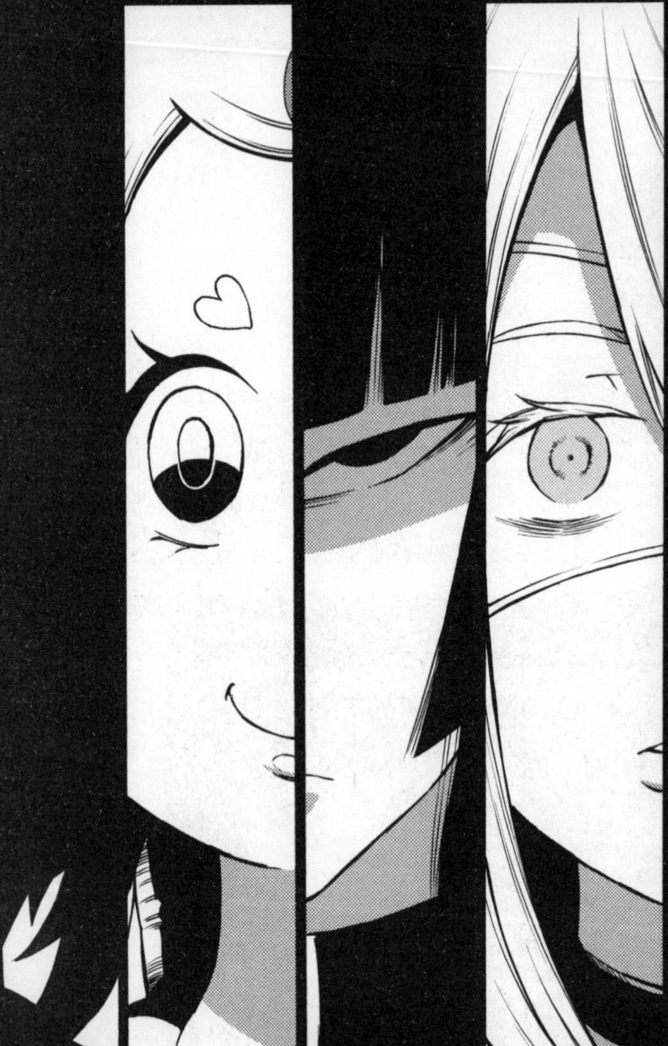

ENTER.23 A MALE MAGICAL GIRL

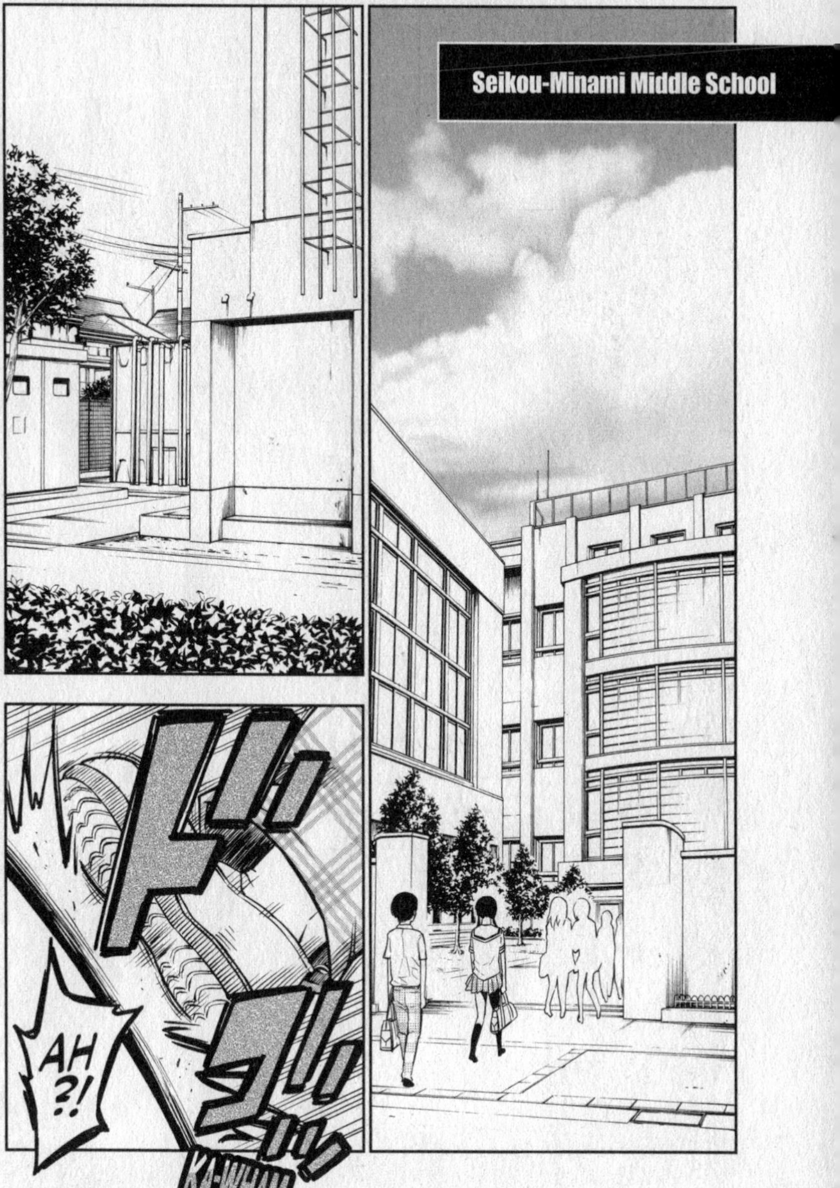
Seikou-Minami Middle School
AH ?!
KA-WHAM

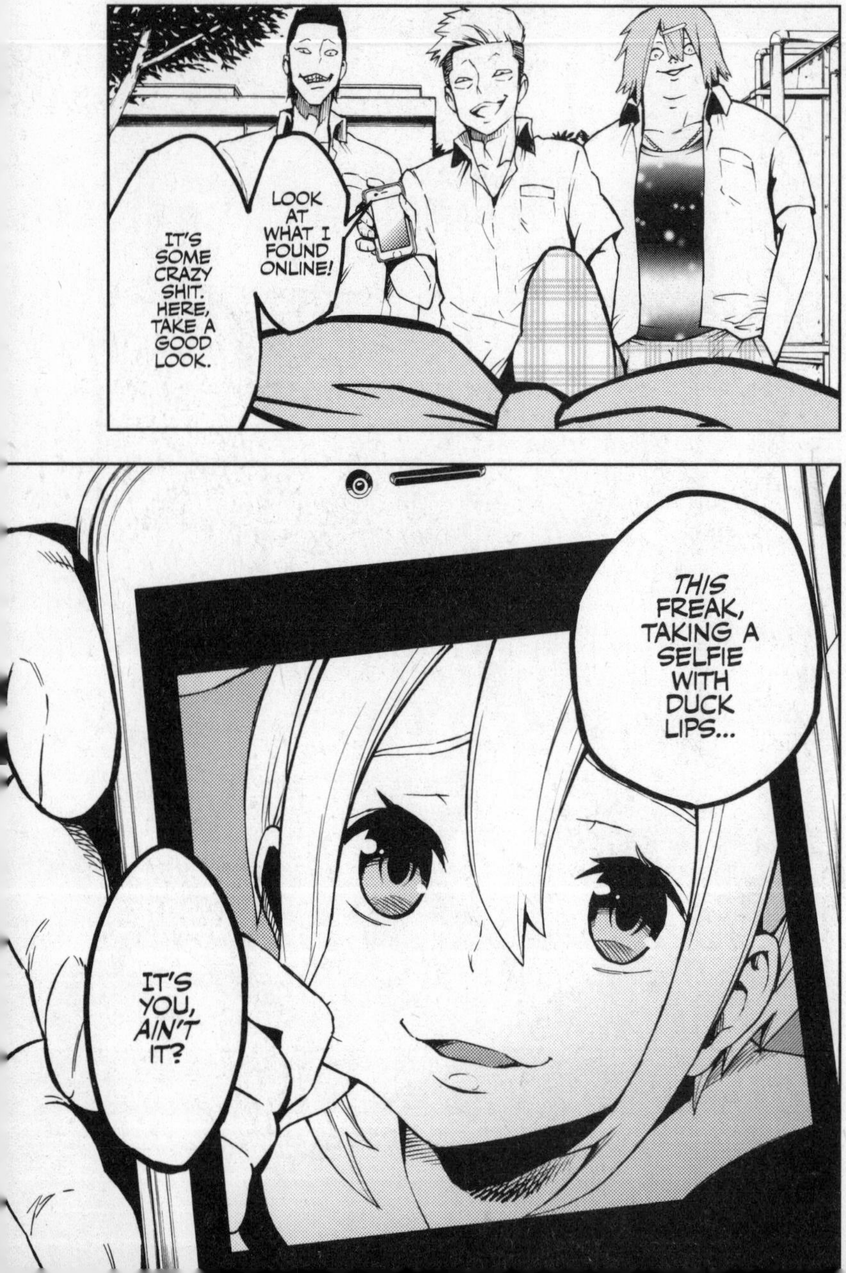
LOOK AT WHAT I FOUND ONLINE!
IT'S SOME CRAZY SHIT. HERE, TAKE A GOOD LOOK.
THIS FREAK, TAKING A SELFIE WITH DUCK LIPS...
IT'S YOU, *AIN'T* IT?

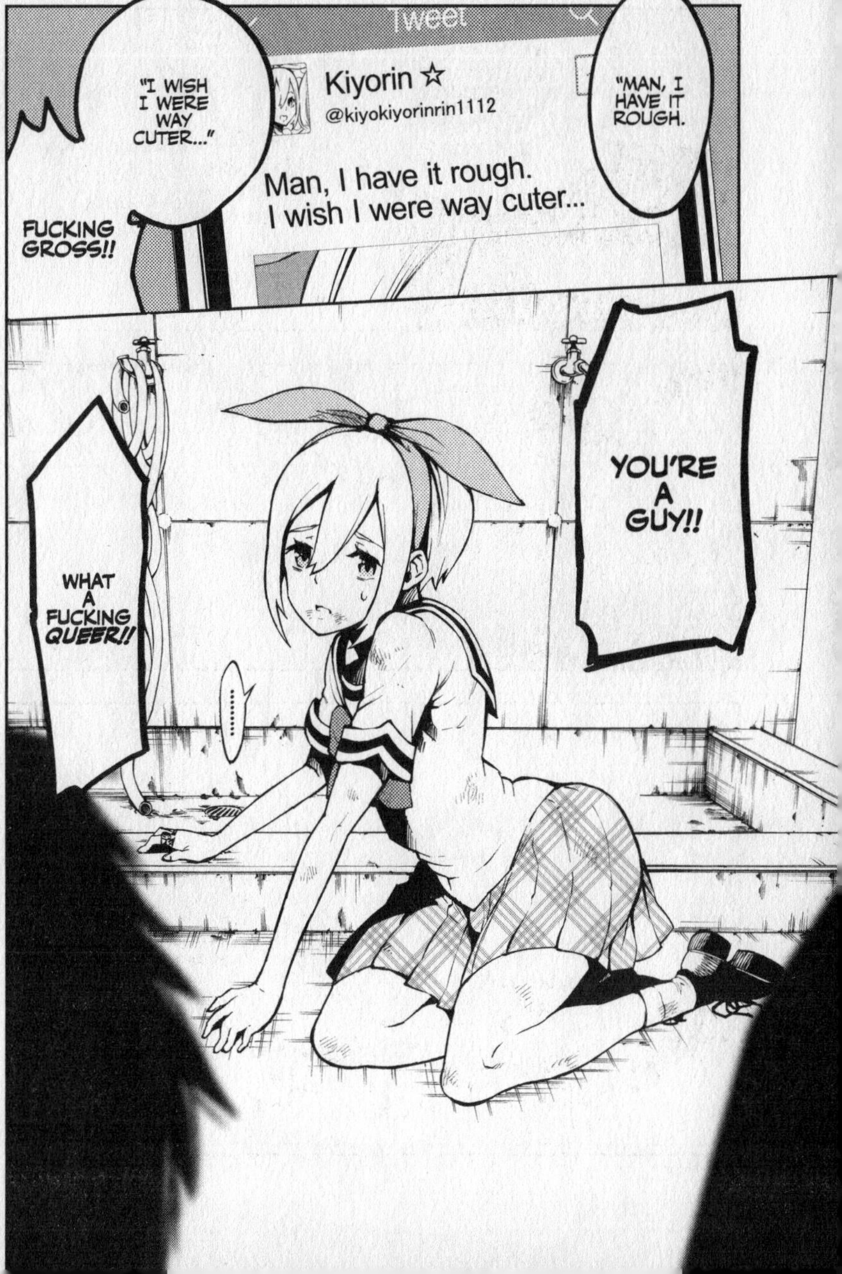
"MAN, I HAVE IT ROUGH.
Tweet
Kiyorin ☆
@kiyokiyorinrin1112
Man, I have it rough. I wish I were way cuter...
"I WISH I WERE WAY CUTER..."
FUCKING GROSS!!
YOU'RE A GUY!!
......
WHAT A FUCKING QUEER!!

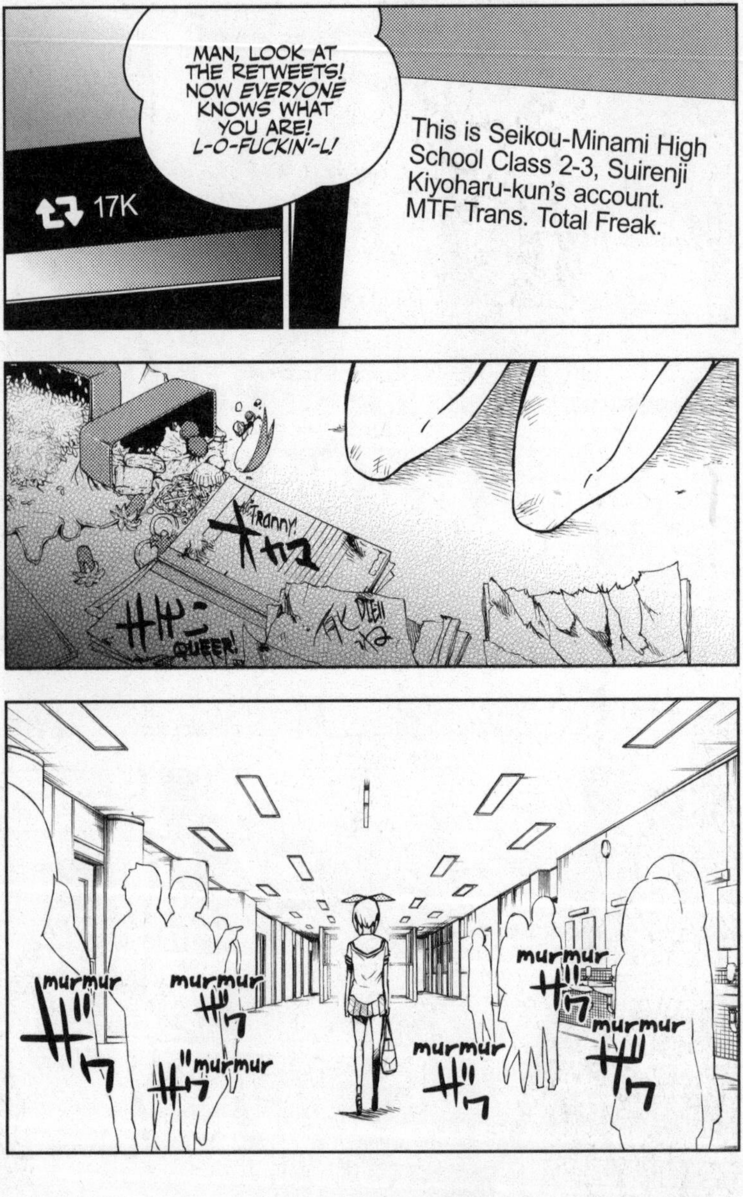
This is Seikou-Minami High School Class 2-3, Suirenji Kiyoharu-kun's account. MTF Trans. Total Freak.
17K
MAN, LOOK AT THE RETWEETS! NOW *EVERYONE* KNOWS WHAT YOU ARE! *L-O-FUCKIN'-L!*
TRANNY!
DIE!!
QUEER!
murmur
murmur
murmur
murmur
murmur
murmur

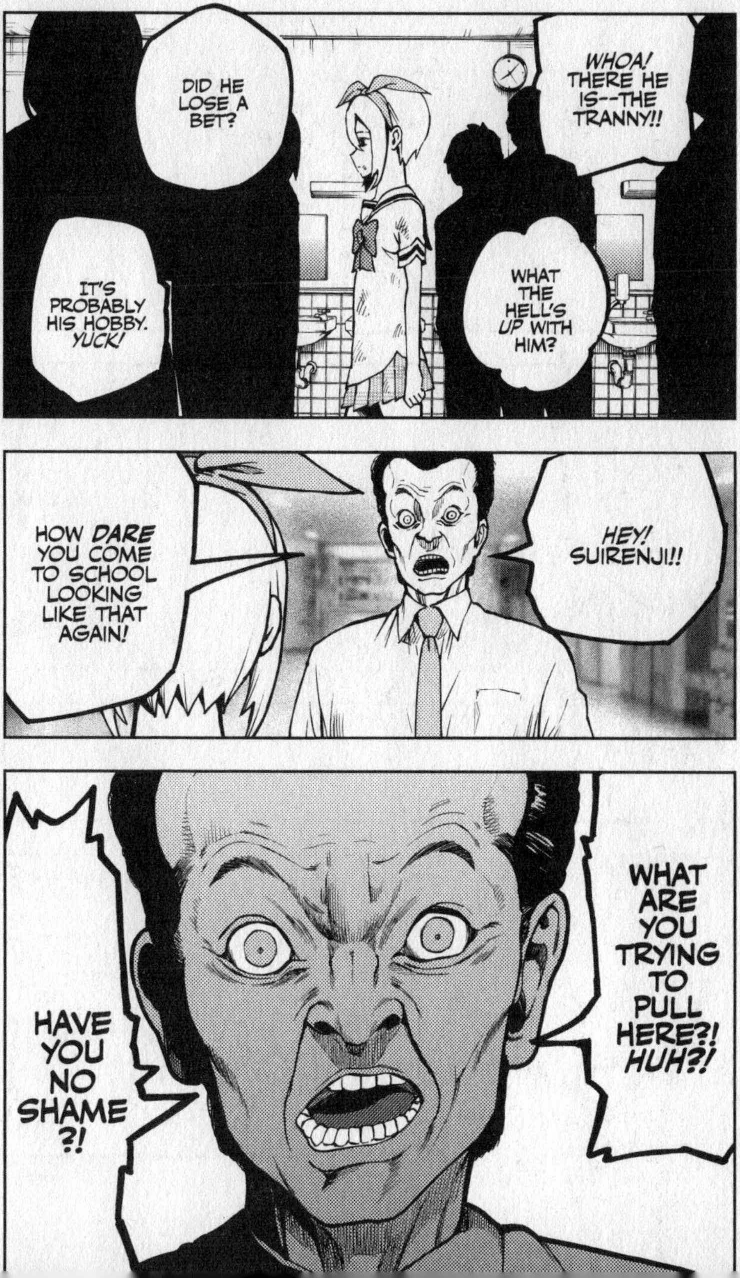
WHOA! THERE HE IS--THE TRANNY!!
DID HE LOSE A BET?
WHAT THE HELL'S UP WITH HIM?
IT'S PROBABLY HIS HOBBY. YUCK!
HEY! SUIRENJI!!
HOW DARE YOU COME TO SCHOOL LOOKING LIKE THAT AGAIN!
WHAT ARE YOU TRYING TO PULL HERE?! HUH?!
HAVE YOU NO SHAME?!

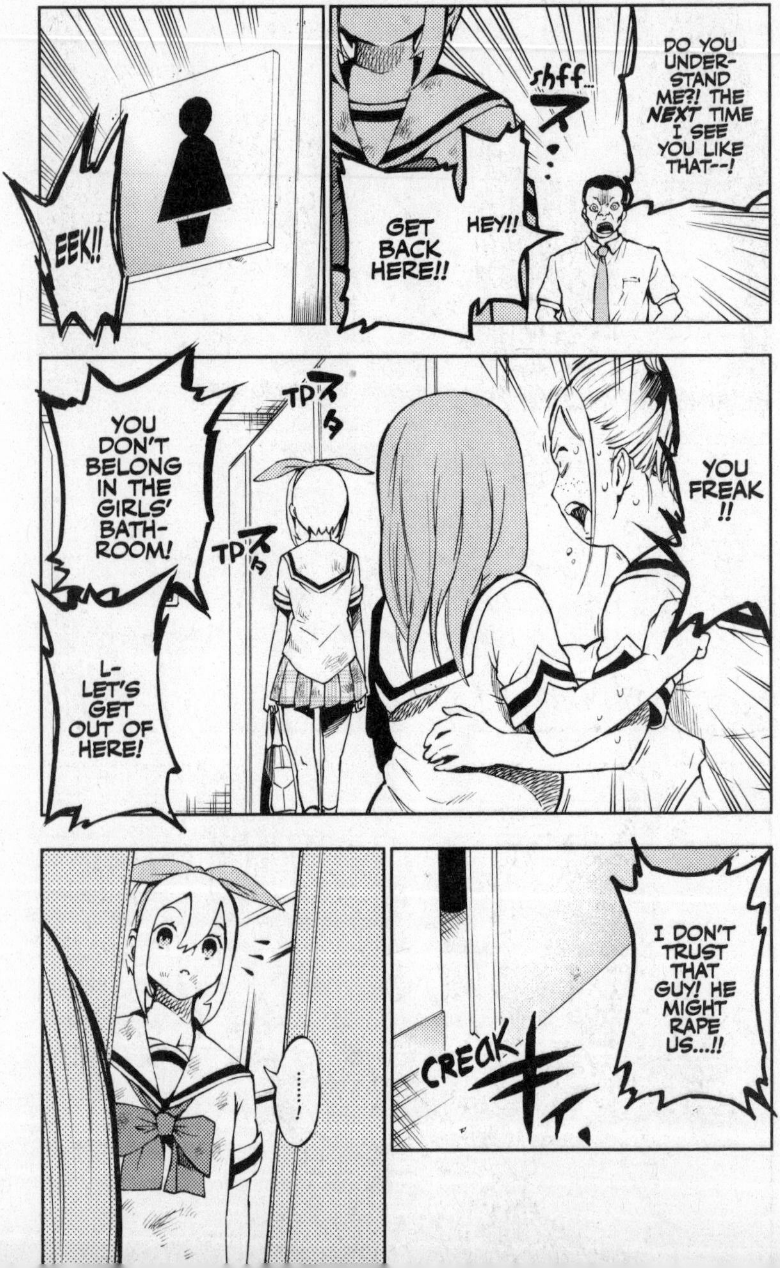
DO YOU UNDER-STAND ME?! THE *NEXT* TIME I SEE YOU LIKE THAT--!
shff...
HEY!!
GET BACK HERE!!
EEK!!
YOU FREAK!!
TP
TP
YOU DON'T BELONG IN THE GIRLS' BATH-ROOM!
L-LET'S GET OUT OF HERE!
I DON'T TRUST THAT GUY! HE MIGHT RAPE US...!!
CREAK
......!

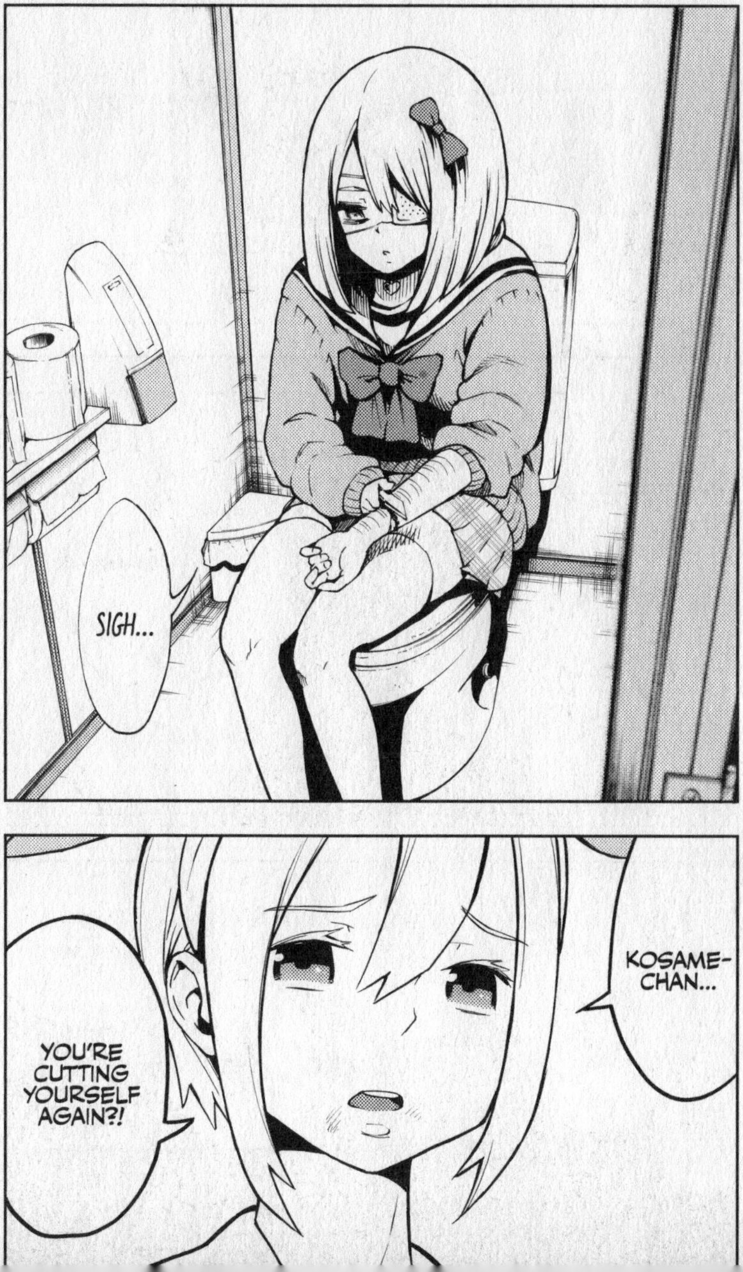
SIGH...
KOSAME-CHAN...
YOU'RE CUTTING YOURSELF AGAIN?!

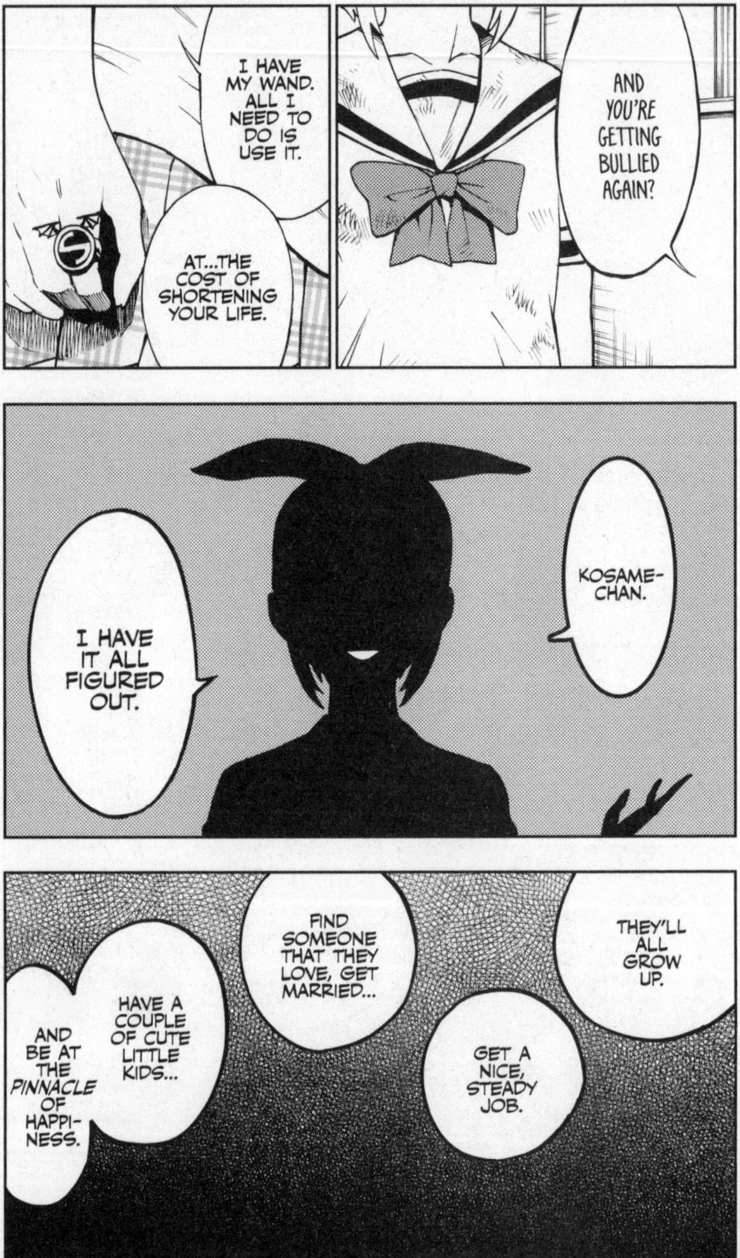
AND *YOU'RE* GETTING BULLIED AGAIN?
I HAVE MY WAND. ALL I NEED TO DO IS USE IT.
AT...THE COST OF SHORTENING YOUR LIFE.
KOSAME-CHAN.
I HAVE IT ALL FIGURED OUT.
THEY'LL ALL GROW UP.
GET A NICE, STEADY JOB.
FIND SOMEONE THAT THEY LOVE, GET MARRIED...
HAVE A COUPLE OF CUTE LITTLE KIDS...
AND BE AT THE *PINNACLE* OF HAPPI-NESS.

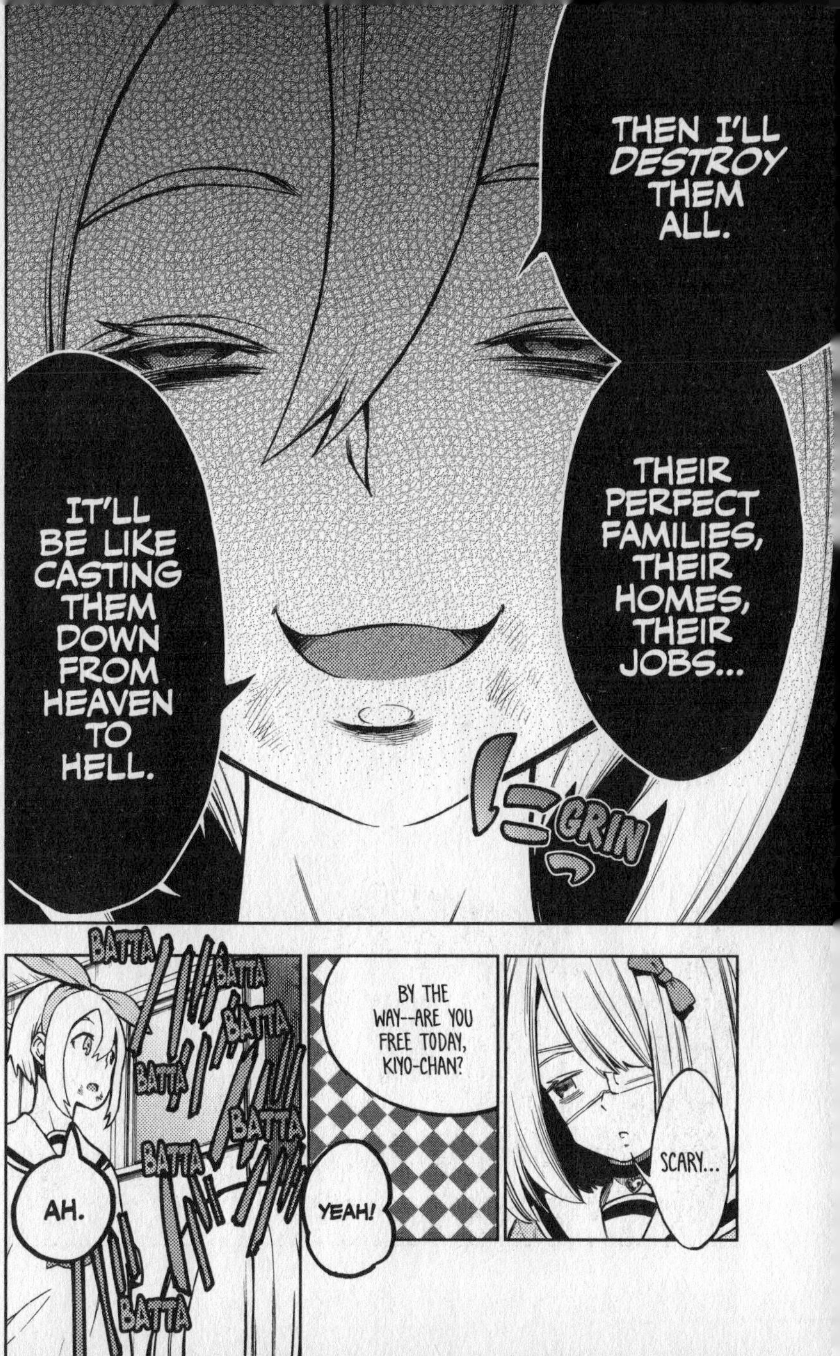
THEN I'LL *DESTROY* THEM ALL.
THEIR PERFECT FAMILIES, THEIR HOMES, THEIR JOBS...
IT'LL BE LIKE CASTING THEM DOWN FROM HEAVEN TO HELL.
GRIN
SCARY...
BY THE WAY--ARE YOU FREE TODAY, KIYO-CHAN?
YEAH!
BATTA BATTA BATTA BATTA BATTA BATTA BATTA
AH.

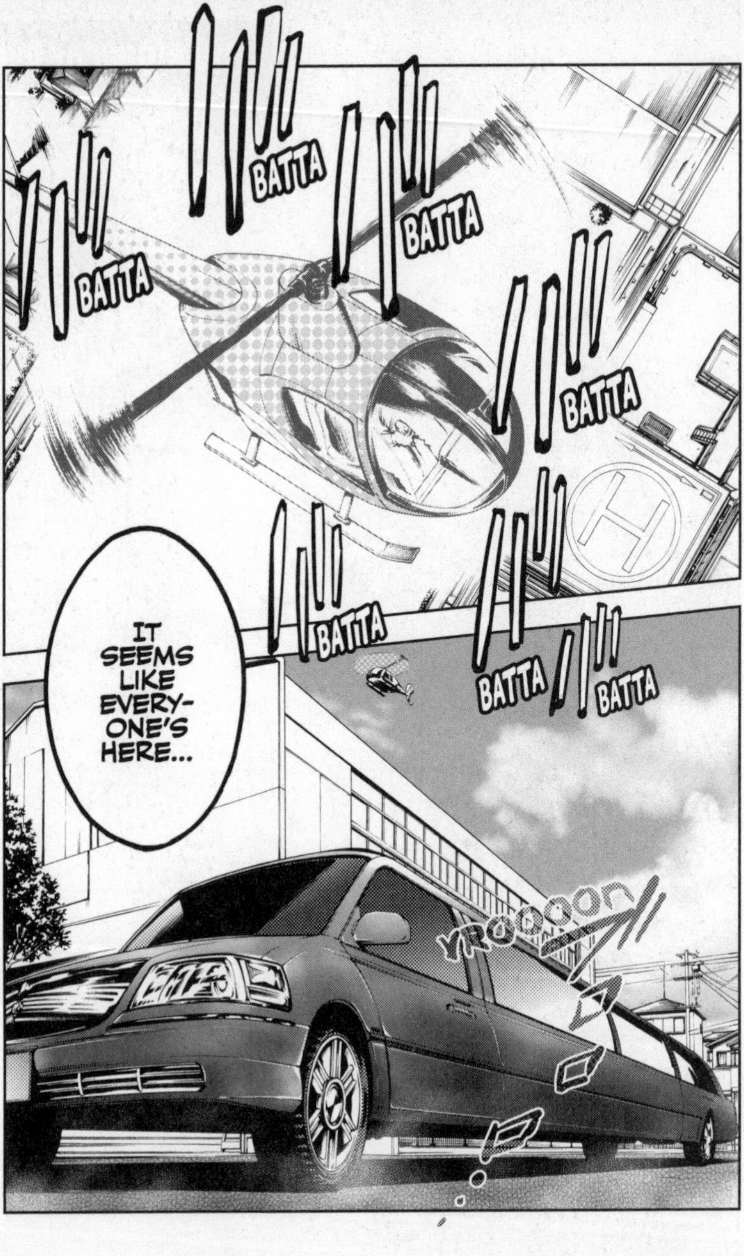
BATTA
BATTA
BATTA
BATTA
BATTA
BATTA
BATTA
IT SEEMS LIKE EVERY-ONE'S HERE...
VROOOOOM

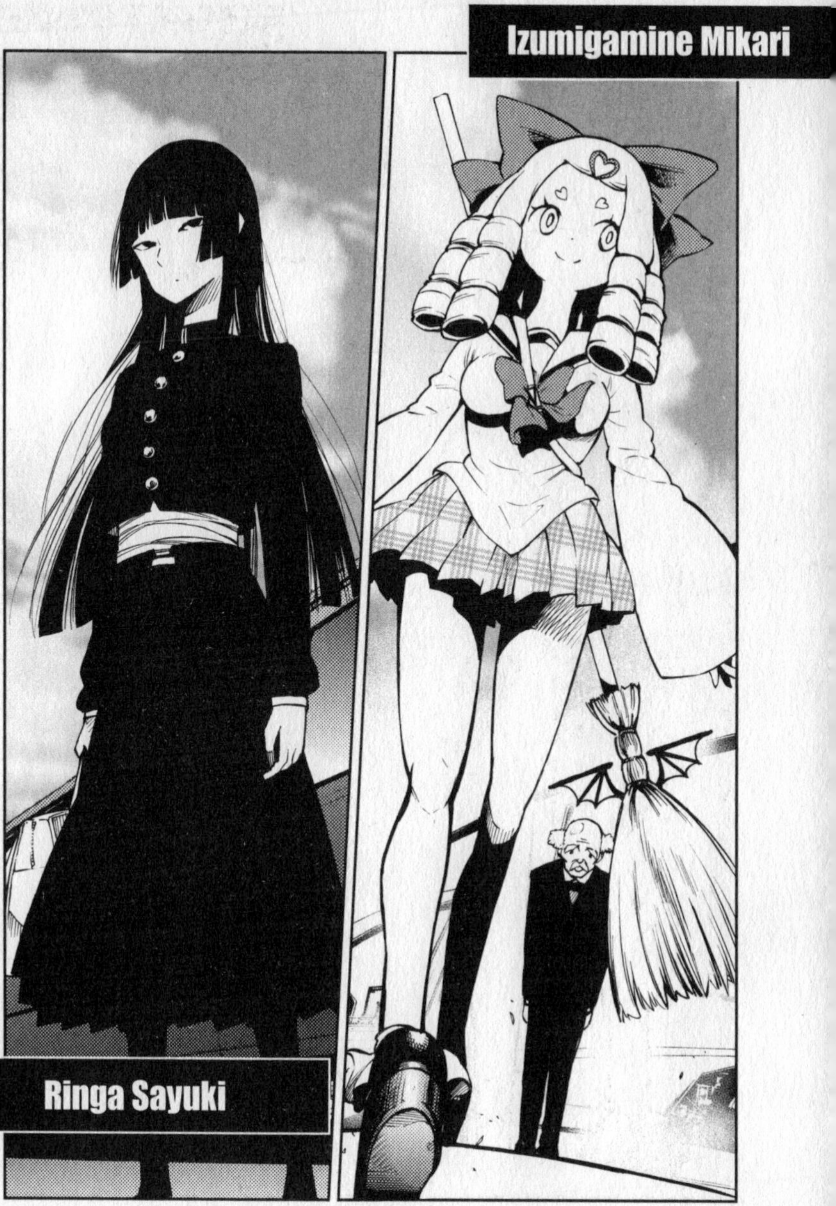
Izumigamine Mikari
Ringa Sayuki

Suirenji Kiyoharu

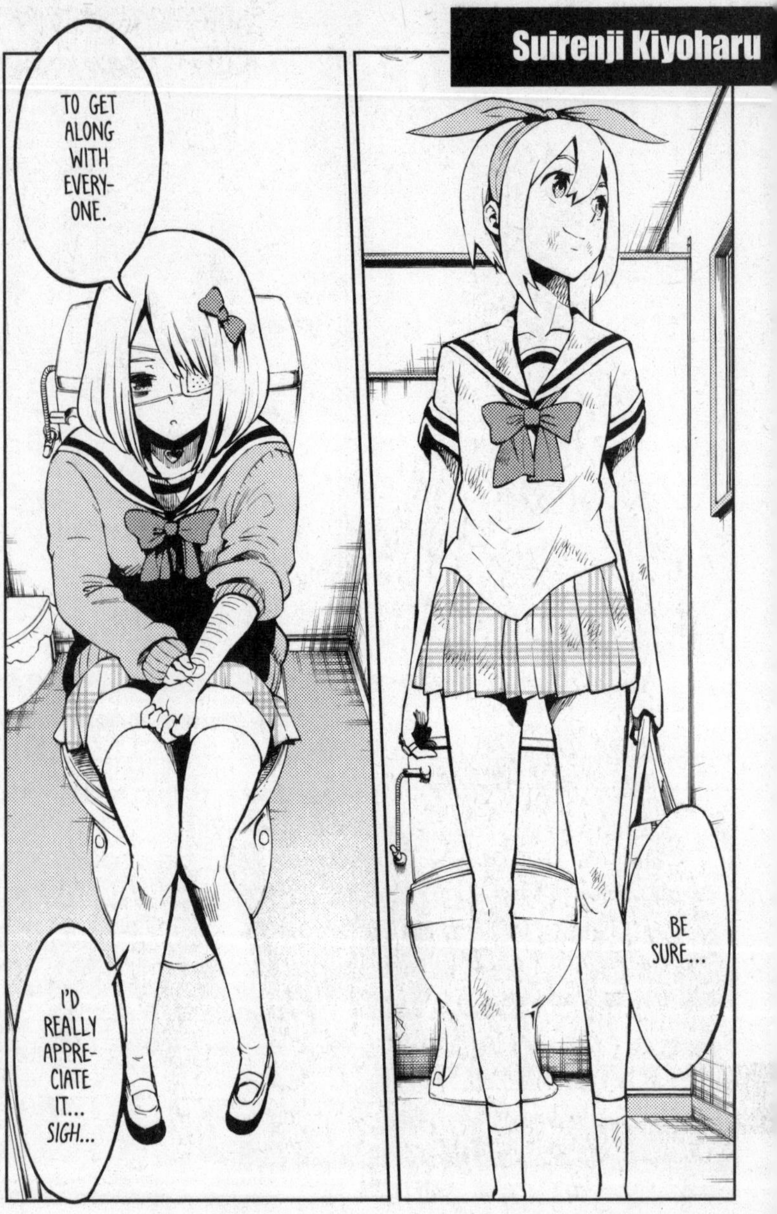
BE SURE...
TO GET ALONG WITH EVERY-ONE.
I'D REALLY APPRE-CIATE IT... SIGH...

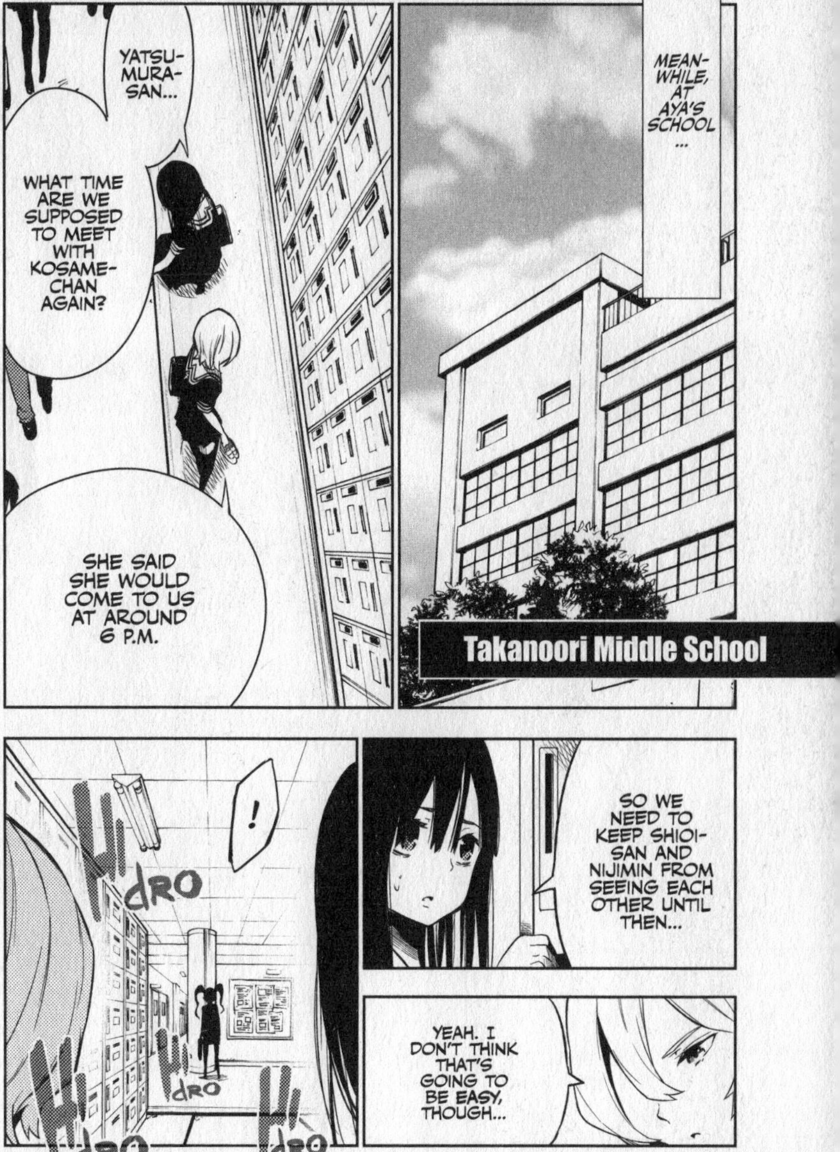
MEAN-WHILE, AT AYA'S SCHOOL ...
Takanoori Middle School
YATSU-MURA-SAN...
WHAT TIME ARE WE SUPPOSED TO MEET WITH KOSAME-CHAN AGAIN?
SHE SAID SHE WOULD COME TO US AT AROUND 6 P.M.
SO WE NEED TO KEEP SHIOI-SAN AND NIJIMIN FROM SEEING EACH OTHER UNTIL THEN...
YEAH. I DON'T THINK THAT'S GOING TO BE EASY, THOUGH...
!
HI dRO
HI dRO
HI dRO
HI dRO

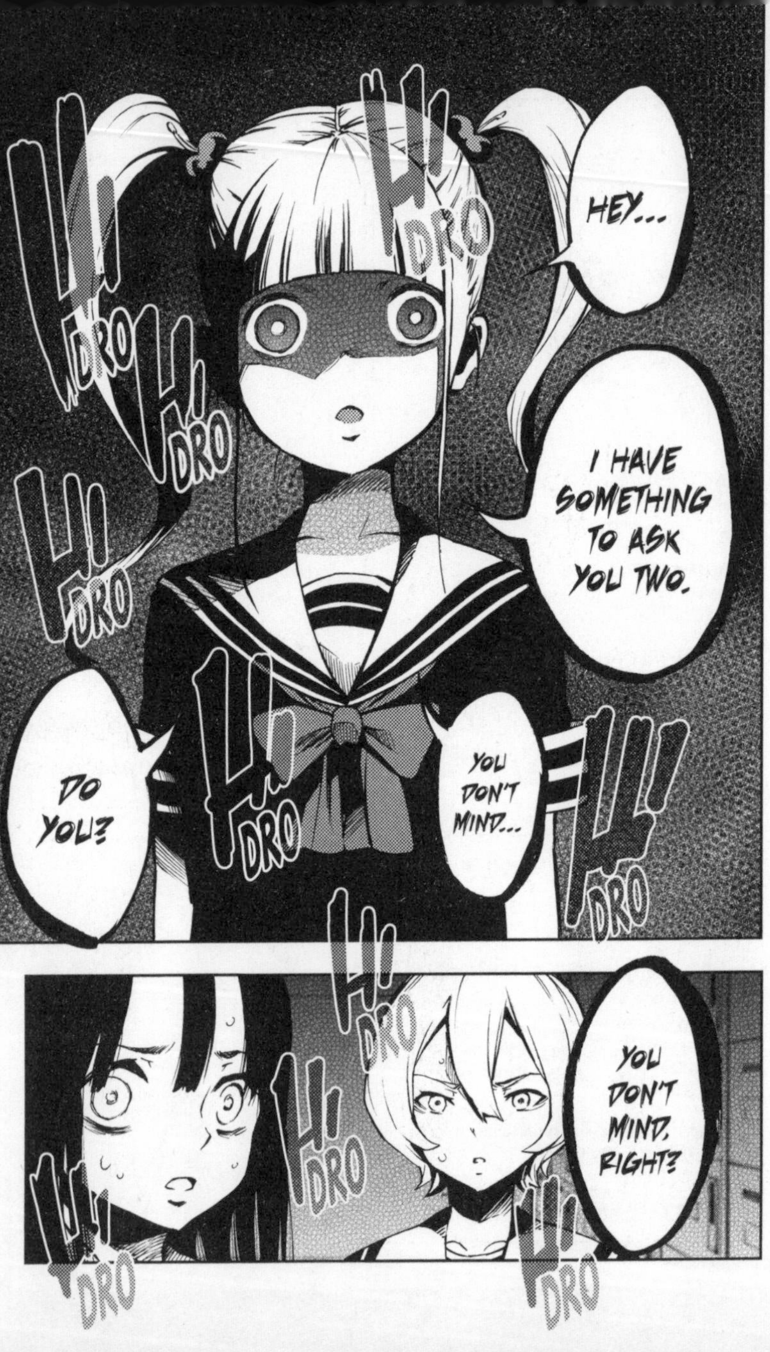
HEY...
I HAVE SOMETHING TO ASK YOU TWO.
YOU DON'T MIND...
DO YOU?
YOU DON'T MIND, RIGHT?

RINGA SAYUKI

Sex: Female
Age: 15
Date of Birth: April 14 (Aries)
Height: 156cm
Weight: 47kg
Blood Type: A
Birthplace: Tokyo

Hobbies/Interests: Tea Ceremony, Kendo, Kyuudo (archery), Karate, Tae Kwan Do, etc... and all sports.

Strong Points: Patient, Extremely Lucky, Beautiful

Weak Points: Thunder, Dogs

Favorite Things: Reading Books, Going to Cafés

- The daughter of a mob boss.

- She has excelled at martial arts from a young age.

- She is so adept at fighting, she stands out far beyond not only those at her own school, but at other schools in the area as well.

- Her current family affairs are secret for the time being.

- Her skin is so beautiful it shines, creating a halo around her.

- Her favorite celebrity is Koji Matoba.

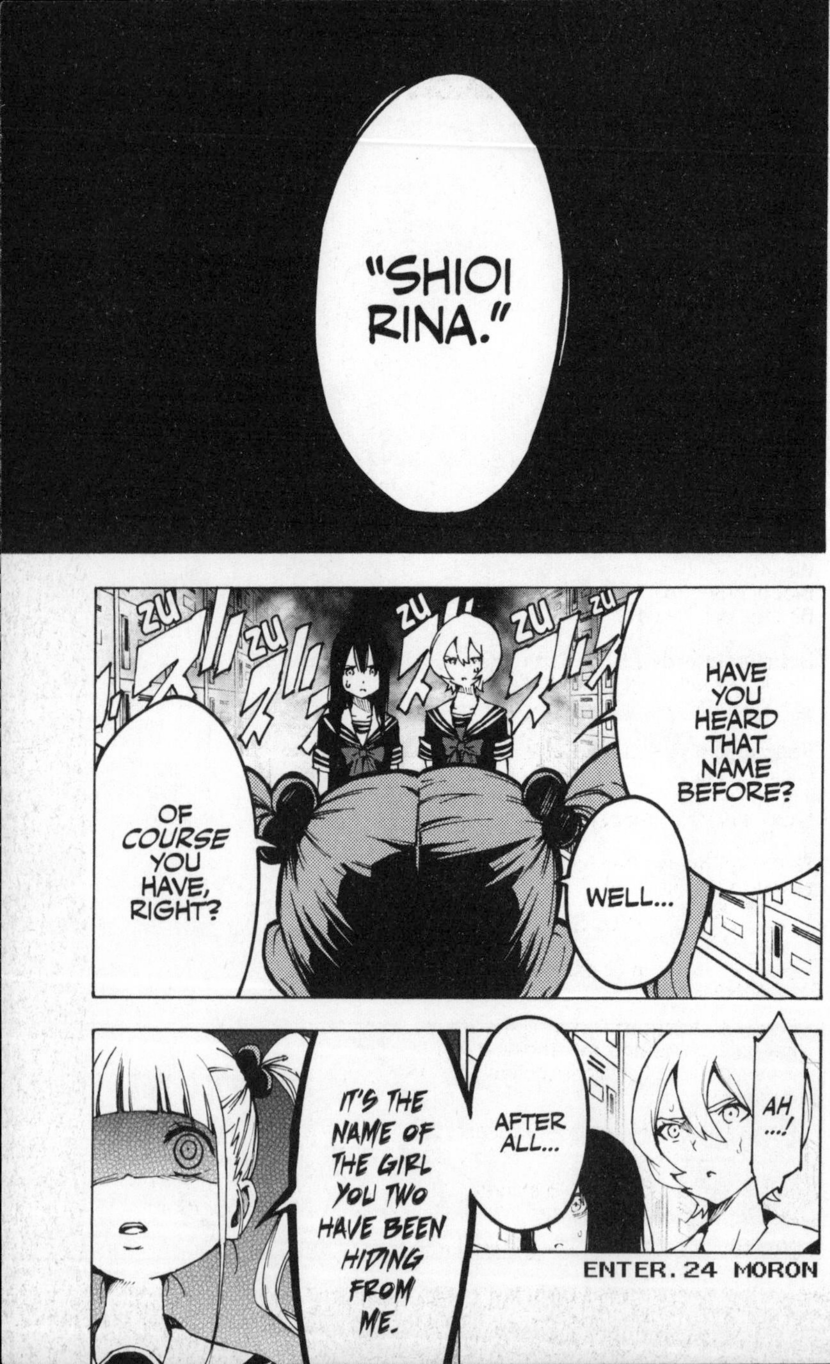
"SHIOI RINA."
HAVE YOU HEARD THAT NAME BEFORE?
ZU ZU ZU ZU ZU
WELL...
OF COURSE YOU HAVE, RIGHT?
AH...!
AFTER ALL...
IT'S THE NAME OF THE GIRL YOU TWO HAVE BEEN HIDING FROM ME.
ENTER. 24 MORON

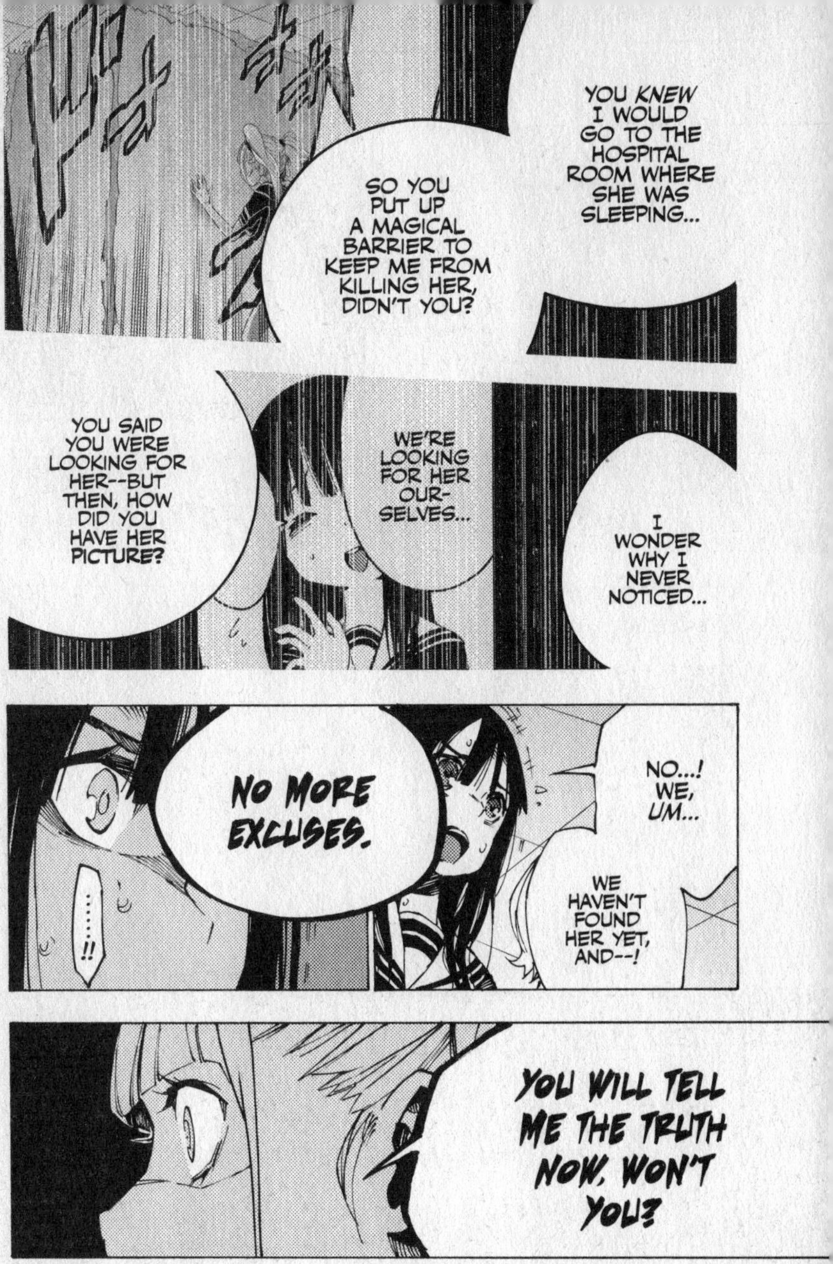
YOU KNEW I WOULD GO TO THE HOSPITAL ROOM WHERE SHE WAS SLEEPING...
SO YOU PUT UP A MAGICAL BARRIER TO KEEP ME FROM KILLING HER, DIDN'T YOU?
I WONDER WHY I NEVER NOTICED...
WE'RE LOOKING FOR HER OUR-SELVES...
YOU SAID YOU WERE LOOKING FOR HER--BUT THEN, HOW DID YOU HAVE HER PICTURE?
NO...! WE, UM...
WE HAVEN'T FOUND HER YET, AND--!
NO MORE EXCUSES.
......!!
YOU WILL TELL ME THE TRUTH NOW, WON'T YOU?

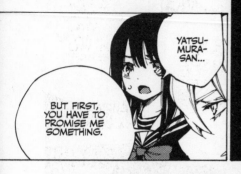

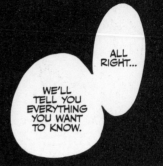

ALL RIGHT...
WE'LL TELL YOU EVERYTHING YOU WANT TO KNOW.
YATSU-MURA-SAN...
BUT FIRST, YOU HAVE TO PROMISE ME SOMETHING.
PROMISE YOU?
WHAT?
YOU HAVE TO PROMISE ME THAT YOU WON'T TRY TO KILL SHIOI WHEN YOU SEE HER.
DRO
DRO
DRO
DRO

ENTER. 24 MORON

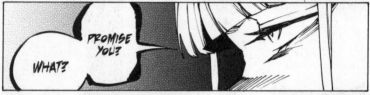

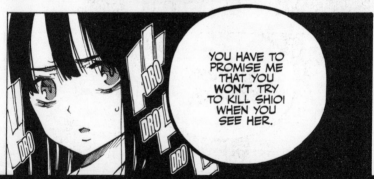

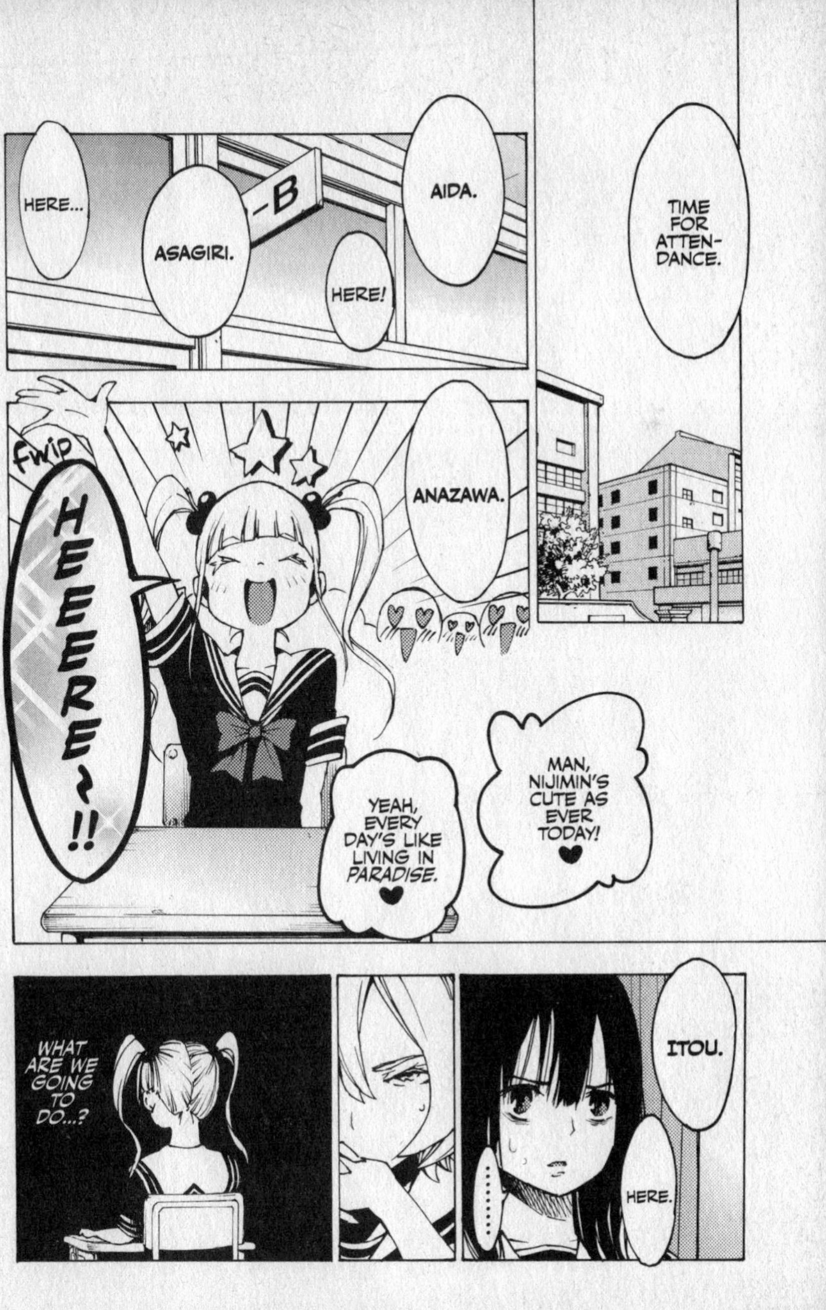
TIME FOR ATTEN-DANCE.
AIDA.
HERE!
ASAGIRI.
HERE...
-B
ANAZAWA.
fwip
HEEEERE~!!
MAN, NIJIMIN'S CUTE AS EVER TODAY!
YEAH, EVERY DAY'S LIKE LIVING IN PARADISE.
ITOU.
...
HERE.
WHAT ARE WE GOING TO DO...?

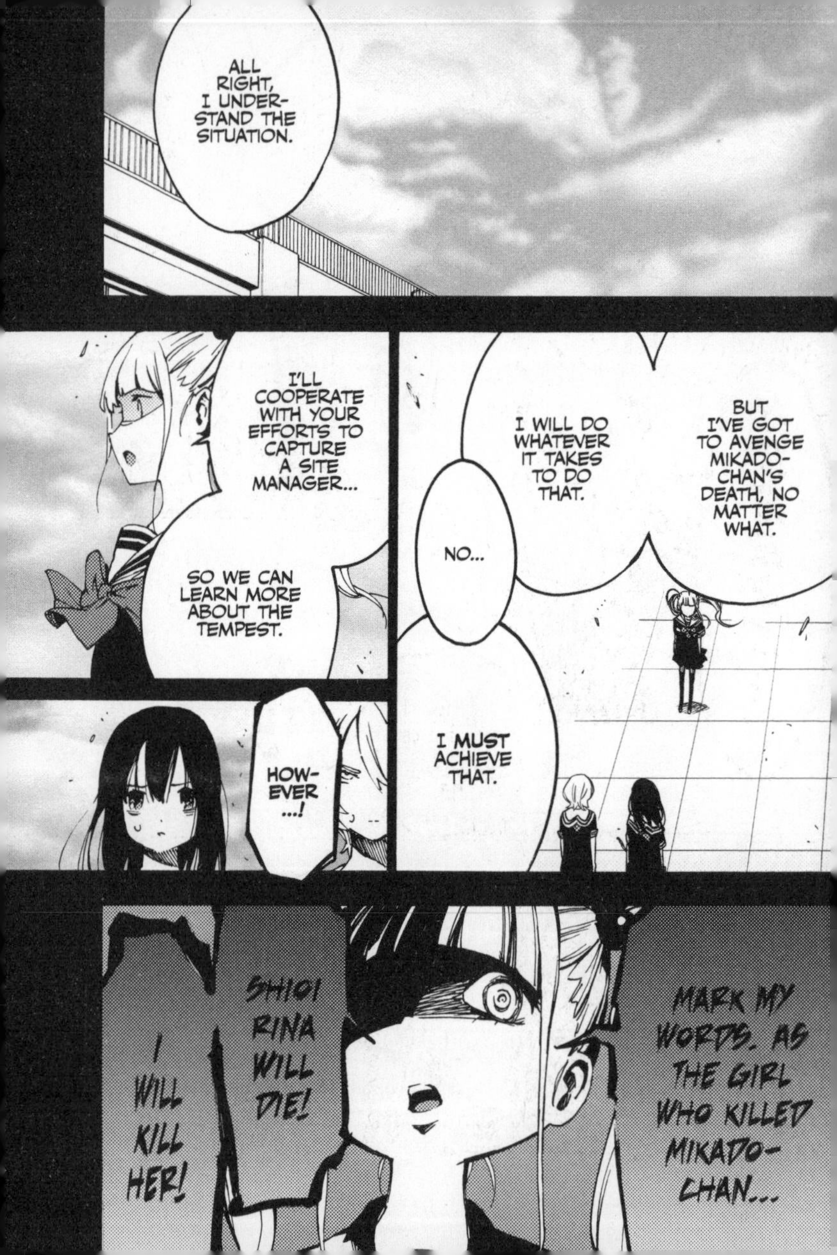
ALL RIGHT, I UNDERSTAND THE SITUATION.
BUT I'VE GOT TO AVENGE MIKADO-CHAN'S DEATH, NO MATTER WHAT.
I WILL DO WHATEVER IT TAKES TO DO THAT.
NO...
I MUST ACHIEVE THAT.
I'LL COOPERATE WITH YOUR EFFORTS TO CAPTURE A SITE MANAGER...
SO WE CAN LEARN MORE ABOUT THE TEMPEST.
HOW-EVER ...!
MARK MY WORDS. AS THE GIRL WHO KILLED MIKADO-CHAN...
SHIOI RINA WILL DIE!
I WILL KILL HER!

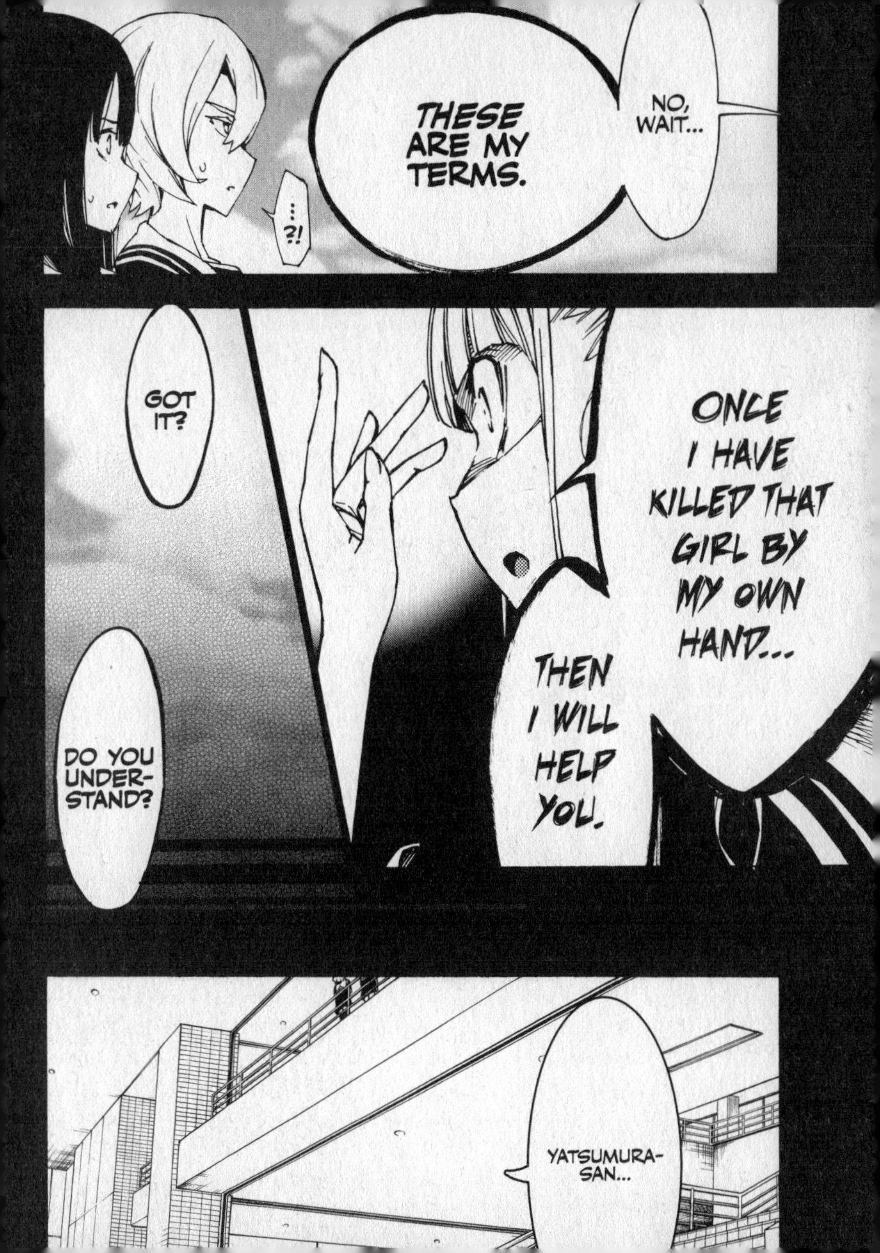
NO, WAIT...
THESE ARE MY TERMS.
...?!
ONCE I HAVE KILLED THAT GIRL BY MY OWN HAND...
THEN I WILL HELP YOU.
GOT IT?
DO YOU UNDER-STAND?
YATSUMURA-SAN...

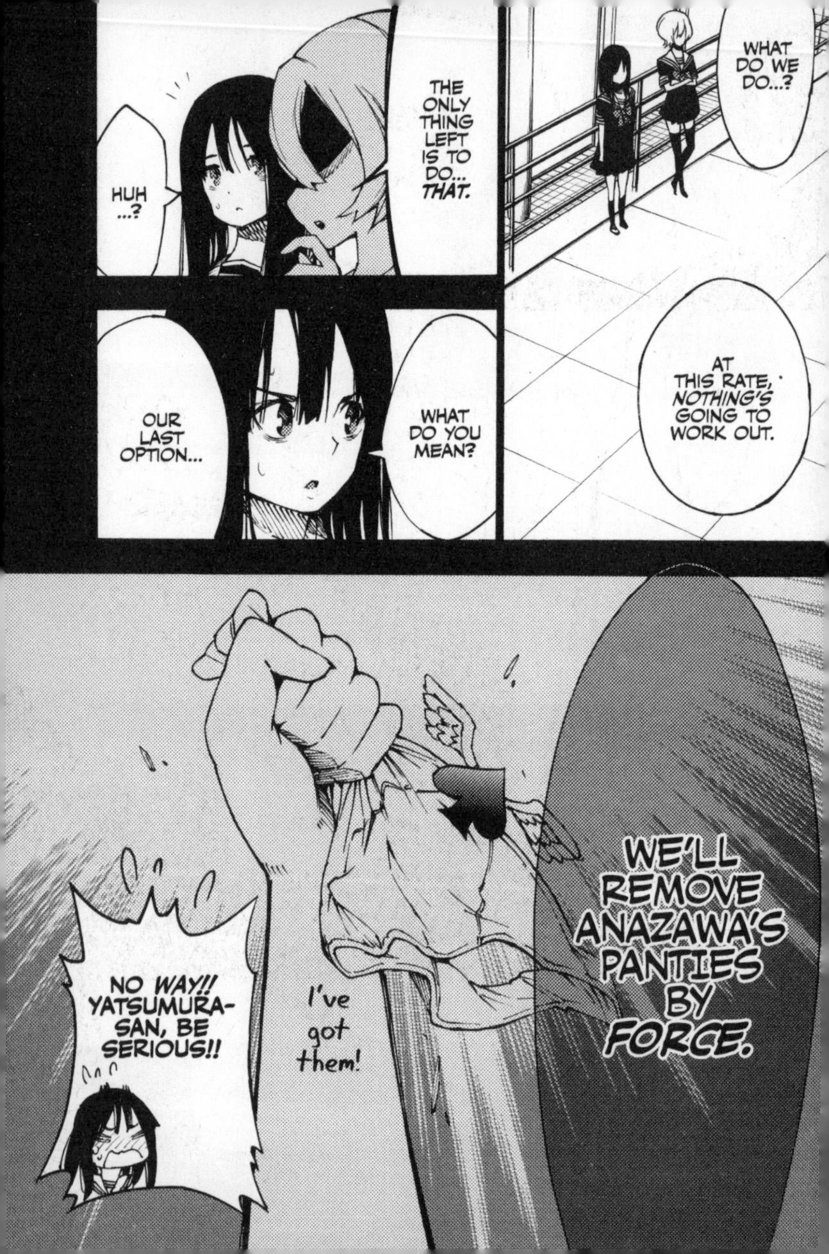
WHAT DO WE DO...?
AT THIS RATE, NOTHING'S GOING TO WORK OUT.
THE ONLY THING LEFT IS TO DO... THAT.
HUH ...?
WHAT DO YOU MEAN?
OUR LAST OPTION...
WE'LL REMOVE ANAZAWA'S PANTIES BY FORCE.
I've got them!
NO WAY!! YATSUMURA-SAN, BE SERIOUS!!

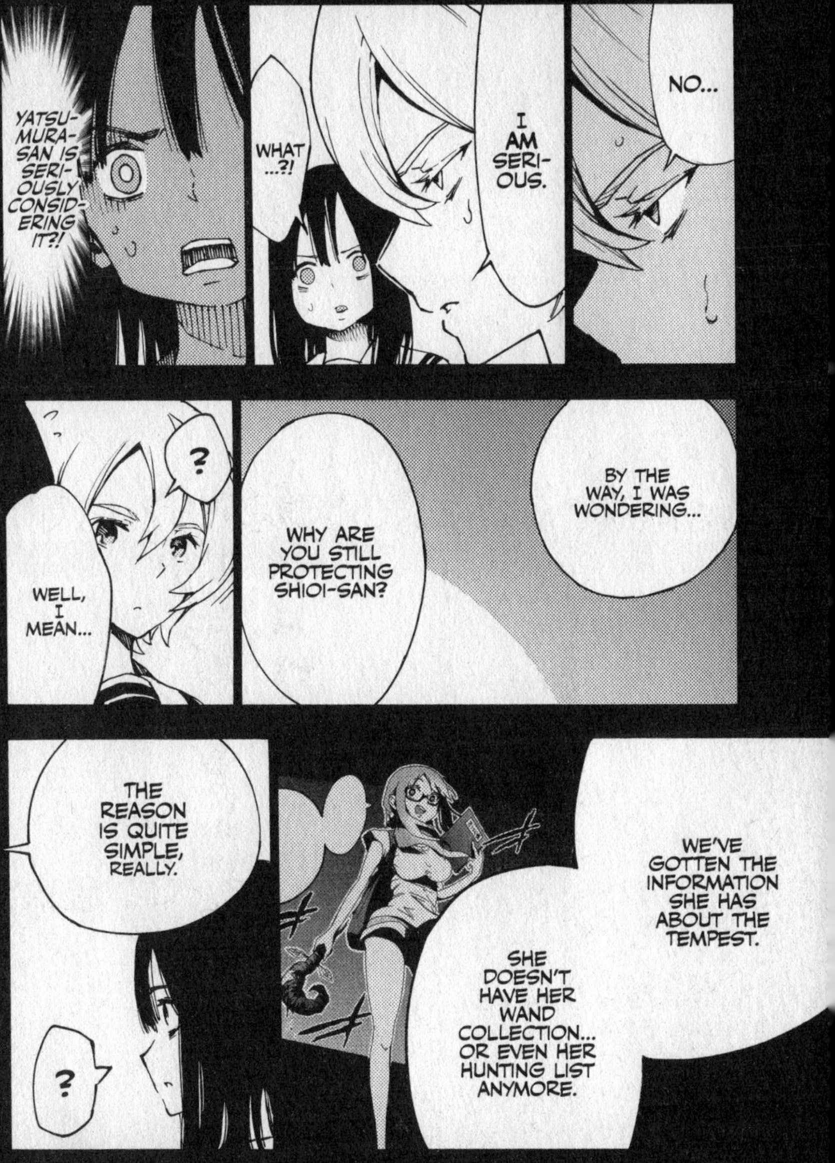
NO...
I AM SERIOUS.
WHAT ...?!
YATSUMURA-SAN IS SERIOUSLY CONSIDERING IT?!
BY THE WAY, I WAS WONDERING...
WHY ARE YOU STILL PROTECTING SHIOI-SAN?
?
WELL, I MEAN...
WE'VE GOTTEN THE INFORMATION SHE HAS ABOUT THE TEMPEST.
SHE DOESN'T HAVE HER WAND COLLECTION... OR EVEN HER HUNTING LIST ANYMORE.
THE REASON IS QUITE SIMPLE, REALLY.
?

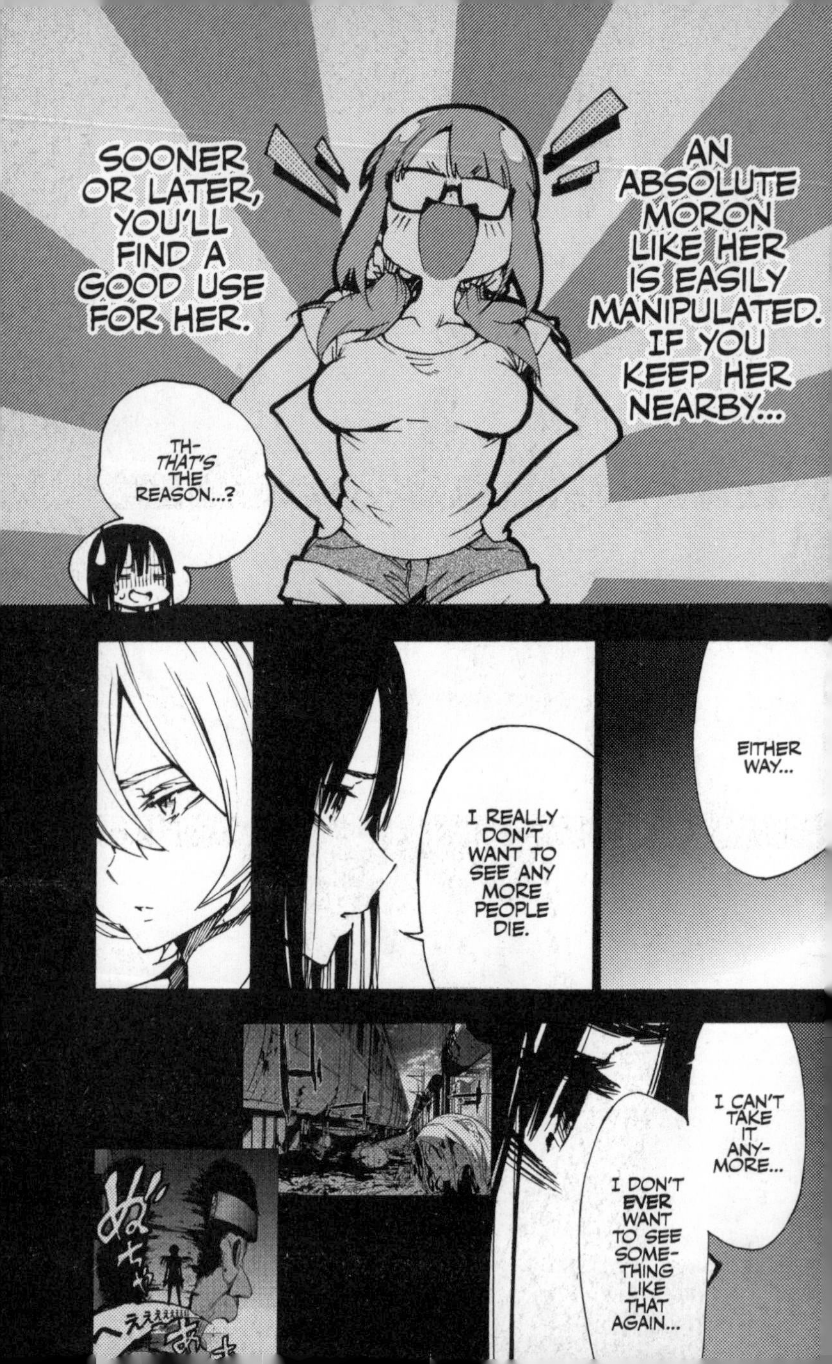
AN ABSOLUTE MORON LIKE HER IS EASILY MANIPULATED. IF YOU KEEP HER NEARBY...
SOONER OR LATER, YOU'LL FIND A GOOD USE FOR HER.
TH-THAT'S THE REASON...?
EITHER WAY...
I REALLY DON'T WANT TO SEE ANY MORE PEOPLE DIE.
I CAN'T TAKE IT ANYMORE...
I DON'T EVER WANT TO SEE SOMETHING LIKE THAT AGAIN...

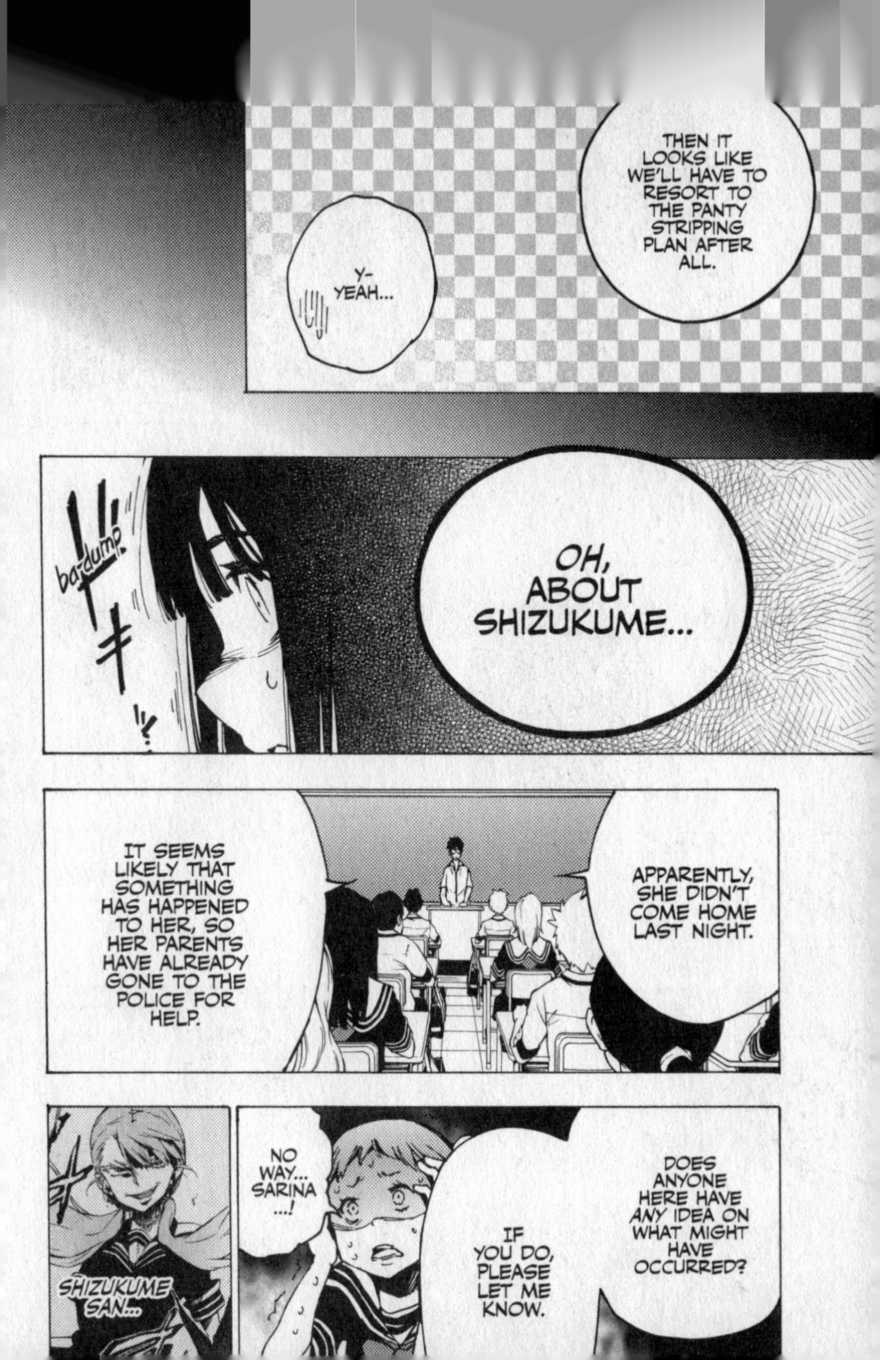
THEN IT LOOKS LIKE WE'LL HAVE TO RESORT TO THE PANTY STRIPPING PLAN AFTER ALL.
Y-YEAH...
OH, ABOUT SHIZUKUME...
ba-dump
APPARENTLY, SHE DIDN'T COME HOME LAST NIGHT.
IT SEEMS LIKELY THAT SOMETHING HAS HAPPENED TO HER, SO HER PARENTS HAVE ALREADY GONE TO THE POLICE FOR HELP.
DOES ANYONE HERE HAVE ANY IDEA ON WHAT MIGHT HAVE OCCURRED?
IF YOU DO, PLEASE LET ME KNOW.
NO WAY... SARINA ...!
SHIZUKUME SAN...

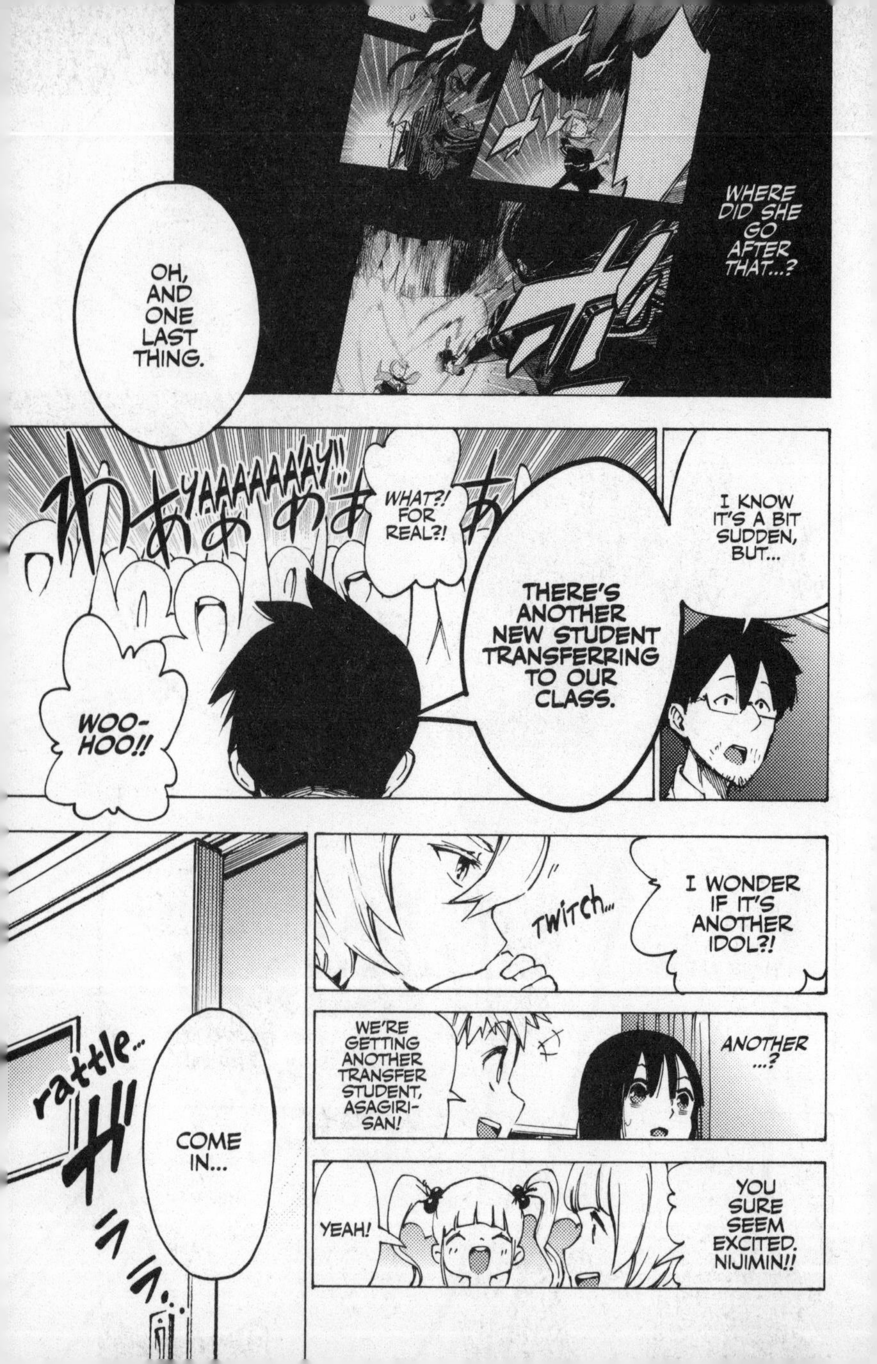
WHERE DID SHE GO AFTER THAT...?
OH, AND ONE LAST THING.
I KNOW IT'S A BIT SUDDEN, BUT...
THERE'S ANOTHER NEW STUDENT TRANSFERRING TO OUR CLASS.
YAAAAAAAY!!
WHAT?! FOR REAL?!
WOO-HOO!!
I WONDER IF IT'S ANOTHER IDOL?!
TWITCH...
ANOTHER ...?
WE'RE GETTING ANOTHER TRANSFER STUDENT, ASAGIRI-SAN!
YOU SURE SEEM EXCITED. NIJIMIN!!
YEAH!
COME IN...
rattle...

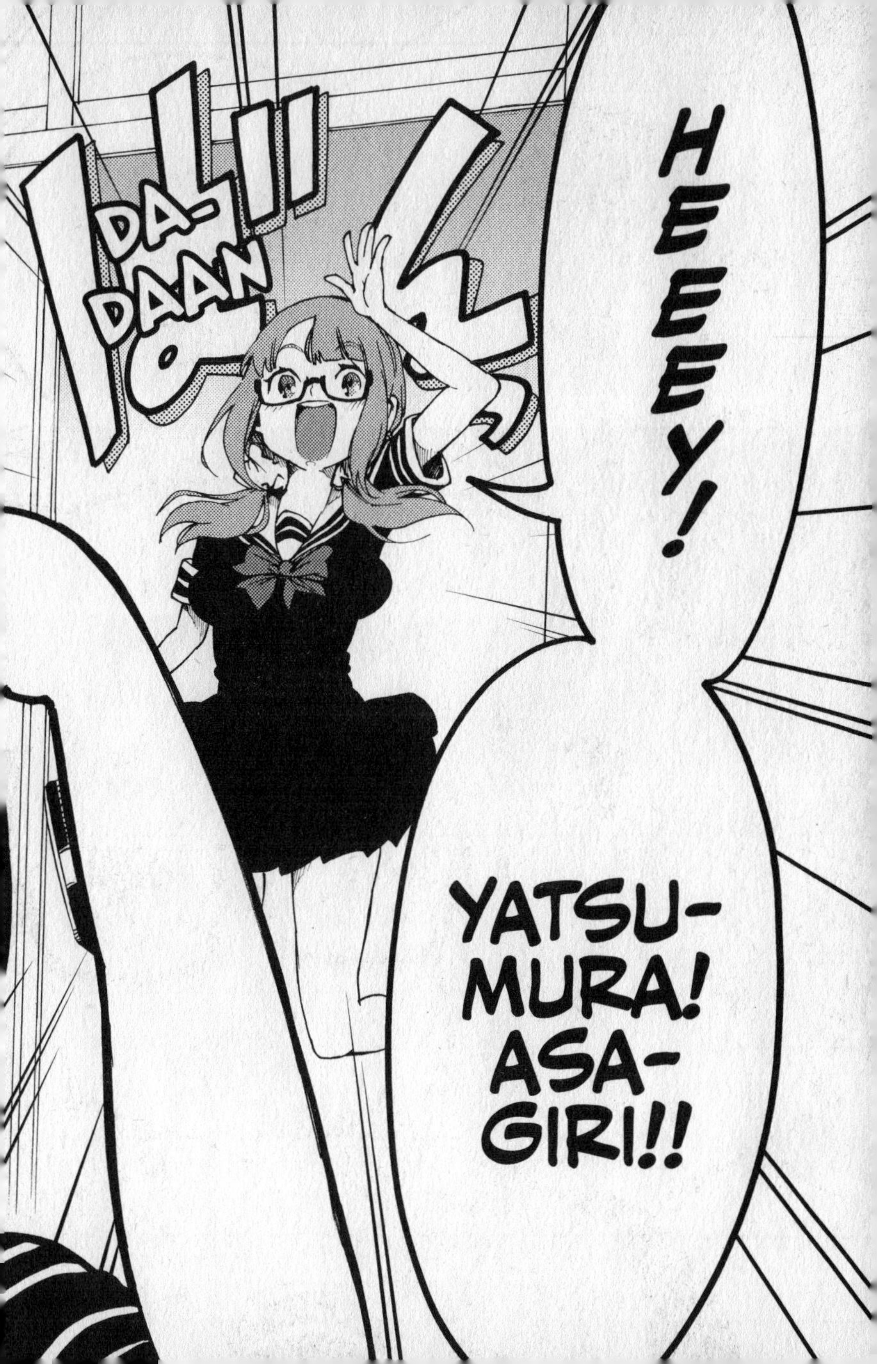
HEEEEY!
YATSU-MURA! ASA-GIRI!!
DA-DAAN

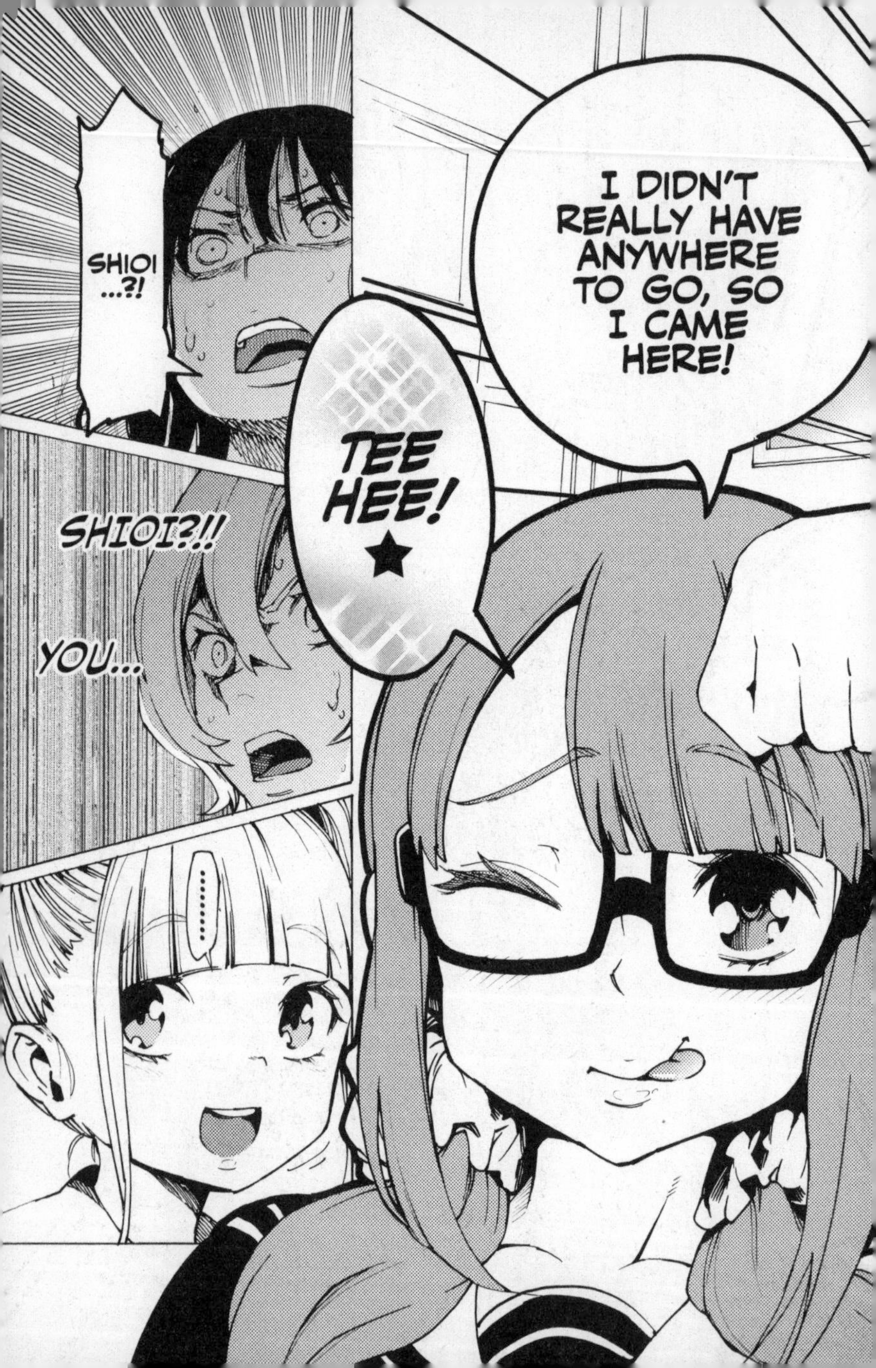
I DIDN'T REALLY HAVE ANYWHERE TO GO, SO I CAME HERE!
TEE HEE! ★
SHIOI ...?!
SHIOI?!!
YOU...
......

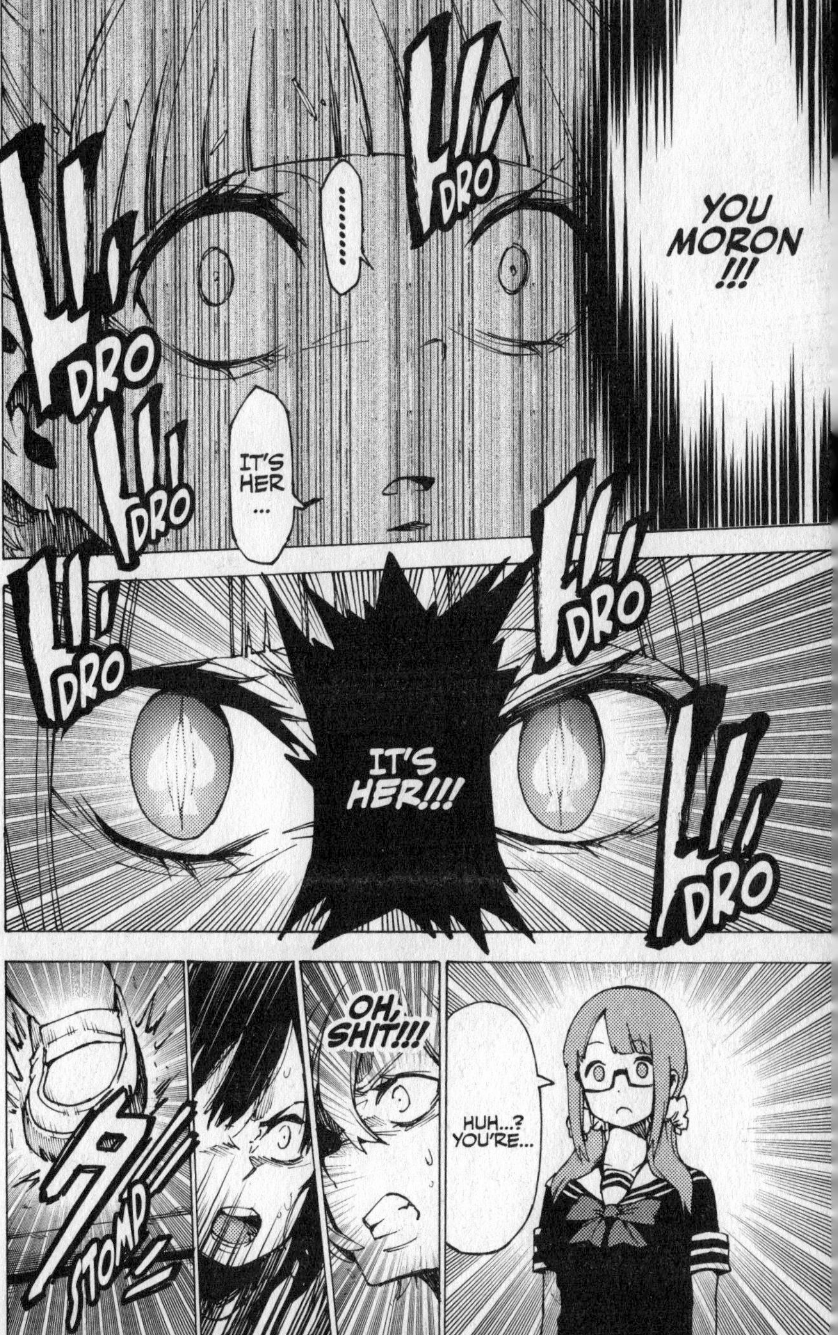
YOU MORON !!!
DRO
......
DRO
DRO
IT'S HER ...
DRO
DRO
IT'S HER!!!
DRO
HUH...? YOU'RE...
OH, SHIT!!!
STOMP

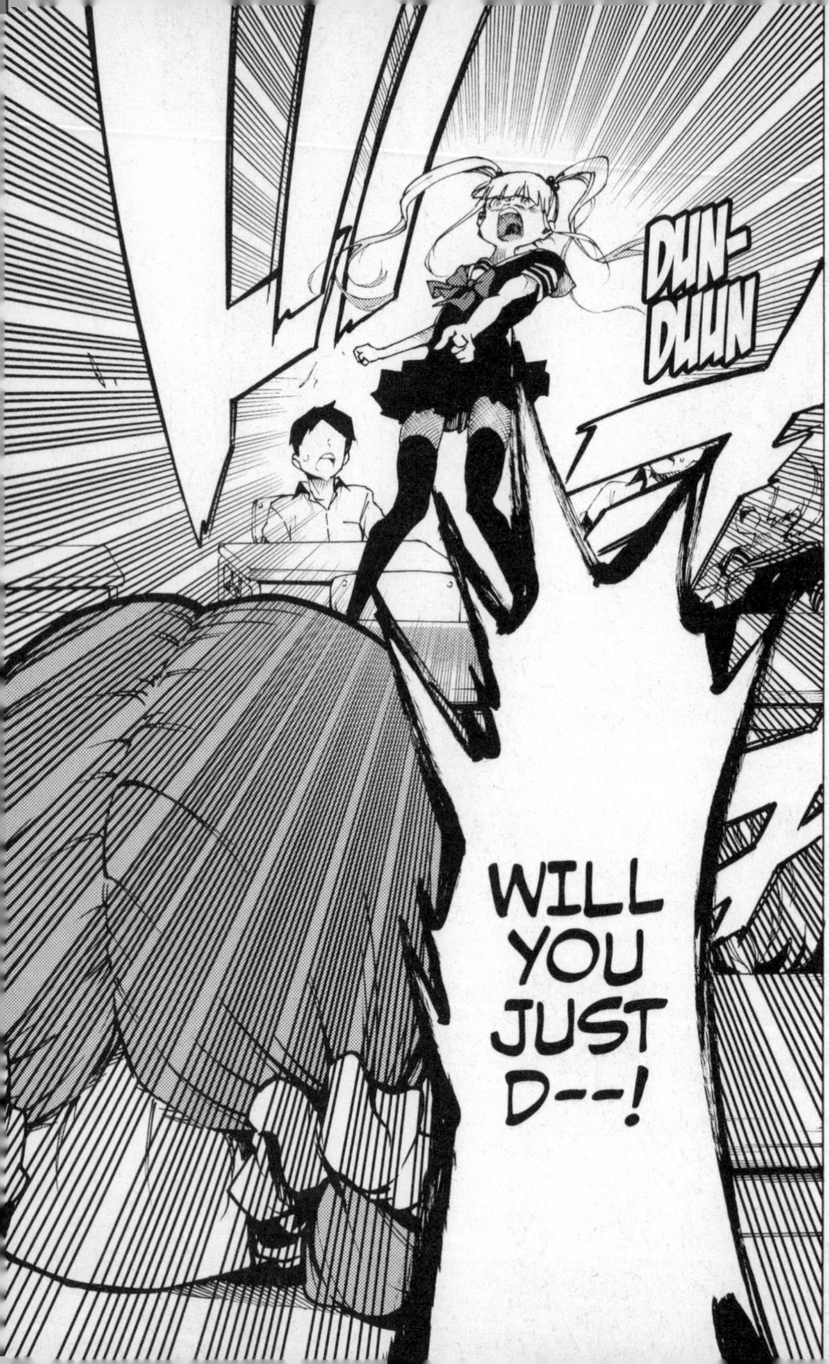
DUN-DUUN
WILL YOU JUST D--!

V

IZUMIGAMINE MIKARI

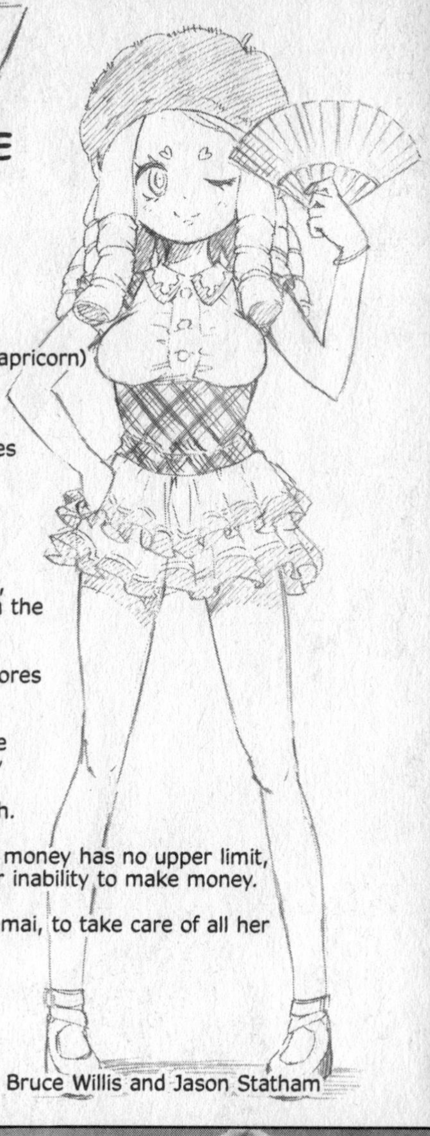

Sex: Female
Age: 14
Date of Birth: January 1 (Capricorn)
Height: 142cm
Weight: 46kg
Blood Type: B
Birthplace: The United States

Hobbies/Interests: Marine Sports, Spending Money, Playing with Servants

Strong Points: Hates Losing, Good at using the "carrot on the stick" routine

Weak Points: Household Chores (all of them), Winter

Favorite Things: Trips to the Beach, Sweet Things, Money

- Her family is extremely rich.

- While her skill at spending money has no upper limit, there is no lower limit to her inability to make money.

- She leaves her servant, Yamai, to take care of all her needs and her chores.

- Extreme Sadist.

- She has fair, white skin.

- Her favorite celebrities are Bruce Willis and Jason Statham

ENTER. 25 THE PANTIES' WHEREABOUTS

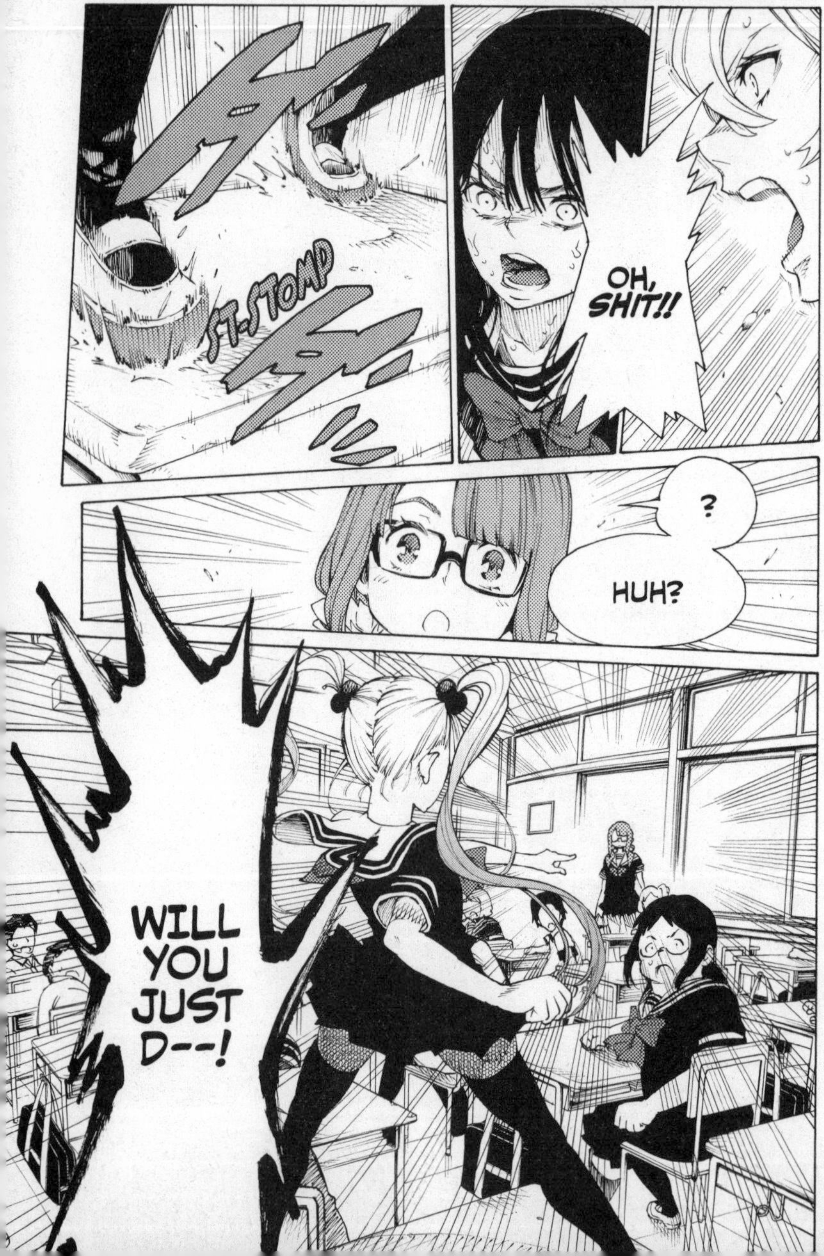
OH, SHIT!!
ST-STOMP
?
HUH?
WILL YOU JUST D--!

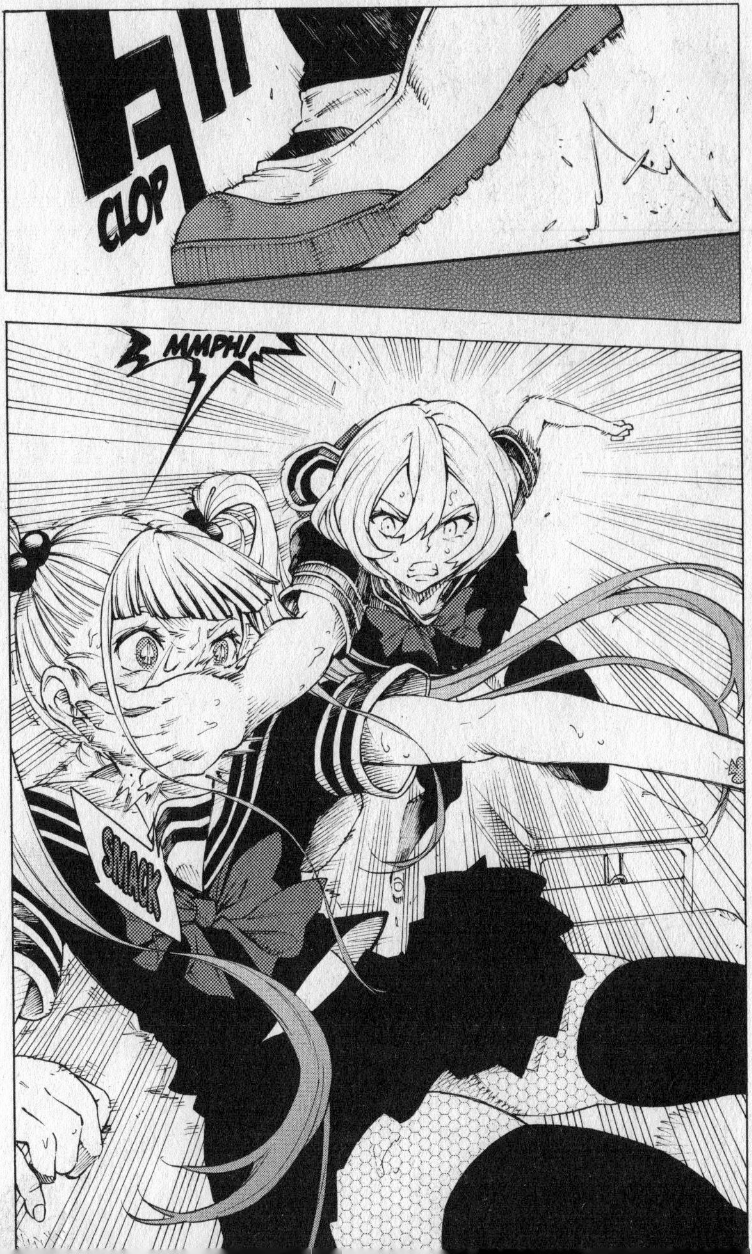
CLOP
MMPH!
SMACK

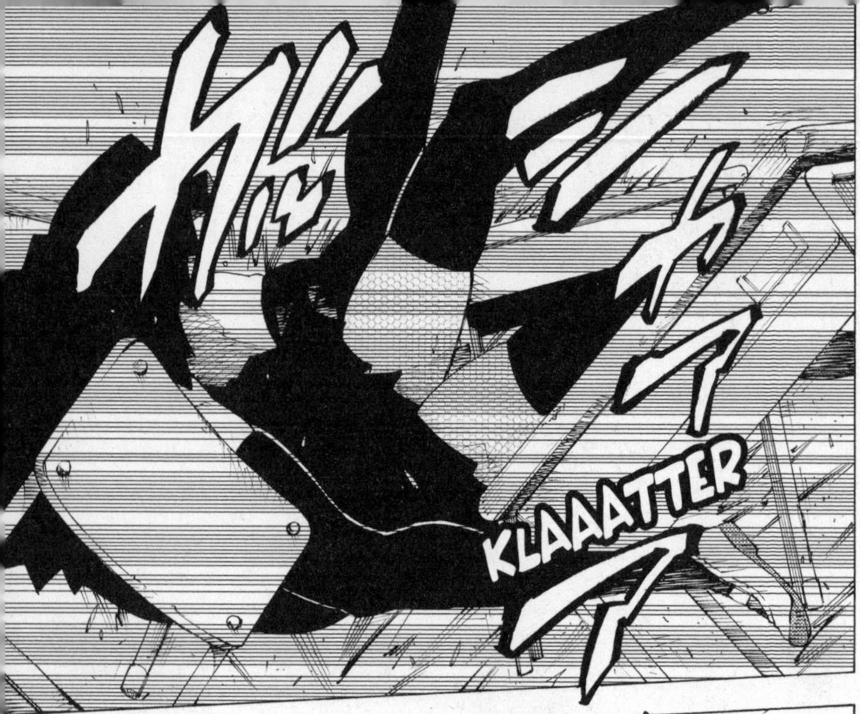
KLAAATTER

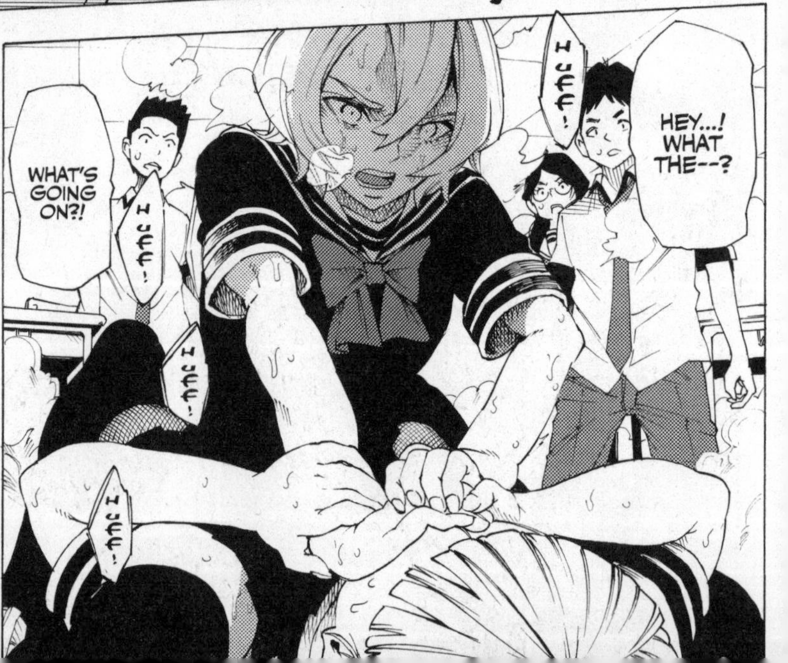
HEY...! WHAT THE--?
HUFF!
WHAT'S GOING ON?!
HUFF!
HUFF!
HUFF!

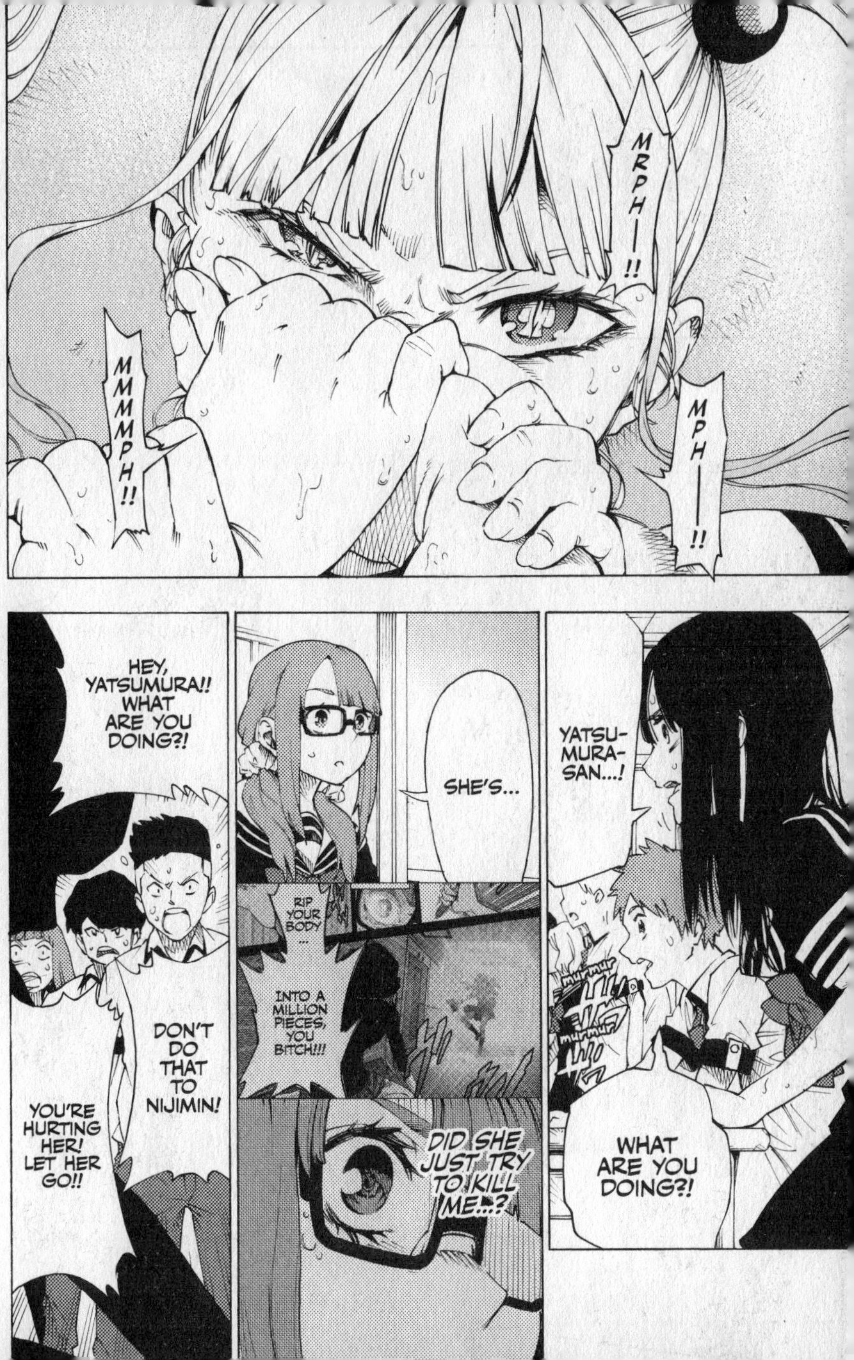
MRPH—!!
MPH——!!
MMMMPH!!
YATSU-MURA-SAN...!
murmur
murmur
WHAT ARE YOU DOING?!
SHE'S...
RIP YOUR BODY...
INTO A MILLION PIECES, YOU BITCH!!!
DID SHE JUST TRY TO KILL ME...?
HEY, YATSUMURA!! WHAT ARE YOU DOING?!
DON'T DO THAT TO NIJIMIN!
YOU'RE HURTING HER! LET HER GO!!

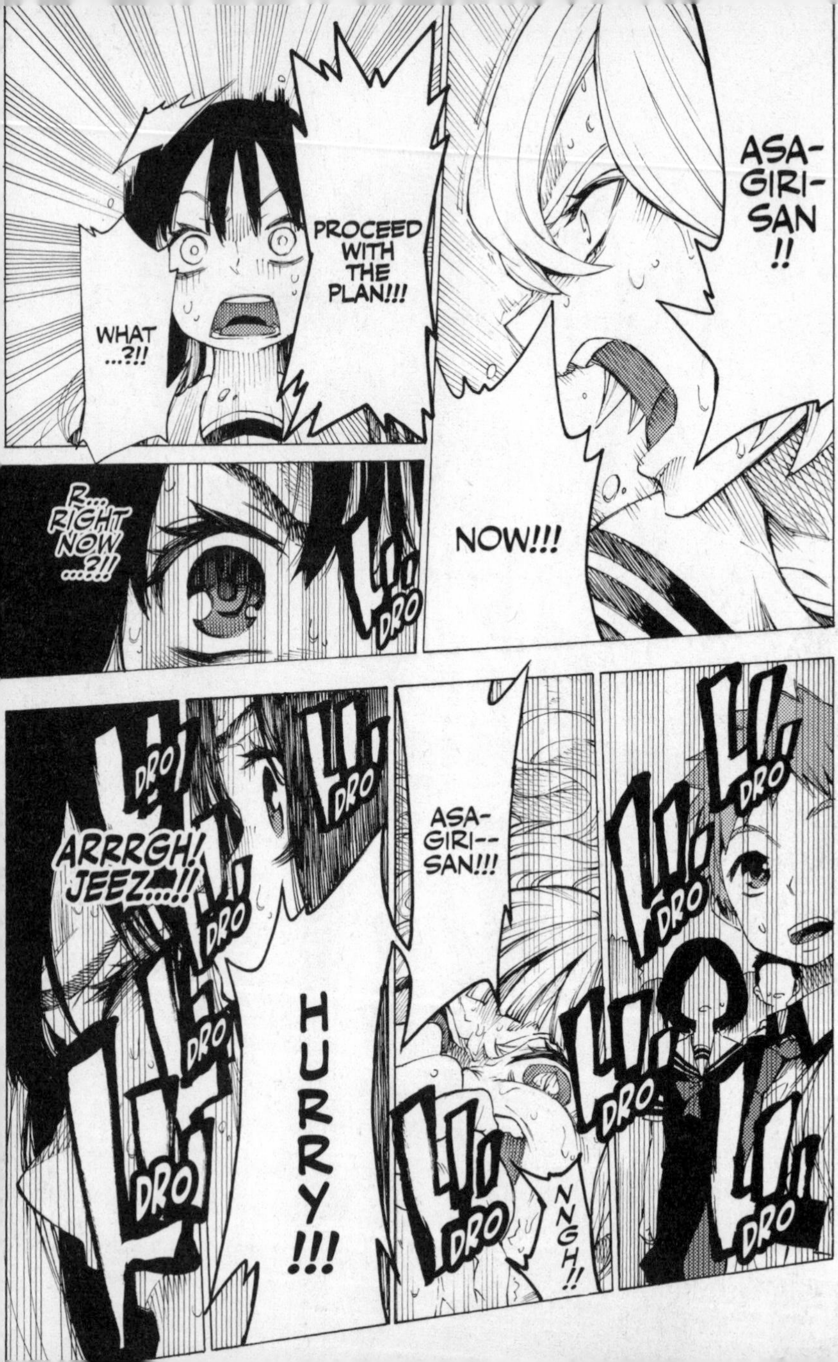
ASA-GIRI-SAN!!
NOW!!!
PROCEED WITH THE PLAN!!!
WHAT ...?!!
R... RIGHT NOW ...?!!
DRO
DRO
DRO
DRO
DRO
ASA-GIRI--SAN!!!
NNGH!!
DRO
HURRY!!!
DRO
DRO
ARRRGH! JEEZ...!!
DRO
DRO
DRO

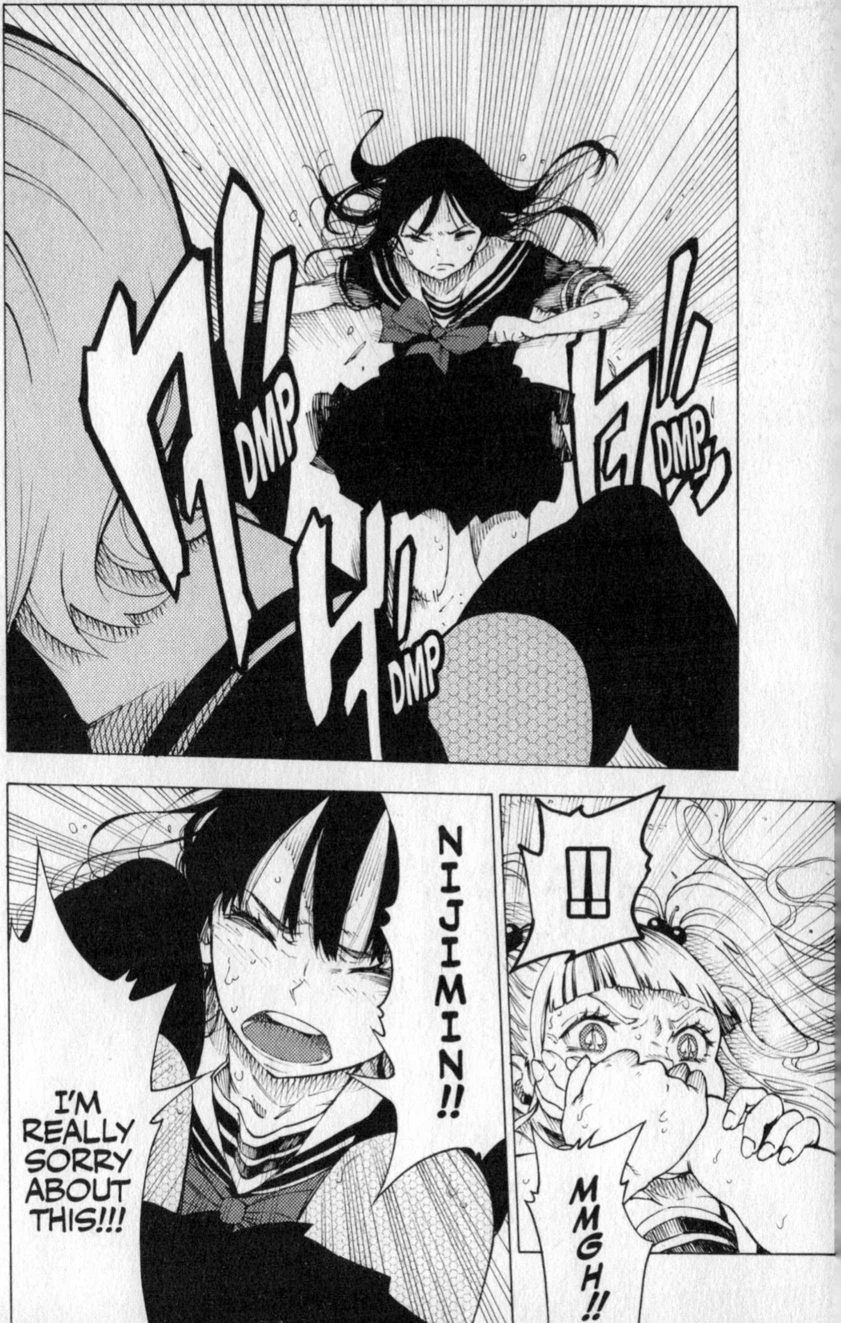

DMP
DMP
DMP
!!
MMGH!!
NIJIMIN!!
I'M REALLY SORRY ABOUT THIS!!!

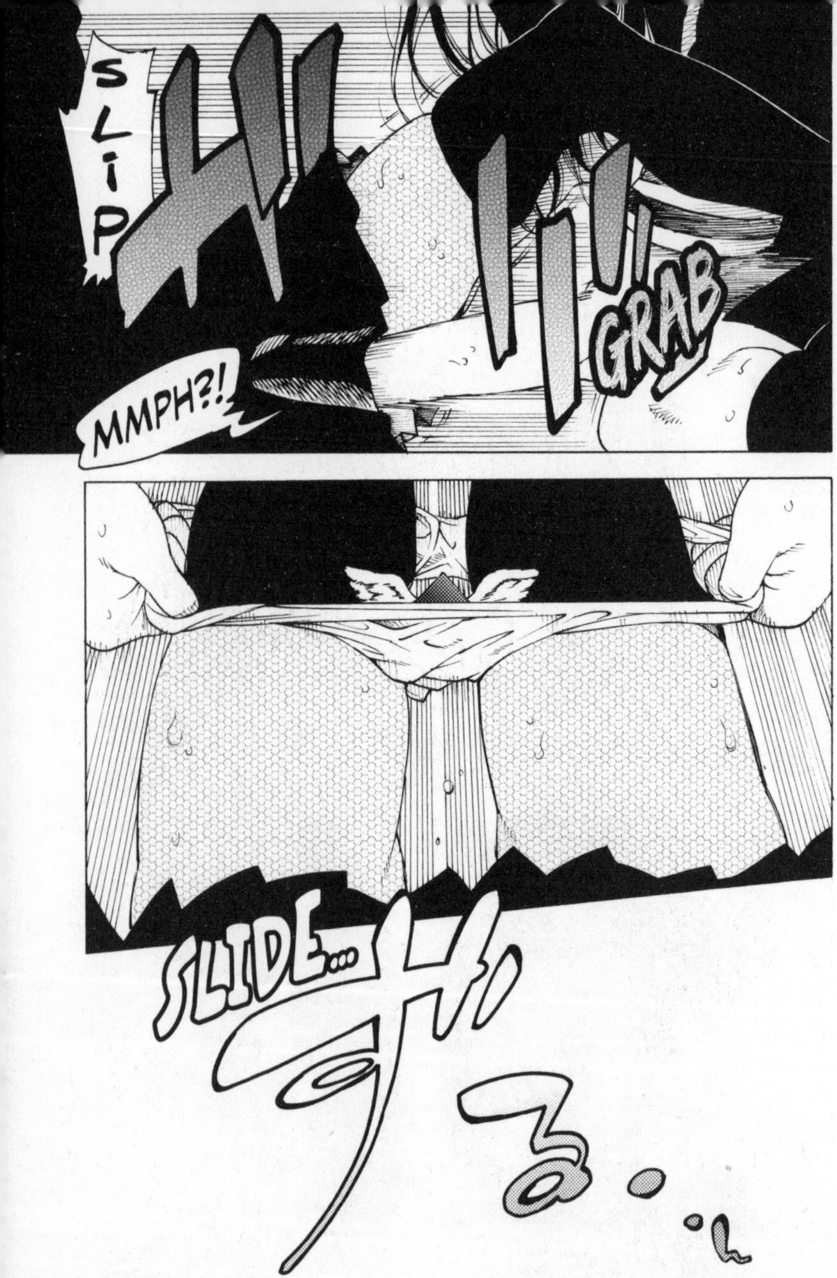
GRAB
SLIP
MMPH?!
SLIDE...

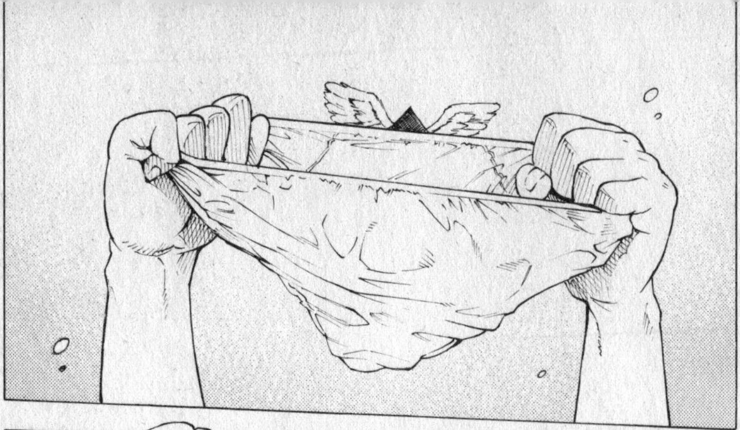

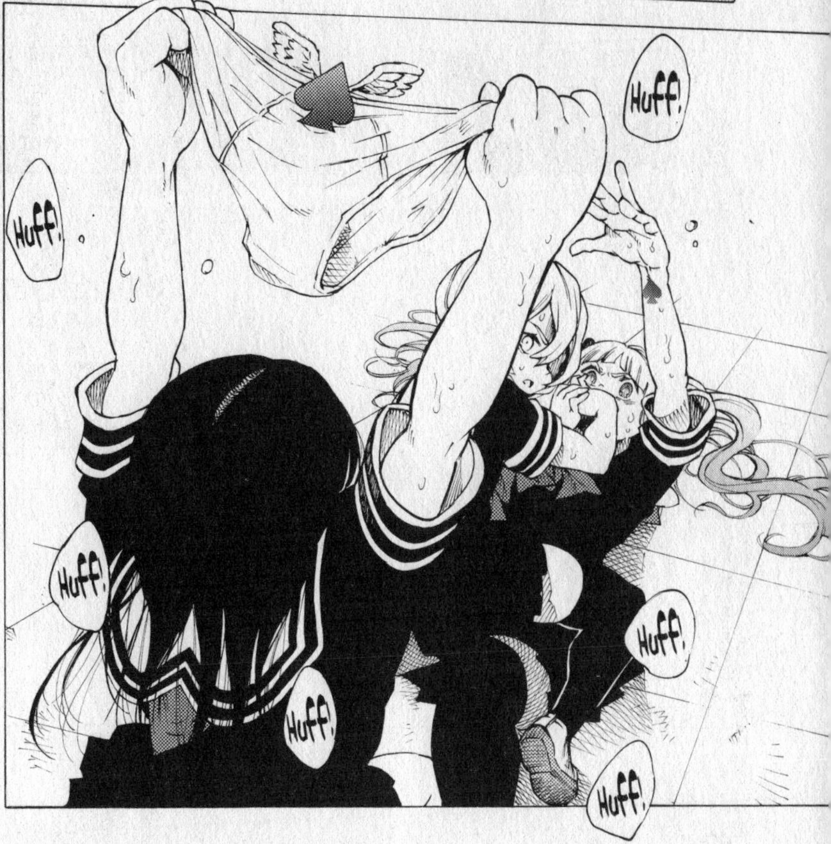
Huff!
Huff!
Huff!
Huff!
Huff!
Huff!

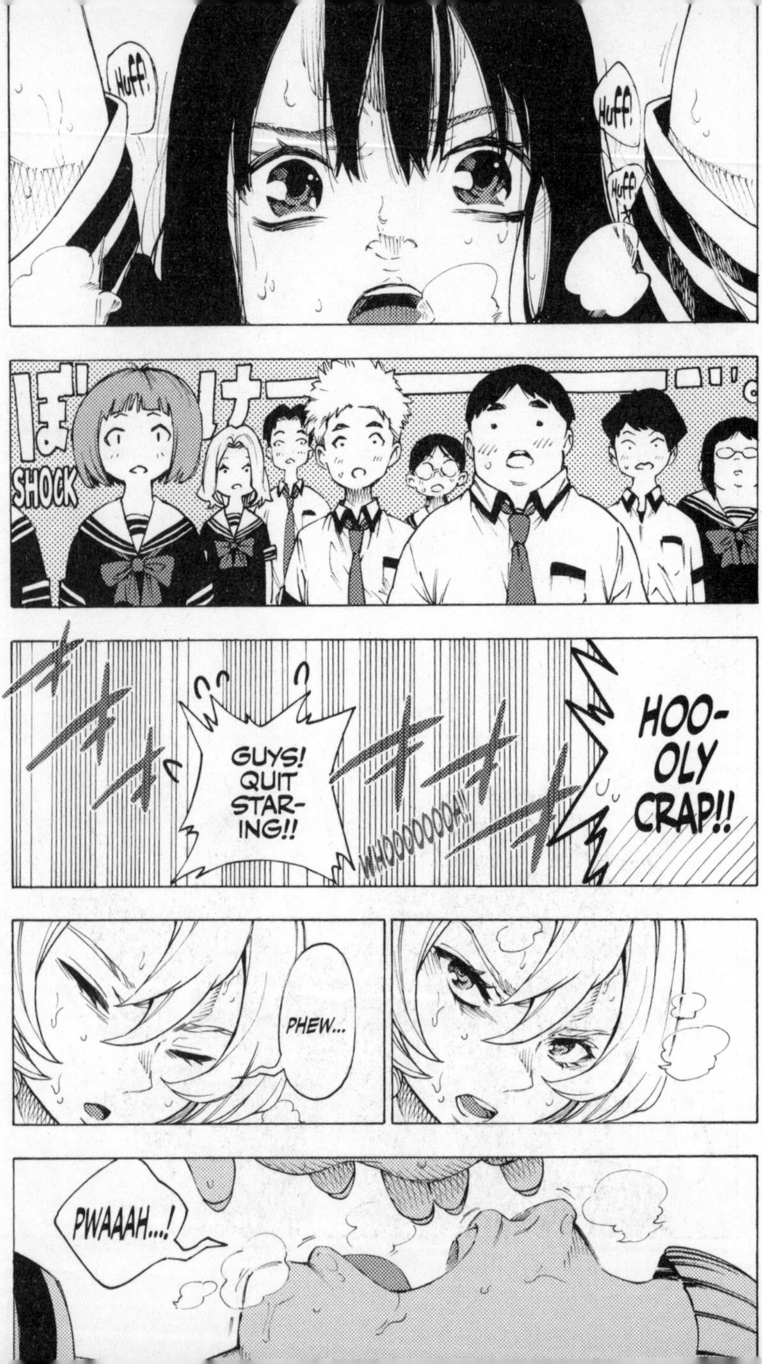
Huff!
Huff!
Huff!
SHOCK
HOO-OLY CRAP!!
WHOOOOOOOA!!
GUYS! QUIT STAR-ING!!
PHEW...
PWAAAH...!

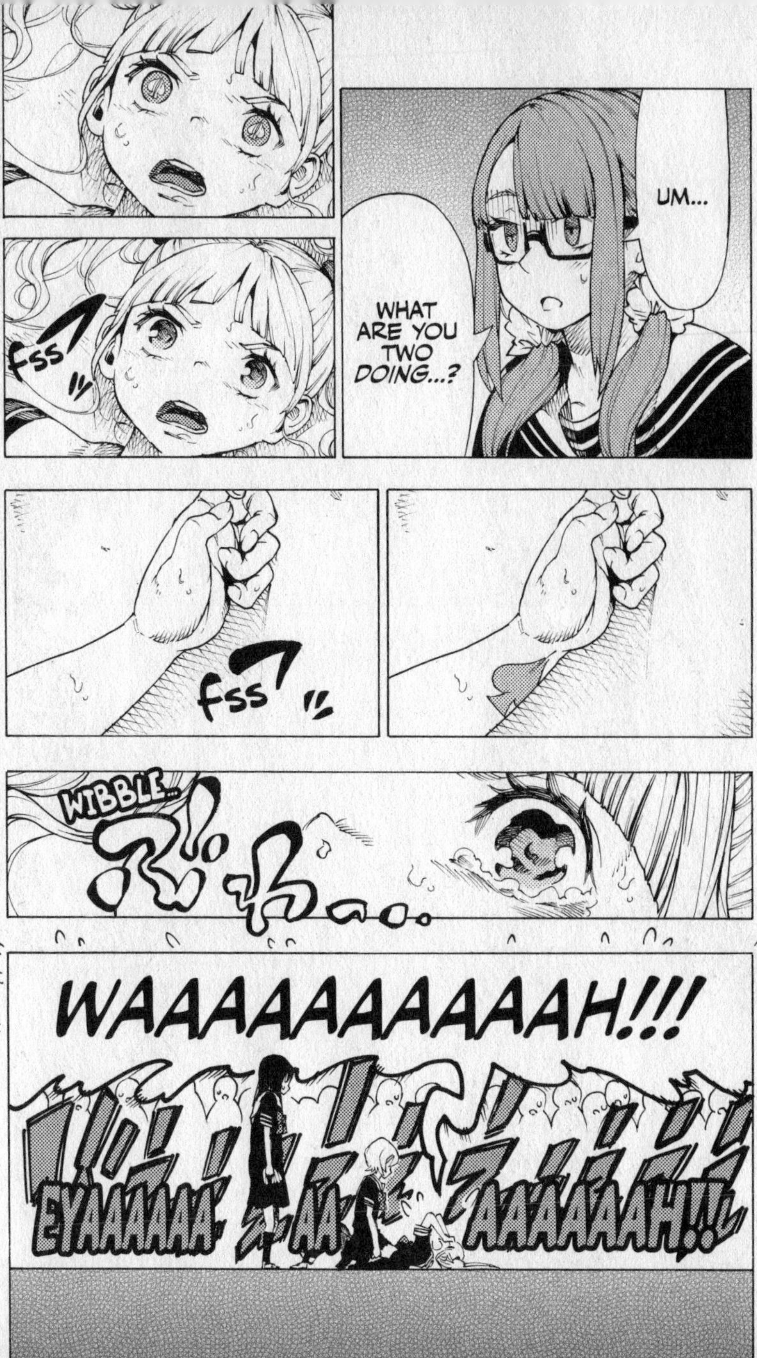
UM...
WHAT ARE YOU TWO DOING...?
fss
fss
WIBBLE...
WAAAAAAAAAAAH!!!
EYAAAAAA AA AAAAAAH!!

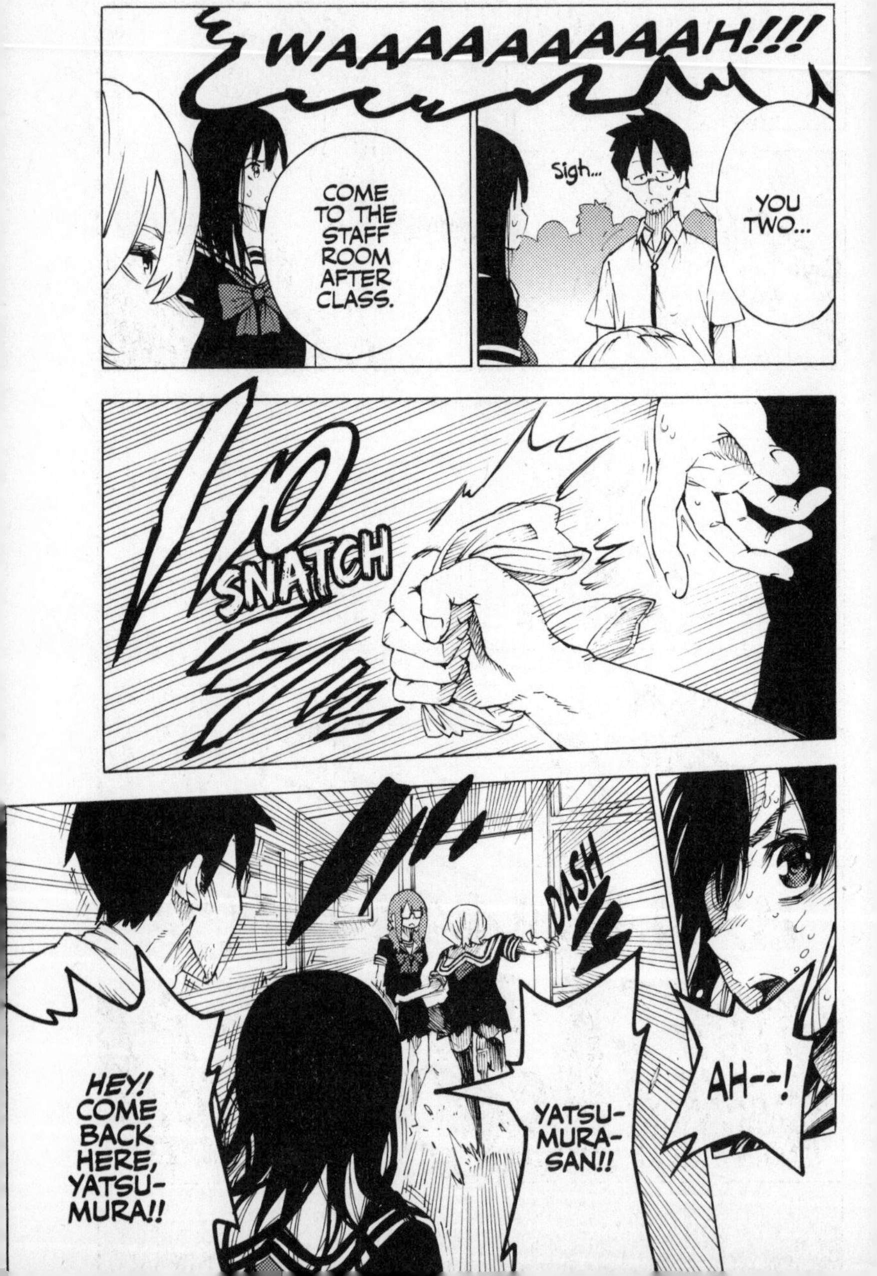
WAAAAAAAAAH!!!
Sigh...
YOU TWO...
COME TO THE STAFF ROOM AFTER CLASS.
SNATCH
AH--!
DASH
YATSU-MURA-SAN!!
HEY! COME BACK HERE, YATSU-MURA!!

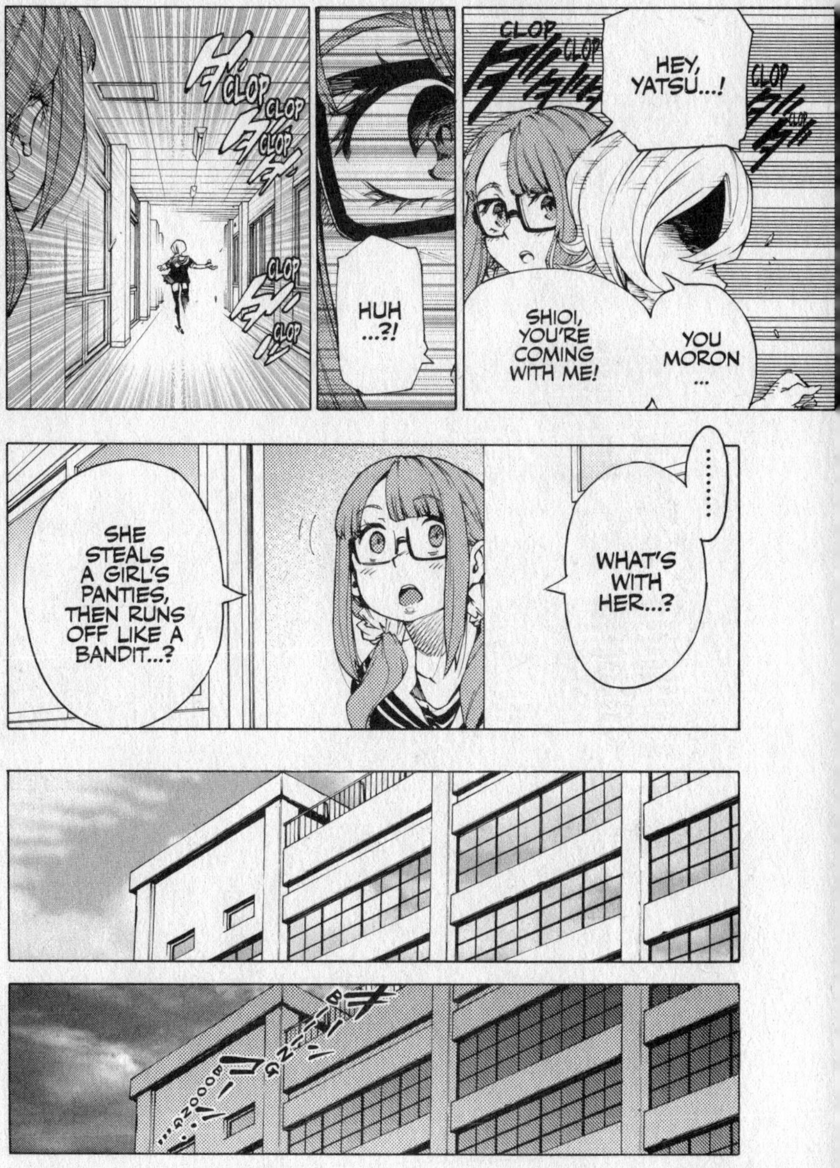
CLOP CLOP
HEY, YATSU...!
CLOP CLOP
YOU MORON ...
SHIOI, YOU'RE COMING WITH ME!
HUH ...?!
CLOP CLOP CLOP
CLOP CLOP
......
WHAT'S WITH HER...?
SHE STEALS A GIRL'S PANTIES, THEN RUNS OFF LIKE A BANDIT...?

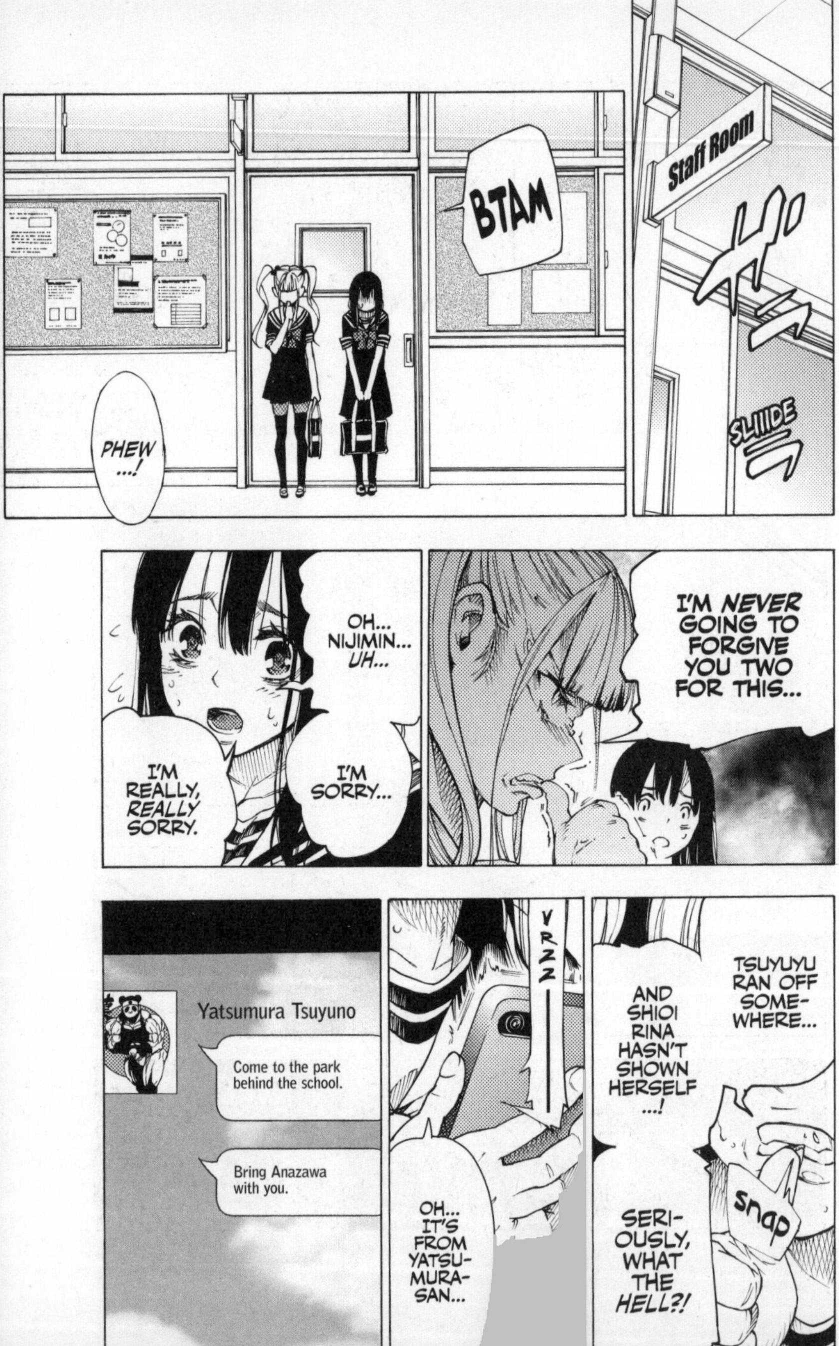
Staff Room
SLIIIDE
BTAM
PHEW ...!
I'M NEVER GOING TO FORGIVE YOU TWO FOR THIS...
OH... NIJIMIN... UH...
I'M SORRY...
I'M REALLY, REALLY SORRY.
TSUYUYU RAN OFF SOMEWHERE...
AND SHIOI RINA HASN'T SHOWN HERSELF ...!
SERIOUSLY, WHAT THE HELL?!
snap
VRZZ
OH... IT'S FROM YATSUMURA-SAN...
Yatsumura Tsuyuno
Come to the park behind the school.
Bring Anazawa with you.

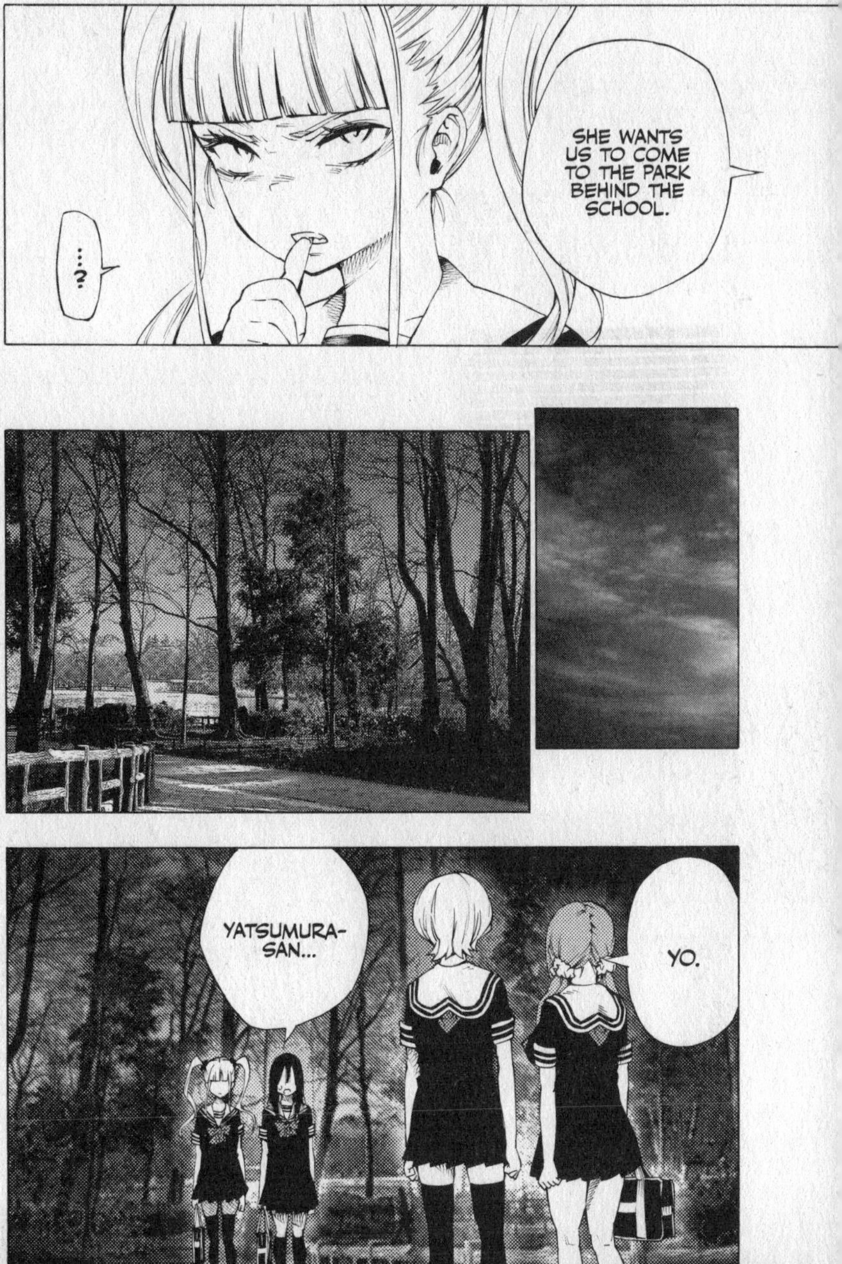
SHE WANTS US TO COME TO THE PARK BEHIND THE SCHOOL.
...?
YO.
YATSUMURA-SAN...

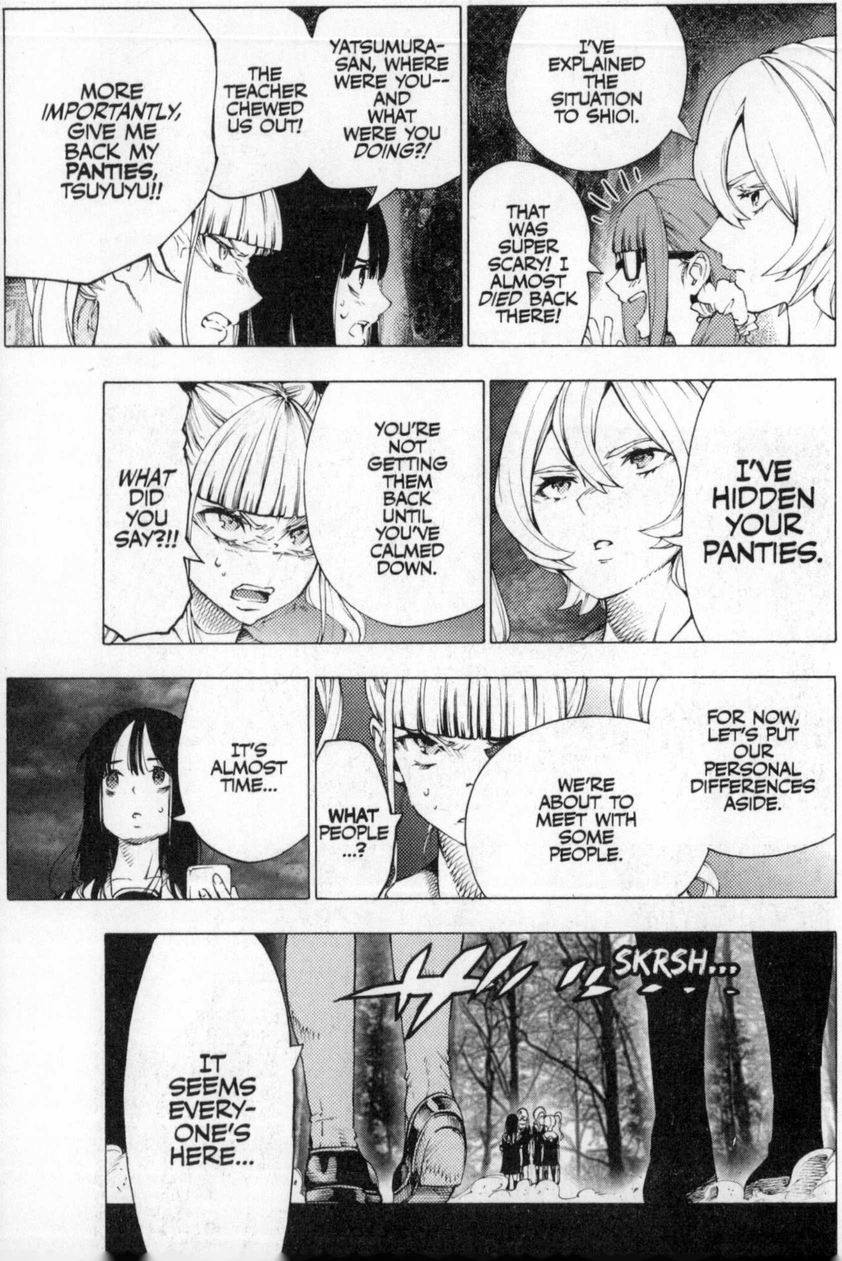

I'VE EXPLAINED THE SITUATION TO SHIOI.
THAT WAS SUPER SCARY! I ALMOST *DIED* BACK THERE!
YATSUMURA-SAN, WHERE WERE YOU--AND WHAT WERE YOU *DOING?!*
THE TEACHER CHEWED US OUT!
MORE *IMPORTANTLY,* GIVE ME BACK MY PANTIES, TSUYUYU!!
I'VE HIDDEN YOUR PANTIES.
YOU'RE NOT GETTING THEM BACK UNTIL YOU'VE CALMED DOWN.
WHAT DID YOU SAY?!!
FOR NOW, LET'S PUT OUR PERSONAL DIFFERENCES ASIDE.
WE'RE ABOUT TO MEET WITH SOME PEOPLE.
WHAT PEOPLE ...?
IT'S ALMOST TIME...
SKRSH...
IT SEEMS EVERYONE'S HERE...

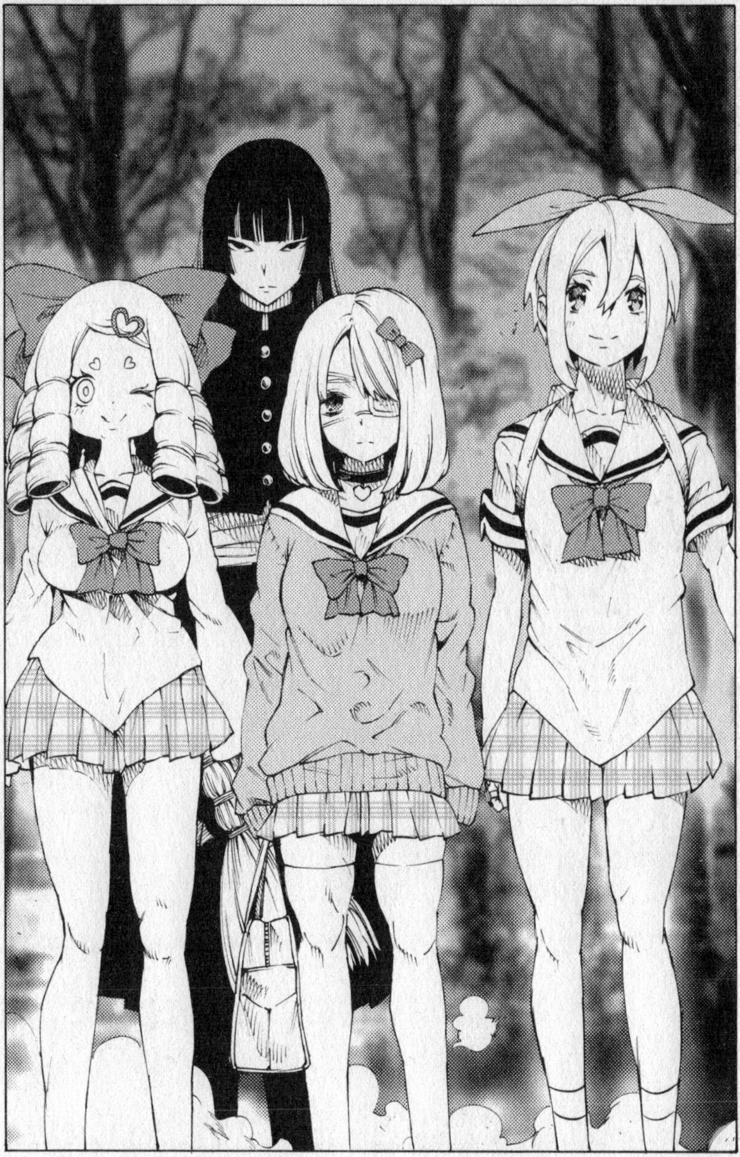

ENTER.26 COORDINATED TACTICS

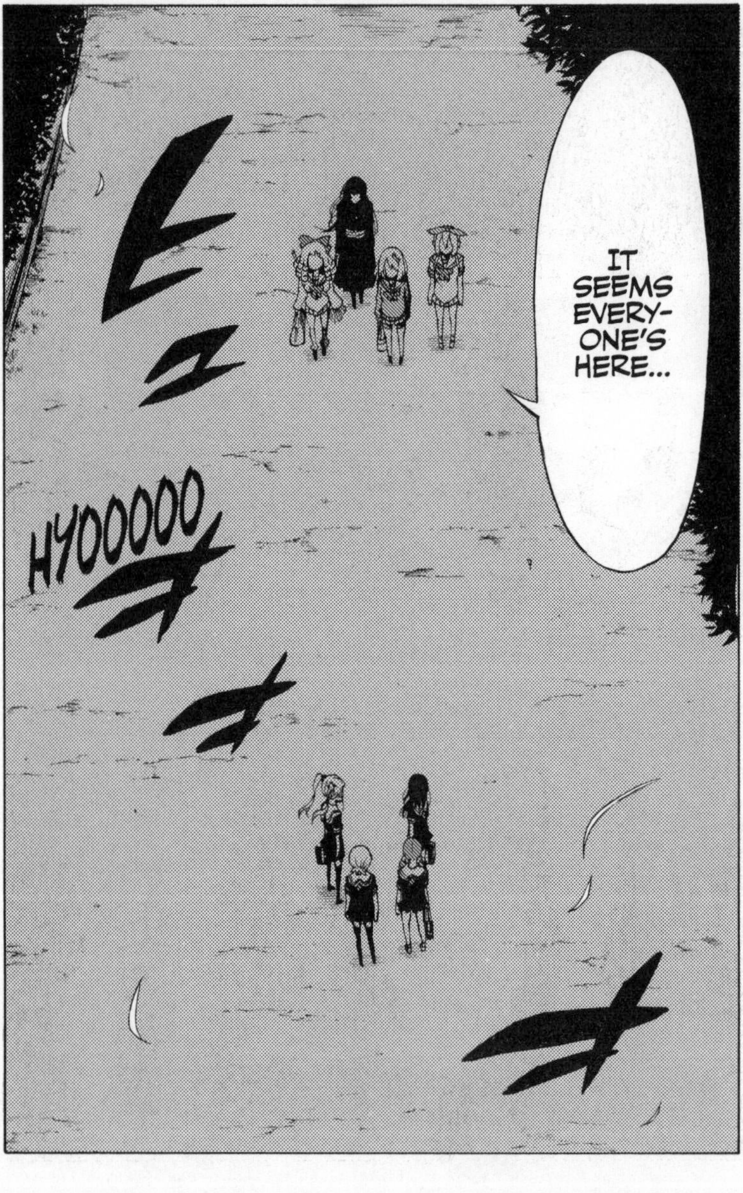
IT SEEMS EVERYONE'S HERE...
HYOOOOO

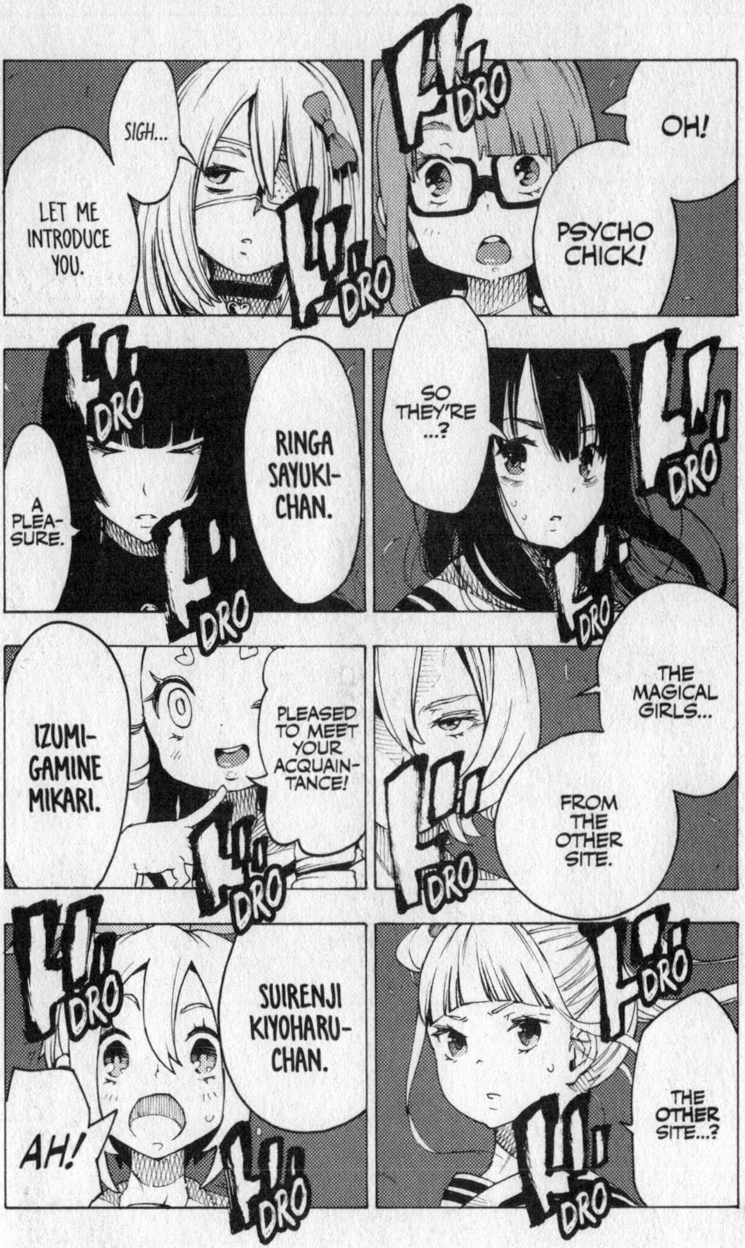
DRO
OH!
PSYCHO CHICK!
DRO
SIGH...
LET ME INTRODUCE YOU.
SO THEY'RE ...?
DRO
DRO
RINGA SAYUKI-CHAN.
A PLEASURE.
DRO
THE MAGICAL GIRLS...
FROM THE OTHER SITE.
DRO
PLEASED TO MEET YOUR ACQUAINTANCE!
IZUMI-GAMINE MIKARI.
DRO
DRO
THE OTHER SITE...?
DRO
DRO
SUIRENJI KIYOHARU-CHAN.
AH!
DRO

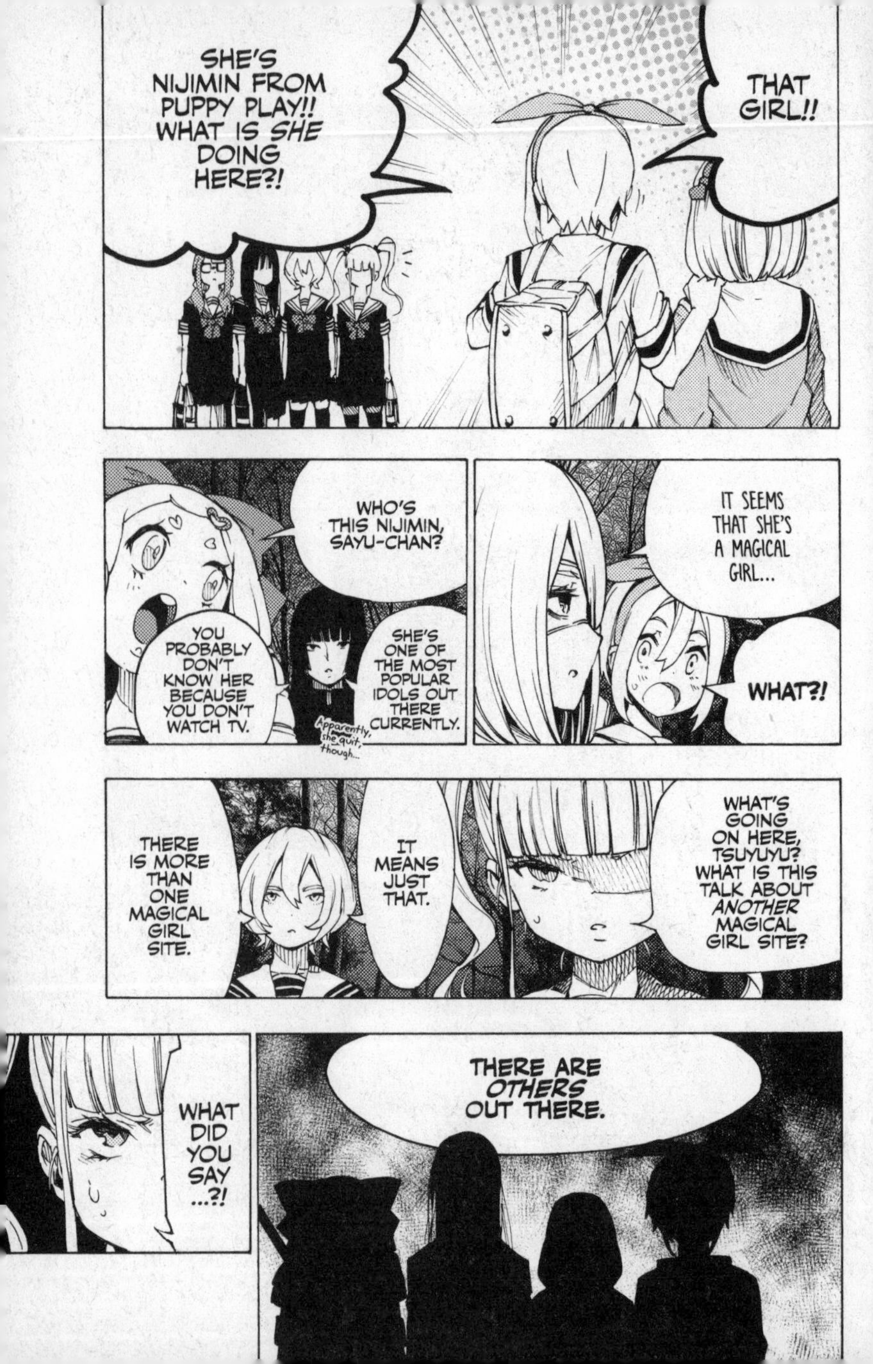
THAT GIRL!!
SHE'S NIJIMIN FROM PUPPY PLAY!! WHAT IS SHE DOING HERE?!
IT SEEMS THAT SHE'S A MAGICAL GIRL...
WHAT?!
WHO'S THIS NIJIMIN, SAYU-CHAN?
SHE'S ONE OF THE MOST POPULAR IDOLS OUT THERE CURRENTLY.
Apparently, she quit, though...
YOU PROBABLY DON'T KNOW HER BECAUSE YOU DON'T WATCH TV.
WHAT'S GOING ON HERE, TSUYUYU? WHAT IS THIS TALK ABOUT ANOTHER MAGICAL GIRL SITE?
IT MEANS JUST THAT.
THERE IS MORE THAN ONE MAGICAL GIRL SITE.
THERE ARE OTHERS OUT THERE.
WHAT DID YOU SAY ...?!

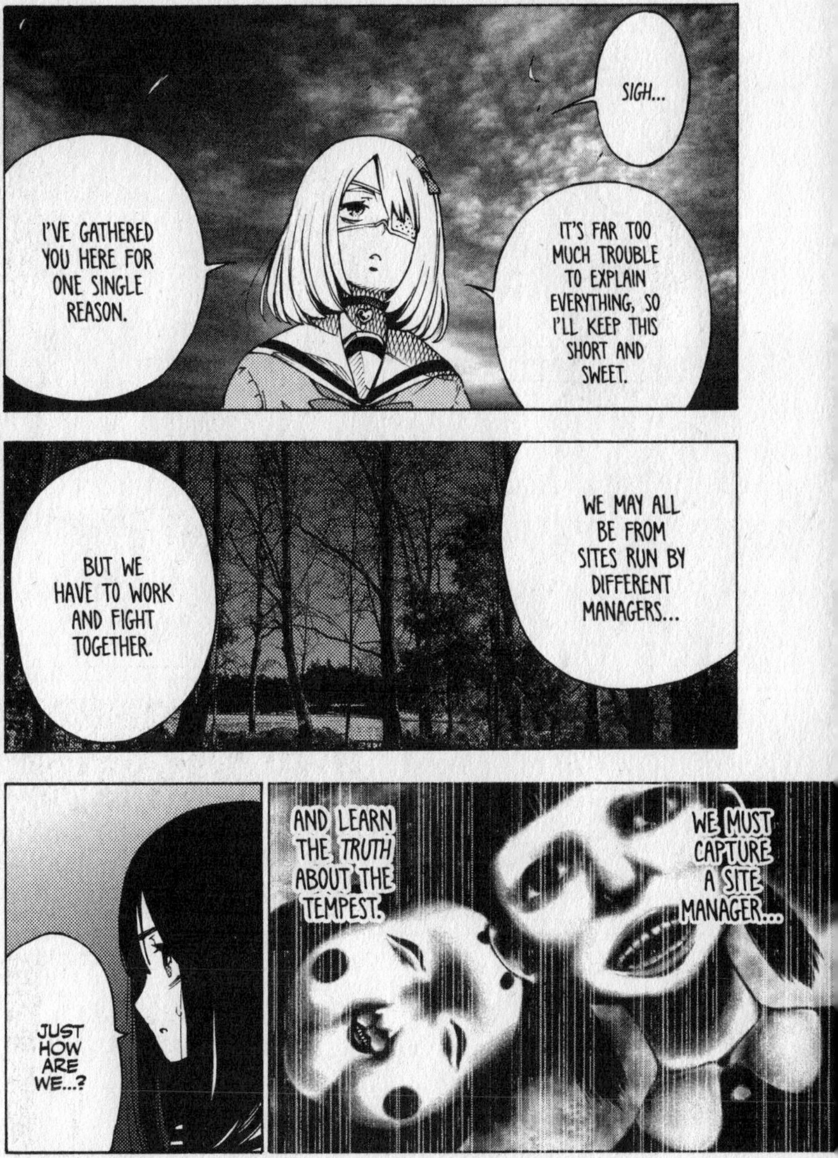
SIGH...
IT'S FAR TOO MUCH TROUBLE TO EXPLAIN EVERYTHING, SO I'LL KEEP THIS SHORT AND SWEET.
I'VE GATHERED YOU HERE FOR ONE SINGLE REASON.
WE MAY ALL BE FROM SITES RUN BY DIFFERENT MANAGERS...
BUT WE HAVE TO WORK AND FIGHT TOGETHER.
WE MUST CAPTURE A SITE MANAGER...
AND LEARN THE *TRUTH* ABOUT THE TEMPEST.
JUST HOW ARE WE...?

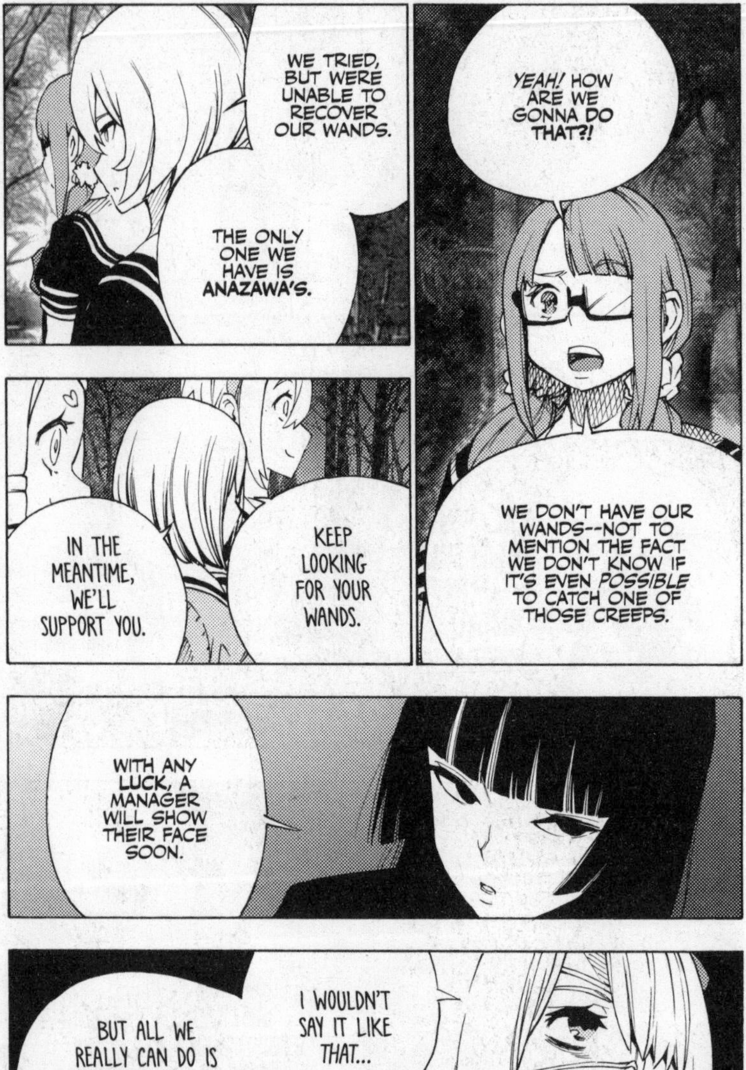

YEAH! HOW ARE WE GONNA DO THAT?!
WE DON'T HAVE OUR WANDS--NOT TO MENTION THE FACT WE DON'T KNOW IF IT'S EVEN *POSSIBLE* TO CATCH ONE OF THOSE CREEPS.
WE TRIED, BUT WERE UNABLE TO RECOVER OUR WANDS.
THE ONLY ONE WE HAVE IS ANAZAWA'S.
KEEP LOOKING FOR YOUR WANDS.
IN THE MEANTIME, WE'LL SUPPORT YOU.
WITH ANY **LUCK**, A MANAGER WILL SHOW THEIR FACE SOON.
I WOULDN'T SAY IT LIKE *THAT*...
BUT ALL WE REALLY CAN DO IS WAIT UNTIL ONE OF THEM APPEARS.

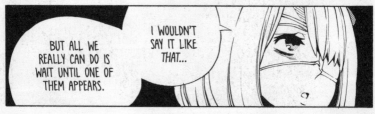

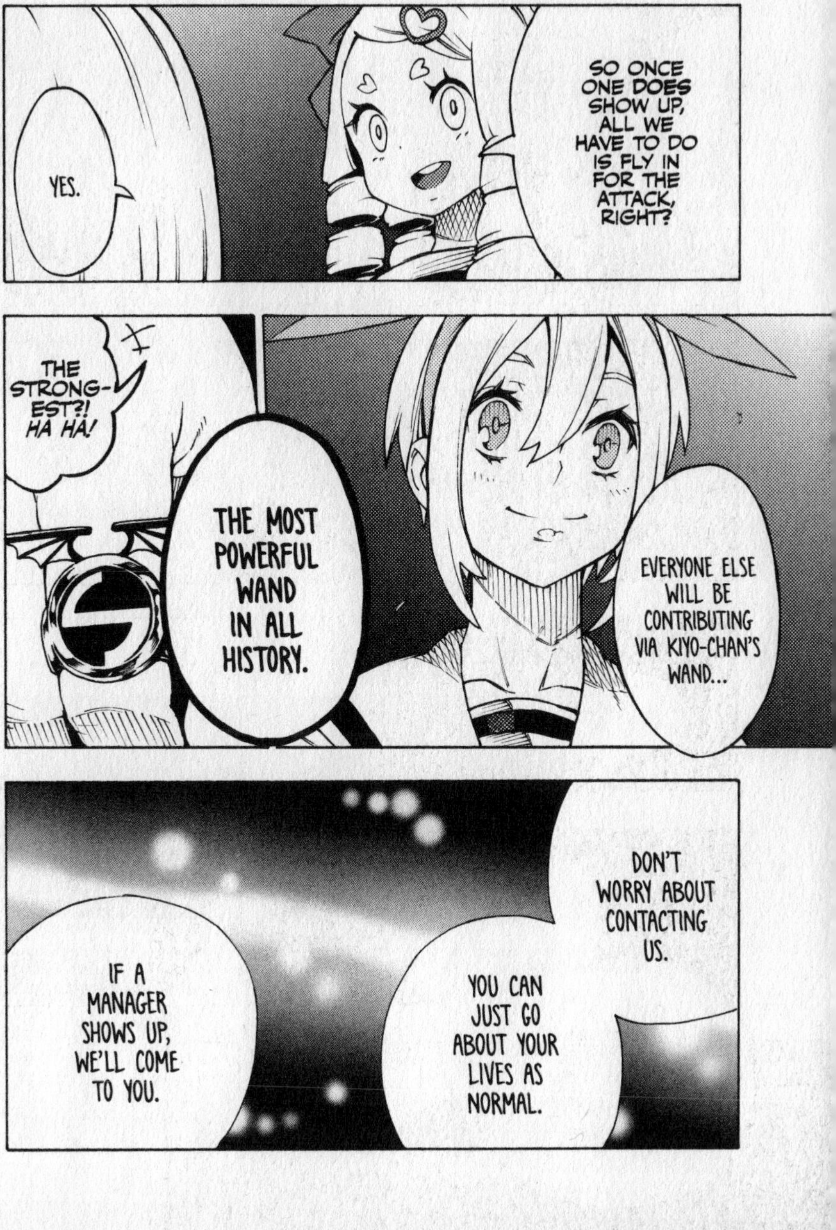
SO ONCE ONE DOES SHOW UP, ALL WE HAVE TO DO IS FLY IN FOR THE ATTACK, RIGHT?
YES.
EVERYONE ELSE WILL BE CONTRIBUTING VIA KIYO-CHAN'S WAND...
THE MOST POWERFUL WAND IN ALL HISTORY.
THE STRONG-EST?! HA HA!
DON'T WORRY ABOUT CONTACTING US.
YOU CAN JUST GO ABOUT YOUR LIVES AS NORMAL.
IF A MANAGER SHOWS UP, WE'LL COME TO YOU.

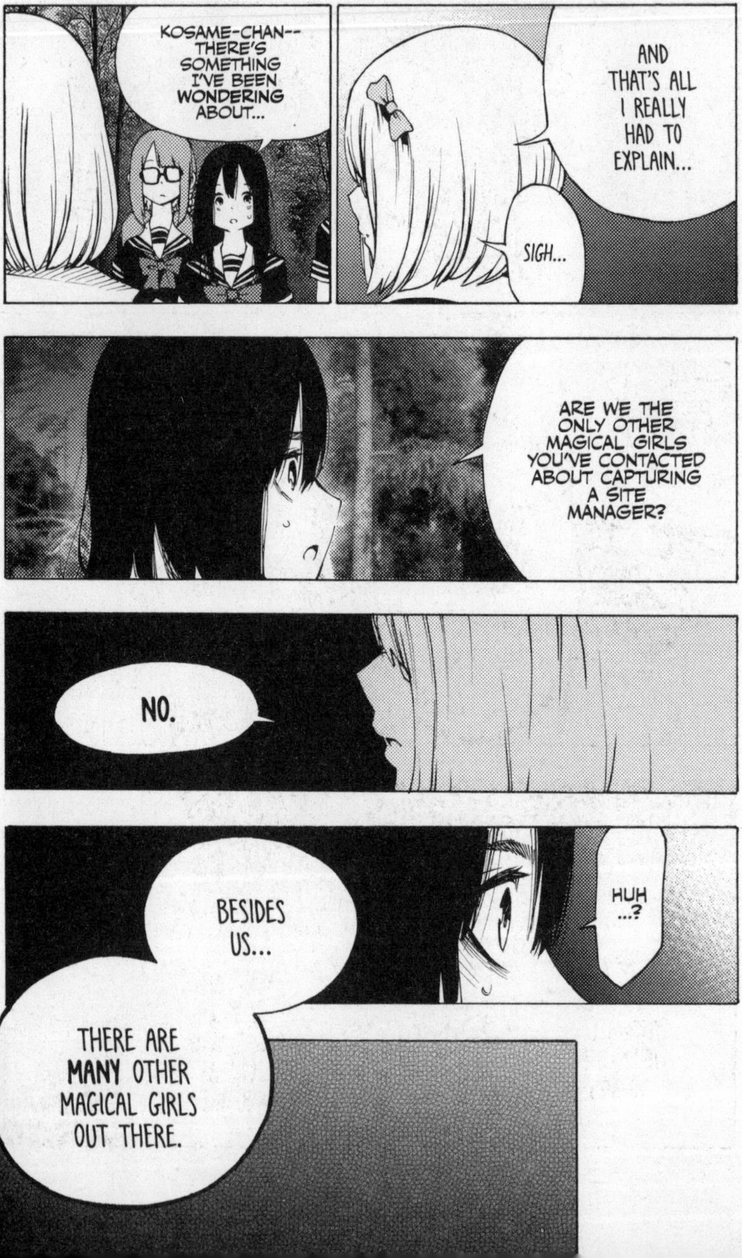
AND THAT'S ALL I REALLY HAD TO EXPLAIN...
SIGH...
KOSAME-CHAN-- THERE'S SOMETHING I'VE BEEN WONDERING ABOUT...
ARE WE THE ONLY OTHER MAGICAL GIRLS YOU'VE CONTACTED ABOUT CAPTURING A SITE MANAGER?
NO.
HUH ...?
BESIDES US...
THERE ARE MANY OTHER MAGICAL GIRLS OUT THERE.

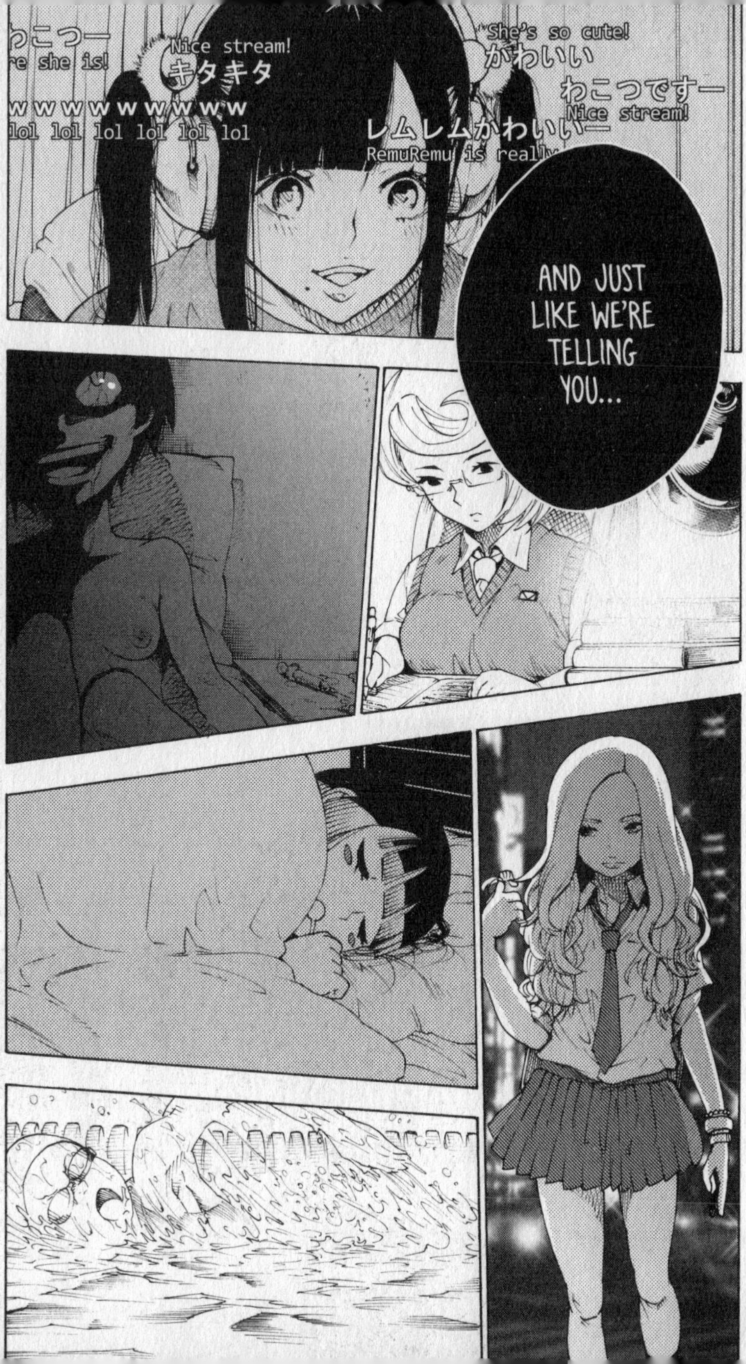
She's so cute!
かわいい
わこつですー
Nice stream!
レムレムかわいいー
RemuRemu is really
Nice stream!
キタキタ
wwwwwwwwwww
lol lol lol lol lol lol
AND JUST LIKE WE'RE TELLING YOU...

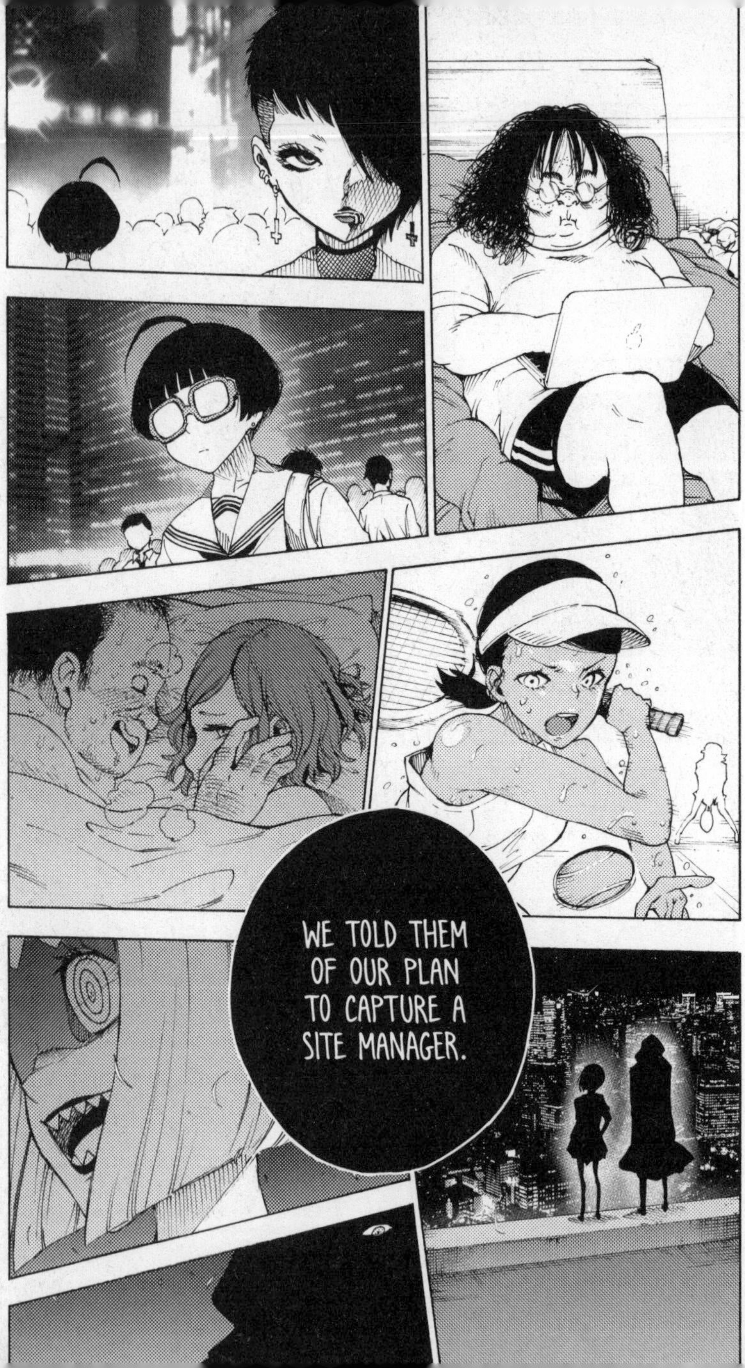
WE TOLD THEM OF OUR PLAN TO CAPTURE A SITE MANAGER.

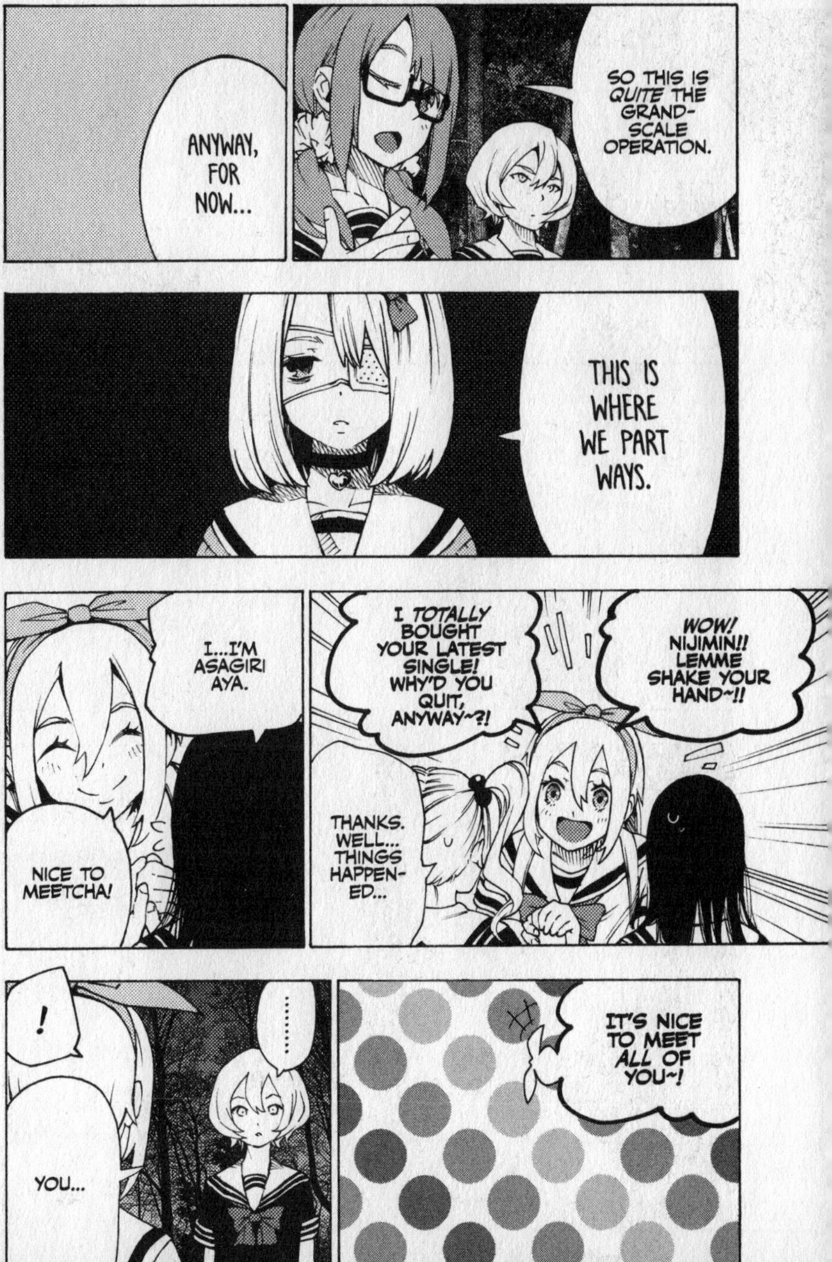
SO THIS IS *QUITE* THE GRAND-SCALE OPERATION.
ANYWAY, FOR NOW...
THIS IS WHERE WE PART WAYS.
WOW! NIJIMIN!! LEMME SHAKE YOUR HAND~!!
I *TOTALLY* BOUGHT YOUR LATEST SINGLE! WHY'D YOU QUIT, ANYWAY~?!
THANKS. WELL... THINGS HAPPENED...
I...I'M ASAGIRI AYA.
NICE TO MEETCHA!
IT'S NICE TO MEET *ALL* OF YOU~!
......
!
YOU...

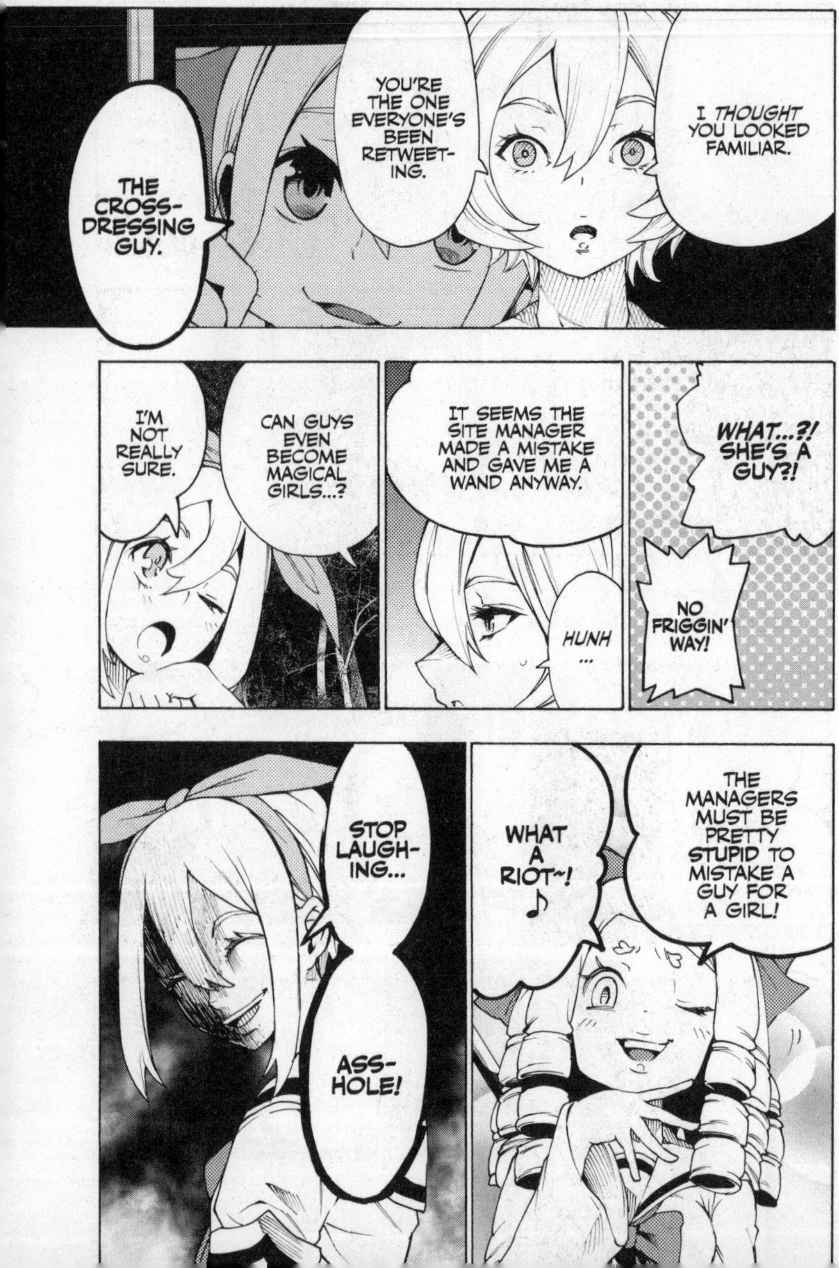
I *THOUGHT* YOU LOOKED FAMILIAR.
YOU'RE THE ONE EVERYONE'S BEEN RETWEETING.
THE CROSS-DRESSING GUY.
WHAT...?! SHE'S A GUY?!
NO FRIGGIN' WAY!
IT SEEMS THE SITE MANAGER MADE A MISTAKE AND GAVE ME A WAND ANYWAY.
HUNH ...
CAN GUYS EVEN BECOME MAGICAL GIRLS...?
I'M NOT REALLY SURE.
THE MANAGERS MUST BE PRETTY STUPID TO MISTAKE A GUY FOR A GIRL!
WHAT A RIOT~! ♪
STOP LAUGHING...
ASSHOLE!

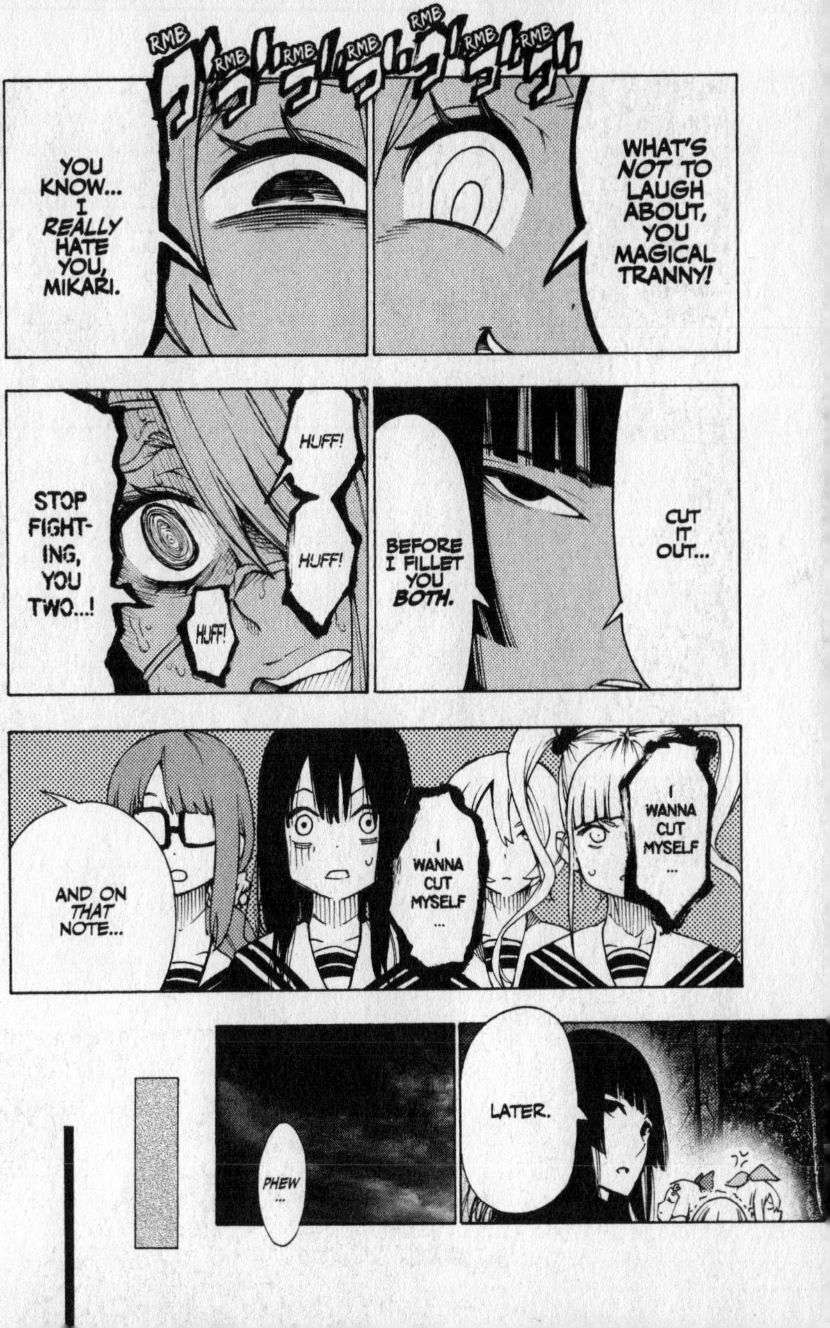
RMB RMB RMB RMB RMB RMB RMB
WHAT'S NOT TO LAUGH ABOUT, YOU MAGICAL TRANNY!
YOU KNOW... I REALLY HATE YOU, MIKARI.
CUT IT OUT...
BEFORE I FILLET YOU BOTH.
HUFF!
HUFF!
HUFF!
STOP FIGHTING, YOU TWO...!
I WANNA CUT MYSELF...
I WANNA CUT MYSELF...
AND ON THAT NOTE...
LATER.
PHEW...

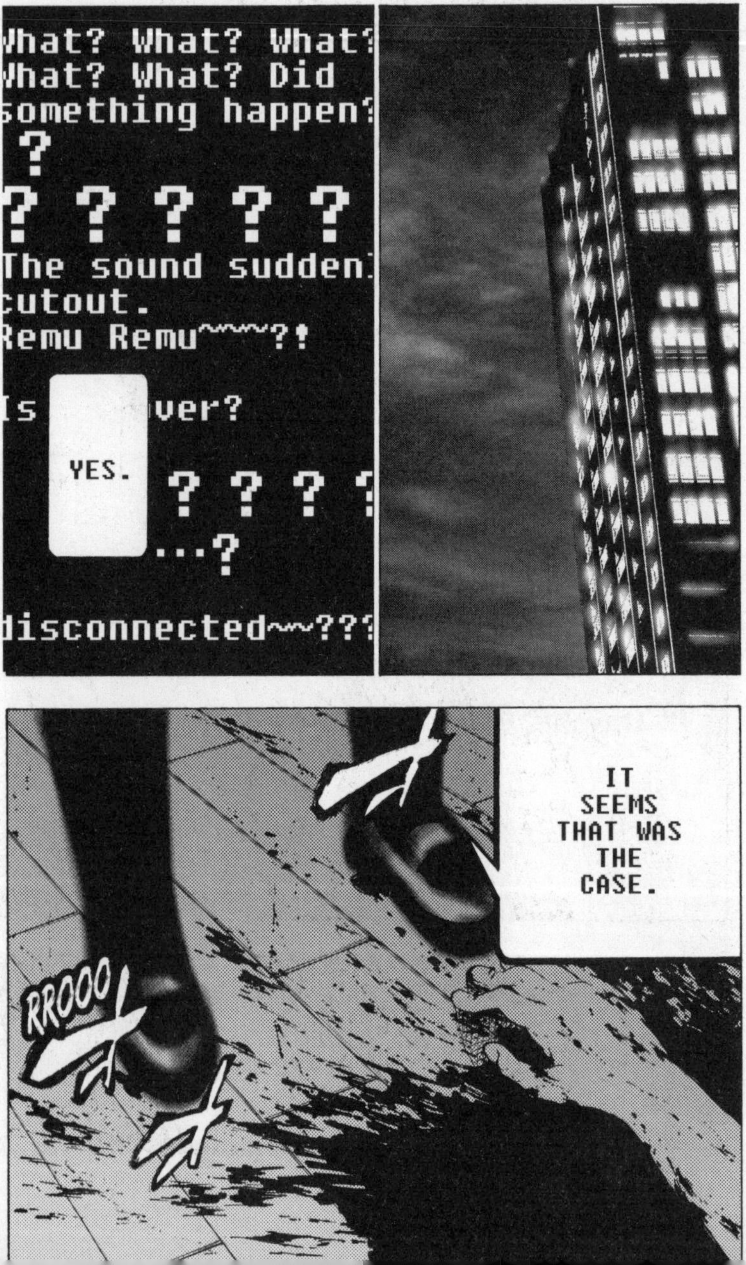

What? What? What?
What? What? Did
something happen?
?
? ? ? ? ?
The sound suddenl
cutout.
Remu Remu~~~~?!
Is ver?
YES.
? ? ? ?
...?
disconnected~~???
IT SEEMS THAT WAS THE CASE.
RROOO

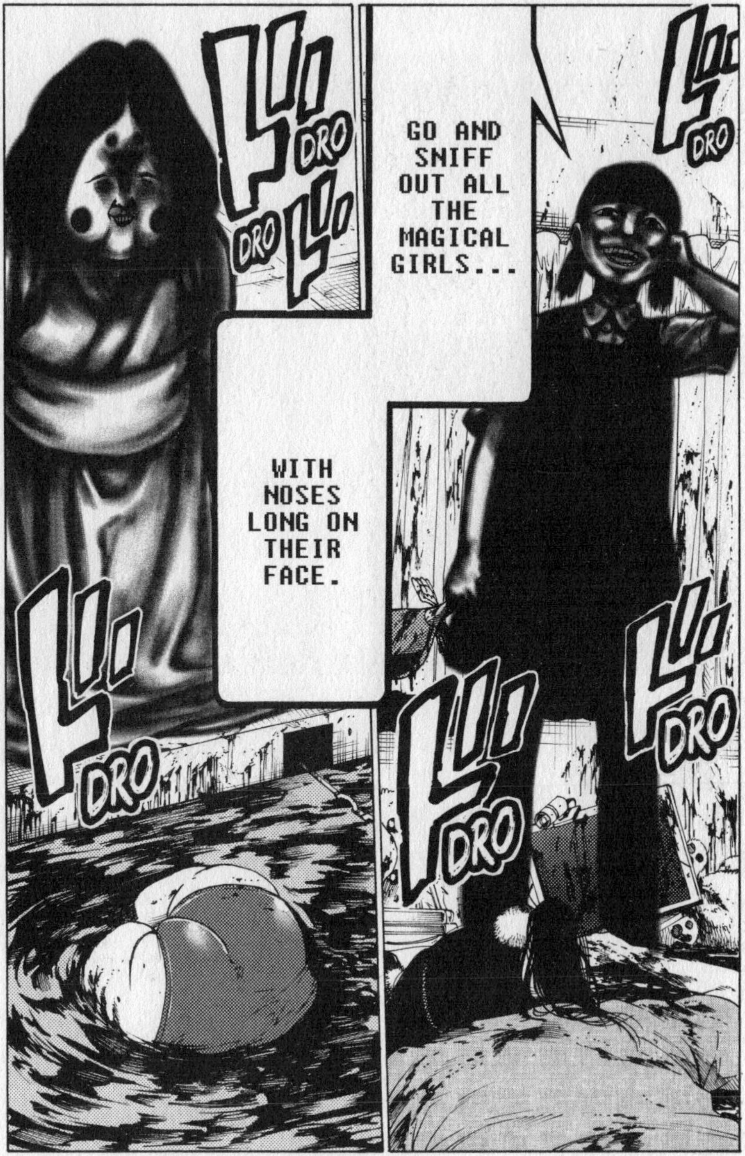
DRO
GO AND SNIFF OUT ALL THE MAGICAL GIRLS...
WITH NOSES LONG ON THEIR FACE.
DRO
DRO
DRO
DRO
DRO

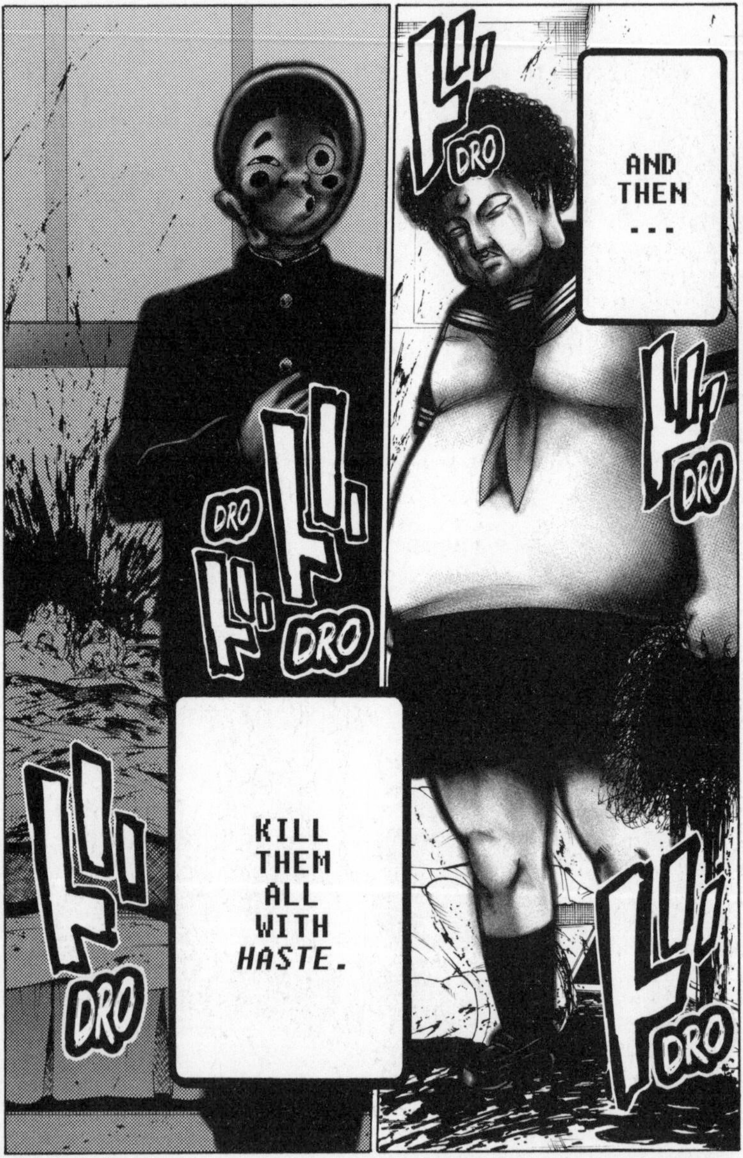
AND THEN ...
DRO
DRO
DRO
DRO
DRO
DRO
KILL THEM ALL WITH *HASTE*.

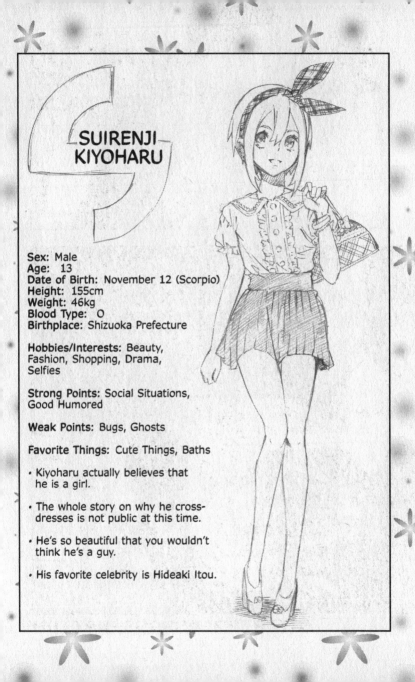

S SUIRENJI KIYOHARU

Sex: Male
Age: 13
Date of Birth: November 12 (Scorpio)
Height: 155cm
Weight: 46kg
Blood Type: O
Birthplace: Shizuoka Prefecture

Hobbies/Interests: Beauty, Fashion, Shopping, Drama, Selfies

Strong Points: Social Situations, Good Humored

Weak Points: Bugs, Ghosts

Favorite Things: Cute Things, Baths

- Kiyoharu actually believes that he is a girl.

- The whole story on why he cross-dresses is not public at this time.

- He's so beautiful that you wouldn't think he's a guy.

- His favorite celebrity is Hideaki Itou.

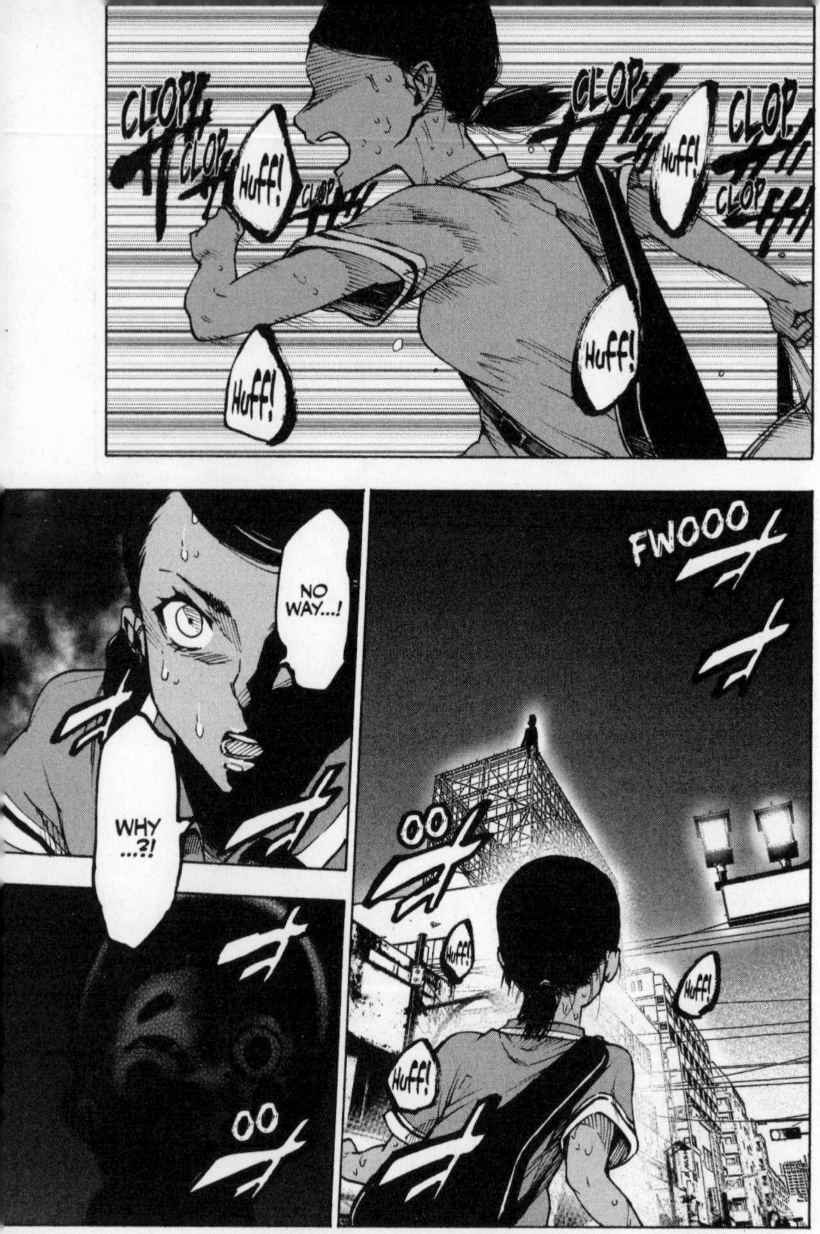
CLOP
CLOP
HUFF!
CLOP
HUFF!
HUFF!
CLOP
CLOP
CLOP
HUFF!
FWOOO
OO
HUFF!
HUFF!
HUFF!
NO WAY...!
WHY ...?!
OO

ENTER.27 ASSASSINATION

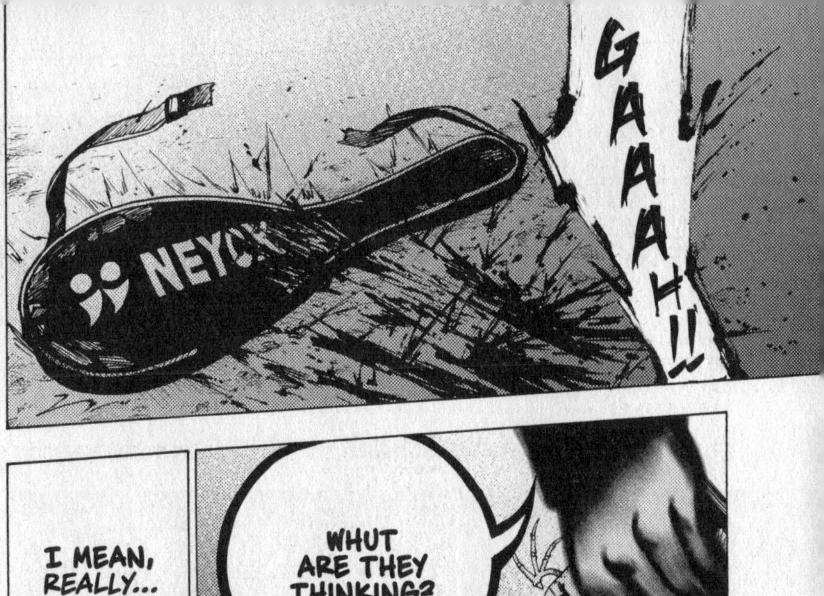
GAAAH!!
NEYC
WHUT ARE THEY THINKING?
SNATCH...
I MEAN, REALLY...

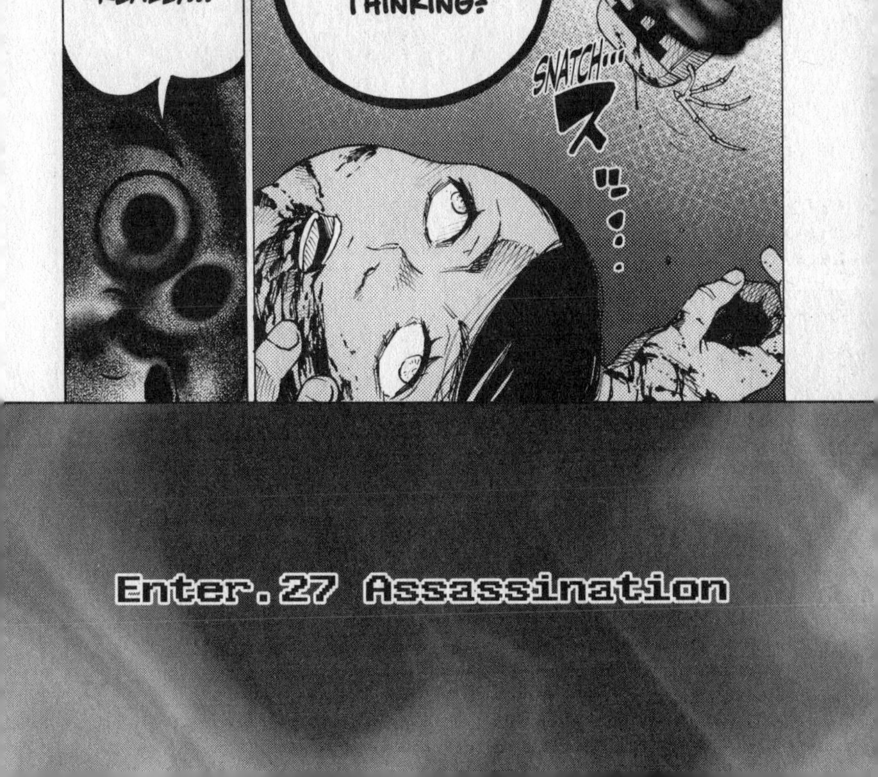

Enter.27 Assassination

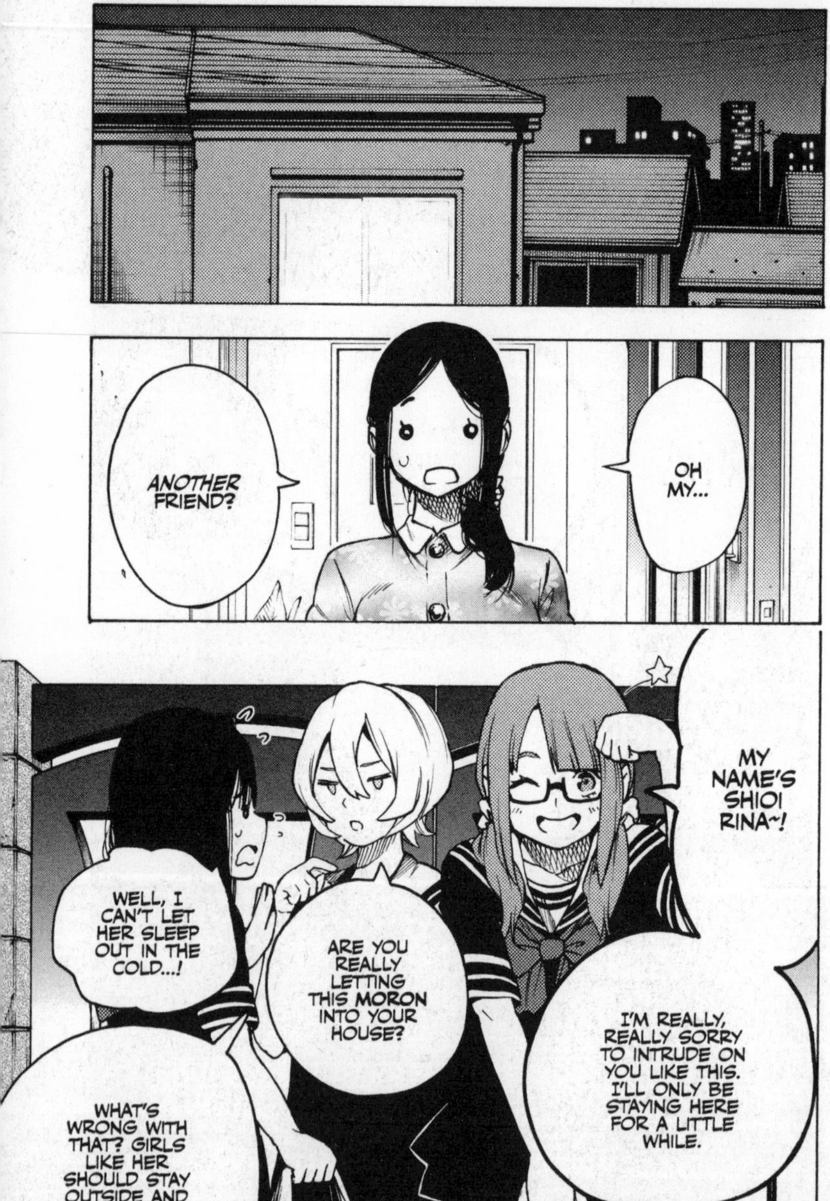
OH MY...
ANOTHER FRIEND?
MY NAME'S SHIOI RINA~!
I'M REALLY, REALLY SORRY TO INTRUDE ON YOU LIKE THIS. I'LL ONLY BE STAYING HERE FOR A LITTLE WHILE.
ARE YOU REALLY LETTING THIS MORON INTO YOUR HOUSE?
WELL, I CAN'T LET HER SLEEP OUT IN THE COLD...!
WHAT'S WRONG WITH THAT? GIRLS LIKE HER SHOULD STAY OUTSIDE AND EAT BUGS.

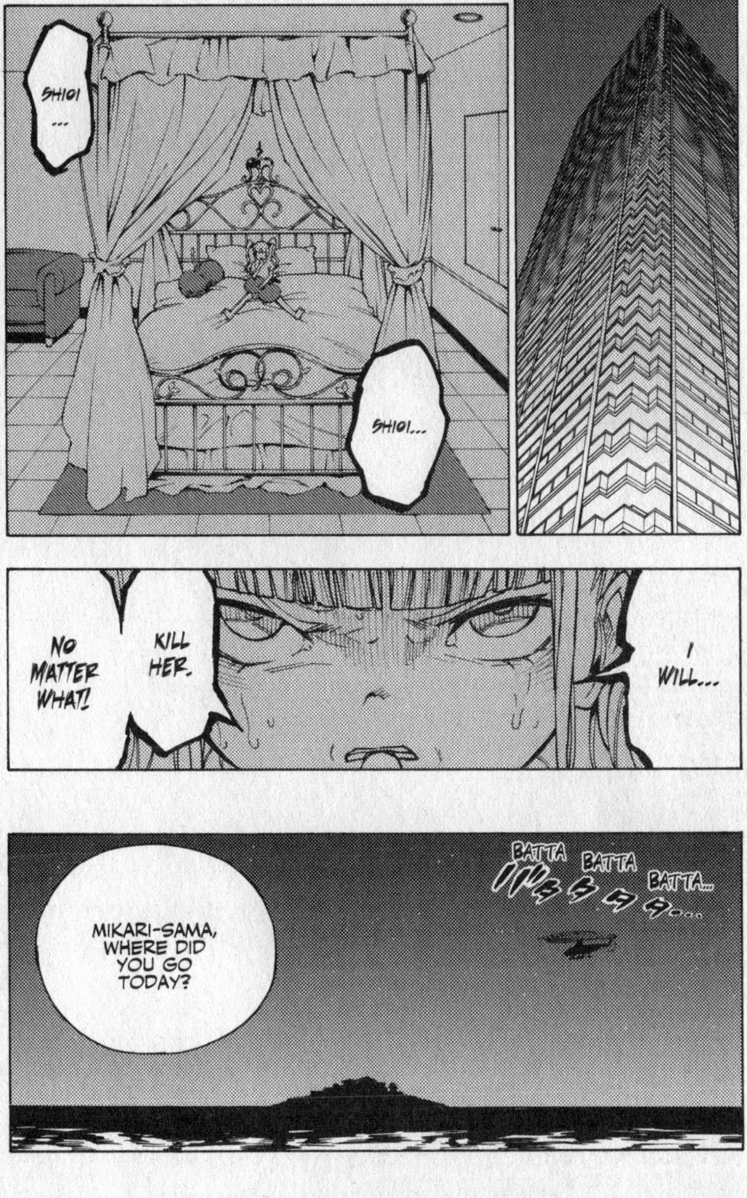
SHIOI ...
SHIOI...
I WILL...
KILL HER.
NO MATTER WHAT!
BATTA BATTA BATTA...
MIKARI-SAMA, WHERE DID YOU GO TODAY?

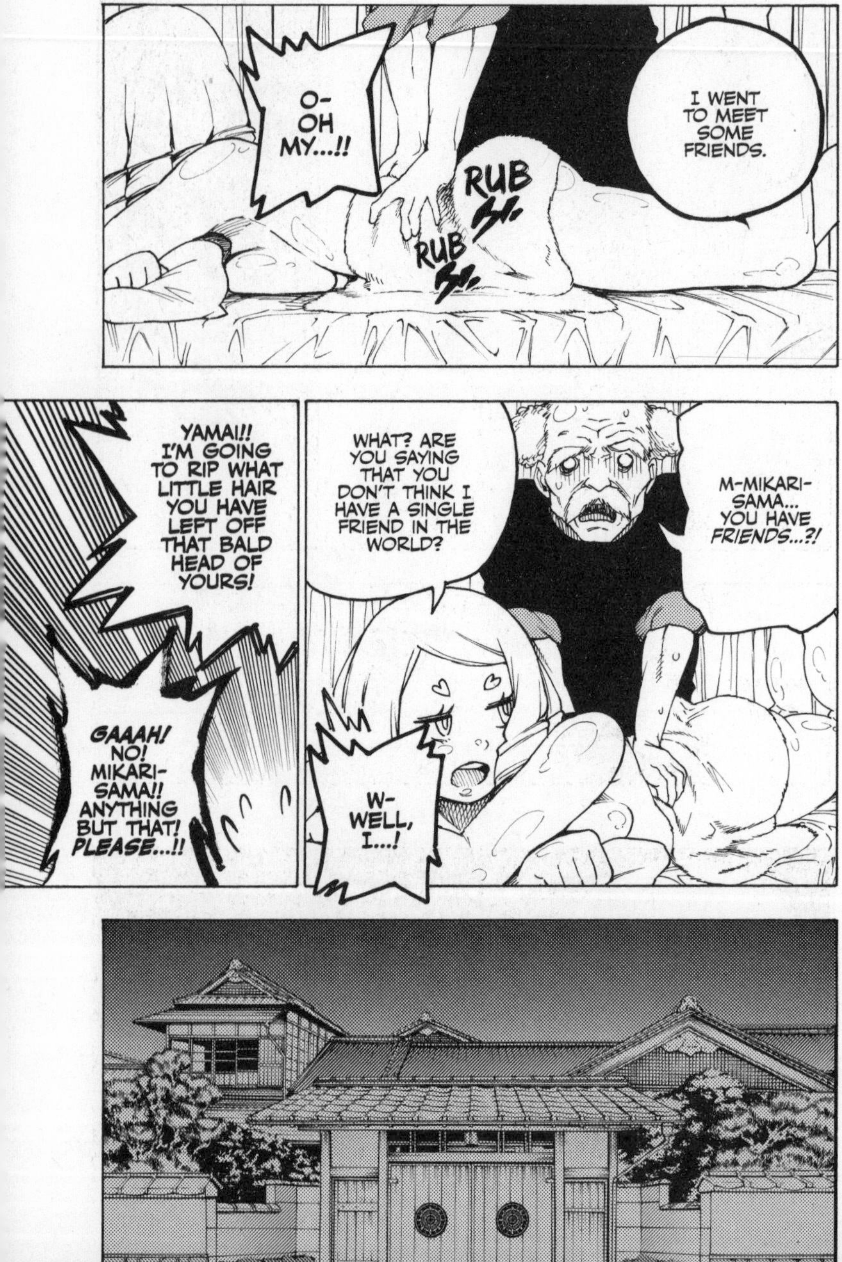
I WENT TO MEET SOME FRIENDS.
O-OH MY...!!
RUB
RUB
M-MIKARI-SAMA... YOU HAVE FRIENDS...?!
WHAT? ARE YOU SAYING THAT YOU DON'T THINK I HAVE A SINGLE FRIEND IN THE WORLD?
W-WELL, I...!
YAMAI!! I'M GOING TO RIP WHAT LITTLE HAIR YOU HAVE LEFT OFF THAT BALD HEAD OF YOURS!
GAAAH! NO! MIKARI-SAMA!! ANYTHING BUT THAT! PLEASE...!!

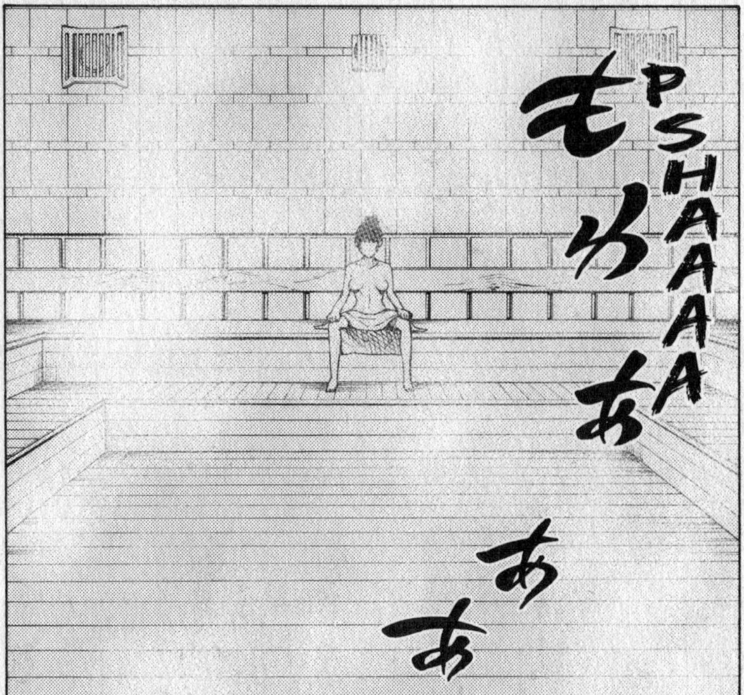
PSHAAAA
もわあ
ああ

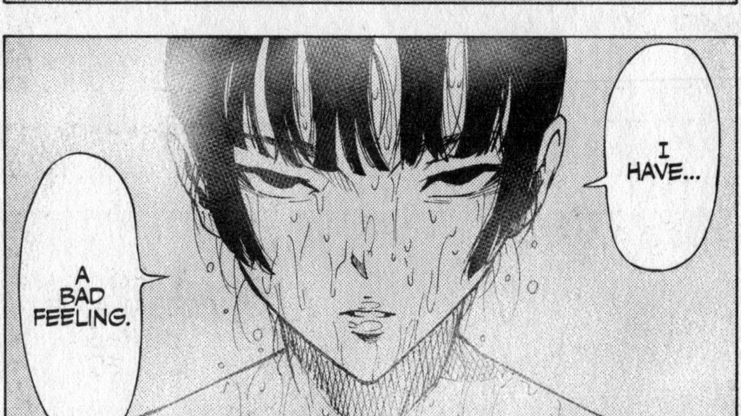
I HAVE...
A BAD FEELING.

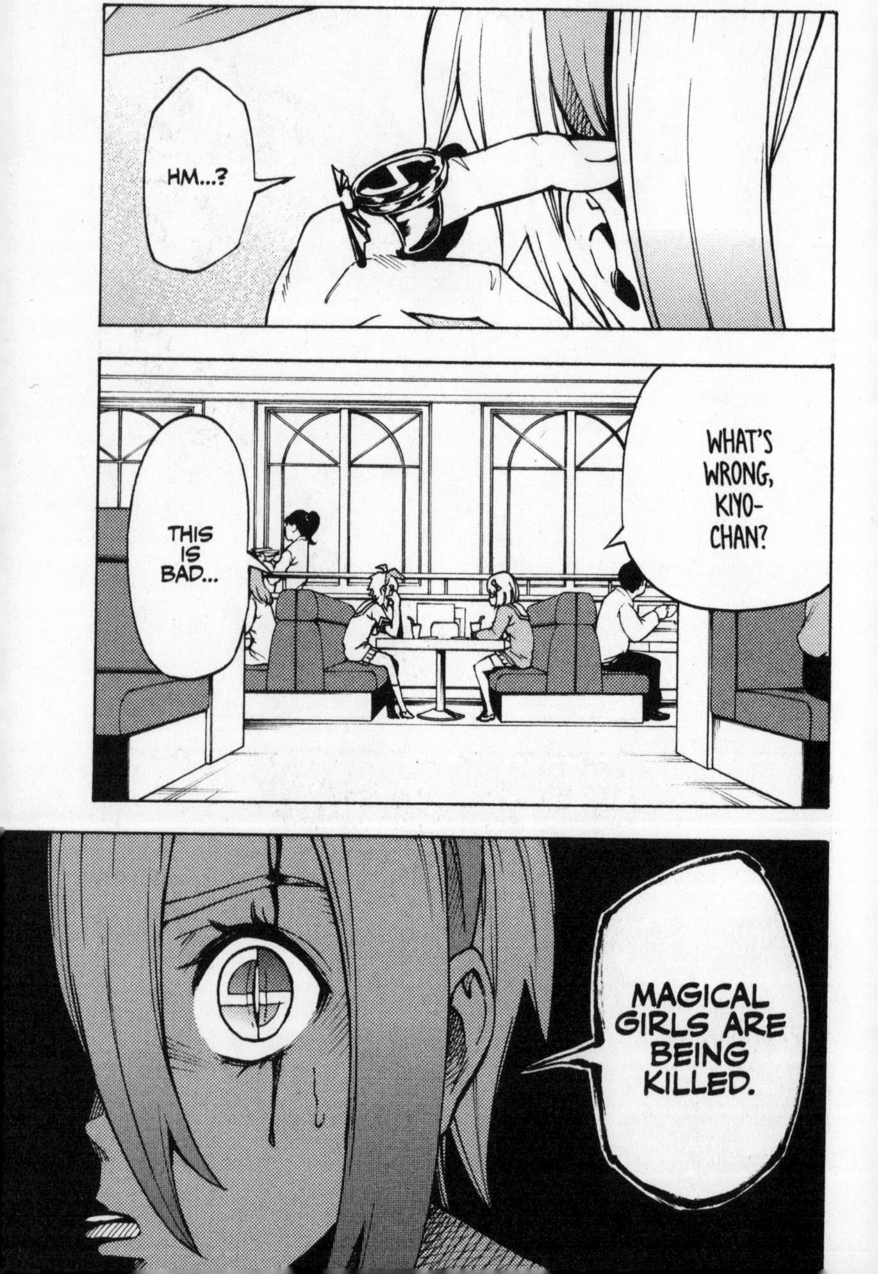
HM...?
WHAT'S WRONG, KIYO-CHAN?
THIS IS BAD...
MAGICAL GIRLS ARE BEING KILLED.

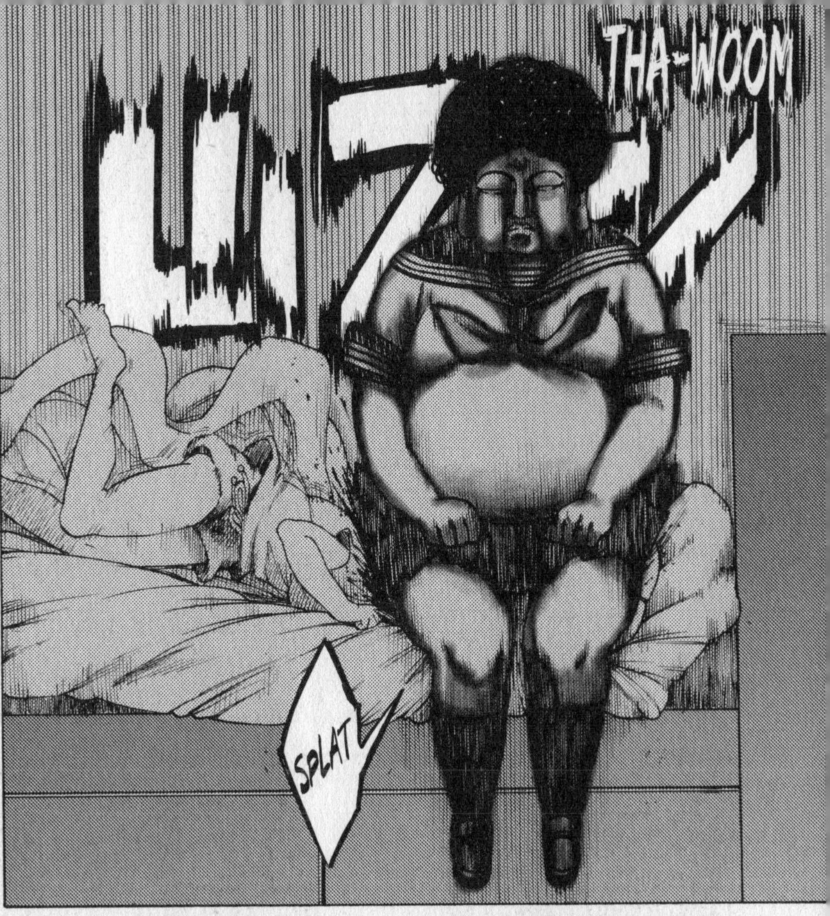
THA-WOOM
SPLAT

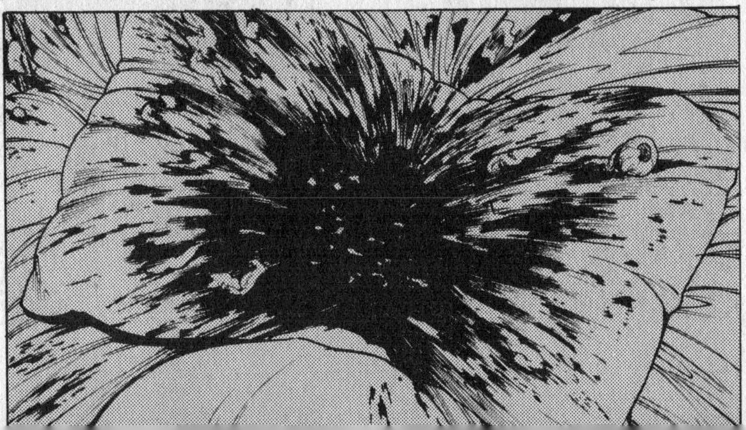

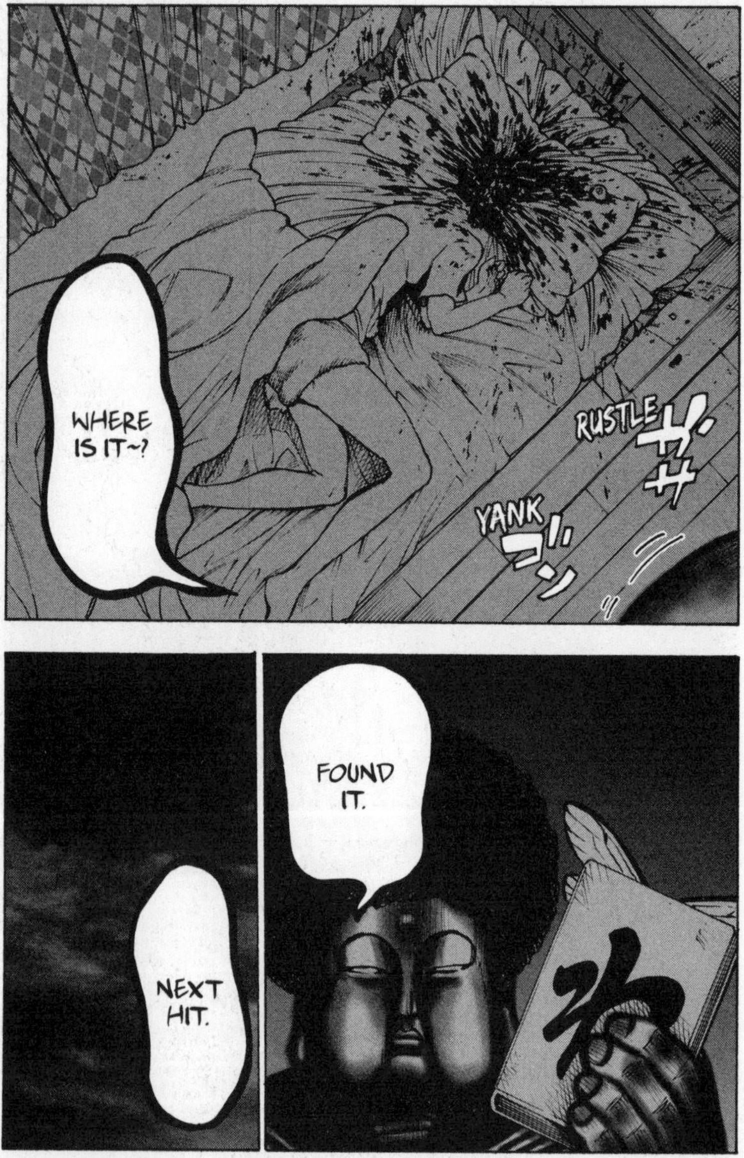
WHERE IS IT~?
RUSTLE
YANK
FOUND IT.
NEXT HIT.

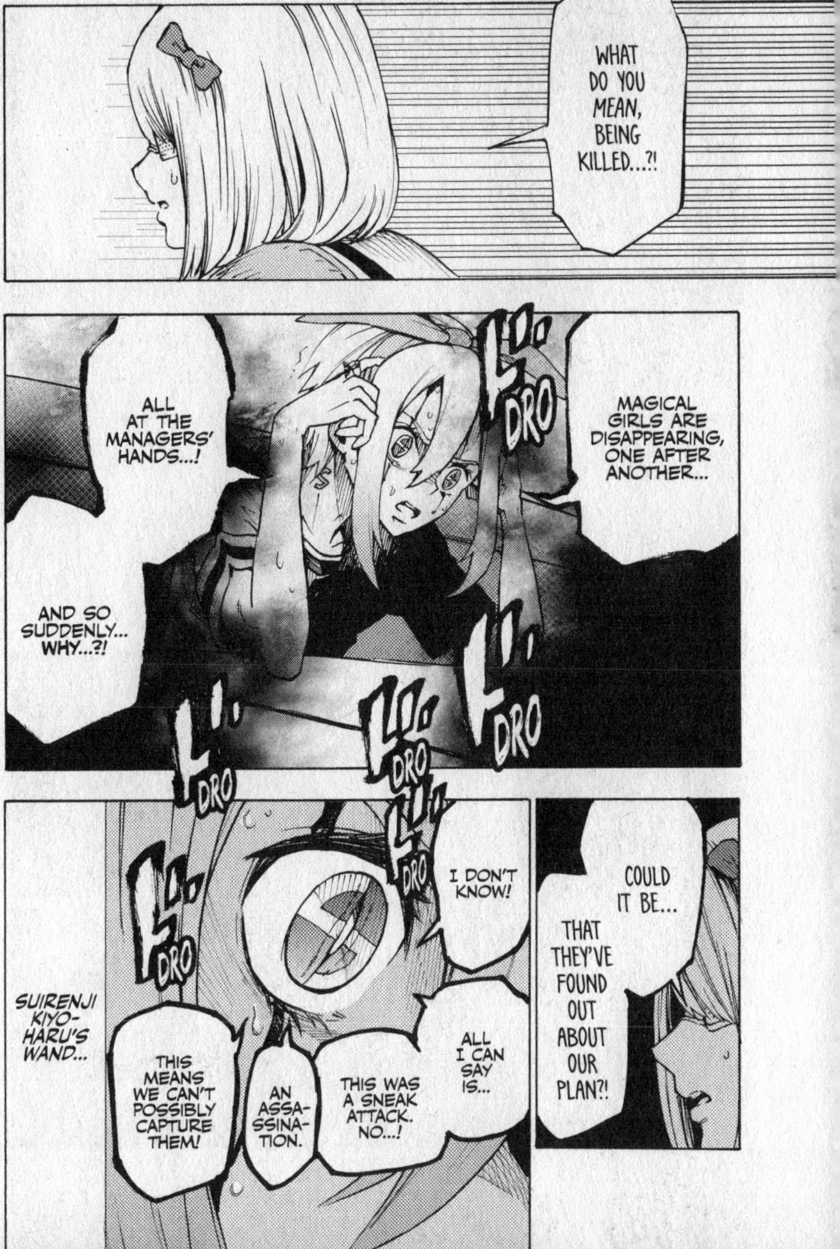
WHAT DO YOU MEAN, BEING KILLED...?!
MAGICAL GIRLS ARE DISAPPEARING, ONE AFTER ANOTHER...
DRO
ALL AT THE MANAGERS' HANDS...!
AND SO SUDDENLY... WHY...?!
DRO
DRO
DRO
COULD IT BE...
THAT THEY'VE FOUND OUT ABOUT OUR PLAN?!
DRO
DRO
I DON'T KNOW!
ALL I CAN SAY IS...
THIS WAS A SNEAK ATTACK. NO...!
AN ASSASSINATION.
THIS MEANS WE CAN'T POSSIBLY CAPTURE THEM!
SUIRENJI KIYOHARU'S WAND...

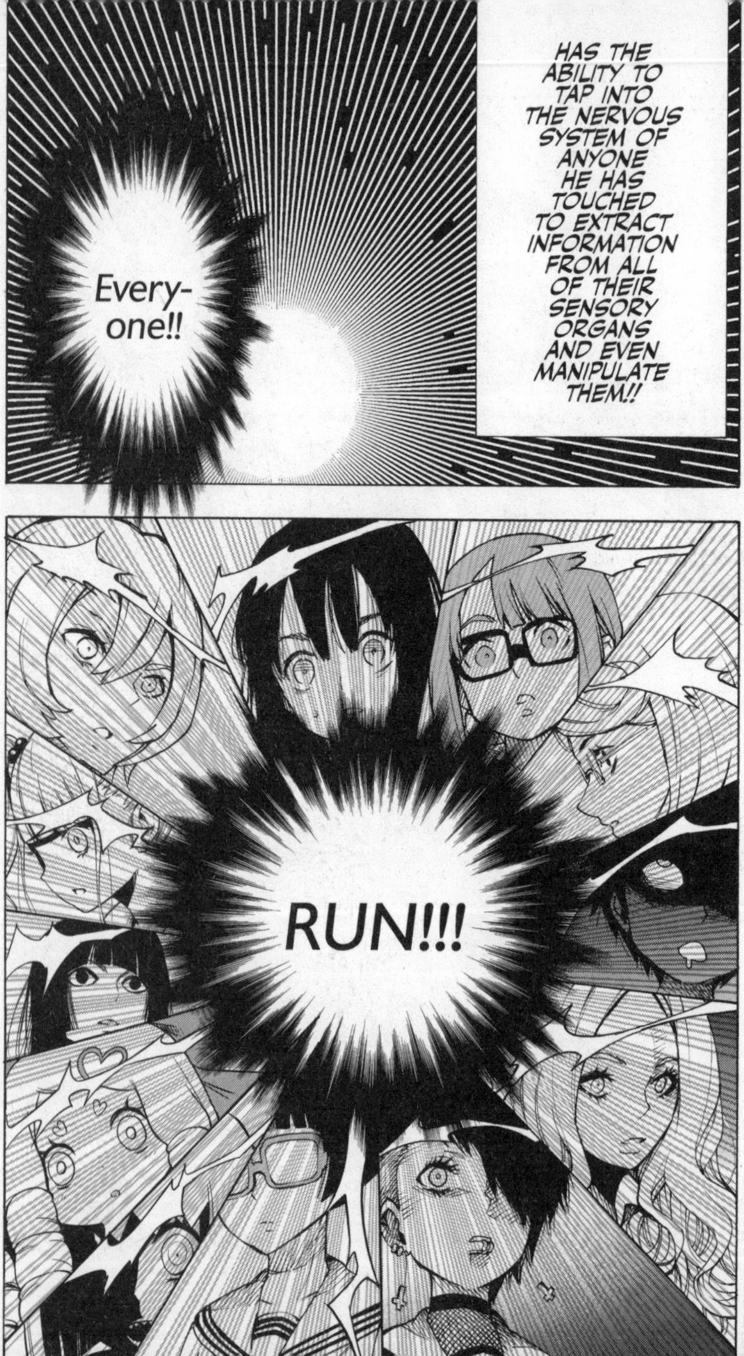
HAS THE ABILITY TO TAP INTO THE NERVOUS SYSTEM OF ANYONE HE HAS TOUCHED TO EXTRACT INFORMATION FROM ALL OF THEIR SENSORY ORGANS AND EVEN MANIPULATE THEM!!
Every-one!!
RUN!!!

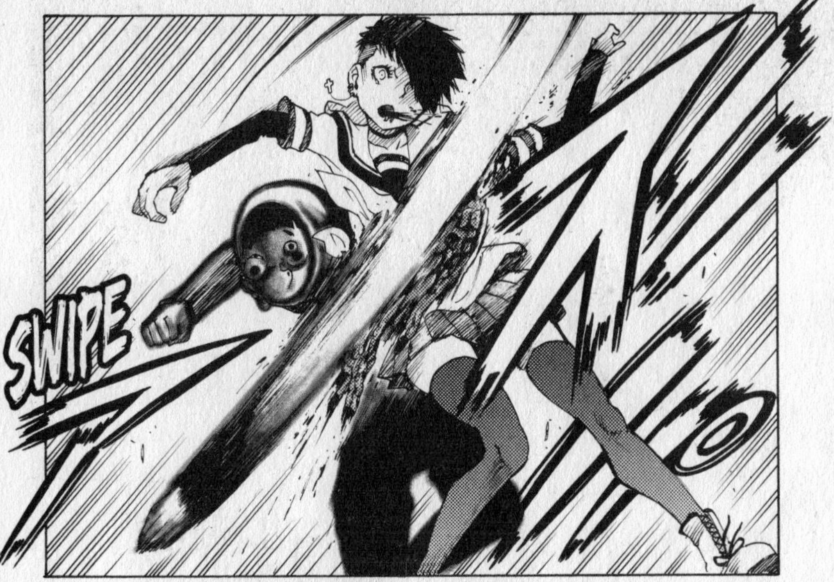
SWIPE

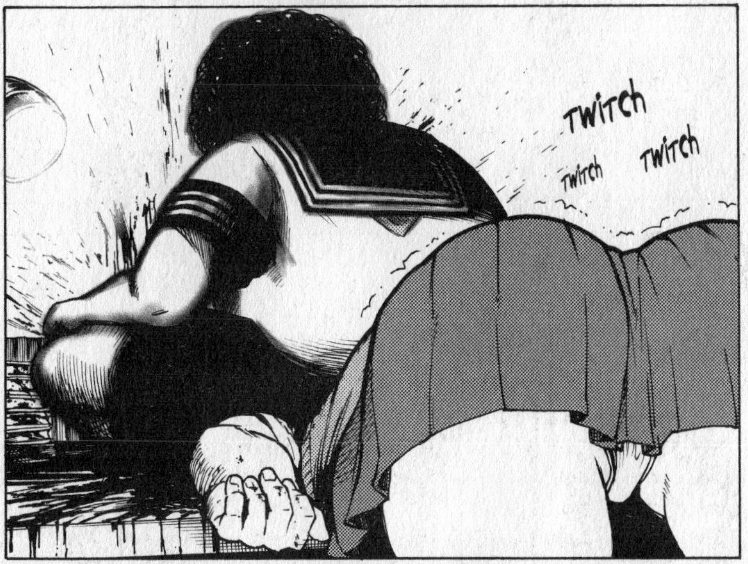
TWITCH
TWITCH
TWITCH

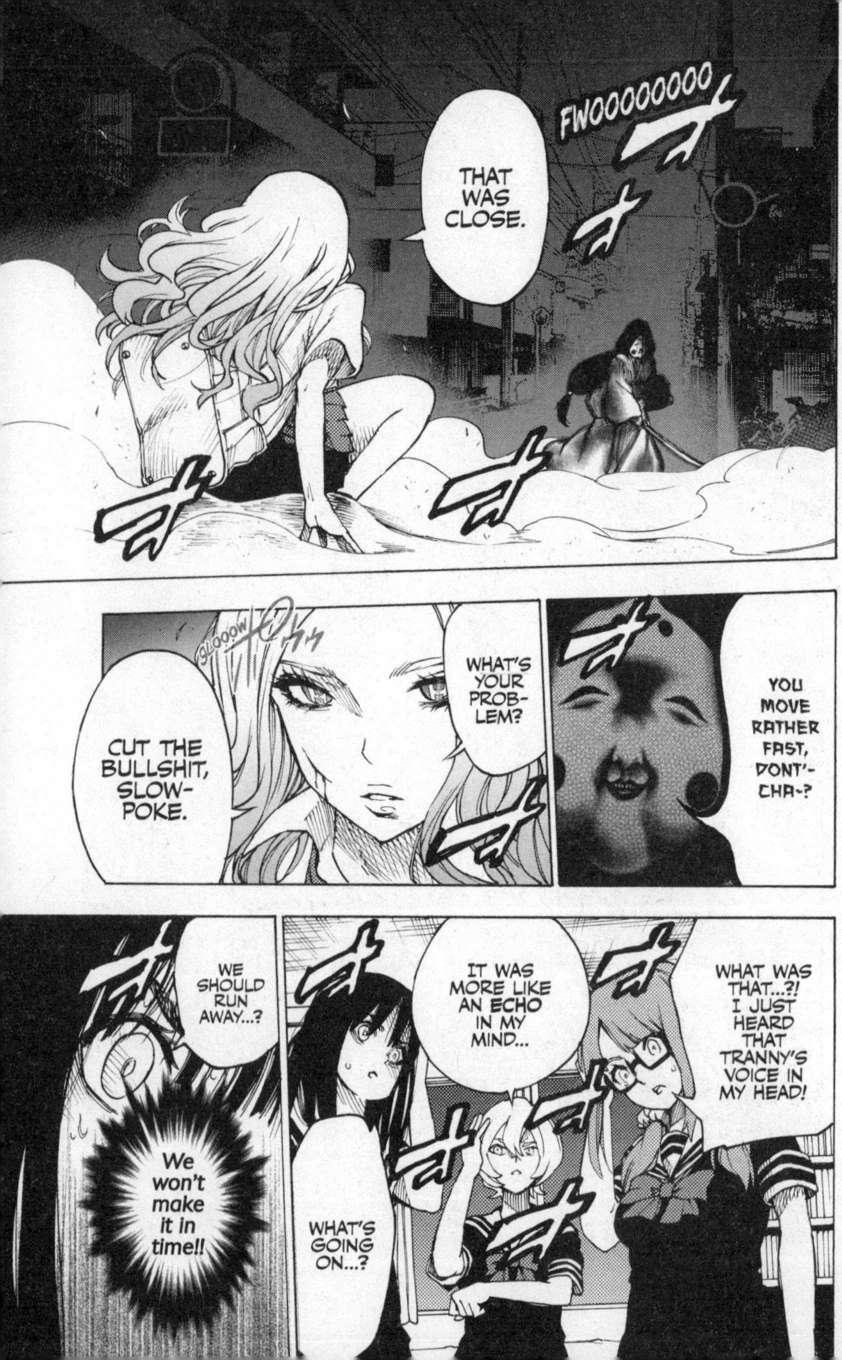
FWOOOOOOOO
THAT WAS CLOSE.
YOU MOVE RATHER FAST, DONT'-CHA-?
GLOOOW
WHAT'S YOUR PROB-LEM?
CUT THE BULLSHIT, SLOW-POKE.
WHAT WAS THAT...?! I JUST HEARD THAT TRANNY'S VOICE IN MY HEAD!
IT WAS MORE LIKE AN ECHO IN MY MIND...
WHAT'S GOING ON...?
WE SHOULD RUN AWAY...?
We won't make it in time!!

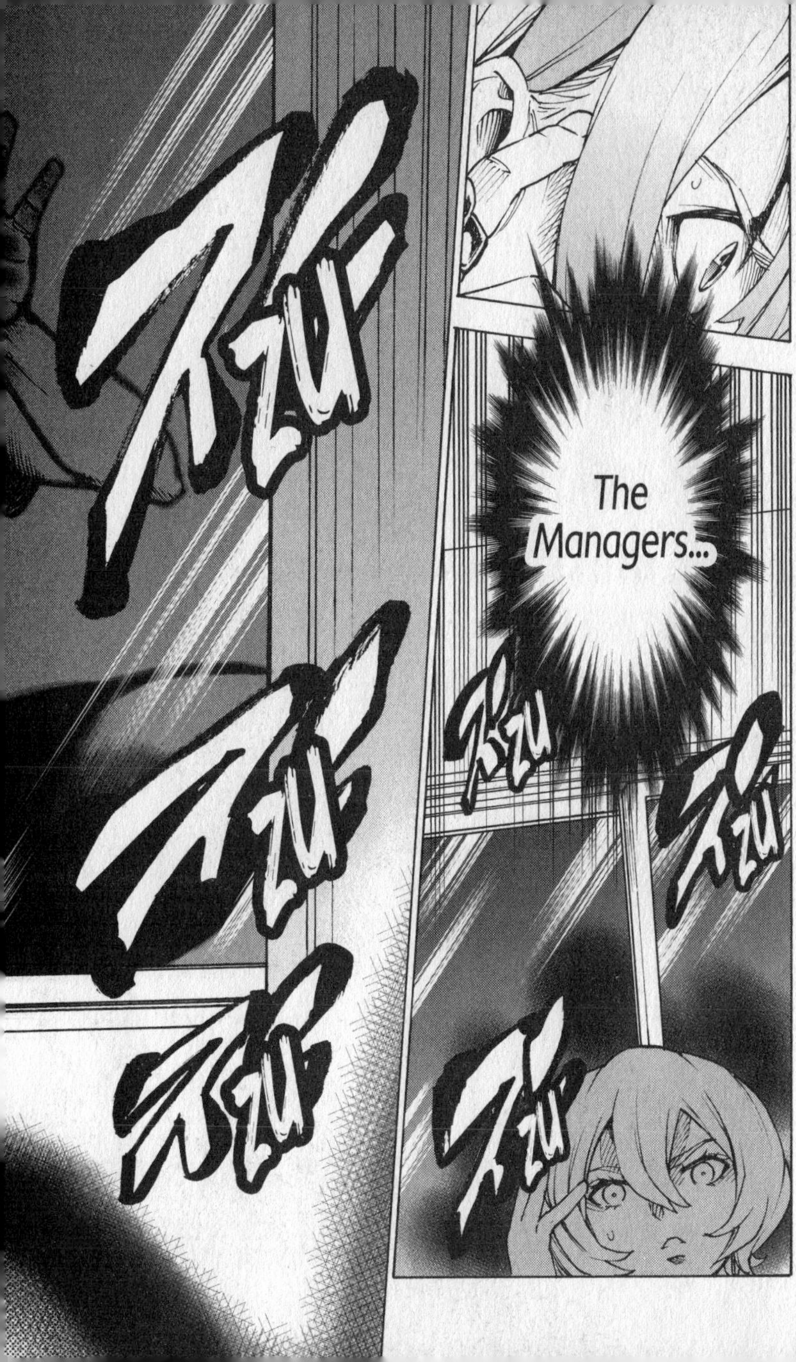
The Managers...
zu
zu
zu
zu
zu
zu

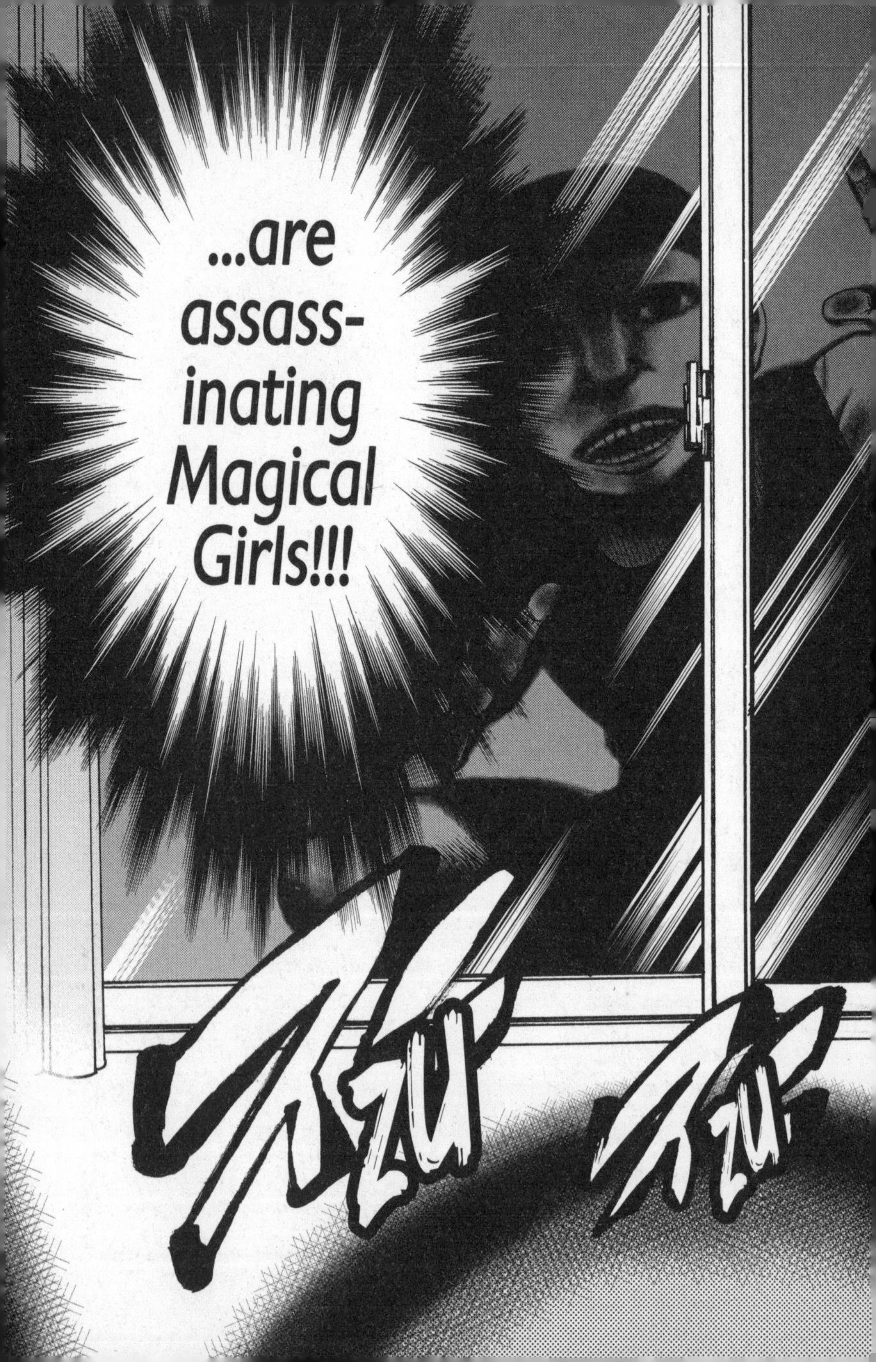
...are assass-inating Magical Girls!!!
ZU
ZU

YAMAI YUMAJI

Sex: Male
Age: 60
Date of Birth: December 24
                 (Capricorn)
Height: 157cm
Weight: 50kg
Blood Type: A
Birthplace: Shimane Prefecture

Hobbies/Interests: Household Chores, Mental Arithmetic, Cooking, Sports, Massaging

Strong Points: Early Riser, Dedicated to his Job

Weak Points: Coriander

Favorite Things: Hot Springs

- Mikari's servant.
- Is often subjected to near-death experiences by Mikari on a daily basis.
- When he gets a Baldie Kiss, all is forgiven.
- Pure Masochist.
- His skin mysteriously became naturally shiny in his 60s.
- He was mostly bald in his 20s.
- His favorite celebrity is Yuriko Yoshitaka.

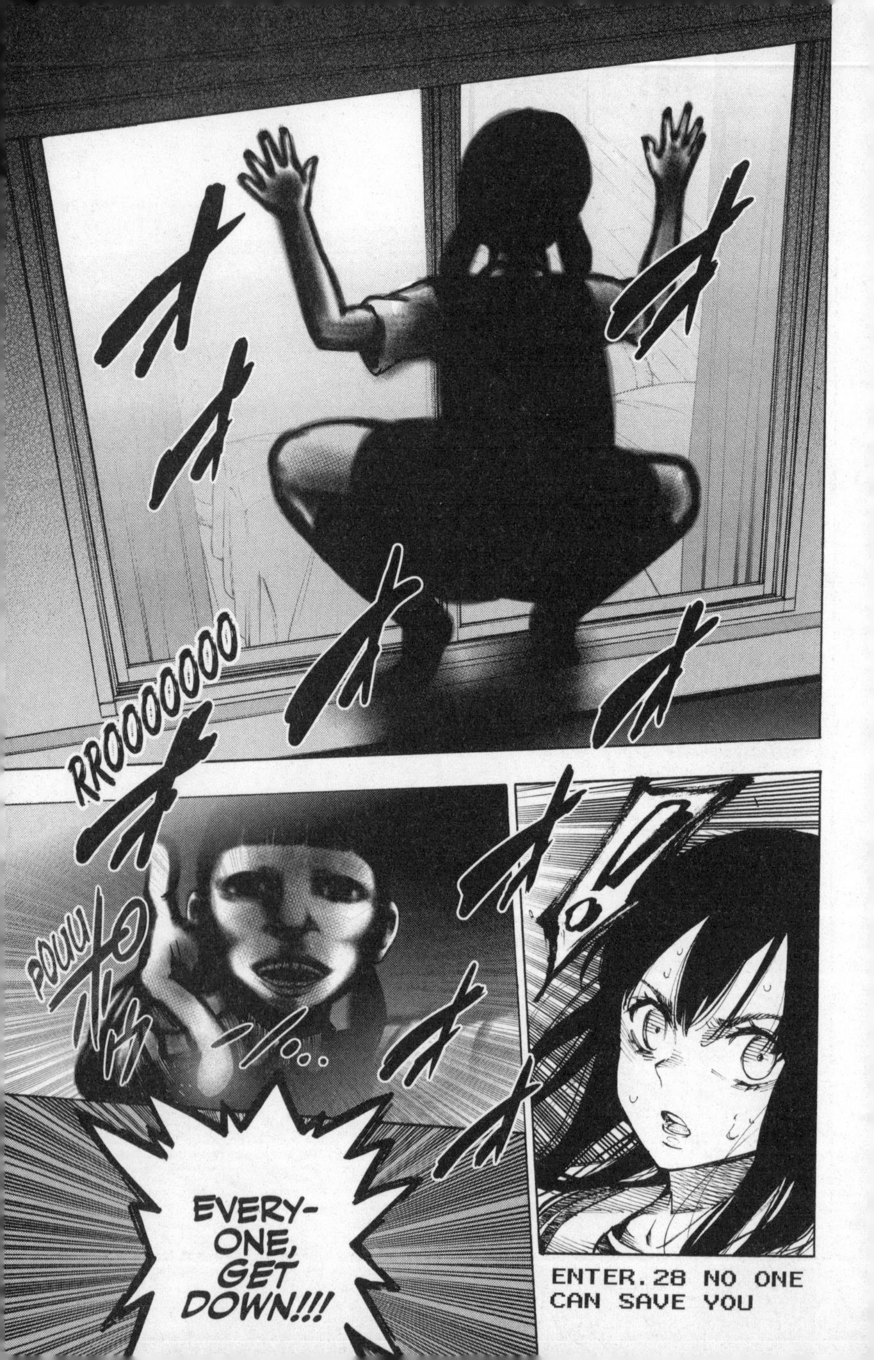
RROOOOOOO
POUUU
EVERY-ONE, GET DOWN!!!
ENTER. 28 NO ONE CAN SAVE YOU

ENTER.28 NO ONE CAN SAVE YOU

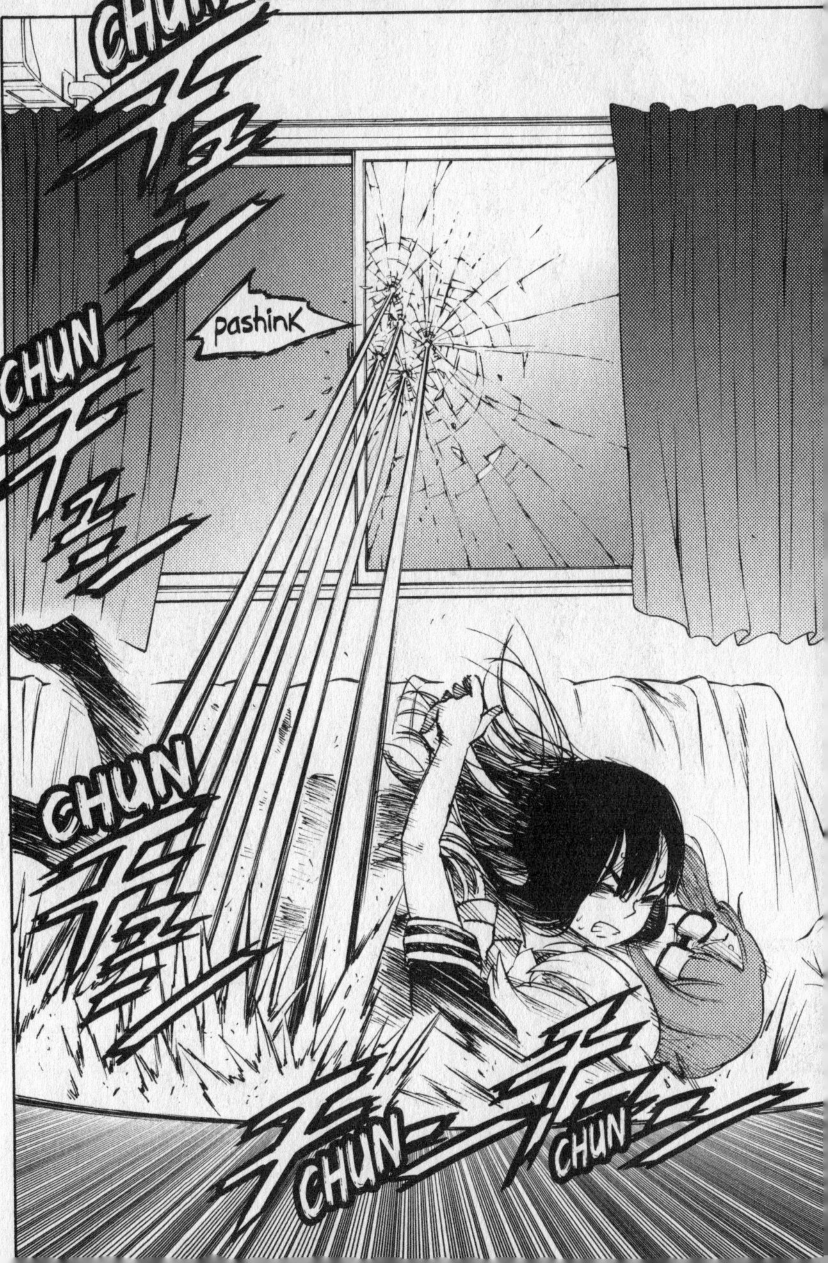
CHUN
pashink
CHUN
CHUN
CHUN
CHUN

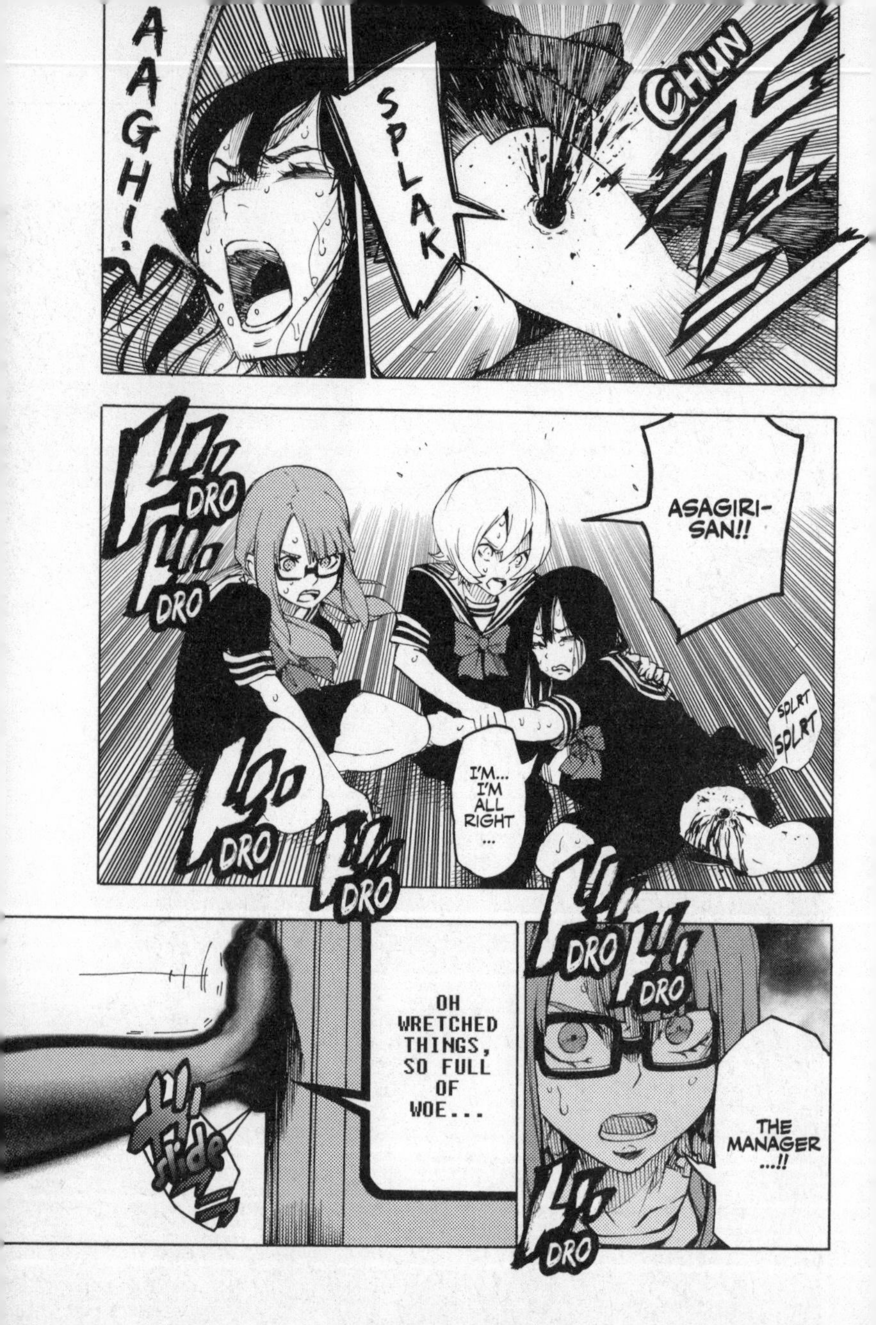
CHUN
SPLAK
AAGH!!
ASAGIRI-SAN!!
SPLRT SPLRT
DRO
DRO
I'M... I'M ALL RIGHT ...
DRO
DRO
DRO
DRO
THE MANAGER ...!!
DRO
OH WRETCHED THINGS, SO FULL OF WOE...
slide

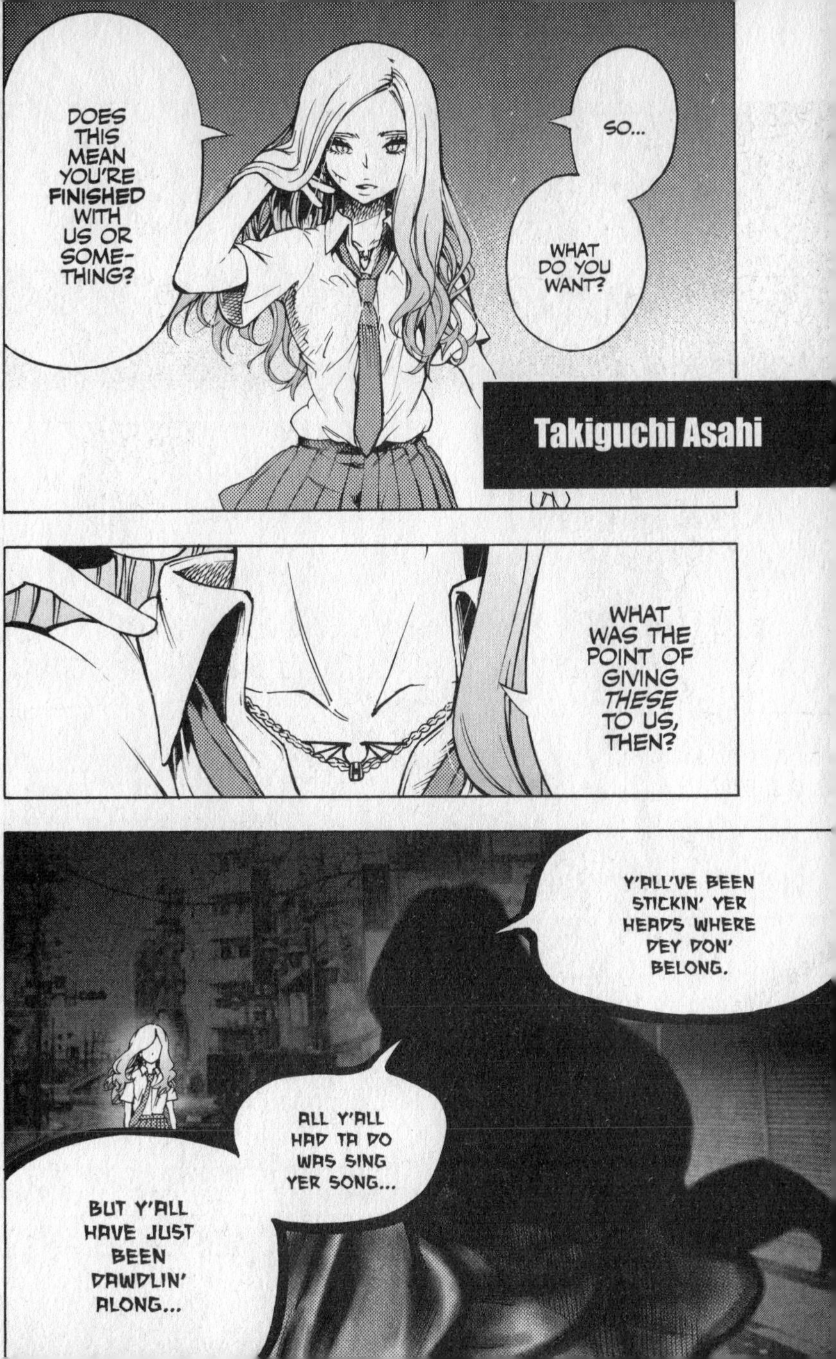
SO... WHAT DO YOU WANT?
Takiguchi Asahi
DOES THIS MEAN YOU'RE FINISHED WITH US OR SOME-THING?
WHAT WAS THE POINT OF GIVING *THESE* TO US, THEN?
Y'ALL'VE BEEN STICKIN' YER HEADS WHERE DEY DON' BELONG.
ALL Y'ALL HAD TA DO WAS SING YER SONG...
BUT Y'ALL HAVE JUST BEEN DAWDLIN' ALONG...

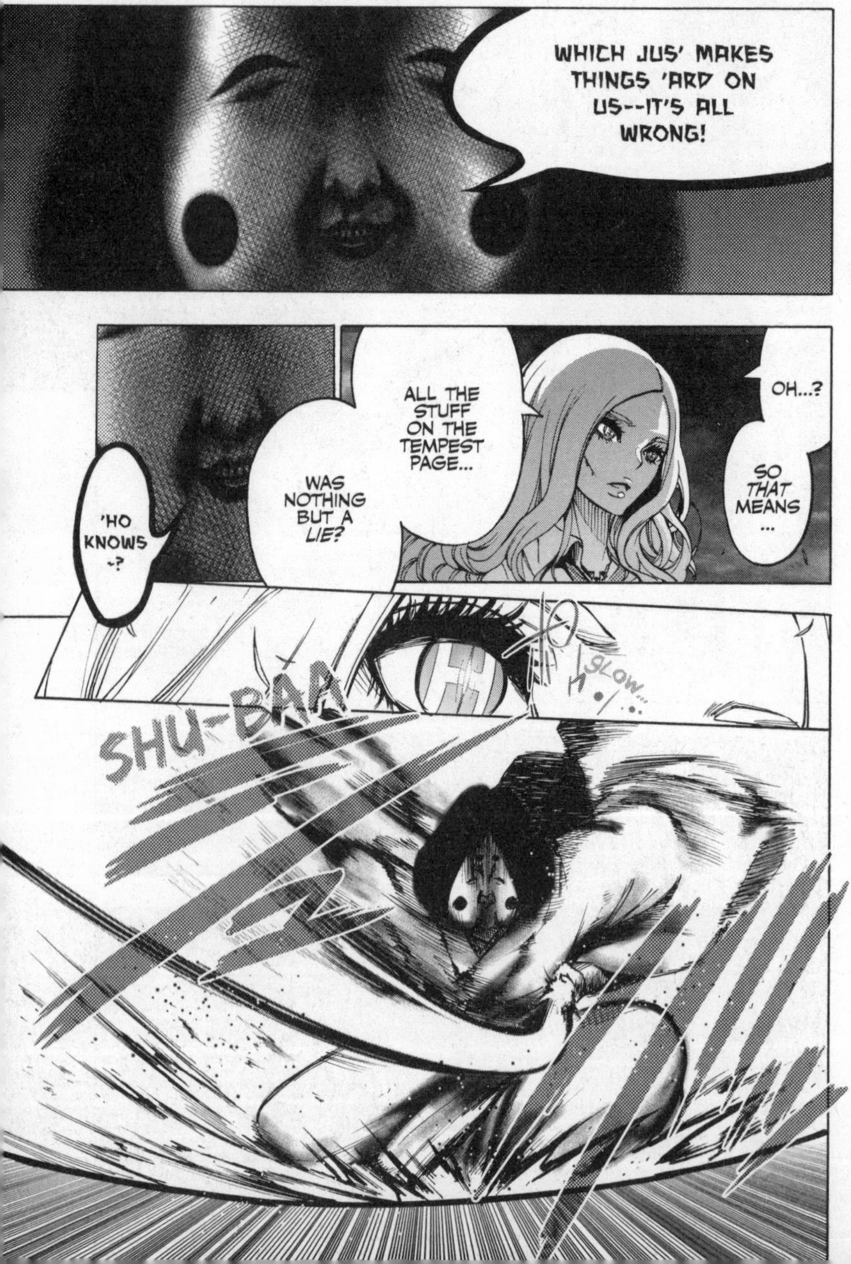
WHICH JUS' MAKES THINGS 'ARD ON US--IT'S ALL WRONG!
OH...?
SO *THAT* MEANS ...
ALL THE STUFF ON THE TEMPEST PAGE...
WAS NOTHING BUT A *LIE?*
'HO KNOWS ~?
GLOW...
SHU-BAA

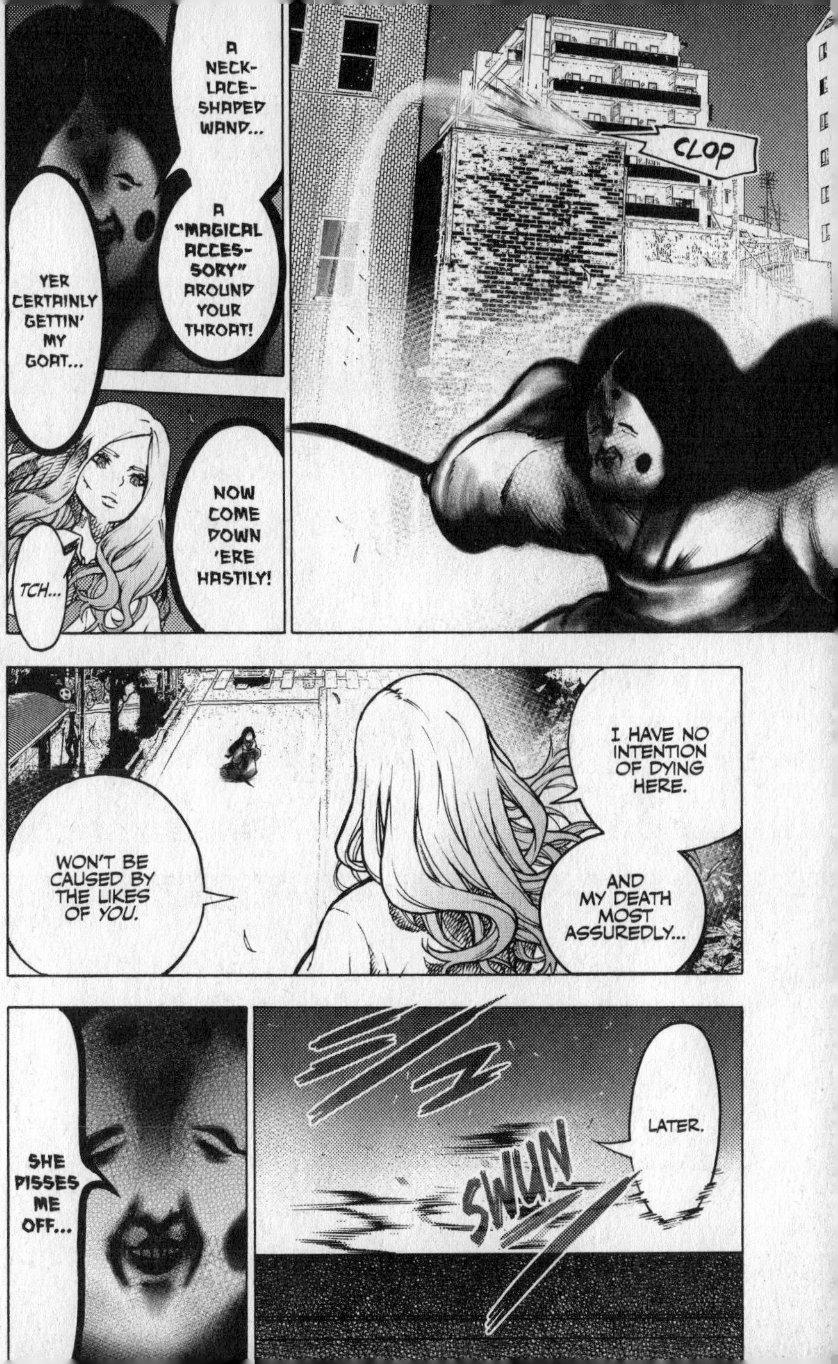
CLOP
A NECK-LACE-SHAPED WAND...
A "MAGICAL ACCES-SORY" AROUND YOUR THROAT!
YER CERTAINLY GETTIN' MY GOAT...
NOW COME DOWN 'ERE HASTILY!
TCH...
I HAVE NO INTENTION OF DYING HERE.
AND MY DEATH MOST ASSUREDLY...
WON'T BE CAUSED BY THE LIKES OF YOU.
LATER.
SWUN
SHE PISSES ME OFF...

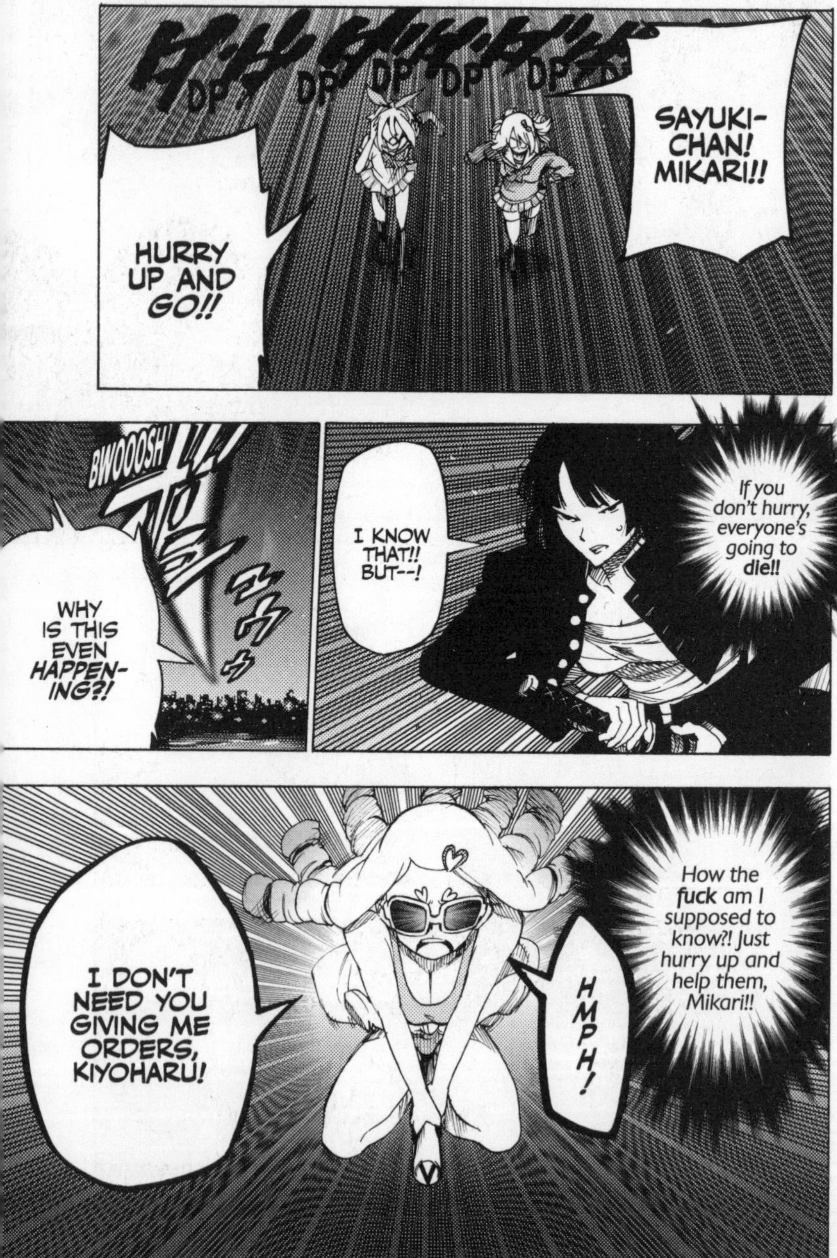
DP DP DP DP DP
SAYUKI-CHAN! MIKARI!!
HURRY UP AND GO!!
If you don't hurry, everyone's going to **die!!**
I KNOW THAT!! BUT--!
BWOOOSH
WHY IS THIS EVEN HAPPENING?!
How the **fuck** am I supposed to know?! Just hurry up and help them, Mikari!!
HMPH!
I DON'T NEED YOU GIVING ME ORDERS, KIYOHARU!

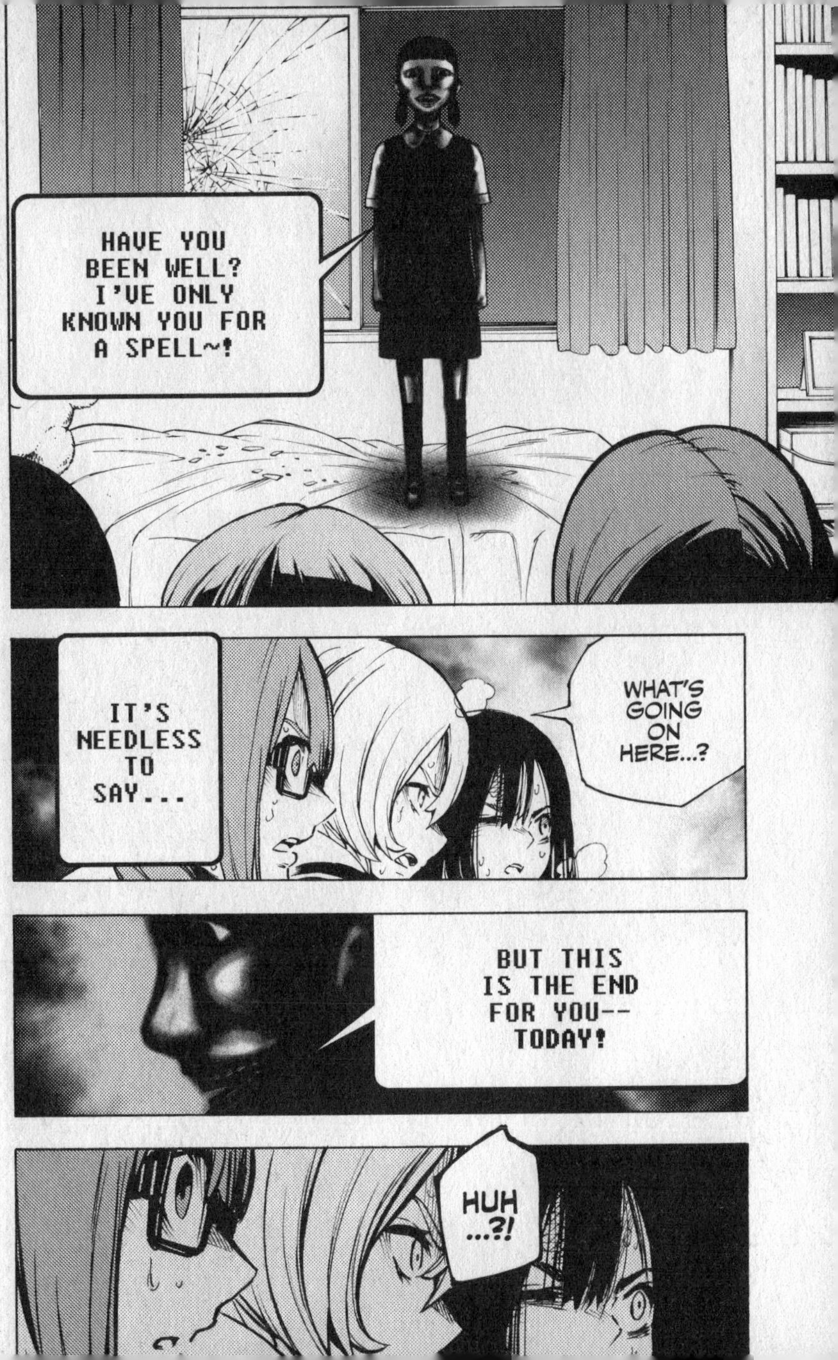
HAVE YOU BEEN WELL? I'VE ONLY KNOWN YOU FOR A SPELL~!
WHAT'S GOING ON HERE...?
IT'S NEEDLESS TO SAY...
BUT THIS IS THE END FOR YOU-- TODAY!
HUH ...?!

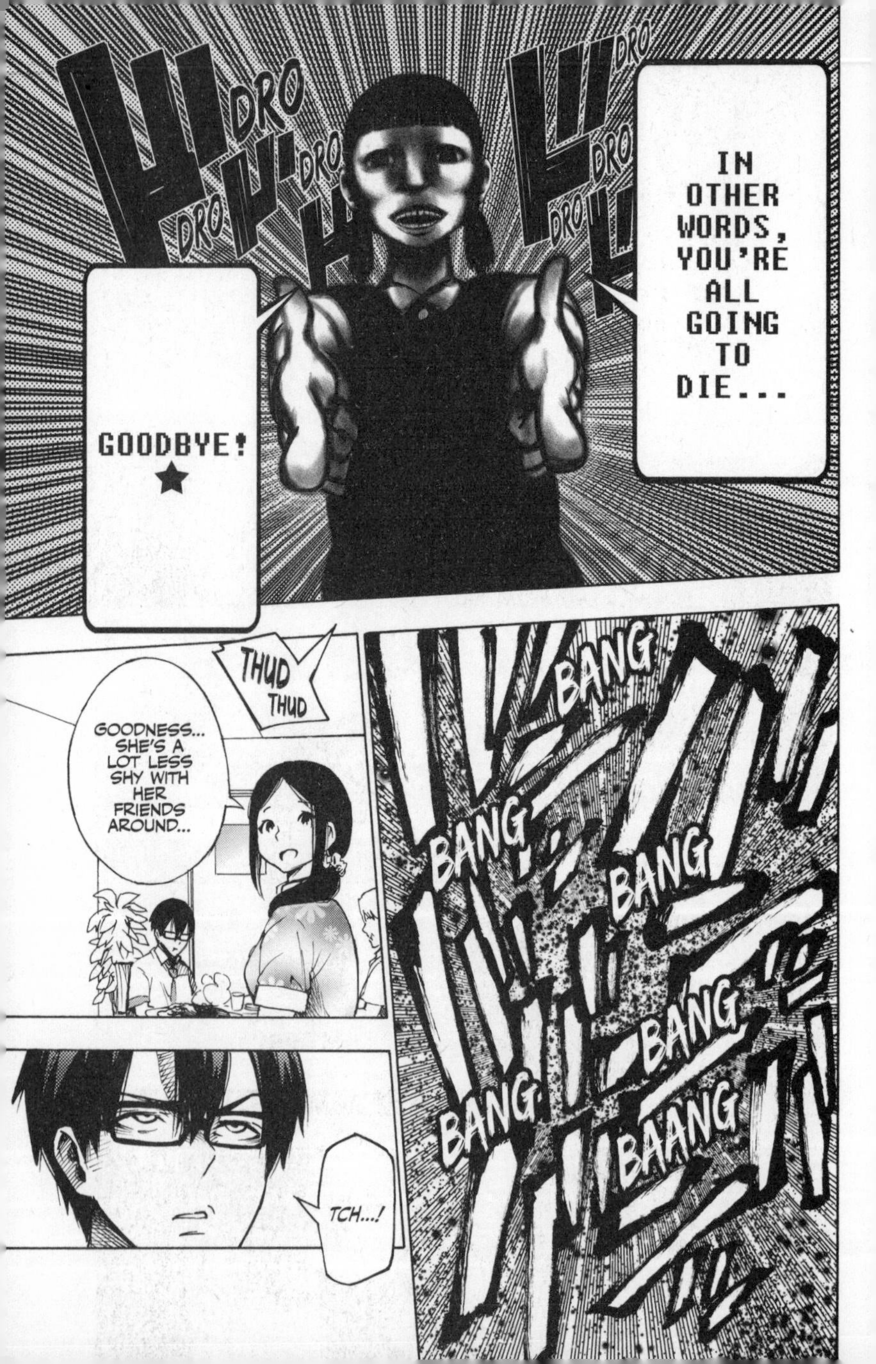
IN OTHER WORDS, YOU'RE ALL GOING TO DIE...
DRO DRO
DRO DRO
DRO DRO
GOODBYE! ★
BANG BANG BANG BANG BANG BANG BAANG
THUD THUD
GOODNESS... SHE'S A LOT LESS SHY WITH HER FRIENDS AROUND...
TCH...!

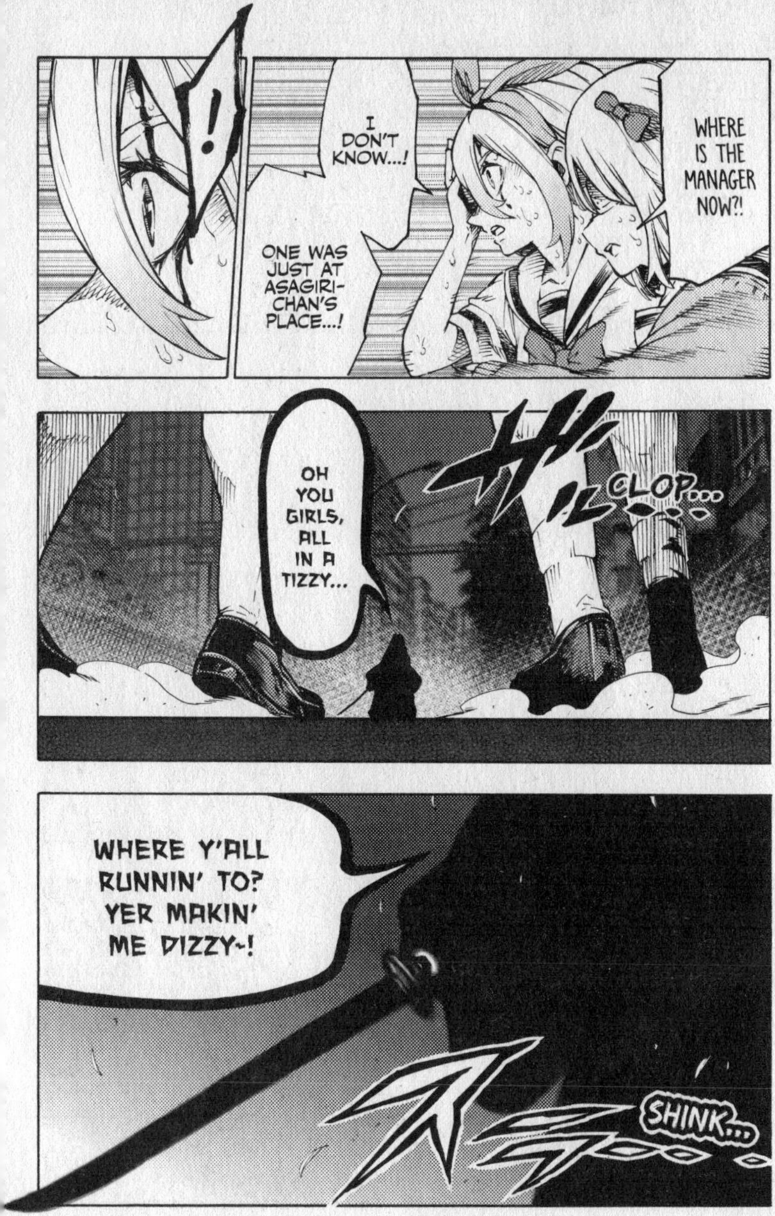
WHERE IS THE MANAGER NOW?!
I DON'T KNOW...!
ONE WAS JUST AT ASAGIRI-CHAN'S PLACE...!
!
CLOP...
OH YOU GIRLS, ALL IN A TIZZY...
WHERE Y'ALL RUNNIN' TO? YER MAKIN' ME DIZZY~!
SHINK...

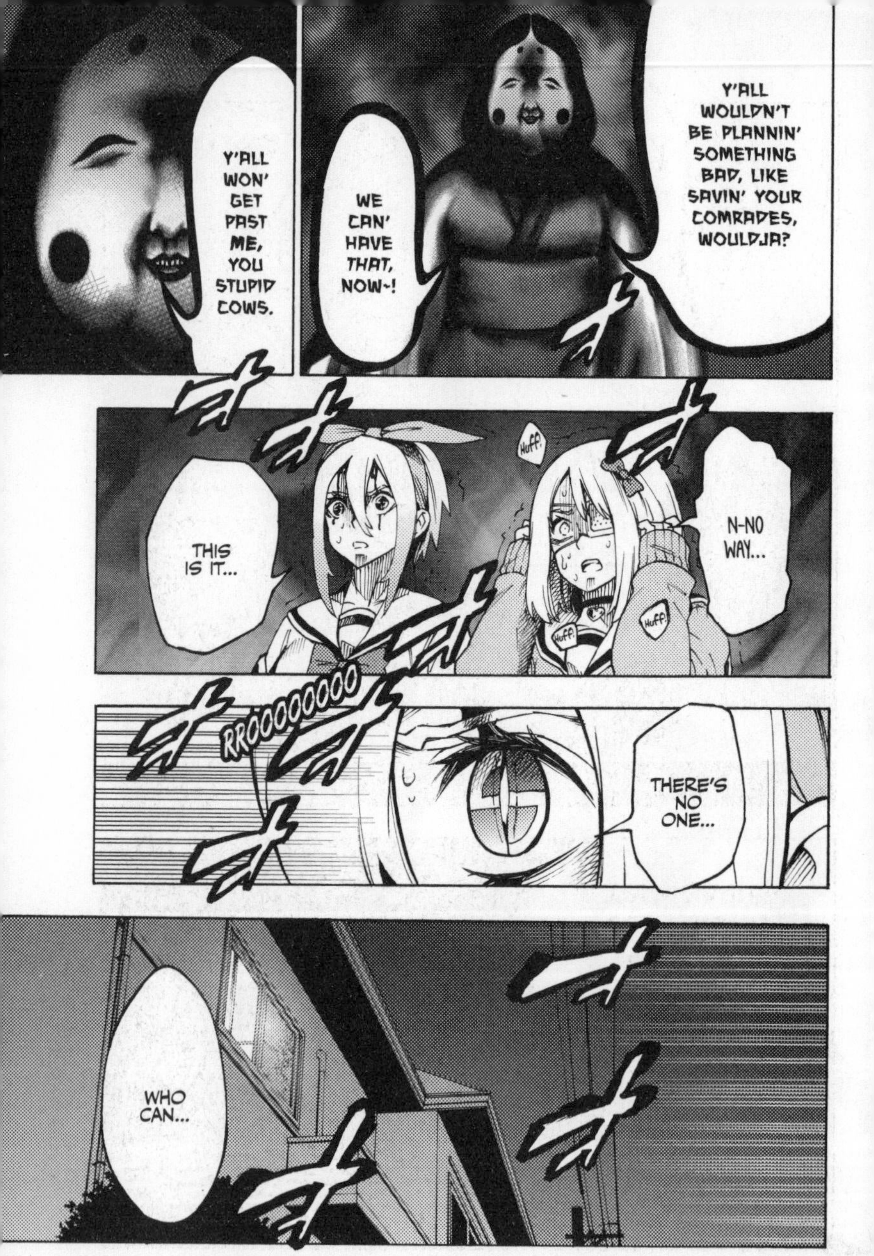
Y'ALL WOULDN'T BE PLANNIN' SOMETHING BAD, LIKE SAVIN' YOUR COMRADES, WOULDJA?
WE CAN' HAVE THAT, NOW~!
Y'ALL WON' GET PAST ME, YOU STUPID COWS.
N-NO WAY...
Huff!
Huff!
Huff!
THIS IS IT...
THERE'S NO ONE...
RROOOOOOOO
WHO CAN...

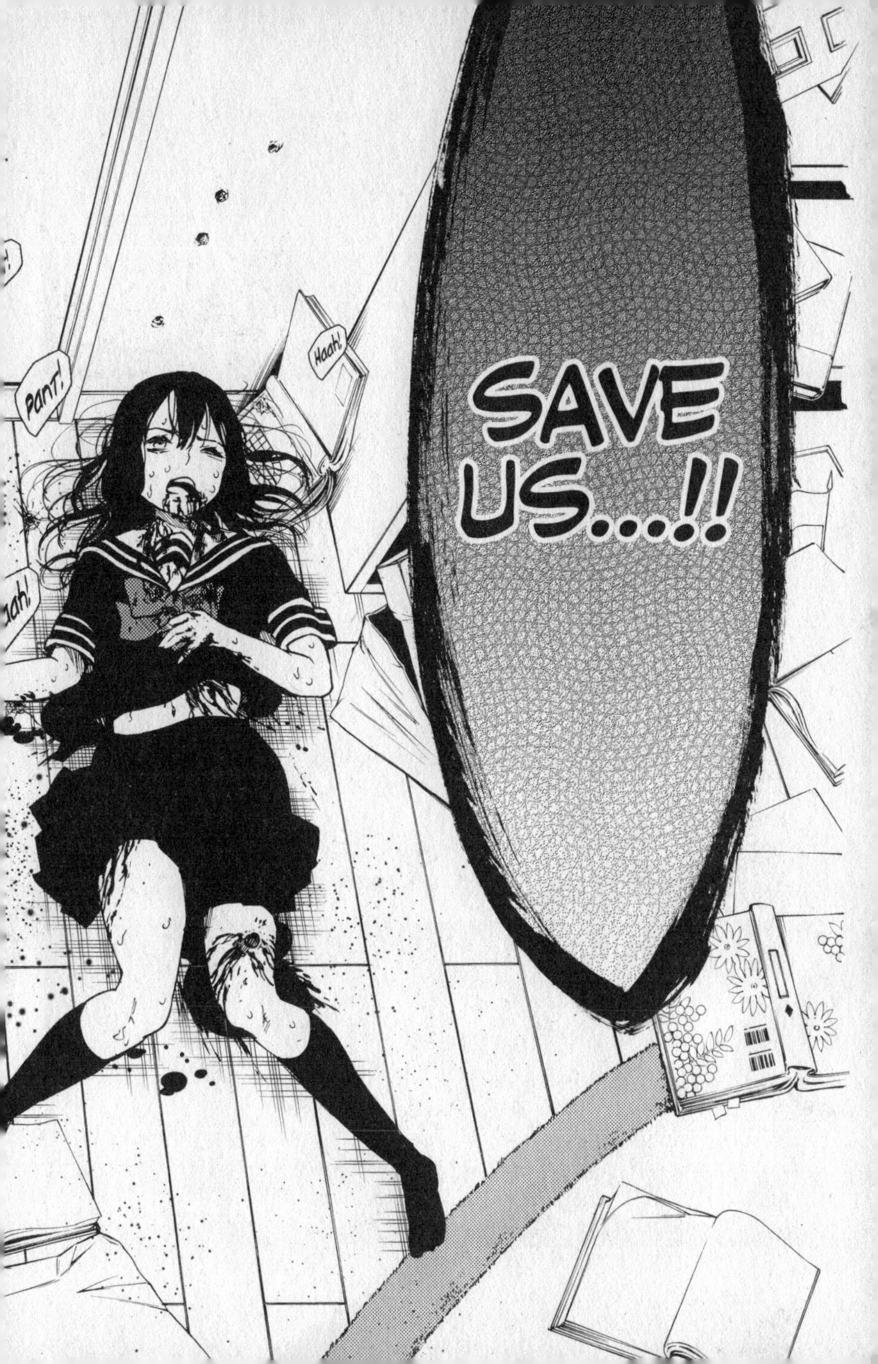
SAVE US...!!
Haah!
Pant!

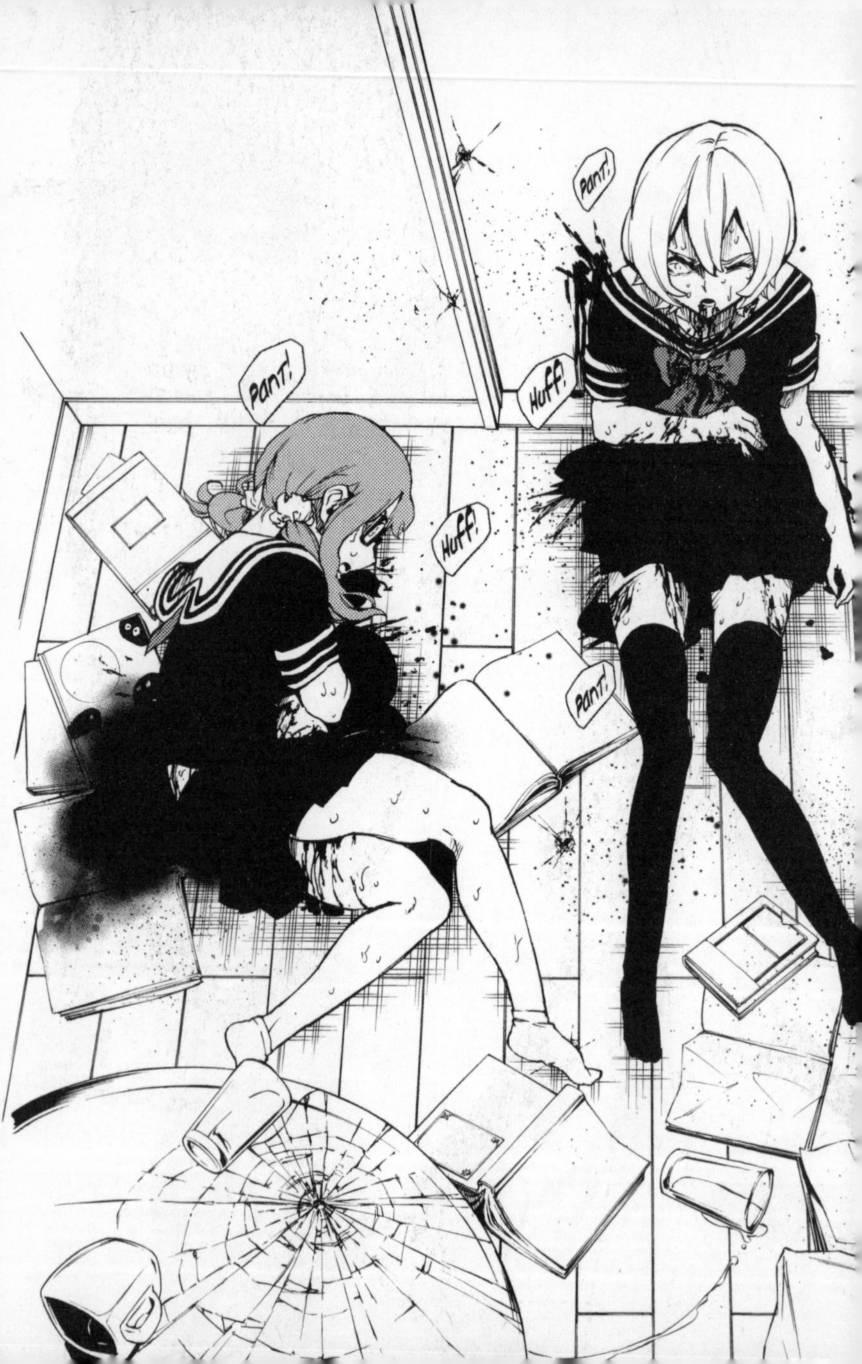
Pant!
Huff!
Pant!
Pant!
Huff!

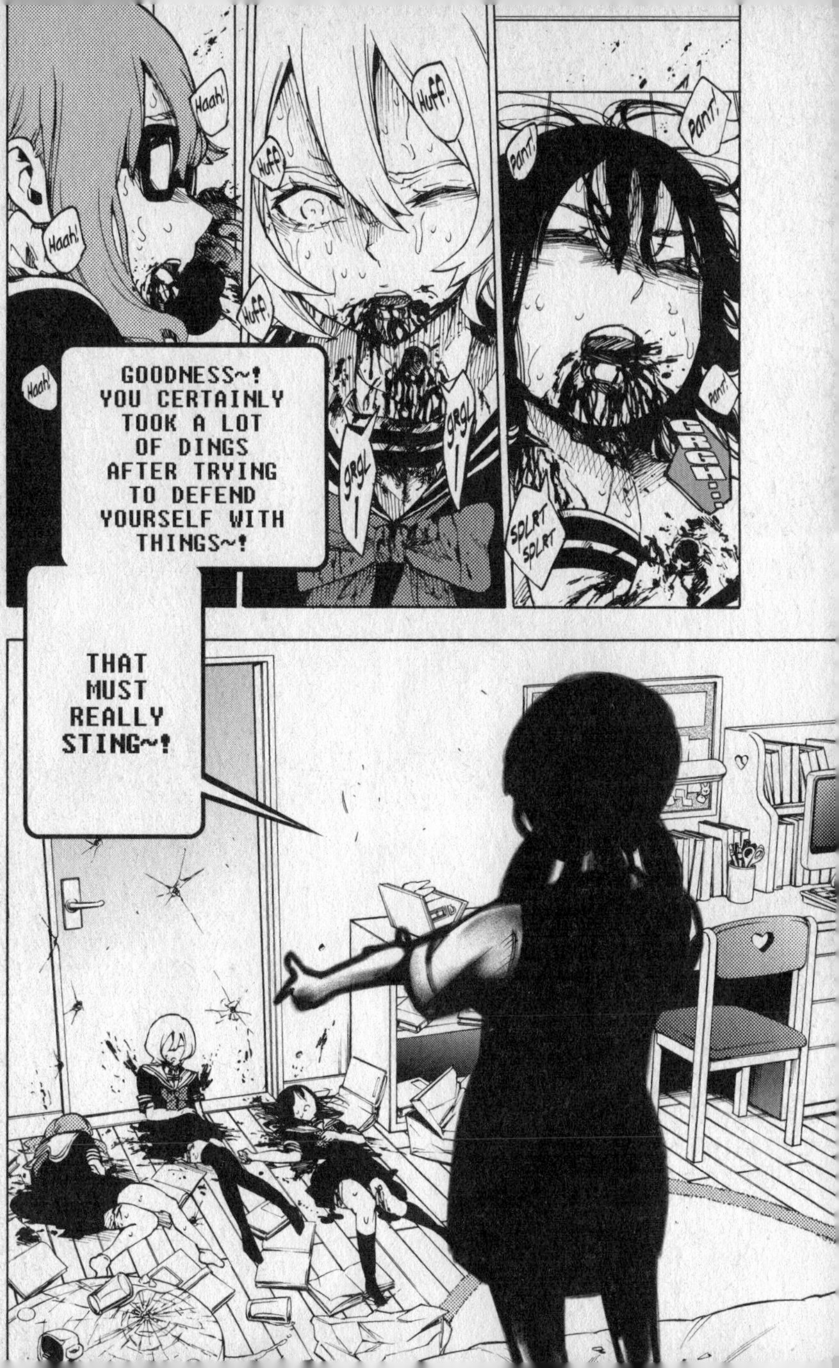
Pant!
Pant!
Pant!
GRGH...
SPLRT SPLRT
Huff!
Huff!
Huff!
grgl
grgl
Haah!
Haah!
Haah!
GOODNESS~! YOU CERTAINLY TOOK A LOT OF DINGS AFTER TRYING TO DEFEND YOURSELF WITH THINGS~!
THAT MUST REALLY STING~!

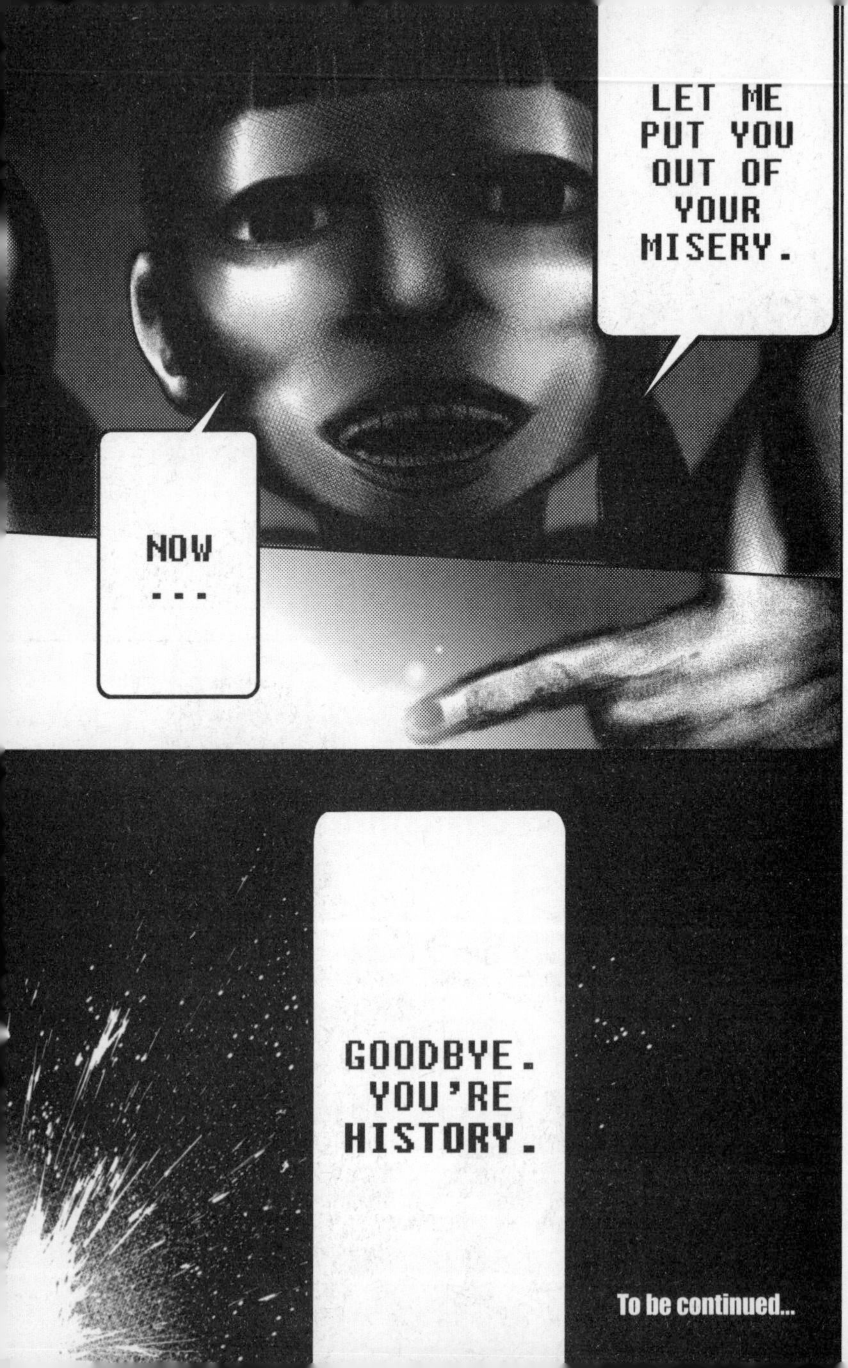
LET ME PUT YOU OUT OF YOUR MISERY.
NOW ...
GOODBYE. YOU'RE HISTORY.
To be continued...

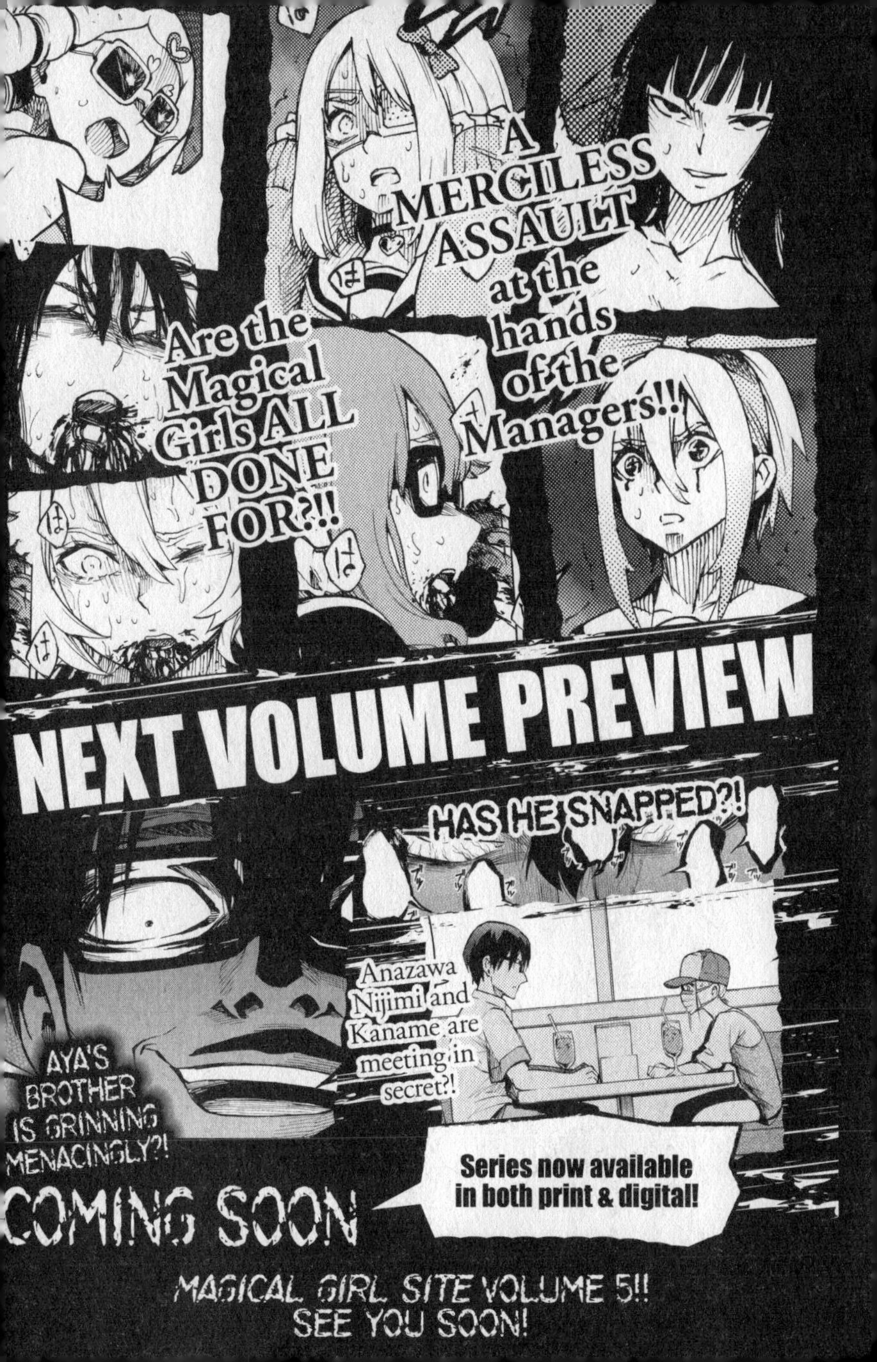
A MERCILESS ASSAULT at the hands of the Managers!!
Are the Magical Girls ALL DONE FOR?!!
NEXT VOLUME PREVIEW
HAS HE SNAPPED?!
Anazawa Nijimi and Kaname are meeting in secret?!
AYA'S BROTHER IS GRINNING MENACINGLY?!
Series now available in both print & digital!
COMING SOON
MAGICAL GIRL SITE VOLUME 5!!
SEE YOU SOON!

Expe... es of

H... n

SEVEN SEAS ENTERTAINMENT

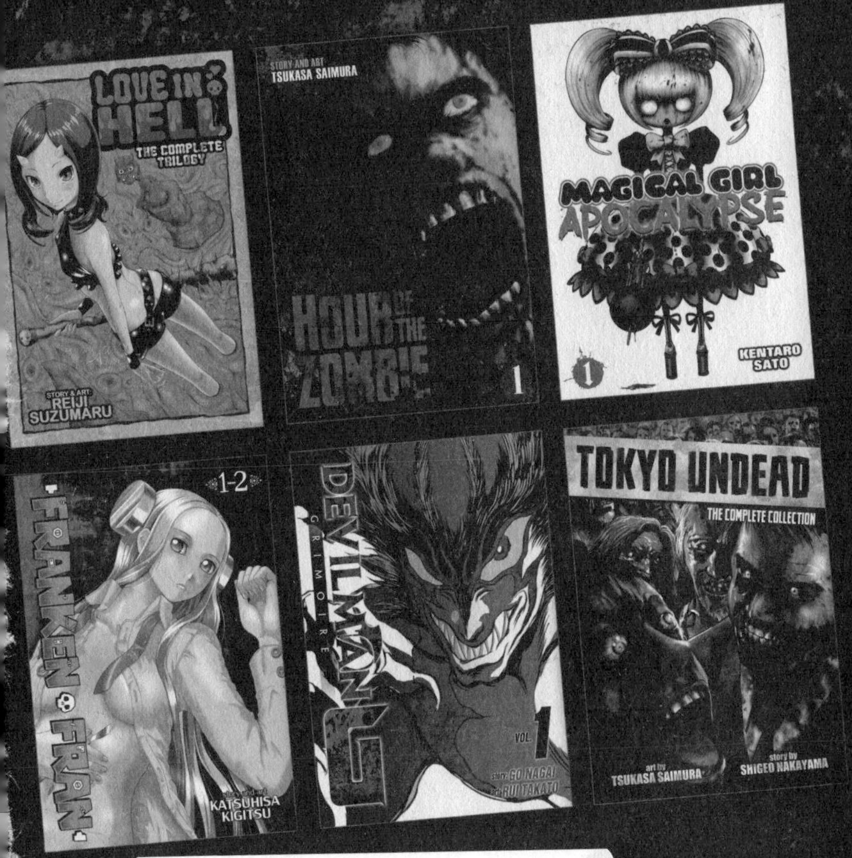

LOVE IN HELL
THE COMPLETE TRILOGY
STORY & ART: REIJI SUZUMARU
STORY AND ART TSUKASA SAIMURA
HOUR OF THE ZOMBIE
1
MAGICAL GIRL APOCALYPSE
1
KENTARO SATO
1-2
FRANKEN FRAN
story and art KATSUHISA KIGITSU
DEVILMAN G GRIMOIRE
VOL. 1
story: GO NAGAI
art: RUI TAKATO
TOKYO UNDEAD
THE COMPLETE COLLECTION
art by TSUKASA SAIMURA
story by SHIGEO NAKAYAMA

See a...

has...

goma...

Seven Seas

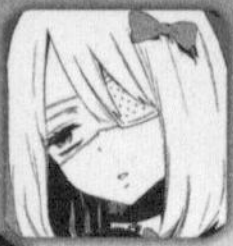

Amagai Kosame

A Magical Girl from a different site than Aya, with a wand in the shape of a box cutter. She takes medicine for her unstable mental condition. relief.

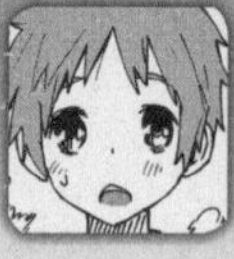

Honomoto Makoto

Aya's classmate. A boy who cares for Aya.

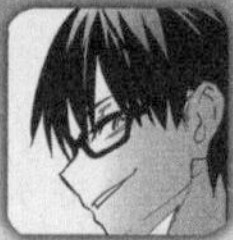

Asagiri Kaname

Aya's big brother. Due to the stress of studying for his exams and living up to his father's expectations, he violently abuses Aya as a source of stress relief.

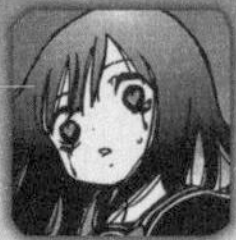

Asagiri Aya

An eighth grader. She possesses a wand that teleports its target to another location.

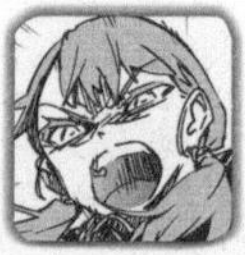

Shizukume Sarina

An eighth grader and Aya's classmate. She became a Magical Girl to get revenge on Aya and Tsuyuno. Her wand is a yo-yo that can cut through anything with its string.

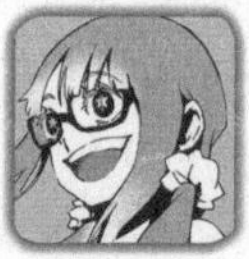

Shioi Rina

An information gatherer. She used a wand to change her appearance and became the "Magical Hunter" who collects wands.

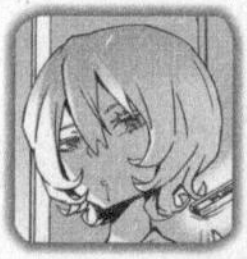

Yatsumura Tsuyuno

An eighth grader and Aya's classmate. She has a wand in the shape of a smartphone that is capable of stopping time.

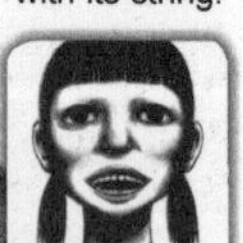

Site Manager Nana

The manager of the Magical Girl Site who gave Aya and Tsuyuno their wands. She has a peculiar way of speaking.

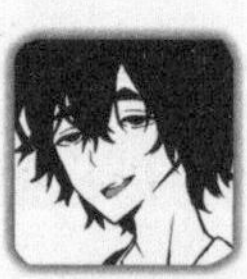

Naoto Keisuke

An obsessed fan of Anazawa Nijimi. His entire life revolves around her and her fandom.

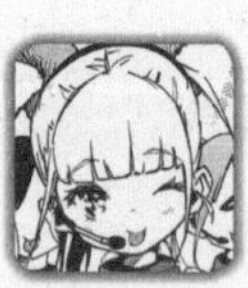

Anazawa Nijimi

An eighth grader and the most popular member of the mega idol group Puppy Play. Her wand is a pair of panties capable of manipulating people.

Magical
Girl Site

VOLUME 4

AUTHOR
KENTARO SATO